QUEER

QUEER

SIMON GAGE

LISA RICHARDS

HOWARD WILMOT

Foreword by BOY GEORGE

THUNDER'S
MOUTH
PRESS

Published in the United States by
Thunder's Mouth Press
An Imprint of Avalon Publishing Group Incorporated
161 William Street, 16th Floor
New York, NY 10038

Originally published in Great Britain by Unanimous Ltd
12 The Ivories, 6-8 Northampton Street, London N1 2HY

Library of Congress Control Number: 2002103623

Project editor: Kate John
Designer: Chris Tate

ISBN: 1-56025-377-0

Printed in China

1 2 3 4 5 6 7 8 9

contents

It's a gay, gay, gay, gay world.

Or, to put it another way, there's nowt so queer as folk. And I don't just mean gay folk either. As you look around you, you realise that everyone these days is gay. And never mind who they're sleeping with.

Gay culture (thankfully!) has seeped into life in general. Children's TV presenters are gay (they always were, but now they're open about it), meaning that kids have a finely developed sense of camp before they reach the 'big school', while old ladies can't seem to get enough of hilarious queeny comedians and presenters, never mind that these guys would have been locked up back in their day. What these new popular culture pin-ups do with their penises in the privacy of their own homes doesn't seem to bother anyone (except right wing politicians and religious nuts, but then they're always raving about something).

But as gay culture in all its forms gets taken on by the mainstream, it's important just to put a bright pink sticker on stuff that is gay, to show young gay people, who are isolated in a way that say black or Jewish kids just aren't, that they do have their own history, roots and heroes, that there is a fine tradition of creativity, power, imagination and success far away from the sad and lonely image of gay men and lesbians the media likes to peddle. From overtly gay artists like Mapplethorpe and Warhol to geniuses like Leonardo Da Vinci and Michelangelo, whose homosexuality is only now being (reluctantly) admitted even though it informed a lot of their work (the naked muscle on the ceiling of the Sistine Chapel simply can't be ignored. It's like a gay disco up there!).

Then there are historical giants like Alexander The Great, Richard The Lionheart and James I, whose sexuality is usually concealed when they become the subject of school history lessons. Madonna and disco and Absolutely Fabulous are great fun, but there's a bit more to gay culture than a couple of sequins and a marabou trim.

But that doesn't mean that it's all very dreary and right-on. If there's one thing the gay sensibility does bring to a grey world is a bit of colour and fun, wit and va-va-voom. I should know. Back at the time of Culture Club my fan base stretched waaaaay across the board: from little kids to grandmas, teen queens to hardened rockers. And there surely can't have been much doubt about which side I was batting for!

But more than culture—though TV shows and movies with gay characters are important when it comes to letting people know that gay folk are living, breathing human beings like them—there is the whole story of the gay struggle for a bit of respect around here. From the drag queens who kick-started the gay rights movement when they laid into the cops who busted their bar one time too often that night back in the late sixties to inspirational politicians like Harvey Milk, the openly gay city official who helped make San Francisco into the happy queer metropolis it is today, there are key characters who deserve to be held in as much esteem as civil rights figures like Martin Luther King but often aren't because the struggle to be taken seriously is still going on.

Although gay men and lesbians are (rightly) famous for knowing how to have a great time, there is a flip side to the gay experience. Apart from the thousands of personal tragedies (suicide among young gay men and lesbians is still frighteningly high), we have gone through the AIDS crisis, which changed the face of gay politics forever, and individual outrages like the murder of student Matthew Shepard, who was literally crucified by a pair of homophobic thugs. It's all a work in progress, something that the current influence of gay culture is helping with. Children no longer grow up thinking they're the only gay person in the world, and that can only be good.

As I say, it's a gay, gay, gay, gay world, with all the triumphs and heartbreaks of a major motion picture, all the sleaze of a great night out, all the glamour of a Paris catwalk show and all the excitement of some of the world's legendary nightclubs. So, whether you enjoy a night in front of Sex And The City or The Golden Girls or a night out in some foxy tight jeans reeking of the latest Calvin Klein scent, you're gay whether you're into the same or the opposite sex. Now, don't make me out you.

Boy George, 2002

Why Queer?

Queer. Funny little word. Queer little word, if you like. 'Eccentric' and 'mildly insane' it says in our dictionary (we don't actually think that's too bad!) but obviously Queer has come a long way since it meant that. It's grown up, moved to the big city and become a star.

Today, more than anything Queer means 'Gay' first as a term of abuse, now as a banner to march under. It's gay with attitude. Gay with quite a lot of "don't fuck with us" approach. But Queer, being the cheeky clever monkey that it is, has moved even beyond that. Queer is now a state of mind, an outlook on life as well as a mere sexual preference.

So we thought that Queer, with its history of contrariness, was an ideal title for a book which challenges perceptions of what gay is and isn't. It's the only word we could think of that went any way towards describing gay and lesbian culture, lifestyles, attitudes and history in one easy "it does exactly what it says on the packet" way. And while we've already reclaimed the word from the knuckle-dragging bigots, it's high time we got it back from the queer theorists whose writings—mostly as dry as Ghandi's sandals—have made it a by-word for dreary and right-on.

But how do you get the whole Queer thing into one book (without lubricant) in a way that both informs and entertains? It's a tough one.

We start off with *Gay Universe*, a roundup of icons, styles, events, works of art (well, Cagney and Lacey) that have shaped the world that homos young and old live in. Everything from Saint Diana, Princess of Wales to the glamfest that is the world of the rock diva is in there.

In *Nature/Nurture* we ponder the timeless question, how did we get to be what we so gratefully are? Was it our mothers' over-protective behavior, our fathers' absence, a gene crawling down through the generations? And what if we want the ultimate makeover from one sex to another?

And while we're on the subject…*Between The Sheets* gets its nose right in there on the sex lives of gay men and lesbians: what we do, what we wear, how we get those huge dildos in there, and how we get away with some of that stuff. Spit roasts, cock rings, glory holes, double penetration… how to have sex with an ugly bug, that kind of thing.

But it's not all about having a laugh and getting your rocks (or lady rocks) off and the party hasn't come without a fight. In *Right On Sister* we move from the struggle from Stonewall to the present day to the outrages like the crucifixion of Matthew Shepard; from martyrs like Brandon Teena to heroes like Harvey Milk, these are our Martin Luther Kings and Malcolm Xs and it's about time the world knew a little more about them.

And let's not forget that there are gay men and lesbians outside New York, London and Sydney: we are everywhere! In *Location, Location, Location* we take you on a whistle stop world tour, telling you where you can live it up and where you should avoid if you want to keep both of your hands.

Not only are there gay men and lesbians outside the major conurbations, we are also outside the 20th and 21st centuries. Men have done men and women have done women since time immemorial and in *The Way We Were* we blow the cover of historical figures from Richard the Lionheart to Florence Nightingale, men and women with certain leanings who have walked the walk, and sometimes in very difficult period footwear. We also trace the evolution of AIDS and keep a beady eye on the Christian New Right.

In *Gay to Straight* you'll see how gay men and lesbians have been targeted by the mainstream with ads and sitcoms and pop groups (yes, Village People, you frauds!). In *The Look* the visual influence of gay men and lesbians on the world in general is explored, whether in terms of uniforms purloined from straight soldiers for our own dirty purposes, piercings that look like they must hurt to top notch bona fide international designers like Gaultier and McQueen worn by pretty much everyone with half an eye.

And for our final bow, we give you *Let Me Entertain You* in which we look at what gay men and lesbians have brought to the cultural table, from artists to actors to musicians to authors to, erm, pornographers.

There you have it. The wonderful world of gay in one easy-to-use package. Flick it, read it in detail, engrave it on your heart or cut all the pictures out and put them in frames. It's your book. And we've already got your money.

Simon Gage, Lisa Richards, Howard Wilmot

Gay Universe

It's a gay old world, but it ain't just homos who produce some of the queerest movies, TV programmes and icons on this planet. The gayest of the gay—and they're nearly all straight!

V

VI

VII

Edin

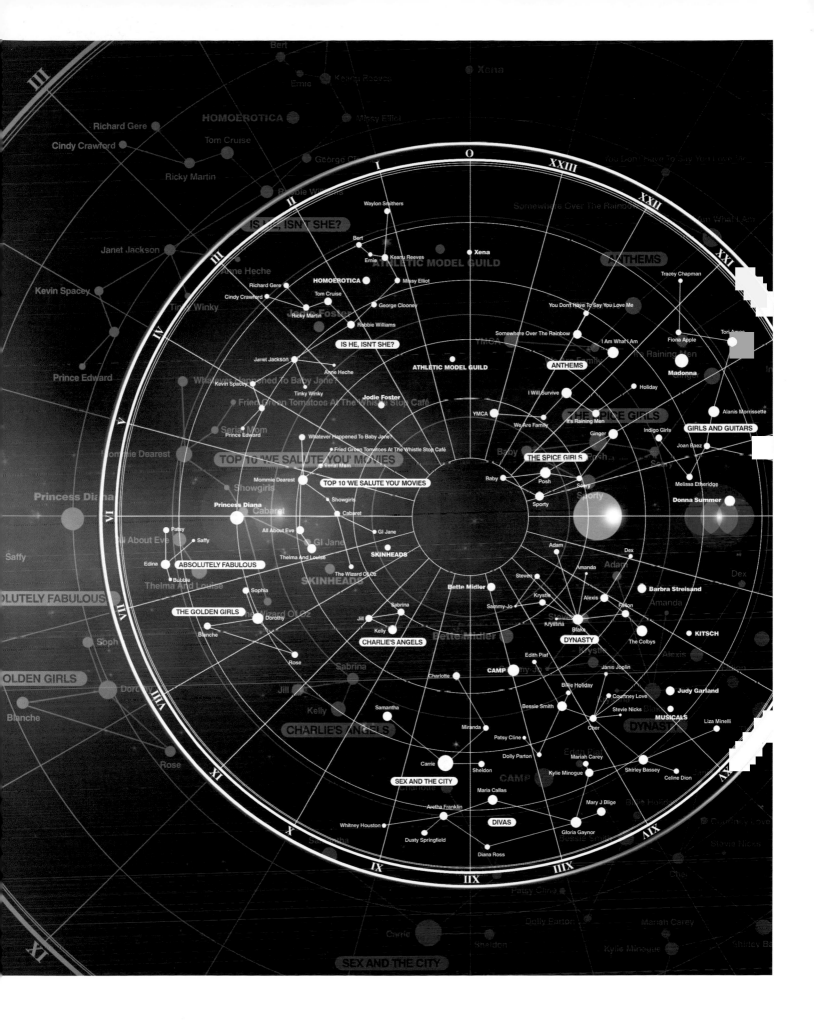

Bette Midler

The Divine Miss M

Don't judge Bette Midler by what she is now. Judge her by what she was then, back in the 70s when she was a prototype and inspiration for Madonna and Sandra Bernhard (who used to pester her with fan letters); when she was shocking and vulgar, edgy and articulate; when she would think nothing of performing numbers in a wheelchair or flashing her tits to the balcony or playing to a room of naked gay men. Don't think of the blousy matron who can still, if pushed, pull a tune and a gag out of the hat, even if it is in some god-awful movie. Think of the ugly duckling fresh from Hawaii, gutted that Barbra Streisand had beaten her to the ugly gimmick (don't blame us, it's her joke), struggling to find her feet on Broadway; the diva who ended up playing for a bunch of gay guys more interested in each other than in the weird, shouty woman with red hair.

Born in New Jersey but raised in Honolulu to the only Jewish family in town (it's the New Jersey that comes through), Midler's Broadway dreams came true when she was promoted through the ranks of *Fiddler on the Roof*. But it was at the notorious Continental Baths, a meeting place (not that they were just meeting) for gay men that Midler earned her showbiz stripes. Performing in front of the men in towels, many of whom would be nipping out every once in a while to take care of business, she created the persona 'The Divine Miss M' who, with the help of Barry Manilow on piano, a black lace basque, and some gold lamé pedal-pushers, would belt out old time numbers, tell some very off-color jokes and generally wow the house down (on good nights, the men would take off their red towels and throw them at her like bouquets.) Dubbed 'the Jewish Tinkerbell,' her gig became so famous that celebrities like Andy Warhol and Mick Jagger starting coming along to what was, after all, not much more than

a gay knocking shop to see her perform. Her gay fans were her only fans to start with, and her first ever interview was conducted by the President of gay rights group The Mattachine Society for New York freesheet *GAY*. She nibbled saucily on a carrot throughout.

The Baths, as well as establishing her core audience of gay men, turned out to be her springboard into the mainstream. Her shows got bigger, but not much classier (her backing singers, including Jocelyn Brown and Sharon Redd, were called the Harlettes, and she still told the dirty jokes) and soon she was travelling the world, appearing on chat shows where she would scandalize whole nations with her vulgarity and Shelly Winters impressions (swimming underwater in *The Poseidon Adventure*, in case you were wondering). In 1972, after a tussle among record companies to sign what had become the hottest act in town, she signed with Atlantic, and was soon being produced by none other than Arif Mardin.

By 1973 she had won a Grammy, and by 1980 had bagged herself an Oscar nomination and a Golden Globe for her debut movie, the story of a self-destructive rock singer, *The Rose*. But it was round about this time that Bette started squandering it. Instead of concentrating on dramatic parts that she had proved she could handle, she went for cheap laughs (and not even good cheap laughs like she used to go for in the Continental Baths) in a series of films including *Ruthless People* and *Down And Out In Beverly Hills*. With the exception of *Beaches*, a campy, tear-jerking 'women's picture' about friendship, cancer, love and forgiveness, Bette's film career never quite recovered, although there were moments, like *The First Wives' Club* with Goldie Hawn and Diane Keaton, that showed she still had it if anyone wanted it. Songs like 'Wind Beneath My Wings,'

from *Beaches*, were still doing the business and her albums pretty much always went gold. But Bette was by now putting most of her energy into her husband and her daughter.

Having been chosen by Johnny Carson to be his last ever guest before he left broadcasting altogether, Bette turned to television to boost her career and in October of the year 2000 started appearing in a CBS comedy show she had developed. It proved not to be the success she was hoping for and was terminated soon after.

Named as one of the 25 coolest straight people by *The Advocate*, Bette has always been there for her original fans, whether it's for a fund-raising show or a walk or even just a little cheerleading: "Open your mouths, for Christ's sake," she told gay men worrying about being too political. "Don't you get tired of being stepped on?" Thirty-odd years after she started putting out for naked gay men, she's still our Bathhouse Betty.

Donna Summer
The first lady of love

There are divas and there is Donna Summer. With a voice of incomparable range and power, she pioneered and defined disco throughout the 70s and, until Madonna—who owes her a helluva lot by the way—was the biggest pop star the gay world had known.

Born Donna Gaines in Boston, she grew up on gospel and took her name from her first husband, actor Helmut Sommer, whom she met in Munich, Germany. It's where she also hooked up with Giorgio Moroder and Pete Bellotte, with whom she recorded the groundbreaking sex disco classic 'Love To Love You Baby' that launched her career in 1975.

She continued to take the sounds of the gay dancefloor to the international charts with songs like 'I Feel Love,' 'Bad Girls,' 'MacArthur Park,' and 'No More Tears (Enough Is Enough)' with Barbra Streisand, which established her as the First Lady Of Love.

Was she comfortable with the overtly sexual image portrayed at the time? "I was doing a bit of a take-off of Marilyn, which I thought was 'sexy' and I was working towards Sophia Loren, but I was actually more like Jerry Lewis or Lucille Ball—that's how I saw myself."

Though her career has picked up recently with 'Dinner With Gershwin' and 'I Will Go With You (Con Te Partiro)' and her collaborations with British producers Stock, Aitken and Waterman, things did go a bit pear-shaped in the early 80s when it was alleged she made a remark along the lines of "AIDS is God's punishment for gays."

This has undoubtedly overshadowed a career that's spanned 25 years, though essentially, it is an urban myth. She has, after all, won court cases on the basis that no footage has ever been found containing the statement, and she has regularly shown her commitment to AIDS benefits and gay causes.

The rumor started no doubt as a reaction to the news she'd re-embraced her faith at what was a difficult time for her personally. She says, "When people say to me I'm homophobic or whatever, it's really offensive on a lot of levels. I just thought people knew me better than that."

Princess Diana

Latter day saint and gay icon or stupid spoilt bitch?

When Princess Diana died in a car crash in August 1997 the gay community went into shock. Diana was our Princess, the first royal ever to flaunt her gay friends, to visit people with AIDS, to go about living her life as if it was glamorous to be one of the richest women in the world and not just lump through her duties like the rest of the royals. She was the ultimate gay icon and, as befits gay icons of that magnitude, her end was tragic.

But not all gay men idolized her. In fact, many gay men were insulted that she should be foisted on them so shamelessly. So she was fabulous and drenched in diamonds, but did that really make her worthy of our respect? Here in two opposing pieces we present the arguments for and against Diana as the biggest gay icon of the 20th Century.

Against: Princess Diana's main claim to sainthood among gay men is that she got involved with AIDS charities. Well, zipadeedoodah. Look closer and you'll find that her always highly publicized 'involvement,' part of a general campaign to turn herself into a Queen of Hearts, was often no more than a quick stop-off to shake a few hands between shopping trips. OK, she didn't have to bother (though she could be assured of great press off the back of it), but it's hardly a life of self-sacrifice and commitment, especially when compared to the full-time carers and Buddies of those affected. But even those people were dazzled by her benevolence. And that's what royalty does—blinds people to the realities of situations.

"It sends out a great message," said her supporters. "It shows that people with AIDS are deserving of love and respect too." True. So why, on the occasion when she, martyr-like, took her two sons to visit people with AIDS, did she tell them that the people they had met had cancer, not AIDS?

Aside from her charity work (how did she choose those charities? Names out of a hat? "Ooh, landmines! That'll mean kiddies with no legs"), Princess Diana was famous for a) wearing supposedly nice dresses—they may have come out of the public funds but most of them were hideous, b) turning really nasty when her husband quite rightly dumped her for being totally out of her box: why

go with dignity when you can wheel in a documentary team and wash dirty linen—something she wouldn't know how to do except in a figurative sense—in public? Well, boo hoo—guess now you'll just have to live the rest of your life holidaying on the yachts of dubious lovers. And c) for choosing her friends among the stupidest and shallowest people on offer.

So, she was beautiful (if big old honkers are your bag), she had tons of cash to waste on designer items, her title meant that she threw mere celebrities into the shade, but are gay men, her main fan base, really so easy to convince? Is that all we require of a heroine, a bit of glitz, a bit of chutzpah and all the exercise regimes and skin treatments (public) money can buy? Honestly, we might as well canonize Ivana Trump.

For: We can never underestimate Diana's contribution to changing the whole climate around AIDS. While the tabloids raged and witch-hunted, the British government put the fear of God into anyone who was considering ever having sex again, and the public at large were petitioning to get anyone even suspected of being HIV-positive moved to Outer Mongolia, Princess Diana was getting ready to visit people with AIDS in hospital. It was a risk. Her strongest weapon was her on-the-streets popularity, and by visiting what were then society's pariahs, she was putting everything on the line. But it worked. Attitudes to people with AIDS changed overnight, with the tabloids finding it very difficult to contradict a message given by the nation's favorite person.

But it's not just Diana's work with AIDS-related and other charities that have made her a gay icon (nor is it the fabulous diamonds). It was her determination to be charming even in the face of vicious adversity. When the whole of the British Establishment seemed to be coming down on her, the reaction was not to run or hide but to be seen going about her business, attending functions that had been looking forward to having the most famous person on the earth turn up for a glass of wine and a vol-au-vent.

And she was no push-over. When her husband Prince Charles went on British television to plead his case, she made sure she was out there in a stunning black dress, which she knew would steal the front pages of all the newspapers.

And as a mother—and gay men love their mothers—she was irreproachable. While royal tradition demanded that her sons be brought up formally, she wasn't above whisking them off for rides at theme parks.

But aside from her basic goodness she was, above all, fabulous. Who can forget images of her being whisked around the dancefloor by John Travolta while her frumpy husband looked on? She was an icon of glamour, appearing on the cover of *Vogue* in a way that would simply be unthinkable for any other member of the Royal Family.

At the end of the day, she was our princess. She had gay friends and, ultimately, in spite of being royally screwed over, she showed style, grace and good old-fashioned manners.

Homoerotica

Material such as pictures, films or literature featuring sexy men, usually with their shirts off.

The adjective homoerotic can be applied to pretty much anything—an image, a movie, an advertising campaign—that features a buff stud usually in a situation that is not overtly gay. A film featuring army cadets in singlets, sweating heavily and running around a lot would definitely be homoerotic even though there wouldn't necessarily be any suggestion of action between them.

Homoerotic art can be traced back to the Greeks, who liked nothing better than to embellish vases and pots and other household sundries with pictures of naked men grappling with each other in an apparently totally non-sexual way. Coming back to the present, Bruce Weber's advertising shots for clothing company Abercrombie & Fitch that feature cavorting football players and the like capture the very essence of the homoerotic.

Kitsch

"So bad it's good" art or design

Kitsch is a word, probably of German origin (the likeliest suspect is *verkitschen* meaning "to sell off"), that was first bandied about in Munich around 1900. It refers to art, design—or anything else, come to that—which could be described as tasteless, garish, sentimental, overblown or cheap. Think flamenco dolls, plastic fruit, 50s advertisements, Catholic paraphernalia and Charo.

It's no wonder that kitsch has always had a special appeal for gay men and lesbians, whose sense of irony dictates that anything generally despised must be OK.

Although kitsch is almost by definition of lowly origin, it has been elevated to an art form by gay movie directors such as Pedro Almodovar and John Waters, and by artist Jeff Koons, famous for his ceramics of Michael Jackson and his chimp, Bubbles.

Skinheads

The neo-Nazi blue collar movement that became a gay sex cult

You have to be careful if you're a gay skinhead. People make assumptions. They spot the uniform—drainpipe jeans, tight fitting Levi's jackets, checked shirts, braces and, of course, knee-high lace-up Doc Marten's boots—and have you down as a neo-Nazi, a racist, a thug. They'll also probably have you down as a homophobe, and there you have the sexual appeal of the skinhead.

Emerging from the working class UK scene as a reaction to the peace and love hippies of the 60s, real skinheads were an offshoot of the Mod tribe and were always trouble. Their working class tribalism and readiness to get involved in a fight at a moment's notice made them perfect fodder for UK fascist groups such as the National Front and the British National Party.

Although the early skins were very much a London thing (their music was even called Oi! after the much-overused Cockney expression), the skinhead movement arrived in the US and Australia and was well established there by the mid-80s, just when its demise was being lamented in the UK. But into the vacuum left by the 'real skins' in Britain moved gay men keen on the iconography—who bought their own skinny-leg jeans (perfect for showing off an impressive packet) and MA1 flying jackets. Even today, most gay men are just 'drag skins,' who feel that the look maximizes their sex appeal. There is a minority that takes the skin identity much more seriously, becoming involved in politics, which is ironically usually of a very anti-racist nature.

There was always a hint of S&M in the gay skinhead movement, even if it never moved beyond a light slap and maybe a bit of piss play, but the look was so pre-eminent, especially in the UK, that you could never make any assumptions at all. Today, the gay skin look has moved on slightly, following the straight football hooligans who were its first inspiration. Now, you might find a gay skin wearing a nylon soccer shirt, combat trousers or even a cheap nylon tracksuit. But the attitude is still the same: Good, dirty, working class, macho fun. But, hey, it's only clothes.

Get the look: Essential skinwear

A pair of bleachers: Tight drainpipe Levi's splattered with bleach.

A pair of Doctor Martens, the higher the better, preferably in an ox blood color.

A pair of soccer socks.

A Ben Sherman checked shirt with a button-down collar.

A pair of red nylon clip-on suspenders, or braces.

A black Crombie overcoat, for formal wear.

A nylon snake-link belt.

A nylon MA1 flying jacket, preferably in olive green.

A tattoo, preferably featuring a national flag.

A gold signet ring.

Electric Wahl hair clippers with a number one setting to keep those locks in order.

White 'dad-style' Y-fronts (though the 'no underwear' dick snaking down the leg look is hot).

White T-shirts for under the Ben Sherman shirt.

An acrylic V-neck sweater, preferably in a light color, by Fred Perry.

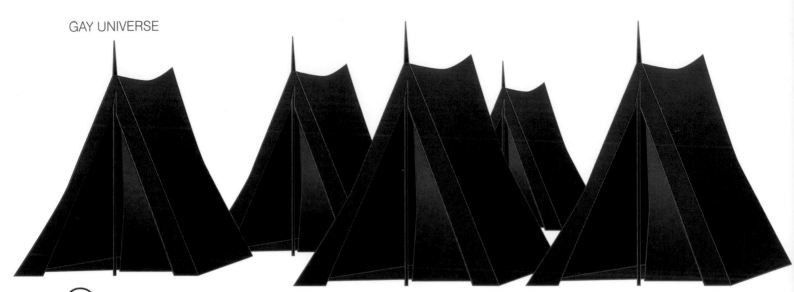

Camp

The lie that speaks the truth

"Camp is terribly hard to define," says Charles Kennedy, a character in Christopher Isherwood's novel *The World in the Evening*. "You have to meditate on it and feel it intuitively."

As far as most people are concerned, camp is anything that has an ostrich-feather trim, a sprinkling of glitter or a funny look in its eye. That could be a daft old game show host with big hair, a pop star like Mariah Carey (so camp it's almost frightening) or pretty much anything in pink: a Cadillac, a pair of shoes, even an entire bedroom (you know who you are!—comments like that, by the way, are also camp).

But there's more to camp than kitsch [see page 18] and effeminate and sarcastic, even though all those things do come into it. Camp is an attitude that refuses to take things seriously; in fact, according to Susan Sontag, the scholar whose 'Notes On Camp' is the definitive article on the subject, it "converts the serious into the frivolous."

If you call anything camp, you invite someone to look at it in a different way. If you say Hitler was camp, you're focusing not on the horror of his actions or the redundancy of his politics but on the ridiculousness of his appearance, the bizarre posturing he used during his speeches, the basic ooh la la of the most evil man of the 20th century. Gay men—the most skilful users of camp—are often attacked for being frivolous about the most serious of subjects but what critics don't appreciate is that camp is an extremely effective weapon. By focusing on the campness of Hitler, you are also belittling him.

Camp is irony, it is estheticism, it is very gay, but the camp approach doesn't necessarily mean that you're not taking something seriously. In fact, you're taking it seriously enough to make fun out of it. Or, as Christopher Isherwood put it, "You're expressing what's basically serious to you in terms of fun and artifice and elegance." In short, camp, when exercised properly, is a total mind-fuck.

"The hallmark of camp is the spirit of extravagance," said Susan Sontag in her 'Notes', and if it's extravagance you're after, you need to get the gays in. Camp also relies on a sense of artificiality, a sense which is very highly developed in gay men, probably dating from the time when it was decided they were somehow separate from the natural way of things. It was as if gay men, realizing that the world in general regarded them as unnatural due to their exclusion from the procreative process, embraced and celebrated everything unnatural they could find. It's the same mind-set that produces gay freaks: "You think I'm a freak, I'll show you what a freak I can be, and here's me inserting saline into my scrotum till it blows up like a balloon just to show you pure freakiness."

The gay relationship with camp dates as far back as the gay identity itself, and probably springs from the feeling of powerlessness, where the most effective way to undermine authority was to refuse to take it seriously. What better way to pop a politician's bubble than to ridicule him?

In the 19th century, Oscar Wilde [see page 176] made the strong connections between homosexuality and irony and estheticism, which are the bedrocks of camp, connections which hadn't necessarily been made before. Irony and estheticism has previously been the preserve of the rich and idle, not of the gay. But when Wilde's famous epigrams, which sought to overturn social morality, were linked with his 'immoral behavior' with boys, this type of arch, sneery, 'amoral' posturing was finally identified as gay behavior.

Camp, it was thought, was proof that gay men found it impossible to take anything seriously. It was also proof that they were devious and sneaky and didn't look at things head on. It is still often seen as evidence of gay men's inability to see beyond the surface, and to engage emotionally. And it's true that there are people who use camp to avoid engaging on a real level. Even Sontag pushed this negative aspect of camp: "Camp is the solvent of morality," she wrote. "It neutralizes moral indignation."

And it's true. It has been noted that the only gay men who can make it in the mainsteam media are those that manage to do exactly what Sontag says, neutralize moral indignation to their homosexuality. They do this by being camp, by neutralizing their own sexuality and emphasizing the playful, the arch, the

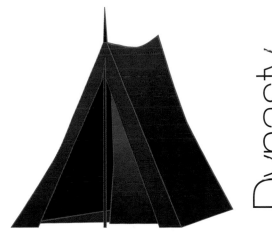

Dynasty

The all-time campest program ever shown

Dallas was all very well but ask any self-respecting homosexual to choose and it's *Dynasty* every time. How could it not be? The Aaron Spelling trash-fest was diva-heavy, crammed with cute guys (some of them gay and willing to get it on) and featured some of the most ridiculous costumes ever to appear on network television. When those vertical stripes started rising up from the bottom of the TV screen accompanied by that parpy old brass music, it was the most ardently awaited moment of the week for most gay men. Gay bars went silent for it.

humorous, the fancy. Camp has become a suit of armor, but, to an extent, it's one that gay men have become trapped in. Unfortunately, it has become something of a chicken-and-egg situation, where the only recognizably gay men that gay kids see as they grow up are camp, so the behavior they learn, the only 'gay' behavior they know, is obviously camp.

Young gay men think, therefore, that this is the way gay men behave, continuing the cycle of camp. In 1960s Britain, when homosexuality was still illegal, radio characters Julian and Sandy, who featured on top show of the time *Round The Horne*, were a screechingly gay couple whose sexuality was indicated by their campness. This meant that not only did gay men have role models—very funny role models as it happens—but straight listeners were let in on a lot of gay slang. And, because their sexuality had been neutralized by their campness, Julian and Sandy were well loved by the public at large. Any young gay man wanting to be well loved just had to camp it up like they did. Or so he thought.

Ironically, especially in the UK, the preponderance of gay men on children's television in the 90s has meant that a whole generation of kids, both gay and straight, are growing up incredibly knowing and arch and, well, camp—meaning that camp is no longer the exclusive preserve of gay men. Now you can hear pretty much everyone giving a camp reading to even the most serious matters, including children as young as six and seven. Maybe our work here is done. What a camp way to finish!

The show, a blatant response to the success of *Dallas*, kicked off with a three-hour pilot on January 12th, 1981 and by 1984 had knocked *Dallas* out of the picture. It focused on the life, loves, family and business of patriarch Blake Carrington, a white-haired bigot played by John Forsyth, the voice of Charlie from *Charlie's Angels*, but it was the female characters that excited most. Carrington's wife Krystle, played by Linda Evans, was embroiled in a week-in, week-out to-the-death bitch fight with has-been British actress Joan Collins, who played Carrington's ex-wife Alexis Colby. No opportunity for the two characters to have a go at each other was left unexplored, with the fight in the lily pond a particular favorite.

But apart from the divas—and they really were wheeled out, with Diahann Carroll brought in to play Dominique Deveraux and Heather Locklear as errant daughter-in-law Sammy Jo—it was the gay characters that most interested the homosexual audience. Despite being married to the foxy and fearless Sammy Jo, Steven Carrington, played first by Al Corely and then, after facial surgery, by the much cuter Jack Coleman, was, much to his father's disgust, gay.

Alexis, our heroine, was always supportive of her gay son, as any bona fide evil bitch diva would be, and he went on to have a happy homosexual relationship—much to the amusement of Sammy Jo—with the equally cute Luke, played by William Campbell. The couple's first kiss caused an absolute furore in a show where terrorists and plane crashes were the daily bread and butter, though any possibility of a happy ending was scuppered by the infamous Moldavian massacre.

More scandal hit the show when special guest star Rock Hudson [see page 184], brought in to provide a bit of romance for Krystle, was diagnosed with AIDS. In the middle of the uneducated paranoia about HIV and its means of transmission that reigned in the 80s, the tabloids had a field day, screaming that Rock had kissed Linda Evans, and now God knows how long she had to live. As it turned out, she lived on to suck face another day.

Dynasty lasted a total of nine shoulder-padded years, many of them near the top of the ratings in countries around the world. It spawned a spin-off series, *The Colbys*, starring British actress (and Alexis wannabe) Stephanie Beacham, and was declared by the influential US magazine *TV Guide* to be the best prime-time soap of the decade, portraying perfectly the greed, extravagance, nastiness, and bad clothes of the 80s.

"Its campy opulence gave it a superb, ironic quality," said *TV Guide*. "In other words, it was great trash."

Madonna

Man-eater, manipulator, monster, bitch, whore. She has been described as all these things. Way to go Madge!

When Madonna Louise Ciccone first appeared on the pop scene in 1983, bumping and grinding her way through happy disco numbers like 'Lucky Star,' everyone laughed hard. It's tricky to remember how much people laughed their heads off at her lame chubby sexiness, at the out-of-date disco ditties, at her small-town Lolita act, and the nude spreads and soft porn movies that started emerging from her hand-to-mouth past. The only people who didn't laugh were gay men. They got it. They loved it. They wanted it.

Just like millions of gay men stifled in home towns that didn't understand them, Madonna had run away from Detroit when she was just 19 years old, landing in New York with just $35 in her pocket and, legendarily, telling the cab driver to take her to the center of everything. He took her to Times Square. From there she apparently picked up a guy who took her to live in his apartment until she eventually found herself a slum dwelling on the scuzzy Lower East Side. She'd come to New York to be a dancer, and was auditioning while working as a waitress, nude artists' model and soft-core starlet to keep hot body and deep soul together.

After a stint in Paris with French disco king Patrick Hernandez, and having infiltrated New York's gay disco scene, Madonna wangled herself a recording deal, had an album masterminded by Reggie Lucas and started to make it on the underground. She had already hooked up—in all sorts of ways—with DJ Jon "Jellybean" Benitez, and had used him to help get her feet on rungs of various music biz ladders, asking him to come in and fiddle with Lucas's work until she had songs like 'Lucky Star' the way she wanted them. Her first dance singles were put out on white labels in the hope that DJs would assume she was black: It seemed to work and hits like 'Borderline' started to have international impact, as did her

post-punk, street urchin style which teamed hair-rags with arm-loads of bangles and dayglo make-up.

For her second album Madonna, always a great collaborator, went to the legendary Nile Rogers. The first single, 'Like A Virgin,' was an international smash and when Madonna performed it at the MTV Awards, rolling around on the floor like a bitch on heat, a star was born. The industry was shocked and the public intrigued.

A role in the Susan Seidelman movie *Desperately Seeking Susan*, where she played a maneater, monster, bitch and whore (her only other successful movie would be in *Evita*, where she played a… guess what?) cemented her as a major new star, while tracks like 'Into The Groove,' from that movie, and great video after great video turned her into a multimedia phenomenon.

From here on in Madonna used whatever skimpy artistic talent she had—a voice so thin you could slide it under a door— to truly shocking effect. Her single 'Like A Prayer,' accompanied by a highly controversial video which saw her kissing a black Christ figure scuppered a deal with Pepsi (though she got to keep the cash), while her book *SEX* set the world against her.

Ridiculed and derided, Madonna had genuinely broken all the rules of celebrity with *SEX*, a collaboration with fashion photographer Steven Meisel. Images of the world's most famous female star naked, being held at knifepoint by lesbians, being raped by skinheads, cavorting with dogs and hitchhiking naked along a freeway were truly groundbreaking, though no one felt in the least bit inclined to give her credit. She had not only blown the whistle on the exhibitionism of celebrities, but had also called the lie to the old chestnut that women involved in pornography were always exploited: This was the single

most successful woman in showbiz, after all. But the world didn't want to hear and laid into her like never before. Madonna was truly unrepentant. In a world where a tearful apology on a big-name talk show will get you off blow-jobs in cars from prostitutes, Madonna refused to back down. On *Bedtime Stories*, the follow-up album to the raunchy *Erotica*, she gave a resounding finger to her critics on the song 'Human Nature,' where she protested that not only was she not sorry, but also that she was no one's bitch and would continue to say what the hell she liked.

Throughout her career, and through an era when, due to the AIDS epidemic, gay men were very much marginalized, Madonna's support never wavered. Many of her closest friends had been affected (her old dance teacher Christopher Flynn, her close buddy artist Keith Haring), and as the sister of a gay man (Christopher), she was determined to do her bit. Madonna's *Like A Prayer* album carried a safer sex information leaflet and an exhortation for people to treat people with AIDS with consideration and dignity, while there was hardly an AIDS benefit danceathon that didn't feature Madonna center-stage.

Already established as the biggest gay icon of the 20th century, Madonna continued to cut edges. Her *Ray of Light* album in 1998 was a critical and commercial smash, as was the follow-up album *Music*. Her *Drowned World* tour in 2001 wowed audiences and critics alike. Yes, she is now a mother of two well into her forties, yes she is on her second marriage, again to a guy suspected of being a borderline homophobe and yes, she is now having her ass chased by a whole gaggle of squeaky blonde wannabes, but Madonna is still doing it and the devotion she's always had from her gay fans shows no sign of declining. She is still, as one UK gay magazine has always called her, Our Glorious Leader.

Five things Madonna plundered the gay community for

Vogue
A black gay dance craze where contestants strike poses, and act like models in fashion magazines. Madonna ripped it off and sent it mainstream.

Sandra Bernhard
She used and abused our favorite lesbian/bi/whatever comic, stole her girlfriend and has spent the rest of her career being dissed for it.

Big fashion
Before Madonna, it was pretty much only gay men that would be caught dead in Gaultier and Dolce & Gabbana.

Out-there sexuality
Imagine anyone other than a gay man with the balls to publish a book not only with her vagina on display but with a dog sniffing round it.

Tony Ward
A bisexual model whom Madonna introduced herself to by burning his shoulder with a cigarette. Previous to being sucked into her orbit, Ward was a nude model in gay mags.

Ten archetypal Madonna moments

1. Demonstrating oral sex with a Vichy Catalan bottle in the documentary *Truth or Dare*.
2. Shouting to an audience of millions that she wasn't taking shit off at the *Live Aid* concert, days after naked photos of her had appeared in *Penthouse*.
3. Simulating masturbation live on stage during her *Blonde Ambition* tour, even though she risked being arrested by Canadian police for obscenity.
4. Appearing at a screening of *Truth or Dare* in Cannes in her underwear.
5. Turning up at the Oscars in millions of dollars' worth of diamonds with Michael Jackson on her arm and walking off with the prize for Best Song.
6. 'Justify My Love,' the first video to be banned by MTV.
7. Posing as a lesbian on *David Letterman* with Sandra Bernhard.
8. Getting her bush out in *Body of Evidence*.
9. Getting schmoozed by Argentinian President Menem.
10. Telling the Pope that if he didn't like her show, he could lump it.

The ultimate showtune diva, Miss Shirley Bassey

Divas

Big mouths, big hair, big trouble

In this day and age, the word diva is used as liberally as 'VWE' in the personal ads; any female singer worth her chops either thinks she's one, or else aspires to be one.

If the definition, according to the *Oxford English Dictionary*, of "a celebrated opera singer" is to be believed, very few ladies actually fit the bill; however the term has also come to include any of the following: a huge voice, an even bigger ego and the balls to use it— throw in a penchant for sparkly dresses, a hint of real life tragedy and "my man done me wrong" torch songs and you've got a very loose definition.

And only gay men can truly understand these defining characteristics. Homos can appreciate the nuances and humor of this image of overblown femininity, they've lipsynched to their voices in front of the mirror more times than they care to remember, and the lyrics…Show us a gay man who doesn't know what it feels like to have tragedy in their life? In a nutshell, these women are who gay men would want to be if they were born a different gender. Ladies, we salute you.

Early diva
Definitive example: Bessie Smith

On the record she was sexually explicit, off the record she was serious trouble; the Empress of Blues was also a well-known bisexual. Discovered by Ma Rainey in Chattanooga, who also taught her everything she needed to know about the love of a good lady, Bessie was soon hanging out with female impersonators and touring with her "All Girl Band." And, apparently, she slept with the lot! Despite getting married, she refused to be bound by any rules and lived her life as large as her ample figure. Also rans:
Billie Holiday—Ex-prostitute, drug addict and tragic diva, though it ain't nobody's business if she did.
Edith Piaf—The Little Sparrow hit with a trail of French torch songs, broken hearts, alcohol, morphine and cortisone.

Rock diva
Definitive example: Cher

Her latest incarnation might have been as a disco diva for the international smash, 'Believe,' but Cher's always been a rocker at heart; leather, tattoos, motorcycles, crazed hair, astride a cannon in chaps… More than that however, she's a ballsy survivor who's notched up almost four decades in showbusiness and has had two ex-husbands, a bunch of boyfriends (some of the toy variety), and three careers (in music, television and film) to her name. Also rans:

Janis Joplin—the greatest white female rock singer of the 60s was an out-there, sweaty sex-beast with more dysfunctions than an episode of Jerry Springer.
Stevie Nicks—Solo artist and Fleetwood Mac member, Stevie is part-ethereal chantoosie, part-grizzled earth mother.
Courtney Love—Rock widow/actress/ desperate wannabe peddling a combo of gratin' guitars and heroin chic.

Dance diva
Definitive example: Gloria Gaynor

Gloria Gaynor was the First Lady Of Disco, and her status as a disco diva is eclipsed only by the Rt. Hon. Queen Donna Summer [see page 15]. She sang with the Soul Satisfiers before being discovered in New York, and was at the forefront of disco in the early 70s with tracks like 'Never Can Say Goodbye,' and the ultimate women's/gay anthem 'I Will Survive' [see page 26]. A vocalist who can really tear the houses down, she's still performing and recording but beware—has also found God. Also rans:

Ultra Naté—'Free,' fierce and rulin' dance diva in the making.
Sylvester—Outrageous, out-there disco star.

Urban diva
Definitive example: Mary J Blige

With the universally-agreed best voice to emerge in the past decade, a former drug problem, an infamous diva-esque moment in *Interview* magazine and, oh yes, Fendi shades, Mary J Blige is the real thing. 1992 was her breakout year when urban cuts like 'Reminisce' and 'Real Love' had her instantly crowned as the Queen Of Hip Hop Soul while her unique style of singing has influenced a generation. The hits have followed almost non-stop as have the traumas, but we're assured she's now back on track. Also rans:

Lil' Kim—Hardcore beats, a pornographic sense of style and a dirty mouth… we love.
Beyoncé Knowles from Destiny's Child—Blond, brazen and ballsy, en route to being the new Diana Ross.
Faith Evans—Once caught in the crossfire between the East and West Coast rap posses, she exudes pure trouble and pain all at the same time.

Showtunes diva
Definitive example: Shirley Bassey

Also known as Bassey the Belter and the Tigress of Tiger Bay, Shirley Bassey [see picture page 24] broke out of Wales in 1955 and launched a series of UK hits with the 'Banana Boat Song' in early 1957. Best-known for her mid-60s big blood-curdling Bond themes like 'Diamonds Are Forever' and 'Goldfinger,' she's since moved into established mainstream territory with lavish Saturday evening television fare and sell-out concerts. She still has enough cachet however, to be found funky, and the late 90s saw a remix album and a collaboration with the Propellerheads. Off stage, however, it's been quite a different story: two husbands (one of whom committed suicide after their divorce) and three children; the first of which, Sharon, was born when Bassey was seventeen and unmarried, the second (Samantha) threw herself from a bridge and the third (Mark) took drugs. Also rans:

Barbra Streisand—No explanation needed [see page 37].
Liza Minnelli—A loser in love and narcotics and oh yes, Judy Garland's daughter to boot.
Celine Dion—With real old-school chutzpah, Celine can reduce the cutesiest ballad to showtune status.

Country diva
Definitive example: Dolly Parton

She may be waaay too nice to be a bona-fide diva-bitch, but singer and songwriter Dolly Parton has certainly got the hair, the hooters and the hard luck stories. Po'whitetrash from Locust Ridge, Tennessee, she's since made real good after a stint at the Grand Old Oprey and the breakthrough single 'Dumb Blonde' (which she's not). The 70s saw her establish herself as a country superstar, and in the 80s, a movie star with films like *Nine To Five*, *Steel Magnolias*, and *Straight Talk*. More gay friendly than is normal, Dolly's been married for 35 years to the same man, Carl Dean, who runs an asphalt-paving business, though rumors of lesbian tendencies still rear their heads. Also rans:

Patsy Cline—'Crazy' country star who sang in the face of tragedy thanks to an abusive hubbie, a car wreck and a plane crash that finally saw her off.
Shania Twain—Homey 'n' hokey chanteuse morphs into country-pop diva with drag queen stylin' and two gay anthems, 'That Don't Impress Me Much,' and 'Man! I Feel Like A Woman!'

Soul diva
Definitive example: Aretha Franklin

With Aretha Franklin, it's all about the voice. A real heavyweight of American music, Lady Soul's roots were in gospel and she first started singing in her father's Detroit church with her sisters Carolyn and Erma in the 50s. But it wasn't until she brought her great gospel voice to an impressive catalog of soul songs like 'R.E.S.P.E.C.T,' 'Spanish Harlem,' and '(You Make Me Feel Like) A Natural Woman' that she found fame in the late 60s. The legacy of these songs is so strong that she's managed to live on the rep ever since. Also rans:

Diana Ross—From Supremes to supreme in one easy move, you don't call her Miss Ross for no reason.
Whitney Houston—From the finest r'n'b pop vocalist of recent times to washed-up wreck. Houston, we have a problem.
Dusty Springfield—Beleaguered lesbo icon and the finest female voice to emerge from Britain, like, ever.

Pop diva Mariah Carey

Opera diva

Definitive example: Maria Callas

The ultimate diva. Of Greek parentage, Maria Callas made her debut as Tosca at the Athens Opera in 1941, but it wasn't until her performance in *La Gioconda* in Verona, Italy, that she hit the big time. Her richly colored voice held audiences captive from New York to La Scala in Milan, but it was her off-stage dramas that really launched her into diva territory; wranglings with a former manager, a lifelong feud with her mother whom she believed had robbed her of her childhood, and a nine-year affair with Aristotle Onassis (who dumped her to marry Jackie Kennedy). But it was her self-critical and temperamental behavior together with persistent vocal issues which meant she'd either sing below par or not at all that really set her apart from the rest. Also rans:

Jessye Norman—One of the world's most celebrated artists, Jessye's talent is real and boundless.

Leslie Garrett—Britain's favorite soprano, otherwise known as the Madonna of opera.

Up and coming diva

Definitive example: Charlotte Church

She might not yet be out of her teens but watch this puppy grow. Finding fame after a TV chat show call-in, Charlotte Church has been fast-tracked into one of the world's megastars with super-soaraway opera-lite albums and performances for presidents, popes and queens. She still manages to work the homespun plain-speaking charm of any Welsh teenager while working an outfit fit for J.Lo. You go girl.

Also rans:

Christina Aguilera—Britney's nemesis with a penchant for trailer trash couture.

Brandy/Monica—The lyrical jousting on 'The Boy Is Mine' reportedly continued out of the studio.

Samantha Mumba—Fierce 'n' feisty Irish wannabe with ever-revealing outfits.

Pop diva

Definitive example: Kylie Minogue

Having wrestled with comparisons to Madonna [see page 22] throughout her 15-year career, diminutive Australian disco-pop diva Kylie Minogue is, however, the ultimate in kitsch gay icons. A former actress in a D-rate Australian soap, she made her mark first with the super frothy 'I Should Be So Lucky,' and cleaned up with some help from 80s über-producers Stock, Aitken and Waterman. There might not be much tragedy in her life—apart from the obligatory 80s hats where she pulled her hair through the top—but after a stint of indie down-the-dumperdom, she's now back with her best albums yet, her tongue firmly in cheek and carefully crafted hotpants. Also rans:

Mariah Carey [see picture page 26]— With a voice that only dogs can truly hear, she became the biggest female vocalist of the 90s but seems to be pissing it all up the wall.

Elton John—Versace schmutter, oversized glasses and an ego to match… you need any other proof?

Jennifer Lopez—Despite her colorful love life being behind her (courtesy of Puff Daddy, P Diddy, whatever), her outrageous demands—"I don't do stairs"—are legendary.

It's like gay icons, every song wants to be a gay anthem. But, just as every has-been drama queen cannot be a gay icon just because she's a tragic case who knows how to apply eyeshadow, not every song with a bit of ballsiness can cut it as a gay anthem. Gay anthems cannot choose themselves, they have to be chosen. Here are the criteria by which they are selected.

1. Any recording with a voice that is big, preferably black and essentially female (and no, Luther Vandross doesn't count). These singers are usually referred to as divas [see page 24] and are mistresses of tearing the goddamn house down with their vocals. Key examples: The entire works of Gloria Gaynor, Patti Labelle.

2. Songs that have some sort of storyline about overcoming hardship, usually in love, being totally mistreated by some cute but unworthy males and coming through the other side more assertive, more kick-ass, and generally a better, stronger person. Think of it as the musical equivalent of a self-help book. Key examples: 'I Will Survive' by Gloria Gaynor, 'No More Tears (Enough Is Enough)' by Barbra Streisand/Donna Summer, 'If You Don't Want To Fuck Me (Then Baby Fuck Off)' by Jayne County.

3. Any record that has a message that brings us together as a community, that makes us feel we're not all alone out there in the big bad world but that we have some other suckers in our corner, and that in times of adversity we could just turn around to our "brothers and sisters," and give them a great big healing hug. These are gay pride anthems and the singers of them see the bookings roll in every summer as those festivals come around again. Key examples: 'We Are Family' by Sister Sledge, 'YMCA' by Village People, 'Sisters Are Doing It For Themselves' by Eurythmics with Aretha Franklin.

4. The flip side of the big old angsty anthem about overcoming adversity in love is the disco ditty where cares, such as they are, are thrown directly to the wind and some usually blonde girl singer who has never had a bad moment in all her life with perfect hair and perfect skin sings about turning beats around, stepping back in time, holidaying, celebrating, feeling alright. Key examples:

'Turn The Beat Around' by Vicky Sue Robinson, 'Step Back In Time' by Kylie Minogue, 'Holiday' by Madonna.

5. The more grown-up, less frothy version of the celebratory anthem [see 4] speaks less of empty good times handed out on a silver platter after just the slightest discomfort and more of hard-won freedom, glamour, beauty and self-esteem, often with a sense that there is still darkness to be overcome. Key examples: 'Free' by Ultra Naté, 'Supermodel' by RuPaul, 'The Greatest Love of All' by Whitney Houston, 'In The Evening' by Sheryl Lee Ralph.

6. The celebration of sheer sluttiness. After years of never getting any (or never getting anything half-decent), the idea of getting all you wanted was worth singing about. Key examples: 'So Many Men, So Little Time' by Miquel Brown, 'It's Raining Men' by the Weather Girls.

7. The Wizard of Oz dream that somewhere there is a land where we can be free to live our lives, where we will get the same respect as everyone else, and can go about our own dirty business without fear or hindrance. Key examples: 'There's A Place For Us' from West Side Story, 'Somewhere Over The Rainbow' by Judy Garland, 'Wouldn't It Be Nice' by the Beach Boys—although gay men don't like this song due to its lack of big, black or female vocals [see 1].

8. The lament, where the singer helps us

indulge our feelings of utter worthlessness and reinforce our secret fear that we are unloveable and will never be able to find a like soul to share our private torment. And even if there's a tiny hope that some other loser may stumble across our weary souls and take pity, these songs should clearly indicate that that hope is in vain and you ain't never going to get it/keep it: 'Maybe This Time' by Liza Minnelli, 'You Don't Have To Say You Love Me' by Dusty Springfield, 'And I'm Telling You I'm Not Going' by Jennifer Holliday.

9. The unashamed pledge, tinged with tragedy, that we are worthy lovers—aka doormats—who will do anything in our power to show that we will be there and that no wind (no wind), no rain (no rain), nor winter's cold can stop us. Key examples: 'Ain't No Mountain High Enough' by Diana Ross, 'Woman In Love' by Barbra Streisand, 'As Long As He Needs Me' by Shirley Bassey.

10. This is the deal, take it or leave it. It's a gay pride thing where you refuse to apologize any more, and expect everyone to either like it or lump it; only if they choose the lump it option they can go the hell somewhere else and lump it 'cause we're not going to have it lumped up here in our faces. Is that clear? Key examples: 'I Am What I Am' by Gloria Gaynor, 'I'm Coming Out' by Diana Ross, 'I Was Born This Way' by Valentino—then Carl Bean.

Cagney & Lacey
A lady-cop twist on the old buddy formula

One of the surprise hit shows of the 80s, Cagney and Lacey broke all boundaries, starring as it did two female lead characters—something never seen on television before. The cop duo comprised of Christine Cagney, a brassy blonde cop with a penchant for pink fluffy mohair, a 50-cigarettes-a-day voice and an alcoholic father, and Mary-Beth Lacey, a brown-haired working class family woman, married to Harvey.

After initial cancellations and cast changes following a pilot in 1982, Sharon Gless and Tyne Daly were recruited as Christine and Mary-Beth respectively. As the series progressed, the viewers became hooked on the show's two stars—gone were the days where shoot-outs and drug deals were the main focus of a police drama, now we actually got to know and love the characters as we explored their relationship to the job and their families.

Despite a distinct lack of homo action within the stories, Christine and Mary-Beth became, unusually, gay and lesbian icons. It was the gun-touting, kick ass way the two women not only beat the baddies but also stuck up for each other that won over homo hearts. Sure those lesbian theorists could try and put a dykey spin on the two women's relationship if they'd tried hard enough, but this straight-down-the-line, fuss-free cop show was a hit with the homos because of its stars—Sharon Gless and Tyne Daly. After all, if you give a woman a dirty mouth and some lip gloss, you're pretty much guaranteed a devoted gay audience.

After its shaky start, the show really kicked off, pulling in Emmy nominations for the pair year after year. She may not have been as glam as Angie Dickenson's Police Woman, but Sharon Gless's diva-esque Christine Cagney had the gay girls and boys wishing they could be her—minus the alcoholism—or be with her, while her loveable, frumpier sidekick, Mary-Beth skilfully juggled a difficult family

life—that damn Harvey never shut up about her job—with dressing up as a prostitute and getting shot at, all in the line of duty.

With storylines touching on drug addiction, hostage taking, sexual harassment and cancer, and even goodie-goodie Mary-Beth being arrested for demonstrating against nuclear weapons, these sisters were certainly doing it for themselves and the viewers were gripped—for nearly an entire decade! The final series ran in 1987 and ended with Harvey Junior being missing in action whilst serving in the Marines, and Mary-Beth's other kiddie being at school with a child with AIDS. No stone was left unturned. The girls did return in the mid-90s for a bash at recapturing the glory, beauty and downright grit of the legendary cop drama in movie form, but Christine was married—like that would have ever happened—and Mary-Beth's marriage was in tatters. Somehow, it just didn't feel right.

Since the glory, glory days, Daly has gone on to musicals, while Sharon Gless, ever the queer icon, went on to perform in the American version of Queer As Folk [see page 147] after begging for the part of the lead character Michael's supportive mother. As Gless puts it: "If anyone ever told me I would be playing a role model, I'd run screaming into the night. But when I read the script, I couldn't get on a plane fast enough." Once an icon…

Whiney wimmin and song

Female folk singers, who do it for females

Folk music is one of the oldest forms of artistic expression, dating back to… well, how long have you got? Oh, OK. Then put it this way: whenever and wherever there's been a campfire, you can be pretty sure there's been a woman with a guitar there to provide the entertainment.

However, it was in the 60s that record companies really cottoned onto this "new" musical genre. Female folk singers like Joan Baez and Joni Mitchell were spurred on by the lovin', livin' and givin' attitude of hippies and the burgeoning women's movement, resulting in protest songs, social commentaries and alternative love songs to the "Be My Baby"s which were cluttering up the charts at the time.

Girls with guitars continue to do the business, but with varied success—they're big for a while when one breaks through into the mainstream, ushering a slew of signings to major labels, but then they disappear again. They are a guaranteed hit with dykes however who—excuse the generalization—prefer female singers. The chanteuses' appeal chiefly lies in strumming their pain with their fingers—their expression of the experience of being female you're unlikely to find anywhere else. It sure doesn't hurt that some are indeed lesbians or at least lesbian-friendly…

Ani DiFranco [see picture page 29]
The poster girl for whiney wimmin and song, bisexual feminist folkie Ani DiFranco has made her mark over the past decade via grass roots touring, female empowerment themes and seriously gritty realism—rape, abortion and sexism, she'd got 'em all covered. By the age of twenty, she'd built up such a word-of-mouth following that she was able to launch her own highly successful record label, Righteous Babe. With further touring and albums, she fast became a figure of fantasy for lesbians, who all bought into her shaven, tattooed and pierced image, but soon got pissed when she married her engineer. Fighting off interest from the corporates, she continues to fly the flag for Do-It-Yourself. You go girl.

Tracy Chapman [see picture right]
A former anthropological and African Studies scholar from Cleveland, Tracy Chapman honed her craft in coffeehouses before a fellow student helped her sign a publishing deal. It wasn't long before her deep voice, powerful melodies, and bittersweet stories concerning human rights, racial equity and economic justice made her 1988 self-titled album a crossover success, and ushered in a new generation of singer-songwriters. Although she's never quite recaptured those moments, she continues to record and sell to a female fan base turned on by the rumors of her relationships with women.

Alanis Morissette
The unlikeliest of earth mothers, Ottawa-born Alanis Morissette was a former child star-cum-disco dolly who, on her move to Los Angeles at the age of twenty, transformed herself into an edgy singer-songwriter with grizzled hair whose international breakthrough, the multi-platinum, Grammy-award winning album, *Jagged Little Pill*, vocalized the rants of a whole generation: "And I'm here to remind you of the mess you left when you went away!" She even got her snatch out—pixellated though it might have been—for 'Thank U' from the much-less successful follow-up *Former Infatuation Junkie*. Kissing Sarah Jessica Parker in *Sex And The City* also upped her lesbian credentials.

Sinead O'Connor
The controversy has always been bigger than Sinead O'Connor. Marrying rock sensibility, traditional Irish vocals, female angst and cute dyke imagery, she scored herself an international hit with a cover of Prince's 'Nothing Compares 2 U' which is still guaranteeing her media coverage over a decade later. Emulating Madonna's headline grabbing tactics, she nevertheless fell flat through over-politicizing, refusing to perform alongside the Star Spangled Banner, ripping up a photo of Pope John Paul II on *Saturday Night Live*, claiming she was first a lesbian then a vicar, then a… oh, whatever.

Indigo Girls
Emily Saliers and Amy Ray are kinda like a slimmed-down Spice Girls, providing something for everyone—as long as you're a lesbian—there's blonde and

dark, raw rock (Amy's department) and sweet melodies (Emily's), but it's that mix of tones and textures that made this "two women with guitars" formula a hit. Emily and Amy became successful as part of the late-80s folky singer-songwriter genre, and although they weren't out then—they didn't want to be pigeonholed—lesbians sure can sniff their sisters out. They've now moved away from their folky roots into more political territory—causing some furore with their rabid fan base—while recent gigs in South Carolina high schools were cancelled when several parents complained that as lesbians they'd be a bad influence. Never mind, it did inspire a song.

Tori Amos
An ethereal vision with flame hair, Tori Amos's art is characterized by piano ballads which fall somewhere between Kate Bush and Joni Mitchell. Her songs are confessional and there's nothing she's scared to commit to record—rape, miscarriage, being screwed up, you name it—no wonder she's brought out the freaks. But they're die-hard freaks, who follow her every move. Despite a false start—her 1987 pop-metal album *Y Kant Tori Read* fell on deaf ears—she's since notched up mega-sales for acclaimed albums like *Little Earthquakes*, *Boys For Pele*, and *Strange Little Girls*—her recent interpretation of male songs from a female standpoint.

Melissa Etheridge
A megastar Stateside, craggy old rocker and two-time Grammy winner Melissa Etheridge is out, loud 'n' proud, while her life has often mirrored and shaped what's going on for gay women in American society. Recent albums like *Breakdown*, *Your Little Secret*, and *Yes I Am* have addressed her sexuality, though she actually came out publicly in 1993 at an inaugural ball for President Clinton. At the time, she was dating Cypher whom she met five years earlier when the filmmaker was still married to actor Lou Diamond Phillips. They went on to have two children, Bailey and Beckett (fathered by fellow musician David Crosby) but caused a storm in 2000 when, hot on the heels of Ellen and Anne's break-up, they also announced their split. Nevertheless she says: "I'm sort of a gay success story, a very inspirational one. What happened to me is exactly the opposite of what closeted people fear: They think they'll lose everything if they come out. This did not happen to me at all. In fact, everything came back tenfold."

Sarah McLachlan
Lilith Fair lovely Sarah McLachlan's atmospheric folky pop, witnessed on her breakthrough oeuvre *Fumbling Towards Ecstasy*, has helped her achieve star status in North America and word-of-mouth success almost everywhere else. But it's her work with the package tour femfest Lilith Fair—which seeks to break women singer-songwriters—that has seriously established her as a force to be reckoned with. Kicking off in 1997, she says of it: "Lilith was kind of this little creature that grew wings and took off..."

Joan Armatrading
A forerunner of Tracy Chapman, the two are similar in many ways: Not only is their music a unique fusion of their influences that was picked up by the mainstream, but both stars are media-shy, resulting in all kinds of rumors projected onto them—one of which is that they are gay. Joan was born on the island of St. Kitts but brought up in Birmingham, UK where, without any kind of role model, she pioneered a blend of soul- and reggae-infused folk that made the androgynous singer a star in 1972. She'll always be renowned for stand-out tracks like 'Love and Affection,' 'Drop The Pilot,' and 'Me, Myself, I'. She continues to record and was recently awarded an MBE in the UK.

Suzanne Vega
Without Suzanne Vega, you probably wouldn't have Michelle Shocked. Or Tracy Chapman. Or the Indigo Girls. Her brand of folk-pop with sensitive lyrics made the genre fashionable again during the late 80s and early 90s, when the album *Solitude Standing* went platinum, and she scored herself massive hits with the niggling 'Tom's Diner' and child abuse-themed 'Luka.' She is, however, straight—sorry girls—but has felt the pain of a broken heart when experimental producer and hubbie Mitchell Froom started seeing *Ally McBeal* chanteuse Vonda Shepard.

Top 10
We Salute You
movies

Ten great films the homos love for whatever reason. Whether it's a film's ultra-kitsch factor, its diva-esque qualities or downright evilness, there are some made-for-straights flicks out there that queer cinema-lovers just can't resist.

Mommie Dearest (1981)

An unadulterated bitch-fest about Hollywood grand dame Joan Crawford based on daughter Christina's autobiography, from which the film was adapted, was written after her mother's death in 1977. Quite blatantly left out of Joan's will, this act of posthumous rejection by a child-beating mother sparked a rage in her daughter that made her put pen to paper. While you'd expect a film about child abuse—both emotional and physical—to be pretty depressing, the camp and theatrical cinematography, teamed with Faye Dunaway's vampish portrayal of the silver screen goddess have turned *Mommie Dearest* into a queer cult classic, with audiences cheering and brandishing wire coat hangers as they watch Joan berate and punish her whining children for minor misdemeanours. Absolute evil—you're not meant to come away loving Joan, but you just can't help it! It's the hats.

G.I. Jane (1997)

It may not be one of the greatest films ever made—despite being a Ridley Scott number—but this lesbo-erotic flick, starring dyke crush Demi Moore hits all the right buttons when it comes to pleasuring queer audiences. Moore plays Lt. Jordan O'Neil who is used as a guinea pig to see if women can make the grade in combat. Looking so hot with a number two crop that she could turn gay boys straight, she takes on the out-and-out prejudice of the army and struggles through rigorous training. Forget the political sub-plot, this film made lesbian film audiences weep when Moore gets her muscles to bulge during one-armed press-ups, beats a fellow trainee to a pulp and tells a misogynistic colleague to "suck my dick." You can practically hear the queens screaming, "You go, girl!"

Whatever Happened To Baby Jane? (1962)

Grotesque, dark and descending into madness, this is quite possibly one of the most evil, campy movies ever made! Downright nasty sibling jealousy is at the core of this black and white classic starring Hollywood icons Bette Davis, and Joan Crawford. Davis is the precocious child star 'Baby Jane' Hudson, whose blossoming career becomes overshadowed by that of her elder sister, Blanche, played by Crawford. At the height of her stardom, Blanche is involved in a terrible accident—guess who's responsible?—rendering her housebound in the home she shares with her nasty little sister. Years later, and the pair are still shacked up in their dilapidated mansion, with Jane terrorizing her sister by serving up rats for breakfast, and removing all routes of escape. The film also picked up on its stars' real-life feuding—Davis hated her co-star and often attempted to sabotage Crawford's solo scenes. Even after the filming, there was no love lost between the pair, Davis remarked on Crawford's death: "My mother always said that it was polite to say something good about the dead. Joan Crawford: She's dead. Good." Meow.

Fried Green Tomatoes (1991)
While lesbian critics were annoyed that the film version of Fannie Flagg's dykey novel (Fried Green Tomatoes At The Whistle Stop Café) reduced the relationship between Idgie (Mary Stuart Masterson) and Ruth (Mary-Louise Parker) to a mere whisper of Sapphic love, it still hits the spot when it comes to those oh-so crucial factors that the gay moviegoer loves. A tale of girlie empowerment, flying in the face of abusive husbands, and fighting against oppression make this a feelgood movie without the side order of cheese.

Showgirls (1995)
In this downright awful, shamelessly kitsch 1990s version of All About Eve (see below) which is so shoddily made and acted that it can only be good, Nomi Malone, played by Elizabeth Berkley, is a dancer whose biggest dream is to be the head of a Las Vegas topless dance revue. Immediately dubbed as one of the worst movies of the 90s, the overblown acting and showbiz glamour meant that the only people making up the bums on seats were the homos! Glitzy, cheesy, a little bit raunchy, it's achieved cult status for obvious reasons, and for Gina Gershon as the dykey Cristal Connors.

Cabaret (1972)
Not only a damn fine film—it scooped eleven deserved Academy Awards—this musical has got it all going on. Based

on a book by gay author Christopher Isherwood [see page 188], it features the perfect diva-like qualities of Liza Minnelli as the vulnerable yet predatory Sally Bowles, a queer love triangle, political commentary on Germany's slide into Nazism and oh yes, some fabulous showtunes! Vulgar and flamboyant all at once, the scenes where Bowles works the audience dressed in a bowler hat waistcoat and boots have become iconic. Deep, dark and really sexy, it's a landmark flick with queer sensibilities.

Wizard Of Oz (1939)
The classic family film is a tale of escaping from a grey old world and making it big and making it happy—even if you are a big old loser at heart. Starring Judy Garland [see page 46] as Dorothy, her performance propelled the young actress into iconic status as she longed to be 'Over The Rainbow'—the ultimate queer anthem. Based on the 1900 novel by L. Frank Baum, the friendship between Dorothy and the motley crew she meets along the way makes it a predecessor to the contemporary road movie genre that homos know and love. With the sissy-like lion to hold dear, as well as those butch little munchkins, this film has been appropriated by homos like no other.

Serial Mom (1994) [right]
A black, black comedy from the genius filmmaker John Waters [see page 206] it stars Kathleen Turner [pictured right] In one of her finest roles, like ever as Beverly Sutphin, the apparently perfect model of a 1950s-esque suburban housewife—cooking, cleaning and always with a smile for her husband and two children (Misty, played by fag hag Ricki Lake, and Chip.) Under the façade however, there's a heart of pure evil as the over-protective mother makes obscene calls to neighbors (check out the "pussy willow" scene), runs people over for giving her family a hard time, and kills someone for not rewinding a rental video tape. A complete and utter satire on clean, genteel suburban living that sees Mr. Waters at his best.

All About Eve (1950)
It's All About Eve's key elements of self-invention, transformation, and utter bitchiness that appeal to the homos. Bette Davis, as Margo Channing,

foolishly helps the apparently naïve wannabe starlet Eve Harrington (Anne Baxter) to make it in the cutthroat world of showbusiness, but before long Eve shows herself for the real nasty piece of work that she is. As well as being a sideswipe at showbiz's cattiness, All About Eve also sees a very early performance by the not-very-good Marilyn Monroe, who plays a dizzy blonde wannabe actress, ironically.

Thelma and Louise (1991)
One of the best road movies ever made, Thelma and Louise's feelgood factor goes right off the scale in this flick about female empowerment, escaping the drudgery of hetero routine and running away in search of adventure and a better life. Ridley Scott's acclaimed drama sees the two stars, Susan

Sarandon and Geena Davis, acting their headscarves off as they roam middle America in a convertible looking for a way out. Murder, rape, thievery and downright naughty minx behavior make it a winner on all levels. It's the kind of buddy movie that makes the homo audience desperate for the two down-on-their-luck ladies to ditch the men for good, and just get it on.

Spice Girls

The girl-powered felsty fivesome

Gay icons have always mirrored gay men and women's status in society. Like Madonna [see page 22] before them, the Spice Girls might have ushered in a sense of 'Girl Power' (even if it was just for preteens), but they also reflected a new sense of gay liberation in the 90s. Here were a bunch of girls who, like us, were feisty, brash and serious trouble into the bargain—and like the rest of the world, we were smitten.

Their rise to fame was meteoric, but like other stars their success was down to the age-old combo of timing, luck and, erm, talent. When they arrived in 1996, there'd been a void in pop music since über-boy band Take That split in 1996 and the demise of New Kids On The Block in 1990. Suddenly here were five girls (Geri, Emma, Victoria, Melanics B and C), from the audition circuit, who could sing a bit, dance a bit, and had quite catchy tunes. But more importantly, they had the marketing budget of Virgin Records behind them, they were tabloid-friendly and embodied something everyone could relate to—whether that was self-empowerment or the feelgood factor of a New Labour Britain (even if they did brand ex-Prime Minister Margaret Thatcher "the first Spice Girl").

In the true tradition of girl groups, the Spice Girls were brought together in 1993 by a management team, who broke them in, made them live together, and created the requisite buzz within the industry to ensure major labels were falling over themselves to sign them.

Yet the Spice Girls were anything but playthings. Spearheaded by the ballsy Geri and mega-mouthy Melanie B, they vocalized their feelings, forged their own identities (though it was a British teen mag that came up with their alter-egos, Scary, Sporty, Baby, Ginger and Posh) and dumped their management in favor of Simon Fuller, who could fulfill their ambitions of becoming an international brand, sorry, band.

The rest of course is recent history; 'Wannabe' kicked off a worldwide chart career and they became the biggest British girl group ever while their booming fortune was increased further by cross-promotions with candy, chips and cameras (disposable of course)—hell, there was even a movie, Spiceworld! Geri and co. were everywhere, never missing an opportunity for self-promotion. You could be sure that if there was a line, they'd be stepping over it in a Buffalo sneaker.

Of course, it couldn't last and in May 1998, Geri, the one with all the chutzpah, left—the reason given was that she wasn't allowed to do an interview for a breast cancer charity. No-one believed it, but despite autobiographies from Geri and Victoria, even now

"Wannabe" kicked off a worldwide chart career and they became the biggest British girl group ever

no-one seems to be any the wiser why she quit. But the spell had been broken, and although another couple of singles were unleashed upon us without her, soon the rest of the Spicers were taking time out to concentrate on solo projects.

There's been little let-up however. Each of the girls has had solo albums with varying degrees of success. Melanie B's did so badly, she was even dropped by her record label, while the girls' reunion album, Forever—without Geri, naturally—was universally panned, even if the girls did buy in the street smart sounds of Rodney Jerkins and Jam and Lewis to realign them with the changing market.

Although their star seems to have well and truly faded, the Spice Girls are still national institutions in Britain—Victoria Beckham, particularly so, since she married English footballer and serious

eye-candy David Beckham, though it's Melanie C and Geri Halliwell who have had the most successful solo careers.

Since the arrival of her solo album, Northern Star, Mel C has suffered a slew of problems (weight, depression, tabloid hell) that would warrant anyone but a Liverpool scally diva status. More interestingly however is the fact that her sexuality has been constantly questioned despite relationships with British superstar Robbie Williams and a string of boy band-members. The evidence for this would seem to lie with the fact she had a close relationship with her PA and well, she just looks like a dyke with tattoos. She has consistently denied it, telling British music magazine Q in 1999: "No wonder I have trouble getting blokes. Of course it's not true. The right man hasn't come along yet."

Always the most gay-friendly of the Spicers, Geri's nevertheless upped the ante since leaving. Initially, she found refuge with George Michael [see page 203] and his boyfriend before launching her own solo career with a bunch of hits worthy of —yep, you guessed it— Madonna in the mid-80s. With a knack for reinvention, an eye on the tabloids and her tongue firmly in her cheek, Geri had us hook, line and sinker—if you were in any doubt, there was even 2001's cover version of gay anthem 'It's Raining Men' to hammer it home.

However, like the other Spicers, her time seems to be running out—and fast. She seems to have lost her sense of humor and it shows: The tabloids have bitten back, her ex-friend Robbie Williams (yes, him again) has branded her a "demonic little girl," and she's even been rumored to be trying to find God.

What the Spice Girls do next is anyone's guess, but until they find the sense of fun that empowered them in the first place, we suspect it's pretty much a lost cause. And that's a shame.

Sex And The City

The Manolo Blahnik-heeled smash hit HBO series

While the four main characters of this global hit TV series may be ladies of a straight persuasion—well, apart from Miranda who has "gone there" with one lady but didn't like it, as did Samantha, the middle-aged tart with a heart who would, quite frankly, "do" anyone! Oh, and Carrie's crush on Alanis Morrisette, and the whispers surrounding actress Kristin Davis in real life—it's the whole looking for love and dressing fabulously while a-searching that appeals to singleton homo boys, and girls, everywhere.

Based on the brilliant book of the same name by Candace Bushell, *Sex And The City* was the brainchild of openly gay TV producer Darren Star, the man behind series such as *Beverly Hills 90210* and *Models One*. In it, the fabulously stylish Sarah Jessica Parker stars as Carrie Bradshaw, a columnist who writes about sex and the single girl in Manhattan. Living the life of an upmarket chick, she plunders her three best friends' lives for stories of sexual shenanigans, serial dating and hopeless men who never want to settle down.

And those best friends are PR executive Samantha, Miranda, the serious lawyer, and the slightly wet, desperate-for-a-husband gallery director Charlotte: four designer-clad gals who, despite their independent and career-driven lives, would actually quite like to meet the right guy. Samantha, played by Kim Catrell, is the honorary gay man of the bunch, an older seductress whose STI-defying scoring card is a match for any gay boy's. She is always on the prowl, always getting off with guys way younger than her, and always has the last word, even when it's drag queens she's exchanging disses with! A kind of latter-day Mae West, she is never short of a bon mot to describe the shoddiness of the men available to a great-looking straight woman in NYC: "It's slim pickings out there. You can't swing a Fendi purse without knocking over five losers."

Carrie also has a gay best friend in the form of Sheldon, a shoe fetish to rival Imelda Marcos', and a fashion sense so "now" only gay men can really understand it.

With its frank portrayal of single life, close-to-the-bone conversations about the ins and outs of sex with all the gory details, and always with an accompanying Cosmopolitan cocktail in hand, *Sex And The City* is not just an aspirational and glamorous series, but a ground-breaking one with gay sensibilities and references. And with their own drag queen impersonators, *Sex And The City* vacation specials to New York filming locations and 'Are You Carrie, Samantha, Miranda or Charlotte?' quizzes doing the rounds on the Internet, it looks like the sexy ladies that lunch have well and truly made gay icon status. And you just know that they would love that.

Golden Girls

US sitcom about four golden oldies sharing a house together

Golden Girls was first screened on September 14th, 1985, ran for seven seasons, and became an instant classic—thanks not only to the fact that women of a certain age had never been portrayed on television in this way before, but also because it was packed with the most hilariously bitchy, if not downright cheap, gags.

The concept was simple, even if it had been tried and tested in different ways in many sitcoms before; four comic 'stereotypes' share a house together. There was Blanche (Rue McClanahan), who was the slut; Rose (Betty White), the dimwit with endless smalltown tales from St Olaf; Dorothy (Bea Arthur), the trout with a nice line in sarcasm; and finally, her (Italian) mom Sofia (Estelle Getty), reprieved from the hell of retirement center Shady Pines, who was just plain rude. Despite a shaky start, the "girls" were soon sharing their problems, stories and slices of cheesecake around the table of their Florida home.

There was little that was overtly gay in the series— Blanche had a gay brother, Clayton and Dorothy a lesbian friend Jean, and the original idea of a gay cook/houseboy had been nixed after the pilot—but we were hooked. As much as the camp sense of humor, we were sold on the idea of four old birds still up for it despite their age—no wonder we were setting up VCRs and screenings in bars across the States and around the globe.

Barbra Streisand

The grande dame of gay icons

If Barbra Streisand can be a major megastar with, well, a face like that, then there's hope for all of us. But then Barbra has made a career out of being all wrong.

Playing the downstairs cabaret joints of Manhattan in the early 60s after having won a talent contest at a Greenwich Village dive at the age of eighteen, Barbra was already working her wrongness. She was so wrong, people flocked. While most of her contemporaries were getting heavily into rock or at least having their hair cut real funny, she was wearing some weird old lady clothes and, if reports at the time are anything to go by, not washing that often. But you couldn't argue with the voice (even if you could easily argue with the material). Reviews of Barbra's boho gigs were ecstatic. People who were there say they knew the moment she came she was a star. But then people who claim to be there often say things like that.

In 1962, she bagged herself a role in the Broadway musical *I Can Get It For You Wholesale*, and was an instant smash hit (even if the show wasn't), releasing her debut (and imaginatively titled) album *The Barbra Streisand Album*—a big old double Grammy-winning top ten LP—the next year, the same year she married actor Elliott Gould. The albums came thick and fast, as did the TV appearances on specials like *The Judy Garland Show*. Then Barbra, turning her nose up at big bucks concert tours, went back to Broadway for *Funny Girl*, the show that gave her her first hit single, 'People,' which featured on her first number one album of the same name. The geeky girl was going places and it

wasn't long before she was collecting her first Oscar for the movie version of *Funny Girl*. But Barbra was a weird one, completely out of step with her rocking contemporaries, and it was this sense of otherness (added to her divaness, strength of character and quirky sense of humor) that endeared her to gay men and, to a lesser extent, lesbians.

By the 70s, Barbra (she started out as Barbara when she was born in Brooklyn in 1942, by the way, but jettisoned one of those 'a's so she could travel lighter) was sporting a bubble cut and vicious nails, acting like she was sexually attractive and starring in smash hit movies like the mega-hit *A Star Is Born* in 1976. The song 'Evergreen' from the soundtrack—her 25th album in fourteen years—was a smash hit, and an Oscar winner to boot. But it didn't turn gay men on half as much as her 1979 collaboration with the First Lady of Love, Donna Summer [see page 15], on the smash disco hit 'No More Tears (Enough Is Enough).'

But enough was never enough for Barbra. She wanted to produce and direct, and in 1983—three years after her 20-million selling Barry Gibb collaboration *Guilty*—took on *Yentl*, the story of a young Jewish woman who drags up in boys' clothes in order to be given access to the secrets of male knowledge. It was a very Barbra role. And that was often the trouble with Streisand's movie projects: she would choose films, like *Nuts*, where she came over as trying to justify her looks or her pushiness, and even though there were triumphs like *Prince of Tides* along the way, audiences were, by and large, turned off.

Live audiences, however, who had always been neglected by Barbra (she was petrified of performing live) were in for a treat. In 1994 she returned to the stage for a mega-sell-out tour. She was, well, simply Barbra: stunning, funny, immaculate; OK, a little on the schmaltzy side, but a winner. There was no doubting that, even though her hair had calmed down a whole lot, she still had what it took. Her gay jokes—about being able to walk around New York during the Gay Games because there was a Barbra on every street corner, for instance—went down particularly well, while the concerts helped her pump millions of dollars into her charitable works.

And gay men, as if they needed one, had a new reason to worship Streisand. It turned out that the very cute son she had had with Gould, whom she had divorced in 1971, was one of the boys. Oh, yes, Jason was gay. But then, how could he ever have turned out NOT gay?

A big old Democrat—and an award winning fundraiser for AIDS charities—Barbra was always very political. It was politics that enticed her back to live performing to raise money to get a total of five Democrat senators elected, and she was always very close friends with President Clinton, standing by him during all his trials.

In 1998, Barbra married actor James Brolin and seemed to be ready to settle down a little. And she deserved it. Not only was she the biggest selling female artist of all time, but was judged by news service Reuters to be the most popular female artist of the 20th century. Not bad for a freaky looking girl from the wrong side of the tracks.

Is He?
Isn't She?

Those gay rumors

Talk is cheap, so are we and hey, we're damn good at it. At a time when it's still a major deal for any celebrity to come out, we've been forced to read between the lines and dig deep for stories which usually start: "Well, you know my friend whose next door neighbor is a stylist? Well, the person they work with slept with _____ (place the name of your celebrity of choice here)."

There are however some celebrities who always seem to be the subject of gay rumors, urban myths or whatever you want to call them. Here we consider the evidence, but before you go pointing fingers, ask yourself: Who really knows what goes on in anyone's bedroom?

Cindy Crawford and Richard Gere
Model and actor
Buddhist Richard has long been the victim of an urban myth about a hamster and his butt, and when he married Cindy in Las Vegas in 1990, rumors started circulating about the true sentiment behind their marriage. Cindy said at the time: "Considering the number of women he's been associated with, when does he have time to be gay?" Stories persisted however, and in response to an article in a French newspaper in 1993, the couple took out a full-page ad in the London *Times* stating: "We are heterosexual and monogamous and take our commitment to each other very seriously." Eight months later, they were divorced.

George Clooney
A-list actor
Rumors seem to stem from the following remark in Australian magazine *Blue* by his *Three Kings* and *Perfect Storm* costar, Mark Wahlberg: "I think George has got a thing for me. I've definitely got a thing for George, so it works out good." George also added his voice to South Park for an episode as Sparky the gay dog. Well, there you go then.

Bert and Ernie
Muppets
Kurt Anderson's book *The Real Thing* made a suggestion that the *Sesame Street* duo are gay in 1980; however, the Children's Television Workshop has consistently denied the rumors. The stories probably stem from the fact that two grown male puppets share a house, a bedroom and the cooking. Neither are they the most masculine of felt toys.

Tom Cruise
A-list actor and producer
Tom has been dogged by gay rumors since 1990 when ex-wife Mimi Rogers revealed that Tom preferred to "maintain the purity of his instrument" than have sex with her. He has however sued anyone who suggests he might not be straight, since it damages his film career. He won a case against London's *Sunday Express*, who suggested that his marriage to Nicole Kidman was a sham, and waged a suit against "erotic wrestler" Chad Slater in 2001, who claimed to be his lover.

Prince Edward
Queen Elizabeth II's youngest son
With a career in theater, rumors naturally circulated about him, but these were put paid to when he married Sophie Rhys-Jones in 1999. She recently told the *News Of The World*: "I had heard something before we met, but I put it down to the fact that he was working in theater and people had presumed he was gay. It is not true."

Missy Elliot
Cutting-edge heavyweight rapper
The rumors seem to emerge from Missy's reported love of fast cars, hi-tech gadgetry and, erm, the "donuts," all of which are stereotypical lesbian interests. They're perpetuated by the fact that Missy never talks about her love life. She was recently rumored to have been outed by Spice Girl Melanie B.

Jodie Foster
Actress. [see page 40]

Anne Heche
Actress
The jury is still out on Anne Heche, even though she says she has never labeled herself straight, gay or bisexual.

She instantly became a household name in 1997 after leaving actor Steve Martin for comedienne Ellen Degeneres [see page 97], whom she met at the Oscars. Until that night she had never slept with a woman: "That was the best sex I'd ever had…" They split up in 2000 and Anne has recently married documentary maker and cameraman, Coley Laffoon.

Whitney Houston
Million-selling, modern-day mega-diva
Almost from the word go, Whitney has repeatedly been linked romantically with her longtime pal and executive assistant Robyn Crawford, though both women have continually denied the rumor. Whitney told *Out* magazine in 2000: "I know what I am. I'm a woman. I'm heterosexual. Period. My mother raised me never, ever be ashamed of what I am. But I'm not a lesbian, darling."

Janet Jackson
Singing sister to Michael
It all started in 1997 on the interlude track, 'Speakerphone' from *The Velvet Rope* album, where Janet indulges in dirty talk with a lady. The same year she said, "I am not gay, but I will stand up for a lot of my friends who are gay, and who are hiding their true feelings." Wild rumors continue to circulate that her separated husband Rene Elizondo has been blackmailing her about her lesbian tendencies.

Ricky Martin
Bon-bon shakin' superstar
The most direct allegation about Ricky's alleged sexuality came as a pointed wicked whisper in the *New York Post*'s gossip column. Rumors of a relationship with Giorgio Armani came after the designer sponsored the *Livin' La Vida Loca* tour.

Keanu Reeves
Actor
The rumor: he married David Geffen in Mexico in 1995, which was followed by a $15,000 shopping spree. Keanu later told *Vanity Fair* journalist: "I've never had a male sexual experience in my life."

Waylon Smithers
Mr Burns' lapdog in The Simpsons
The case for: an intimate though unrequited relationship with his

employer C. Montgomery Burns; a collection of Malibu Stacy dolls; vacations at single men's resorts; has even been seen frolicking with the Village People. The case against: erm...

Kevin Spacey
Actor
Talk about Kevin's sexuality started long before *Esquire*'s infamous October 1997 cover story entitled, "Kevin Has A Secret" in which he was pseudo-outed. Kevin slammed the feature calling it "dishonest and malicious." He started dating his secretary, and affirmed his heterosexuality in *Vanity Fair* where he said that the gay rumors had improved his sex life: "Women want to be the one to turn me around. I let them."

Bugs Bunny
The world's most famous rabbit
Although we never see Bugs engage in buck-on-buck action, speculation about his sexuality has always been rife since he consistently dons drag and uses sexual wiles to get his way.
His adversary Elmer Fudd is usually the object of his affection. During the *Rabbit of Seville*, Bugs even rushes him up the aisle after a rendition of "I'm your little Senyeree-ter; yooou are my type of guy."

Robbie Williams
The biggest pop star in Britain
Despite tabloid tell-all tales from Robbie's female conquests, eyebrows have recently been raised at the closeness of his relationship with longtime mate Jonathan Wilkes. Fuel has been added to the fire by Nicole Kidman (who he duetted with on 'Something Stupid'). When quizzed about their relationship, she reportedly said she thought everyone knew he was gay.

Tinky Winky
Purple Teletubbie
Like Bert and Ernie, Tinky Winky has been attacked by right wing Christians for subverting the innocent minds of kiddies. The evidence? He's purple (the gay pride color), his antenna is shaped like a triangle (the gay pride symbol), and he carries a purse/magic bag.

Jodie Foster

The actress, movie mogul and celebrity hermit

Right, let's set the record straight: Jodie Foster is, without a doubt, most definitely a lesbian, erm, icon. While you can read tens of dull old manuscripts on lesbian theory and representation in the arts which all conclude that Ms. Foster is indeed a lady who sups from the furry goblet, it's far more fun to look at how members of the dyke community have, at various times, outed her, adored her, awarded her with iconic status and wished, hoped, prayed that if Ms Foster did ever come out (that's, like, if she is gay) that they could be her girlfriend.

Born in Los Angeles in 1962, Foster has become a talented, beautiful and powerful mover and shaker within Hollywood. She's been a part of the movie industry since she stepped into the limelight as a precocious child actor back when she appeared first in a Coppertone advert at the age of two—where a dog pulled down her pants—and then in a suitably tomboy-ish role in the 1972 film *Napoleon And Samantha*. Ever since, she's had every single one of her starring moments appropriated and consumed by lesbians—the gritty teen prostitute in *Taxi Driver*, the boyfriend-less Clarice Starling in *Silence Of The Lambs,* and flicks like *Little Man Tate* and *The Accused* where Jodie's characters have been without a sniff of male love interest. And then there are her lesbian roles: in *Hotel New Hampshire*, which has become a must-see classic for dykey fans of Foster everywhere, *Siesta*, and *Carny*, where she pretends to be a dyke and flirts with a female customer. That proves it then, she must be gay.

Since the assassination attempt on former US president Ronald Reagan by John W. Hinckley Jr., a crazed fan of Foster's who was trying to impress her, she's become one of the most elusive and private stars in Hollywood. Even with

two Oscars under her belt, for *The Accused* and *Silence Of The Lambs*— she was the first actor to win two Oscars before the age of thirty—and a respected directing and producing career, Foster's close-knit team have managed to keep stories about the actress's life off-screen under wraps. Even close family aren't aware of the ins and outs of her private doings—her brother Buddy, upon the release of his biography on Jodie, told *USA Today*: "I have always assumed Jodie was gay or bisexual." In an uncharacteristic retort, Jodie told the media: "I don't know him well. I certainly have never spoken to him about my personal life, as I and my entire family consider him a distant acquaintance motivated solely by greed and sour grapes." Meow. But still no denial.

Two aspects of her life that were impossible to keep quiet were her pregnancies. A shock to the news-hungry media who knew that Foster had never denied or accepted the rumors about her homosexuality, with her having no current male partner they wondered just how it all could have happened. Her first son, Charles, was born in 1998 and Foster has never let slip who the father is, or if she knows the father at all. While most assume that Foster was artificially inseminated, what is known is that she's bringing up Charles and son number two, Kit, with the help of her close friend Cydney Bernard. Bernard is another person involved in Foster's life under heavy press speculation and scrutiny, especially when Foster and Bernard were allegedly spotted wearing identical wedding bands. Surely a coincidence? According to the more salubrious tabloids in the US, Bernard and Foster have been a couple since 1998, and don't hide their relationship from close friends and family; instead they enjoy

their co-parenting responsibilities of Charles and Kit.

Whatever it is that makes Foster a dyke icon—her early tomboyish roles, an absence of concrete information as to her sexuality and her lesbian-esque screen persona in a number of films— the lesbians can't get enough of her. With lookalike competitions in—you guessed it—*San Francisco*, a short film by British independent filmmaker Prathiba Parmar about her "dykonic" status and fan websites all over the Internet, it's an odd juxtaposition that someone so private about her life has had to live with it being dissected, analyzed and obsessed about. But then you can see the appeal—as lesbian comic Lea de Laria puts it: "If I was Hannibal Lecter, it wouldn't be her liver I'd want to eat." Enough said.

▷ **Take it further:** Jodie Foster: An Icon, *1996. A short film by Prathiba Parmar.*

Xena: Warrior Princess
The ass-kicking, leather-clad
lesbian icon

While the media world's jaw dropped when it became
apparent that Xena: Warrior Princess had become a cult
dyke icon, the lesbians just shrugged. What did they
expect? An almost six-foot tall Amazonian beauty, with
mythical breasts and sexual tension between her and
her blonde sidekick, Gabrielle, so thick you could slice
it with a butter knife—of course was going to be a hit
with lesbians.

Running over five years and numbering more than 100
panty-wetting episodes, the show starred New Zealander
Lucy Lawless, and American Renee O'Connor. Originally a
spin-off from *Hercules*, Xena managed to throw the original
into the shade as she high-kicked her way through
marauding gangs.

As the show reached cult status, lesbian bars and clubs
the world over—especially in the States—held Xena nights,
look-alike competitions, and "Xena calling" contests. Cue
many a dyke squeezed into leather, brandishing a plastic
sword in a nylon wig, desperate to find her own Gabrielle
in the crowd.

Desperate and deserving of more positive lesbian
characters on TV, dyke fans embraced the "will they, won't
they?" subtleties of Xena and Gabrielle's relationship. While
detractors would argue that the pair were just good friends,
lesbian fans hung on to every hint of their possible
relationship—and boy, did the producers milk it. With out-
lesbian Liz Friedman on the production team, and feedback
from fans on the Internet who were concentrating on a
lesbian interpretation, Friedman says the show started to
consciously play with the lesbian sub-plot: "We started
having fun with it," she says.

With hundreds of fan sites, the stars and the makers of the
show sat up and took note. With cross-dressing girls and
eventually a girl-on-girl kiss creeping into the script, it
became pretty clear that even the straight writers were
starting to become very vocal about the prospect of Xena
and Gabrielle being more than just good friends. As Ms.
Lawless herself says of their potential Sapphic relationship:
"We found that so amusing, and intriguing, that we started
to pepper scenes with ad libs. We fanned the flames and
then there were things that the producers wrote that were
definitely ambiguous or not even ambiguous. I like the fact
that she might or she might not be. "'What's it to you?'
That's our attitude."

Now the series is defunct, with the "lesbian vampire disco"
episode living on in lesbian video players everywhere, the
rest of us are enjoying the re-runs of the kick ass duo with
their leather outfits and double entendres. Those wanting
double-enders will just have to wait for a X-rated spin-off.

Absolutely Fabulous

The sitcom that made two mad cows into international gay icons

It all started quietly enough. The UK sketch show *French and Saunders*, starring comedians Dawn French and Jennifer Saunders, featured 'Modern Mother and Daughter,' a skit—not even a particularly funny skit—where French plays a teenage schoolgirl trying sensibly to get on with her homework while her immature trendy wannabe mother tries to distract her with tantrums and threats. It was classic role reversal comedy of the type that had made French and Saunders household names in the UK.

But no-one could have imagined what that sketch would grow up into. In the hands of Jennifer Saunders, the painfully trendy mother would mutate into the monster of selfishness and shoddy parenthood that was Edina Monsoon, while ex-*Avengers* actress Joanna Lumley, very much a has-been by this time, would be drafted in to play Edina's booze- and drugs-addled nymphomaniac pal Patsy, and be transformed into probably the best-loved actress in Britain. The sensible daughter became Saffron while other characters— dotty mothers, gay ex-husbands, nightmare magazine editors, inept secretaries—would be brought in to flesh out this monstrous portrait of London media life in the 1990s.

Debuting on the more niche BBC TWO, the first episode of *Absolutely Fabulous*, or *Ab Fab* as it would become known to homosexuals across the globe, opened with a hungover Edina trying to organize a celebrity fashion show, establishing *Ab Fab*'s targets: the worlds of PR, fashion, celebrity and art (many women from the London scene parodied by *Ab Fab* have been in the frame as inspiration for Edina, from fashion designer Edina Ronay to PR guru Lynn Frank).

The gay sensibility of the show, whose script was edited by old gay favorite Ruby Wax, was spot on and by the end of series one, gay men were freely ordering Stolly-Bolly (a made-up Stolichnaya vodka and Bollinger champagne cocktail) and calling everyone "Sweetie Darling" (Edina's moniker for her daughter, whose real name she could barely remember through her constant drunken haze).

There was no question about the commissioning of a second series, with *Ab Fab* being immediately promoted to the more mainstream BBC ONE and lots of talk about an American series being commissioned (the UK series, with its smoking, drinking, drug-taking, general bad behavior and filthy language was deemed too risqué for the major networks, although the original show was broadcast by HBO, which led to *Ab Fab* parties taking place in queer bars and homes across America).

In Australia the impact of *Ab Fab* was so great that there were hundreds of marching Patsies at the Sydney Mardi Gras [see page 117], while in France a movie based on the characters was soon in production (it was called *Absolument Fabuleux* and was panned by critics upon its release). Back in London, Saunders and Lumley turned up, in character, at the stellar Equality Show—an annual queer event—to join the likes of Elton John and Kylie Minogue to promote gay rights. And with Roseanne Barr after the American rights to *Ab Fab*, Patsy and Edina even turned up—drunk!—on an episode of Roseanne.

With record audiences and celebrities and has-beens like Marianne Faithfull,

In Australia the impact of Ab Fab was so great that there were hundreds of marching Patsies at the Sydney Mardi Gras

Britt Ekland and Ivana Trump clamoring to appear on *Ab Fab*, it was always going to prove a hard one to give up on. After the end of the third series, which had concluded with a glimpse into a future that had Eddie and Pats living in a granny flat together with just the hope of next door's dog sniffing their crotch, it seemed that the characters were finally being laid to rest for good.

In 2000, however, Saunders went back to the drawing board and, with the same actors she had worked with on *Ab Fab* in mind, set about writing a brand new comedy series called *Glitterball*, set among London's theater set. It was an absolute disaster, and even she admitted that she had found it impossible to get away from Edina and Patsy, Bubble and Saff.

And so she caved and wrote a fourth series of *Absolutely Fabulous*, even though she had promised she wouldn't, afraid that it would turn into pantomime instead of satire. But we cheered its return. In the US, HBO even organized a series of parties in gay bars to celebrate the reprise of the two best-loved post-menopausals in comedy history.

And at first it seemed like it had worked. The new series gained a healthy one-third share of the UK audience the night it aired, but those who tuned in noted that some of the magic was gone. The jokes were as well honed— Botox, the disposability of pop groups— but as the series wore on, the show started to revisit themes covered in previous series (fatness, the need to impress old friends). "I did it too late," admitted Saunders in UK newspaper *The Guardian*. "I was too frightened of it. Of failing with it. The feeling that if I left it and did it another time it might be better. It also lacks structure. That was my failing."

EXHIBIT #1 **EXHIBIT #2** **EXHIBIT #3**

Musicals

There's no theater like musical theater when it comes to gay appeal

There's something about a song, a dance, a long frock, a couple of tear jerkers, and a rousing end that appeals to gay men (the rousing end, by the way, comes from the fact that British society always arrived at the theater really late, meaning impresarios saved their best till last).

Gay men were familiar with the format of musicals from opera, where the overblown emotion and sheer quality of the fabrics had had opera queens rapt in their boxes for centuries. Downgraded through operettas like the extraordinarily camp ones turned out by British duo Gilbert and Sullivan, with a bit of vulgarity from vaudeville thrown in, the medium ended up custom-made to a good-time gay man's tastes, much more than something Italian and blousy.

After Gilbert and Sullivan had conquered Broadway in the 19th century, local impresarios reckoned they could produce homemade versions of the highly popular musical entertainments. One of the first to make his mark was Florenz Zeigfeld, who opened his first Broadway show, which was very much influenced by Paris's *Folies Bergere*, in 1895. By 1907 he had his own *Zeigfeld Follies*, which hoped to rival British imports like *Floridiana*, the show that was setting the tone for future musicals by focussing on a young woman seeking romance. Gay audiences projected like crazy.

By the First World War, big stars like Al Jolson were being lured onto Broadway, and Zeigfeld eventually secured the talents of Fanny Brice, W. C. Fields and any lady with legs up to here who didn't mind walking around with a huge headdress on. Meanwhile, eventual masters of the art like Jerome Kern were originally brought in to pump some decent songs into other shows.

By the 1920s, a real heyday for the musical, Zeigfeld was lavishing up to a quarter of a million dollars on shows, something hitherto completely unheard of, and the real stars of the musical were starting to make their presence felt: in the UK, the gay blade Noel Coward was becoming a great success, while on Broadway the likes of Rodgers and Hart, George and Ira Gershwin, Cole Porter and Fred Astaire were shining and productions like *Showboat* were upping the ante. By the 40s, the medium was fixed with productions of classics like *Oklahoma* and *Carousel* setting the paradigm for the next decades.

Rodgers and Hammerstein ruled the 50s with musicals like *The King and I*, and *The Sound of Music*; Lerner and Loew's *My Fair Lady* and the Bernstein/Sondheim collaboration *West Side Story* becoming the only other shows to get a look in. Hollywood meanwhile was taking them and turning them into big old Technicolor crowd pleasers. The world had gone musical crazy.

But it was short-lived. By the 60s, the whole scene was looking tired. Kander and Ebb breathed new life into the format with harder-edged shows like *Cabaret* and *Chicago*, but rock had made the running and jumping, the gushing and the swooning all look hopelessly outdated. Cue rock musicals like *Hair*, *Jesus Christ Superstar* and *Godspell*—none of which particularly interested gay men, who still hankered after the swooning. Thank God for Sondheim, the *West Side Story* lyricist, whose *Follies* in 1971 proved that musicals could be dark and modern, and still use some great sparkly costumes.

But as far as musical purists were concerned, the dark ages were upon us. The British were coming back in the form of Andrew Lloyd Weber, while Disney was payrolling Brits like Elton John and Tim Rice to turn their cartoons (sorry, animated features) into stage extravaganzas. By the 90s the only real hope was in revivals, especially the sexy re-reading of Kander and Ebb's *Chicago*, which blew Broadway and the West End's socks off. Unless you count *Mamma Mia* that is. We don't.

The Ten Gayest Musicals of All Time

1. Cabaret
Based on *Goodbye To Berlin* by gay Brit Christopher Isherwood [see page 188], this featured bisexuality and a big old drag queen of a leading lady complete with green nails, fur coats, black panties and bowler hats. Divine decadence!

2. Sweet Charity
The ultimate loser, dance hall hostess and general tart with a heart Charity appeals to gay men because all she wants out of life is a big strong man to treat her right. The fact that nice (read "straight") men always dump her is not incidental.

3. Sound of Music
Overcoming adversity with a couple of great songs and a haircut to kill for is actually the book and score to most gay men's lives. No wonder they fell for this story of a nun falling for a Baron in Nazi Austria.

4. My Fair Lady [pictured above]
Low self-esteem at the ready in this musical update of George Bernard Shaw's *Pygmalion*. Nasty old professor (who is quite cute if you go for that sort of grizzled look) drags spirited scamp out of the gutter and makes her a lady. Ten gay points out of ten.

5. Evita
Dirty little whore shags all the right guys and eventually sleeps her way to the top of a whole country, now which gay men's dreams aren't made of that? Add to the mix Madonna in the movie, and you've got a gay all-time classic.

6. Chicago
Nasty bitch murderesses try to beat the rap by becoming famous in probably the darkest, most cynical musical outside the work of Stephen Sondheim. But oh, what tunes and what smart-ass lines like, "So I fired two warning shots. Into his head."

7. La Cage Aux Folles
Based on the brilliant gay movie (yep, the same one *The Birdcage* is based on), this is the showbiz-tastic tale of a gay couple trying to play it straight, albeit in drag. Includes the gay anthem, 'I Am What I Am.'

8. Funny Girl
Barbra Streisand [see page 37] stars (on stage and screen) as wild old musical hall star Fanny Brice who, besides being a game old bird and probably the best fun in town, struggles to find a decent man. Where have you heard that story before?

9. Dreamgirls
Apparently the Diana Ross and the Supremes story (although Ms. Ross is having none of it), this musical brings the big dresses to the little people and includes the gut-wrenching showstopper 'And I'm Telling You I'm Not Going.'

10. Company
You can't beat Sondheim's tale of a single man—it's not made clear why he's single—beating off the attentions of women and getting worn down by the relentless coupledom of his friends. Presses all the right buttons.

Also rans...
Kiss of the Spiderwoman
Victor/Victoria
Mame
Sunset Boulevard
Hair (you get to see naked guys in it!).

Token lesbian musical

Calamity Jane [pictured above]
If the spangles and the sequins don't do much for lesbians, put a tomboy in a bit of buckskin and you've got them. Made famous by Doris Day who appeared in the movie, this has clear Sapphic undercurrents.

Judy Garland

Movie star and gay icon extraordinaire

Superlatives are not wasted on Judy Garland. With a forty-five-year career that spanned vaudeville, movies, records, radio and television, she was indeed a phenomenon, but as much as her talent, it was the way she embodied both vulnerability and strength which had gay men hooked. Compounded by the gay subtext of her trademark movie, *The Wizard Of Oz*, her status as a gay icon was unquestioned by the 50s and 60s—hence the gay terminology 'Friends of Dorothy'—while her death in June 1969 is cited for the high emotions which sparked the Stonewall Riots [see page 87].

Judy was born Frances Ethel Gumm on June 10th, 1922, in Grand Rapids, Minnesota. Her parents were former vaudevillians running a theater in Grand Rapids, which was where Frances made her debut at the age of two singing 'Jingle Bells.' Shortly afterwards, she joined her sisters Mary Jane and Virginia as the Gumm Sisters vocal group where her strong voice stood out. The sisters started making appearances at small theaters in the area, and continued to do so when they moved to California in 1926, where they went on to secure a handful of small roles in movies and rename themselves the Garland Sisters. Frances took the name Judy because she liked the Hoagy Carmichael song of the same name.

When the group split up in 1935 Judy auditioned for MGM, where she was the only person to be contracted without a screen test. She didn't make much headway until she performed 'Dear Mr Gable' for said star at an MGM party—a part was immediately written into *Broadway Melody* for her. She was instantly signed to a recording contract while the movies she made with Mickey Rooney established them as the Teen King and Queen of Hollywood.

The release of *The Wizard Of Oz* [see page 31] in 1939 upped the ante still further, and she scored a miniature Oscar for outstanding performance as a juvenile. Although it was pitched as a family movie, gay men have always loved it because it's all about leaving the black and white

behind and finding acceptance on your own terms.

The early 40s saw Judy married (briefly) to conductor David Rose with whom she worked on the soundtrack to *Little Nellie Kelly*. Together with *Strike Up The Band*, *Babes on Broadway*, and *For Me And My Gal*, it saw her become a bankable star. For the rest of the decade, Judy's film work became less frequent, though on average she knocked out a movie a year, including *Meet Me In St Louis*, on which she met Vincente Minnelli, father to Liza who was born in 1946. However, by this time she was fast establishing herself as a pain in the ass to work with. When she was a child star at MGM, her mother had started her on diet pills to control her weight, uppers to boost her energy, and barbiturates to help her sleep, so it was no wonder she often wasn't up to the job. By the late 40s, she was fired not once, but three times—after which she made a feeble attempt at suicide. Divorce from her second husband, Minnelli, followed.

Judy turned her attention to the stage, first at the London Palladium, then at New York's Palace Theater, a run that resulted in a Tony Award and a hefty salary. A third marriage to manager Sid Luft, with whom she had babies Lorna and Joey, came in 1952. Two years later, in 1954, Judy had a serious hit on her hands in the shape of *A Star Is Born*, in which she'd previously appeared on radio. Scoring her a top ten soundtrack album and an Oscar nomination, it was a part that only Judy could have played: she knew only too well the trials and tragedies of being a star and, considering her background, some might argue it was an act she milked.

For the rest of the decade Judy concentrated on her concert career with performances everywhere from London to Las Vegas. In 1959 however, she was taken into hospital suffering from hepatitis and was warned off performing for good. Judy, of course, had more resilience than that, and just over a year later, she was at the top of the tree again with the double Grammy award-winning live album, *Judy At Carnegie Hall*.

By this time, Judy's status as a gay icon had been acknowledged, albeit tacitly. While her performances were widely lauded for the sheer emotion she gave to each song, her concerts were attended en masse by gay men because she was the quintessential diva, although Daniel Harris argues otherwise in *The Rise And Fall Of Gay Culture*: "The answer to the proverbial question 'why did gay men like Judy Garland so much?' is that they like not her so much as her audience, the hordes of other gay men who gathered in her name to hear her poignant renditions of old torch songs that reduced sniffling queens to floods of self-pitying tears."

Judy then returned to movies, scoring herself a further Academy Award nomination for her role in *Judgement At Nuremberg*. The concerts, television performances, movies and hit records continued, as did *The Judy Garland Show* (1963), which was only held off the number one spot by cowboy caper *Bonanza*. Nevertheless, the series was not renewed and she suddenly found herself broke, in litigation and in increasingly ill health. The rest of her life was taken up by consistent touring, though she married first actor Mark Herron in 1965 (but divorced him when she found out he was gay), and then, in 1969, nightclub manager Mickey Deans.

She died on June 22nd, 1969 in London from an accidental overdose of barbiturates—the same day a tornado hit Kansas, go figure!—and when her body was brought back to New York, 22,000 people filed past her glass-covered coffin over a 24-hour period. The day of her funeral, June 27th, 1969 will remain legendary as the birth of gay rights, thanks to the storming of the Stonewall Bar. There were even rainbow-colored wreaths.

In retrospect, Judy's life story reads like that of a tragic old queen, and she herself said: "When you have lived the life I've lived, when you have loved and suffered and been madly happy and desperately sad—well, that's when you realize that you'll never be able to set it all down… maybe you'd rather die first." While she touched gay men's lives on various levels, she was also a true multimedia star, someone today's wannabes couldn't even hope to emulate.

Nature/Nurture

Is gayness chosen, taught, in-bred or just learned in some mysterious karmic way? Gays and society, flirting and even reproduction.

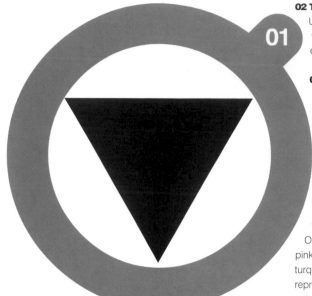

Signs and symbols

How gay men and lesbians have identified themselves to each other with badges and motifs

It takes one to know one and it's not hard to know if you can read the signs. Gay men and lesbians have, over the years, adopted a number of logos both to help recognize each other, making it easier to hook up, and to identify themselves in a political sense. The most significant are:

02 The Black Triangle

Used by the Nazis to identify "difficult women," this was the lesbian equivalent of the pink triangle.

03 The Freedom Flag

Designed in San Francisco (where else?), the Rainbow Flag has become the internationally recognized symbol of the gay and lesbian community, even if bars can still get away with using it without any straight folk being any the wiser. Gilbert Baker came up with the idea back in 1978, but the flag has mutated since then.

Originally there were eight stripes: hot pink, red, orange, yellow, green, turquoise, indigo and violet. The colors represented sexuality, life, healing, sun, nature, art, harmony and spirit. Gilbert approached the city's Paramount Flag Company to mass-produce it, but unfortunately hot pink just wasn't available, meaning the flag had to be reduced to seven stripes. Things changed once again when the Pride Parade dropped the indigo so they could distribute the colors evenly along the 1979 parade route. The flag is now recognized by the International Congress Of Flag Makers, which means it's official.

04 Freedom Rings

Designed by David Spada and based on the Freedom Flag, the Freedom Rings consists of six aluminium rings which can be worn on a finger or on a chain round your neck. And it goes with everything. Or nothing.

06 The Labrys

A double-edged axe adopted by lesbians from matriarchal societies like the Amazons, the labrys symbolizes lesbian strength and self-sufficiency. Demeter, the ancient goddess of the earth used a labrys as a scepter and as ceremonies in her honor included lesbian goings-on, it kind of felt appropriate.

07 The Pinkie Ring

Prince Charles, the Prince of Wales may wear one, but the pinkie ring was a secret sign of gayness in the 50s, 60s and early 70s when it was replaced by a single sleeper earring in the left ear. Then, as with many gay trends, it entered mainstream fashion and lost its special significance.

01 The Pink Triangle

The Nazis made gay men wear a pink triangle with the point turned down in the concentration camps to identify them as the lowest of the low. It also identified homosexuals to the Allied "liberating" forces so that they could relocate gay men from the concentration camps to a regular jail. Gay men and their families were never compensated in the way that other concentration camp victims were.

05 The Lambda

Not to be confused with a South American dance craze, the eleventh letter of the Greek alphabet was adopted in the 1970s by New York City's Gay Activists Alliance; it was worn on lapels only by the bolshiest of gay activists. In 1974 it was adopted by the International Gay Rights Congress but, despite the official stamp of approval, never quite crossed over into mass use.

08 The Red Tie

Subtle almost to the degree of pointlessness, the red tie was a secret sign at the beginning of the century that male-on-male advances would not necessarily be rebuffed.

09 Four Diamonds in a Diamond Pattern

Introduced by the Mattachine Society, a gay pressure group from the 50s, this failed to cross over.

Slogans

Queer slogans for every occasion. And don't forget your whistle...

While marching and demonstrating feels like something we used to do way back when (it's all about parading, Mardi Gras-ing and getting drunk in an open space these days), queer slogans still serve a purpose, even if it's only for slapping on the nearest cheap cotton mix T-shirt for a quick buck. Classics like the "Hate is not a family value" bumper sticker may still manage to stir things up a little, but the days of wearing your "Closets are for clothes" T-shirt must surely be over.

Don't Panic T-shirts

Sure, it was kind of funny when Axl Rose, the ginger-haired lead singer of once popular rockers Guns'N'Roses wore a "Nobody Knows I'm A Lesbian" T-shirt. And it almost raised a chuckle when, back in the early 1990s, you spotted that middle-aged lesbian couple, with matching homemade tattoos and mullets, with the butch one sporting that infamous Don't Panic T-shirt boasting the slogan "I'm Not A Lesbian, But My Girlfriend Is." While still on sale to queers who've never been to a big city or queer resort before [see page 105], it seems that the queer slogan T-shirt will shortly be making its way to a bargain bin or thrift store near you.

Top 10 classic
Don't Panic slogan T-shirts

We're not saying good, we're saying classic.

01 **I can't even think straight**
02 **4 out of 5 cats prefer lesbians**
03 **Anything with rainbow colors/ rainbow flags**
04 **Tell your boyfriend I said thanks!**
05 **Dip me in honey and throw me to the lesbians**
06 **Nobody knows I'm gay**
07 **2QT2BSTR8**
08 **It happens in the best of families**
09 **Xena rules!**
10 **Straight but not narrow**

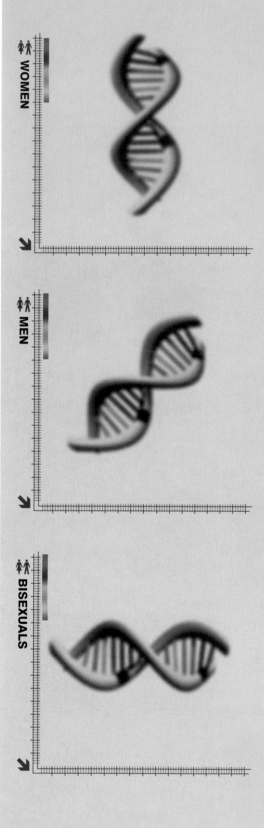

Gay Gene

A highly contentious scientific claim that gayness is physical not psychological

The latest installment in the age-old nature versus nurture argument—were you "born this way" or did your mother make you a homosexual?—the gay gene was meant to establish a link between your physical make-up and your sexual behavior.

In 1991, Salk Institute researcher Simon LeVay claimed he had found significant physical differences between the brains of gay men and straight men (something to do with an enlarged third interstitial nucleus of the anterior hypothalamus in straight men, apparently). Other scientists begged to differ. The most recent research, reported in journals such as *Science and Nature*, claims that although 90% of the human genome had been put under a microscope (a very big, strong microscope), none of the 30,000 genes were looking obviously gay.

But the significance of the argument goes way beyond scientific. Supporters of the idea of a gay gene claim that it will prove that we are not "unnatural" and that we have not "chosen" to be gay just to spite our parents or appear fashionable. Others fear that if a gay gene is isolated, eradication of that gene will not be far behind. At the very least it is feared that tests will be done to determine whether a fetus has the gene so that it can be aborted to prevent the birth of homosexuals, male or female— something Emmanuel Jakobovits, the former Chief Rabbi of Britain, welcomes: "Homosexuality is a disability, and if people wish to have it eliminated before they have children, I do not see any moral objections to using genetic engineering to limit this particular trend."

Some hoped that under US constitution, gay men would be afforded protection from discrimination (such as the above) if their sexuality could be proved to be natural rather than nurtured.

But while many conservatives in America have embraced the notion of a gay gene not only as a possible "final solution" to the problem of homosexuality but as "proof" that gay men and lesbians are different and should therefore be treated differently, others have denounced it, citing the many cases of homosexuals who have been "converted" or taught to curb their desires.

Turkey Basters

How to get a girl pregnant in ten easy steps. Not necessarily using a turkey baster

You've all heard the urban myth about the woman who bought a plant in foreign climes that released thousands of poisonous spiders, right? Or the one about the man who bit into a burger to find a patty containing something other than prime American beef? Then there's the even more laughable tale of the lesbians who gave birth to a bouncing baby boy courtesy of a cup of warm sperm that had been on a low-light since Tuesday and a turkey baster sterilized in hot water.

The turkey baster will go down in the lesbian hall of urban legends. And though the story of a tattooed dyke who had to hold the receptacle while a gay male donor jerked off with his one good arm (he'd had a bicycle accident the previous day) is apparently true, the bit where a turkey baster is used to plant the seed where the sun don't shine probably isn't. A syringe, yes. A common or garden turkey baster, no—although its sheer size would at least give the girl a thrill while she prayed for the pattering of tiny little feet.

While we can laugh at the stories of just how the girls got the sperm to the place it normally doesn't go, artificial insemination has become big business, raking in millions of dollars from both gay and straight couples desperate to have kids. While modern clinics decked out in Ikea furnishings are bringing in kiddie-hungry customers from the world over, guaranteeing clean sperm for hard-earned money, some folk still prefer the good old 10-step Do-It-Yourself method that makes the bun-to-oven process so simple:

1) Place an advertisement in a gay paper seeking a potential sperm donor.

2) Check the guy out to make sure he is clean and has good dress sense and ask for official papers ensuring his HIV-negative status.

3) Keep an ovulation diary, and work out the day when the lady is at her most fertile.

4) Get your chosen donor to do the "deed" in a paper cup. Sex mags may need to be supplied.

5) Do not hover, and do not knock the bathroom door to "make sure he's OK." Pressure is not conducive to a swift, clean ejaculation.

6) Keep the ejaculated liquid at body temperature (the cleavage is a good place for extra warmth on cold days), and transfer to the lesbian in the receptacle from which it came as quickly as possible. Be careful not to spill.

7) Inject the milky-in-color substance with a syringe (minus the needle, naturally) into the soon-to-be-mom, who is standing on her head to help the semen on its merry way. While you could in theory use a turkey baster for this part of the process, bear in mind that boys actually only produce about a teaspoon of the sticky stuff when bringing themselves off.

8) Get the mum-to-be to stay in this legs-in-the-air-like-she-just-don't-care position for as long as is possible.

9) Keep your fingers crossed and look out for bizarre food cravings and morning sickness.

10) Wipe out the next eighteen years in your diary and kiss goodbye to early morning sex.

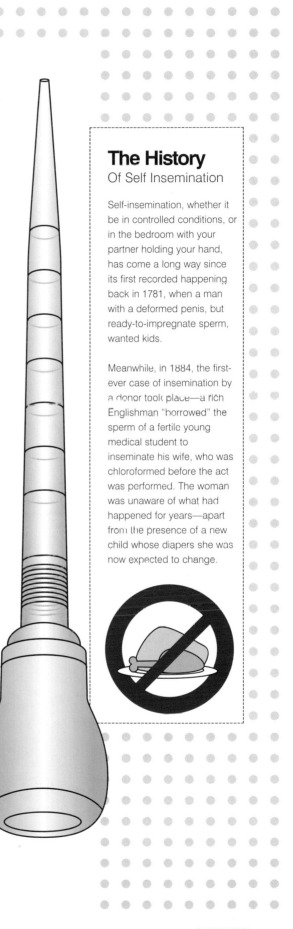

The History
Of Self Insemination

Self-insemination, whether it be in controlled conditions, or in the bedroom with your partner holding your hand, has come a long way since its first recorded happening back in 1781, when a man with a deformed penis, but ready-to-impregnate sperm, wanted kids.

Meanwhile, in 1884, the first-ever case of insemination by a donor took place—a rich Englishman "borrowed" the sperm of a fertile young medical student to inseminate his wife, who was chloroformed before the act was performed. The woman was unaware of what had happened for years—apart from the presence of a new child whose diapers she was now expected to change.

M to Fs, F to Ms

The truth about transsexuals

There are some folk who just don't feel at home in their body, who believe their sexual identity doesn't fit with their anatomic gender, and who undergo processes of varying degrees to change it. They're called transsexuals.

But before we start, let's clear up a few common misunderstandings. Transsexuals are not "gay" and they're not "transvestites." Transvestites are actually happy with their bits and content with doing the cross-dressing thing. Neither are they "transgenderists" who may dabble with minor surgery or hormones to acquire the secondary sexual characteristics of the opposite sex (though of course, this is a stage transsexuals go through en route to acquiring their new gender) but don't want major replumbing and all on-site garbage removed.

Transsexuals, whether male to female (MTF) or female to male (FTM), actually want to transform themselves into the opposite sex and rid themselves of the genitalia they were born with. This is something they'll have felt since they were little kids. The condition is called Gender Dysphoria.

Nothing much physically could be done about gender dysphoria until after the Second World War, when advances were made in sex hormones and plastic surgery. The first procedures saw MTF's sexual organs being removed before a vagina was constructed using skin grafts taken from the thighs or buttocks. Christine Jorgensen was among the first of a small group of transsexuals to be operated on, and her story became a major sensation Stateside in 1952 when the media discovered it.

It was in the late 50s that great advances took place, pioneered by a French doctor Dr Georges Burou who came up with "penile inversion" for MTFs. Variations of his technique have been used ever since, though the following decade saw Dr. Harry Benjamin taking it all a step further with the concept that gender identity and sexual orientation are two independent dimensions in humans, thus requiring a combination of innovative surgical and hormonal treatments.

So what exactly happens when someone wants to change sex? Well, sex reassignment surgery is not a procedure any Tom, Dick or Harriet can choose to have at the drop of a hat. Yes, the ultimate decision rests with him or her, but first he or she must obtain approval for the operation from a surgeon and two psychiatrists.

Having satisfied the professionals that they are serious about this, the patient starts hormone treatment to physically alter their body.

Men will be prescribed oestrogen and/or progesterone to make their voices and faces more feminine, increase their tit mass and decrease body hair—though it can't shift facial hair. It'll also shrink their dick and balls. Meanwhile, women take androgen, which butches up their bodies. They stop having periods and sometimes experience a weakening of breast tissue.

For the following one to two years, the patient lives as a member of the opposite sex while continuing hormone therapy, all the while monitored by their doctors. This is called a "real life test."

At the end of this phase, surgery can take place—and this is where it gets really serious as there's no going back. For MTF operations, as well as performing boob jobs, surgeons remove the patient's balls and use the scrotum to make labia. Meanwhile the penis is hollowed out and inverted. You might not want to think about that too much—just be content with knowing that it all

Female To Males (FTMs) want to transform themselves into the opposite sex and rid themselves of the genitalia they were born with

requires extensive surgery and lots of follow-up visits. However, the result is top quality and pretty damn lifelike. And yes, the patient will be able to orgasm as the sensitive nerves of the penis are now inside her body, while the prostate is left intact and can still spasm as it did before.

The FTM usually gets the gear after one year of cross-dressing as the mental jump from female to male isn't as drastic as the other way round, apparently. Most patients visit a plastic surgeon to have their breasts removed while a gynaecologist will remove the womb. A surgeon will then do the "phalloplasty," which is where they get their dick sorted, though if the patient's been on androgen for a long time, they might have had so much clitoral enlargement, they might be happy with just that.

It is however not as easy to make a penis as it is a vagina! A prosthetic strap-on or glue-on penis is made lifelike by a medical sculptor with skin being taken from the lower abdomen or inner thigh, then peeled, rolled and attached where a penis should be. The clitoris is left intact and embedded at the base to maintain sexual sensitivity, while balls are made from gel, much like the stuff used in breast enhancement.

The age-old argument that preferring a grapple with someone of the same sex is a "crime against nature" has been blown out of the water with the discovery of a whole range of gay and bisexual activities in animals.

According to research, approximately 450 species have been found to possess a preference for the same sex and, as with humans, these gay animals often form life-long relationships, the best example being the bottlenose dolphin, which is more likely to form a gay coupling (including full-on gay sex) than a straight one. Other animals, like bison and gazelles, prefer one-off gay flings. Just because they can. While the bottlenose dolphin flippers down the path of monogamy, walruses prefer to indulge in a spot of same-gender boy walrus sex out of the breeding season, usually reverting to their lady duties during the "normal" breeding season.

And bisexuality is rife in other species. According to Bruce Bahemihl, Ph.D, the bonobo chimpanzee, for example, prefers to dabble with both sexes rather than swing exclusively one way or another.

Even zookeepers have come forward to acknowledge the existence of gay animals. There is now even a gay zoo in Amsterdam—a favorite location for sons and daughters to take parents they've just come out to—that boasts flamingo orgies on its pond, gay monkeys, geese and bulls and a lesbian chimp. The zoo has proved to be a popular attraction, with the geese often taking part in their own gay marriage "ceremonies." According to the zoo's director Maarten Frankenhuis, "the idea is to show that homosexuality is a natural phenomenon." The male animals in the Dutch zoo have willingly taken male partners, even when there are cute females on offer. Sometimes, however, the animals only go gay when removed from females, "like in English boarding schools," adds Frankenhuis.

So homosexuality is not a rare occurrence in the animal kingdom. It seems that boy-on-boy and girl-on-girl animal action is actually rife. These animals have gay sex, show affection towards each other and even, as in the case of female barn owls that were artificially inseminated without a male partner, co-parent their offspring.

We do it, over 130 species of birds do it, and even the southeastern blueberry bees do it. It's natural.

Gay Animals
Whole zoo-loads of animals have demonstrated homosexual behavior

Classified adverts

The acronym- and code-filled ads used by boys and girls looking for love, or just a quick one

Classified adverts make up the bulk of most queer magazines these days. Leaf through the rear end of any gay boy newspaper and you'll find very little news and rather a lot of adverts for men seeking men, and not just for long-term relationships, but also for a cheeky one-off with a professional.

It's not all about just getting your end away with a toned straight-acting bloke with an impressive appendage. Gay girls and boys looking for true love also use these ads to advertise their availability and get down in print just who it is they're looking for.

Use some of these fool-proof terms to bag the boy or girl of your dreams

VGL—very good-looking. There's no point in being modest.

VWE—very well endowed. You won't be disappointed by this boy's package.

XXWE—extra, extra well endowed. Enough to bring tears to your eyes.

Cut—this boy's dick sports a neat little circumcision.

Uncut—an *au naturel* penis.

Smooth—this boy spends more than most girls do on waxing, sugaring and shaving his body hair.

Versatile—these boys, usually of a rent variety, can either top you or play bottom. The choice is yours.

Hairy—this man's ideal for boys who prefer their fuck buddy hirsute.

8"—a modest little measurement so that you won't be disappointed when you go a-knocking.

SA—straight-acting. Don't expect this one-night stand to play it camp.

WE—just plain old well endowed. Contrary to popular opinion in London, this does not refer to boys residing in the West End area of the city.

28yo—28 years old.

In/out—the service provided by rent boys that can either be performed chez toi, or in the tradesman's own home.

Active—this boy is in charge and on top.

Swimmers body—exactly what it says. Big shoulders and a toned physique.

WLTM—would like to meet. This one's looking for love, and not just a one-off.

Professional—only queers with a "proper job" need apply.

N/S—a nonsmoker is preferred.

Must like cats—usually found in the lesbian sections of the "looking for love" classifieds.

Seeks—a more desperate sounding plea.

Gaydar

The intuitive built-in system that gay men and women use to spot other queers

So a "gaydar" is a machine for straights to check out who's homo and who ain't, right? Au contraire. Our gaydar system, which only recently gained its groovy moniker, is a built-in, can't-buy-in-the-shops ability to spot a fellow gay boy or lady lesbian.

So why gaydar?
It comes from the happy marriage of two words: "Gay" and "radar." Radar, from "Radio Detection And Ranging" is a system for detecting the presence, speed and direction of common day items like an aircraft or a ship, while gaydar is our very own system for spotting the presence of queers, moving or otherwise.

But how?
We don't know, it just kind of happens. Show us a homo at thirty paces, and we'll spot 'em, give them a rating out of ten, and eye them up all in the same movement.

That's so handy…
With just 10% of the population to choose from, it really helps to separate the wheat from the chaff, so to speak. None of those horribly embarrassing hitting on a straight girl/boy faux-pas moments.

So is it a foolproof way to meet fellow homos when you're out and about?
Foolproof, no. Handy, yes. It's a great way to make your day-to-day movements around town so much more pleasurable.

Is this just a made-up thing, or is it a scientifically proven skill?
Well, until recently it was mere gay propaganda, but a bunch of science types at the University of Harvard, with way too much time on their hands, found that gaydar actually does have some basis in scientific fact.

So what happened?
The Harvard researchers showed a group of gay and straight men and women silent videos and photographs of other men and women of various sexual persuasions and ask them to play Spot The Queer. In this cute little experiment, gay men and women were better overall at identifying gay people, with the dykes being the most accurate. Differences between the groups, however, were reported to be "slight."

I'm surprised no-one's made a pocket computer that spots your fellow homos?
Well, gay men tend to be born with a pocket computer that does that job for them, but of course, when there's a sniff of money to be made the gay community is first in there to reap the profits. Apparently there's an attachment you can add on to your Palm Pilot to help you recognize fellow queers and there was a strange invention that you'd program and keep in your pocket which would "go off" if someone else with a similar contraption came close. But going for a beer in a designated gay bar is generally far more fun and a lot cheaper.

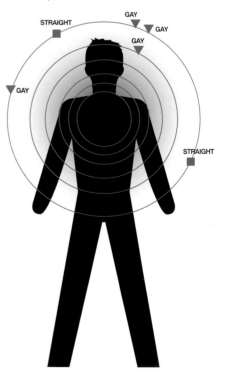

A-Gays

High society homos

Every community needs a pecking order, and as perhaps the snobbiest minority of all, the gay community has got the mother of all pecking orders, albeit with a slightly different selection process.

A-Gays are anointed by virtue of a high social standing, which may depend on fabulous connections (David B. Mixner may be a great activist but it was his "in with the Clintons" that A-ed him), fabulous wealth (David Geffen is excellently connected but oh those billions…!), fabulous celebrity (Elton John is the most visible A-Gay) or just fabulous fabulousness (John Galliano, Karl Lagerfeld, any other Paris-based major fashion designer you care to mention).

In contrast to most gay pecking orders based on, well, pecs, a beautifully muscled or visaged gay man or lesbian cannot make their way onto the list by looks alone. To get on there they must hitch their wagon to a star, like David Furnish, the filmmaker boyfriend of Elton John, who swept to the top of the list like a society wife in a Henry James novel.

In the UK, gays can reach A status by excelling in their field—even a really humdrum field—and getting themselves honored by the Queen. Already pretty A-list, actor Sir Ian McKellan turned a corner when he was knighted for acting and activism, while gay television executive Waheed Ali went one better and got Tony Blair to recommend that Her Majesty dub him a Lord.

Alternatively, you can make your own power. Tony Blair's UK cabinet included A-Gays such as Chris Smith—the first out gay Member of Parliament—and the creepy but powerful Peter Mandelson. US Senators like Allan Spear also qualify, as does Cheryl Jacques, who became the first openly gay person to announce her candidacy for Congress.

Obviously, as far as class conscious Brits are concerned, there's no A-Gay as A as a member of the royal family. Take it back a few hundred years and you have a gay monarch, King James I, complete with a fully fledged A-Gay boyfriend in the form of the Earl of Buckingham, who used to sign himself "Your most humble slave and servant and dog." More recently, Queen Victoria's grandson and heir to the throne Prince Eddie was a very sociable A-Gay to the extent that he was even caught red, ahem, handed in a male brothel.

Rumours that the Queen's son Prince Edward—now safely married—is gay are unconfirmed. If it were true it would be A-Gay nirvana.

Sex Types

How gay men and lesbians identify themselves by what sex they like to have

You'd think that the old "opposites attract" rule wouldn't apply to gay men and lesbians. Well, they're into same-sex stuff by their very definition. But that doesn't take account of the sex types that exist in the gay world. If you're a smooth-skinned Twinkie with a mop of blond hair and a scrotum as smooth as a baby's bottom, what could be more "opposite" than a big old hairy Bear that gives you beard rash just looking at him?

1. The Leatherman

He bases himself on old Tom of Finland pictures, which apparently date back to when straight men used to wear leather chaps with just a jockstrap underneath, funny little Muir Caps and harnesses (it's a biker thing, don't worry about it). The Leatherman can be of any age—though it's a good last refuge for the grizzled—but they do often define themselves sexually by age: older leathermen go on top, younger become greedy bottoms. They are often pretty out there sexually—fisting, spitting, biting even punching around—and are the sex type most likely to identify their sexual appetites using the time-honored colored handkerchief code [see page 82]. In fact, with Leathermen, it's all about accessories.

2. The Twinkie

Smooth, young, clean-cut and fresh, the Twinkie is usually in his late teens or early 20s and is generally thought of as dirty blond, both in hair color and general behavior. It is the Twinkie's responsibility to keep his body as free from hair and muscles as possible to maintain his boyish appeal, meticulously shaving his testicles and making sure that any work-out routines don't bulk him up (get that muscle-shake out of here!). Catch him in corny college sweaters or in soft-punkwear (you know, spikey surfey hair, skatewear, that kind of thing). In bed, he's generally believed to be a bottom, but don't bet on it.

3. The Daddy

Think the silver fox, the smooth-talking moneyed man about town with a college education, a position somewhere high up in finance and a house in the Hamptons (and probably a couple of big Irish dogs and the complete Ralph Lauren homeware collection). The Daddy can be blue-collar but frankly, if a Twinkie is into that, he'll probably go the whole hog and have a bear. Handsome and solid and oozing experience, the Daddy dreams of being a bottom but is usually top though he has been known to be fucked, though only in the credit card.

4. The Bear

Big and hairy with a huge potbelly—not necessarily an anti-aphrodisiac—the Bear is an incredibly popular sex type (incredibly because we can all be bears with just a few extra pounds and a shaving embargo). Usually kitted out in jeans and a checkered lumberjack shirt with a huge pot, the bear's biggest challenge is not to lapse into girlish chatter and giggling as masculinity is the essential ingredient for the bear. The bear tends to be a top (if they are mating with non-bears that is), and must keep his pubic hair in a state of wild disarray to be convincing.

5. The SM Dyke

You'll know her by her shaved head, extensive piercings (especially below the panty-line, not that she would dream of wearing panties you understand), and enough tattoos to fill a Sear's Catalog. The palette is strictly black, the fabric of choice either leather or rubber (or, in some cases, a weird Nazi uniform she once saw in an old Jane Birkin film). She'll have a whole arsenal of sex toys—mostly frightening—and will love to pinch and handcuff and generally slap about any of her much femmer playmates.

6. The Lesbian Dominatrix

She may be working the same furrow as the SM Dyke, but with the Lesbian Dominatrix the accent is firmly on style. The silhouette will be tall and willowy but not without enough haunch and bosom to make for a dramatic waistline. Her clothing will be black, tight-fitting and immaculate quality-wise and she may even be sporting a phony pony. Expect her to come fitted with a riding crop, vertiginous heels and a sneer that could curdle cream. Call her Madame but don't ever maintain eye contact, not if you know what's good for you. Girl!

7. The Pig

This is an equal opportunities sex type, which welcomes both ladies and gentlemen. Their proximity can usually be detected by a strong smell of rubber and urine as these guys dress in clothes seemingly designed to emphasize body odor. Big in Europe, you'll find them usually shaved of head and genitals, wearing rubber costumes so tight they feel like party balloons, and so pierced you could probably lace them up. They will do anything no one else will do: lick the soles of your shoes, drink your piss, let you fart on them, they've even been known to exchange all the major body fluids — and solids!—through the post by using condoms (and think about that one for a moment!).

8. The Beefcake

Not to be confused with the Bear, this sex type is rippling with muscles and will not miss any opportunity to take that shirt off to show anyone who wants to see. Basically narcissistic, the Beefcake wants to have sex with anyone who looks exactly like him (which is why when you go to a Beefcake bar everyone looks exactly the same). Known for their very small penises and pea-size balls (steroids) and for their copious drug use, this is the "no pecs, no sex" brigade and they have one big dirty secret: they are all big old bottoms who just want someone with even bigger breasts than them to flip them over and call them Martha.

9. The Baby Dyke

She dreams of turning into a big old Diesel and eyes up the sexy little femme behind the bar like a dirty old man. She is the Baby Dyke—a top by nature, doing the bottom thing as a kind of apprenticeship. She is hungry for learning and doesn't mind letting the big dykes—the alpha females of their tribe—much her as part of that learning experience. You'll find her looking like a boy but trying to look like a man, holding her cigarette between her thumb and forefinger and treating the femmes with the sort of panache you'd expect from a construction worker, and just praying she can pull it off. She is trouble, but not half the trouble she's going to be.

10. The Swinger

This one's probably not even gay but will still go there (well, he'll pretty much go anywhere). He may identify as gay but still be into a little light girl action, just for old-time's sake. Or he may be straight but like nothing better than the thought of a big old dick up his ass. Or he may be very organized and check into swingers' clubs because he gets off on the whole atmosphere of guys humping girls. He was brought up on it, buys straight (or, at a push, bi) pornos and is generally up for anything. Looks-wise, he can be a little confused, not quite wanting to opt for gay uniform but wanting to make a bit of a suggestion of his sexual tastes, and getting it all wrong and doing something like growing his hair long.

QUEER

Boys

1. arse bandit, 2. ass burglar, 3. batty boy, 4. bowler from the pavillion end, 5. brown hatter, 6. bum chum, 7. butthole surfer, 8. chocolate starfish poker, 9. chutney ferret, 10. cocksucker, 11. daisy, 12. doughnut puncher, 13. faggot, 14. fudgepacker, 15. gayola, 16. Hairy Mary, 17. invert, 18. Jessie keester, 19. bandit, 20. lavender cowboy, 21. moll, 22. nelly, 23. oofterpa, 24. pillow-biter, 25. poof, 26. queer, 27. rear admiral, 28. sausage smuggler, 29. sissy, 30. three dollar bill, 31. tooti frooti, 32. turd burglar, 33. uphill gardener, 34. vegemite driller, 35. woofter

CARPET-MUNCHER POOF LES
R ADMIRAL WANKER
FINGER ARTIST
ASS BA
R
BO M
B MUNGHER
UNGHER LESBYTERIAN

Girls

1. Amazon, **2.** bean-flicker, **3.** beaver eater, **4.** carpet-muncher, **5.** crack-snaker, **6.** daughter of bilitis **7.** dutch girl, **8.** finger artist,
9. gay lady, **10.** gusset-nuzzler, **11.** he-she, **12.** jasper, **13.** kissing fish, **14.** Lebanese, **15.** les-be-friends, **16.** lesbyterian,
17. lezza, **18.** manwijf, **19.** muff diver, **20.** no-nuts, **21.** pussy-puller, **22.** quim, **23.** ruffle, **24.** sapphist, **25.** split tail lover,
26. tit king, **27.** tunaface, **28.** urningin, **29.** vagetarian, **30.** warme Schwester, **31.** zamie

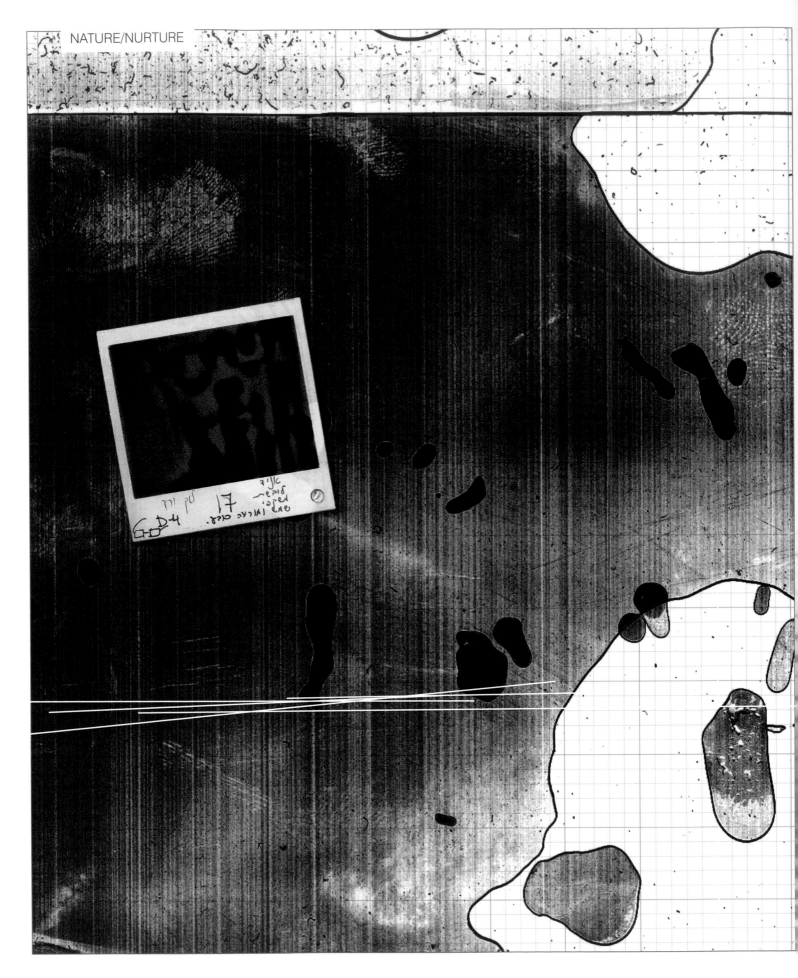

Gay Serial Killers

It's not a gay "thing," but the gay community has had its fair share of killers on the rampage

Serial killing is a male thing (93% of serial killers are male), a white thing (even though black men are over-represented in murder figures generally), and often a gay thing. Mind you, although 43% of serial killers have reported homosexual experiences, a percentage of them also reported having humped their mothers' severed heads, so we're not talking your gay man on the street here. In fact, scientists have said that sample groups are so small—and "homosexual activity" so hard to establish as a factor in a person's identity—that the figures are probably next to worthless. Still, a gay serial killer is a stereotype that has proved very attractive to a number of filmmakers [see page 206].

Most gay serial killers (and be careful with the term: in the UK, Colin Ireland was dubbed The Gay Serial Killer, the "gay" describing his five victims and not himself) choose other gay men or else young boys as their victims.

The first recorded gay serial killer was Gilles de Rais, a companion of Joan of Arc no less, who was held responsible for the sadistic killings of more than three hundred young boys. Since then, gay serial killers have varied as much as their straight counterparts, running the gamut from the sexually sadistic and socially arrogant John Wayne Gacy, to the totally inadequate Jeffrey Dahmer. Here are five of the best known.

1. Jeffrey Dahmer

A sad, lonely child with an interest in animal biology, Dahmer became America's most reviled serial killer when his Milwaukee apartment was raided by police who found a veritable Black Museum: heads in the refrigerator and freezer, torsos in a barrel, genitals and sundry severed hands all over the place, and plans under way for a shrine made of body parts. A sexual inadequate, Dahmer dreamt of turning young men he had picked up in bars into his sex slaves, which is why some of his victims had had holes drilled in their heads and battery acid inserted. Cutting a very pathetic figure in court, where he tried to apologize to his victims' families, Dahmer was eventually murdered in prison in 1994 by a fellow inmate.
➪ **Take it further:** *The Shrine of Jeffrey Dahmer* by Brian Masters

2. John Wayne Gacy

A vile, arrogant businessman and local "man of influence," who dressed up as a clown to entertain children in his spare time, Gacy chose his victims among drifters and young men who came to him for work. He would play drinking games with them, get them to put handcuffs on as part of a trick he was going to show them and then submit them to hours of torture and sexual abuse before killing them and burying them in the crawlspace below his house. Gacy became something of a cult figure, with rock stars scrambling to buy his kitsch paintings of clowns, before he was eventually executed in 1994.
➪ **Take it further:** *Buried Dreams* by Tim Cahill.

3. Carl Panzram

The story of Panzram is so extreme it's almost funny, especially as it takes in stints in the Foreign Legion, feeding people to crocodiles and marauding the high seas as a pirate. Raped by four bums as a child, Panzram went on to live a flamboyant life of crime, which included once hiring a yacht, drugging a bunch of sailors on it, sodomizing the lot of them, then dumping their dead bodies overboard. By the time he was captured—for robbery!—he admitted having killed at least twenty-one men (including boys), and sodomizing over

1,000. "For all these things I am not in the least bit sorry," was his final statement. He was eventually hanged in 1930 with insults for the executioner and the priests still on his lips.

4. Dennis Nielsen

Dennis Nielsen—a mild-mannered civil servant by day—was apparently set in his murderous ways by the sight of his grandfather's dead body at a very impressionable age. He would pick up young men from gay pubs in London, take them back to his home and, while they were sleeping, strangle them, usually with a tie. He would then keep the corpses around the house for as long as feasible "for company." The bodies were eventually dismembered, boiled up and disposed of by being flushed down the toilet. Nielsen was eventually caught when the drains became blocked with human flesh. With sixteen victims, he is the UK's most prolific serial killer and is currently residing at Her Majesty's Pleasure, aka in jail.
➪ **Take it further:** *Killing for Company* by Brian Masters.

5. Aileen Wournos

Of the 7% of serial killers who are female, a third work in collaboration with a man, which is what makes lesbian Aileen Wuornos an exceptional case. When she was eventually picked up in a biker bar in 1991, Wuornos was suspected of having put .22 bullet holes into no fewer than seven working men. Eventually admitting to five of the murders, Wournos, a prostitute with a major attitude problem and a history of violence towards men, claimed that she had been attacked by her victims and was acting in self-defence. As she was found guilty, she shouted at the jury: "I hope you get raped! Scumbags of America!" They recommended the death sentence shortly after.

Bisexuality

Sexual attraction to members of both sexes

"Being bisexual doubles your chance of a date on a Saturday night," said Woody Allen, which sounds handy but doesn't take into account the amount of trouble you have to be accepted as bisexual in the first place. Especially in a society obsessed with finding a clear line between gay and straight, and ignoring the idea of a continuum between the two. Most gays will think you're just too chicken to come all the way out as gay, while most straights will think you're somehow sexually confused or going through a funny phase. So, what does being bisexual actually mean? Theories on what exactly constitutes bisexuality vary greatly, from the "we're all bisexual really" argument espoused by the daddy of psychiatry Sigmund Freud, who thought that we simply repressed the side of our sexuality we were least happy with, to the narrow definition of a bisexual as someone who has had sex with members of both genders within a twelve-month period. The University of Chicago discovered that if you apply the one-year rule, only 0.7% of men and 0.3% of women qualified, while it's thought that most of us would qualify if the definition stretched to sexual contact with both genders over a lifetime.

Definitions of sexuality in general usually boil down to three ways of looking at the thing: identity (who you say you are), behavior (what you actually get up to), and attraction (which may never get beyond the fantasy level). All of which means bisexuals are pretty tricky to pin down.

"Given the diversity of human sexual responsiveness, it may be as artificial to use a three-category system to describe individuals as it is to employ a two-category system," says psychologist Jay Paul, which is why some sex researchers have gone even further in their attempt to classify different levels of bisexuality. In the 1980s psychiatrist Fritz Klein developed a 'Sexual Orientation Grid'—an upgraded version of a scale first invented by legendary sex researcher Dr. Alfred Kinsey—where you plot Sexual Attraction, Sexual Behaviour, Sexual Fantasies, Emotional Preference, etc. between one and seven, one being exclusively heterosexual and seven being exclusively homosexual, taking in your ideal situation, your current situation, and your past history. But then the old problem of untangling identity from behavior from attraction (you may identify as bisexual though you only have sex with women but are really only attracted to men, for example) always rears its ugly head. It's a problem the authors of *Sex In America: A Definitive Survey* found they had when they discovered that only 2.8% of men and 1.4% of women identified as bisexual or homosexual, while 4% of women and 9% of men had had same-gender sex, and that's without taking same gender fantasies into account. It's interesting, by the way, that men always come out of these surveys, however they are worked out, as more bisexual than women.

With so many variables operating, it's not surprising that bisexuality is often thought of as sexual confusion in a "biphobic" society, though it should be pointed out that in many non-Western societies (or even Western prisons!), sex between members of the same gender—often due to the unavailability of the opposite gender, though not always—is not thought of as unusual, confused or defining in any way. It's just a means of getting your rocks off.

Palare

British gayspeak from the 60s

Palare, palyaree, palary or polari was a slang language—never very complete—used by British gay folk back in the burgeoning gay milk bar scene of the 60s to differentiate themselves and identify each other. It was also, in what was then a viciously homophobic environment, a very handy way of discussing how sexy another omi palone (gay gentleman) was. Despite that, its origins seem unlikely to be purely queer.

Linguists are still divided as to where Palare originally came from, though large parts of the vocabulary are certainly Italian in origin. Some language experts believe it was imported by sailors and traders from the Mediterranean and trickled down to entertainers and fairground people with whom they hooked up after they retired from the navy. Others are more convinced it arrived with the large number of Italian travelling showmen in the 1800s. Whichever of those theories is true, Palare also contains a variety of slang terms from sources including English (backwards slang, rhyming slang), circus or theatrical slang, canal-speak, Yiddish and Gypsy languages.

In the late 60s, Palare reached a kind of mainstream status thanks to the Julian and Sandy sketches on the BBC radio program *Round the Horne*, which featured actors Kenneth Williams and Hugh Paddick being seriously camp and peppering their dialog with the slang, which was by this stage recognizable to the British public at large.

As a language, Palare has almost died out, though some words still live on and have even been absorbed into the English language itself. Here's a selection of the ones that have survived as well as a few of the downright weird ones…

barney—fight
beancove—young queen
bencove—close friend
bevvie—drink
bingey—penis
bijou—small
bona—good
carsey—house
charver—to have sex
chicken—young boy
clobber—clothes
corybungus—arse
cottage—public toilet
dizzy—scatterbrained
drag—women's clothes
Eine—London
fruit—gay man
glossies—magazines
kaffies—pants/trousers
lally—leg
mince—walk effeminately
mish—mouth
naff—boring, straight
omi palone—gay man
on your tod—by yourself
palone—woman
rattling cove—taxi cab
scarper—escape
slap—make up
striller—piano
trade—sexual partner
troll—to cruise
trundling cheat—car
vada—to look/see

MBAs

An MBA? What's that? Some new-fangled degree or a credit card company?
No, but it's something that, if done the wrong way, could cost you even more than your debauched years at college, and seriously damage the credit card.

Put us out of our misery… what does it stand for?
Mutually Beneficial Arrangement.

A what, sorry?
Also known as a "marriage of convenience," it allows gay men and lesbians to marry each other, thereby getting our hands on hard-to-come-by immigration permits entitling you to residency in your boyfriend or girlfriend's country of birth. It also allows you to benefit from tax relief and insurance benefits, and get free ironing boards from clueless relatives.

I'd quite like to live in Sydney. How do I go about finding me a homo spouse?
It's not something to be taken lightly. Most people only use MBAs if their partner is at risk of deportation. One option is to get a homo friend of the opposite sex to marry your partner for a small sum of cash. Another popular way is to put a classified advert in either your local gay newspaper, or a gay newspaper in the city where you're looking to move to.

Saying what? "Bride for sale?"
No, no, no. Remember, a marriage of convenience or MBA is illegal. That's the point. You're attempting to duck under these laws that ignore gay couples in order to stay living in your partner's country of residence. Marrying any old queer could set you up with a fair few legal problems: Check out some of the penalties you could face for either helping a non-citizen become a resident, or trying to get hold of residency in your country of choice. And remember, due to the nature of such an arrangement, some gay men and women have set

themselves up for nasty cases of blackmail.

OK, so talk me through this classified ad that I saw in the *SF Weekly*…

> ■ **European/American couple,** GWMs, WLTM a lesbian for a MBA Must be willing to move to London

Meaning: A gay, white male couple, one of European descent, one of American, living in San Francisco, would like to meet a lesbian couple for a mutually beneficial arrangement so that the European man can obtain legal papers to allow him to stay in the US.

I've seen them before. Loads of them in fact. How come?
Well, as you well know, gay couples are rarely recognized in the eyes of the law [see page 112], so when your partner is not an official resident of your country, getting a job, a flat and all the things that come with being an illegal alien make life, and the prospect of a long-term partnership, incredibly difficult. Many lesbian and gay couples use MBAs as a last ditch effort to keep their loved ones in the country. It invariably means months of cohabiting with your intended husband/wife-to-be, government checks and the questioning of your friends and family which can not only cause stress, but if you're found out to be taking part in a false marriage, could lead to deportation. Scary stuff.

But what other options do we have?
Well, none. But most countries do have gay groups that offer free legal advice for those of you with no other option. As with all legal goings-on, seek advice, get it all down in a contract, and prepare yourself for a good year or so of hassle and annoyance. It's a rocky road, but it might just mean a happy ever after for you and your partner.

Gay Marriage

While some gay men and women see getting married as a sub-standard version of the straight ideal, others the world over are putting on white lacy numbers and are tying the knot

Even though a gay or lesbian couple getting formally hitched is only recognized in the eyes of the law in a few countries [see page 112], that hasn't stopped thousands of couples exchanging rings and drawing up a gift list for their nearest and dearest.

As anyone knows, getting married is an expensive business, and there's a growing gay wedding industry to prove it, so it's important that you get it right—it is, apparently, one of the most stressful things in life, but don't let that put you off.

Some couples see a ceremony as a cutesy way of letting their friends and family know they're going to be together for the foreseeable, while others see it as a damn good excuse to throw a wild old party and receive all the cutlery and crystal sets they could ever need. Here are a few hot tips and pointers to make sure that the 'best day of your life' is stress-free and memorable.

1. What do we call it?

Most queer couples can't get legally wed, and as walking up the aisle at your local church might not be to everyone's taste (including the parishioners), and exchanging a marriage contract at your synagogue might not go down too well, there are a whole bunch of alternative ceremonies that you and your loved one can take part in.

First of all, give it a name. How about a commitment ceremony or lifelong commitment vows? Others prefer a union ceremony or the beautifully schmaltzy ceremony of hearts. Ahem. Whatever you call it, and whoever you get to marry you, remember it's all about you.

Right, now you need to choose a suitably gorgeous location where you can exchange rings and cut that over-priced wedding cake.

2. Whom do I invite?

Whomever you damn well like. This may seem like a stupid question, but so many queer couples, keen to please their family members, end up inviting everyone in their family tree including that evil great aunt who'd rather you'd have married Satan than be gay. Think about it—does your family know you're a big old homo? If not, then the news of your impending gay betrothal might a) come as something of a shock and b) might not be the best news they've ever heard. It's a party so invite people who are going to love it.

3. Do we get presents?

Yes ma'am! You don't even need to have a boyfriend or girlfriend in tow to start fine-tuning that wedding list. One of the biggest bones of contention for queers regarding marriage laws is that they don't get to throw a big old party and get presents for it just because they've met someone they think is half-decent. Think about what you need—is that cut-glass crystal decanter in the shape of a swan really going to look hot in your minimalist loft apartment? Do you really need those purple velour scatter cushions everywhere? How often will you be using that canteen of cutlery with your ready-made micro meals? And make sure you give your friends who don't earn as much cash as you the choice of something affordable. Not everyone has the budget for Versace silk bed linen.

4. What do we wear?

Whatever you want. While you may look hot in your jeans and a lycra skinny shirt, think about making an effort. And just because you're a lady lesbian doesn't mean you have to wrap yourself up in lace and white silk and go to your own wedding looking like a hefty fairy. It's all about taste, and whatever people might say, not all homosexuals possess it.

5. So what happens on the big day?

Again, it's all about preference. How about a quiet little ceremony or speech for you and your nearest and dearest? How about a poetry reading on the beach? Choose someone to read out a few choice words, and then you and your intended can announce your vows. Exchange rings, kiss the bride or groom and hey presto, you're now happily wed. A big old party afterwards is almost obligatory.

6. How can we let everyone know we're married?

Wear those rings with pride. Legal experts recommend you draw up some kind of agreement or contract—this can include information about property and money matters, or it can just be something signed by both of you saying you are together. Other ways of gaining recognition for your partnership is to open a joint savings account, put both of your names on all of your subscriptions to saucy magazines, get a joint doctor, put your partner's name as your spouse onto all medical records and legal documents, and make a will.

7. So what do we call each other?

Good point. Is your girlfriend still your girlfriend? Does your boyfriend become your husband? Or do you refer to them with that dry old term "partner?" While wife and husband sound so hetero, significant other just sounds stupid. And would you really introduce your lover to your boss as your "soulmate?" We don't think so. Whatever you choose, remember that some people ain't going to like it.

8. Can we go on honeymoon?

Naturally. You'll need a holiday after all that! Go check out a gay old destination [see page 108], and book that honeymoon suite.

Stereotypes

How gay men and lesbians boil down into easily recognizable sub-categories

1. Trolley Dolly
Recognizable characteristics: A rock-hard coif, scattered with highlights, low-lights and any other lights he can think of, manicured nails, orange complexion and eyebrows tweezed to give a permanently surprised effect. His clothes are slim-fitting, recognizable Italian labels only, though he may wear cheap shoes (well, who's looking down there?).
Behavior patterns: Not just an airline steward, the trolley dolly can work in any service industry—smart shops, hairdressers—where getting on with older ladies (who adore him!) is at a premium. They adore his fussy service, faultless turn-out, bitchy comments and saucy anecdotes.
Find him: Eyeing up the boys in The Stud, San Francisco before his morning flight.

2. Disco Bunny

Recognizable characteristics: He —or she (this category includes baby dykes)—will have an alcopop in one hand and a light stick in the other and will be decked head to toe in skinnywear, usually made of Spandex. Look for body glitter, cute, cropped T-shirts with words like "Angel" or "Pussycat" and big old stacked sneakers, usually with a bit of a silver trim.

Behavior patterns: An inveterate podium dancer, no raised surface is safe from the disco bunny's eternally dancing feet. See him or her doing all the right dance moves from the video, screeching, snogging, or eventually slumping in a corner out of it on sugary drinks and a pill their mate gave them.

Find him or her: Going for it like it's New Year's Eve at G.A.Y. in London or Pop Rocks in New York.

3. Diesel Dyke

Recognizable characteristics: Not one to worry too much about girth—especially when there's a lumberjack shirt to disguise it—the Diesel Dyke can be spotted by her short back and sides haircut, her tattoos (often home-made, of the "jail" variety) and her tendency to hold a cigarette between her thumb and forefinger. Also look out for pink or black triangles, and, on fancy occasions only, labrys earrings, a smart pair of chinos and a waistcoat.

Behavior patterns: When not fighting in bars over girls who don't even like her, the Diesel Dyke can be found hanging with the guys, or driving her pick-up truck, the one with the 'Hate is not a

family value' bumper sticker.

Find her: Queuing for the pool table at Henrietta Hudson's in New York

4. Muscle Mary

Recognizable characteristics: Rarely seen sporting clothing on the upper half of their bodies (do the muscles make them really hot or something?), the Muscle Mary will often have a nipple ring and some sort of Celtic tattoo, usually in a position to accentuate a muscle (round the biceps, across the shoulder). He will wear jeans or combats with boots or trainers. Not necessarily great looking: muscles are the last refuge of the ugly.

Behavior patterns: Pumping iron, pumping arms in the air or pumping the ass of another slightly less muscular Muscle Mary, the MM has simple tastes. His limited activities include looking at the pictures in exercise magazines, mixing up power shakes and popping the pimples he gets through steroid abuse.

Find him: At any gym, on the circuit party scene, at Crash in London or at any beach or location where he can take most of his clothes off.

5. Euro City Dyke

Recognizable characteristics: If it's new and urban, she wants it, whether it's ludicrously twisted up jeans, a revolutionary haircut with a fin on top or a pair of trainers specially smuggled across the borders from Far Eastern countries, even if they do cost her a week's wages. There may be some vestiges of a "right on" past (a feminist T-shirt for

instance) but only if it falls within strict fashion parameters.

Behavior patterns: Usually employed in the media as a web designer or writer, she spends her money on weekends out, her minimalist apartment and travel to other cool queer cities. She will spend all her "quality time" with her beloved gadgets: a mountain bike, maybe, a little scooter and obviously downloading hot new tunes on her iMac.

Find her: At the Candy Bar in London or the new Prada Sport store in New York's SoHo.

6. Clone

Recognizable characteristics: The most globally recognizable of the gay stereotypes— mainly due to Tom of Finland who drew him and the Village People who made him dance—the Clone can be spotted by his moustache, white T-shirt, leather jacket, jeans that show off his equipment in unnecessary detail and various chains and rings and leather accoutrements. He may be pierced, maybe even through his nose, and will probably have a tattoo of some description.

Behavior patterns: Cruising is everything to this critter, whether it's on the streets, late night in the bushes or round the more spit 'n' sawdust drinking dens of whatever city he lives in. Due to the fact that he is generally an older gentleman (though in Europe they still manage to breed a younger model), he will be experienced in the ways of the flesh and big on large glasses of beer.

Find him: In New York's Village (everyone else is in Chelsea), London's Earl's Court (everyone

else is in Soho), and Argos (or anywhere else) in Amsterdam, Holland.

7. Florida Dyke

Recognizable characteristics: A big-haired breed of her own, this East Coast American lovely defies all lesbian stereotypes. Hardly ever out of a dayglo bikini (or at least a T-shirt you can see her nipples through) teamed with lots of showy gold jewelry, light pink lipstick, and long manicured nails to make your eyes water.

Behaviour patterns: These girls never seem to work and you'll usually find them on the beach, working on dark brown tans or at the gym, getting a little definition in those arms. And then there are those nail salons and hair studios… Big on fantasy of the Dungeons and Dragons variety and on skinny little g-strings that go right up.

Find her: At the Xena lookalike contest at Key West Women's Week

8. Military Gear Queer

Recognizable characteristics: As un-camp as they come (or so he likes to think), the MGQ sports the ultra-butch look and will wear anything that comes in camo colors. Also available in a skinhead variety (rolled up bleach-splattered jeans, suspenders, knee-high workboots, tattoos on their shaved scalps), the MA1 flying jacket works for all MGQs.

Behavior patterns: The ultra-aggressive male is the image he's going for and, as like often seeks like, he can usually be seen in packs or with a matching boyfriend. He tends to hang out in old-style bars or

boozers and can also be found masquerading as heterosexual by going to football games and riding motorbikes.

Find him: In Boot Camp in London or at Pork in New York.

10. Tweedy Lezzer

Recognizable characteristics: She almost certainly won't be out so you will have to try and spot her for her tweedy masculine

suit (if she wears a skirt it will be boxy and unflattering), sensible shoes, upturned collar, and short straightforward hair that never needs the aid of a roller or hair-drier. She won't wear enough make-up to satisfy a forensic team and will smell vaguely of cats and whisky.

Behavior patterns: Her job as a schoolteacher (fairly

high up) will mean she can excuse her single status by pretending she's married to her job. She's in fact married—in all but name—to the "cousin"—who shares her modest home. Her interests include gardening, fishing and vintage cars and she can shoot a rifle.

Find her: At home or watching women's sports.

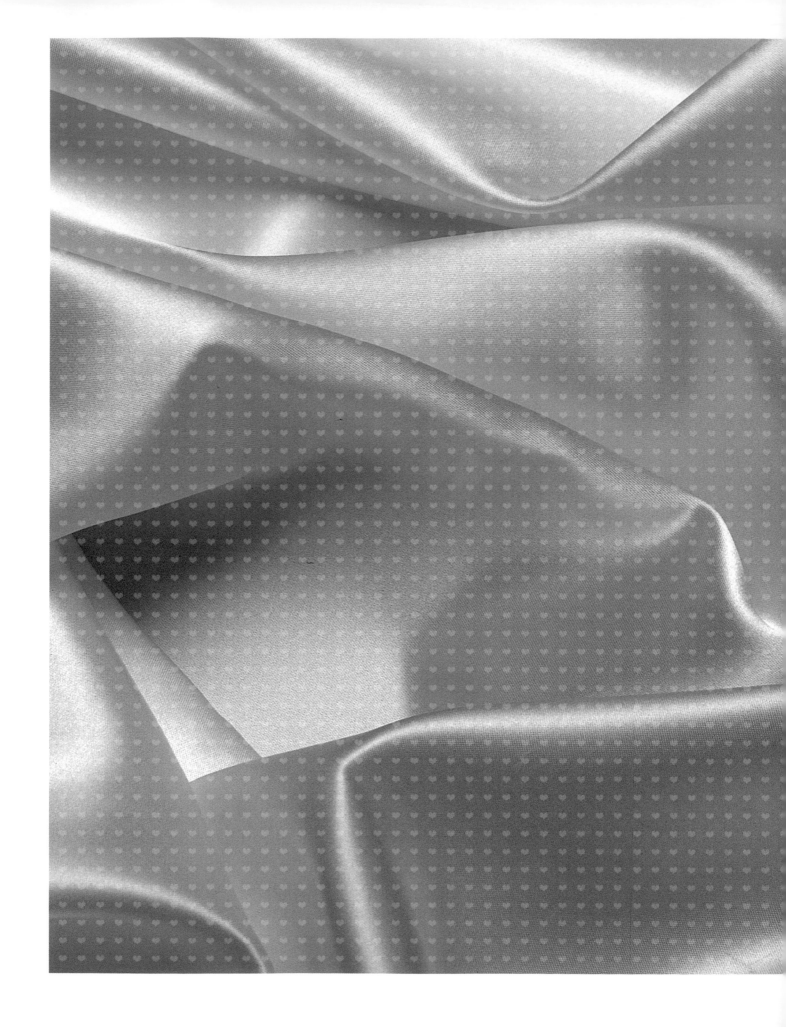

Between the Sheets

Being gay may not be all about the sex, but that doesn't mean to say there's not a whole lot of sexy sex going on. 'Cause there is!

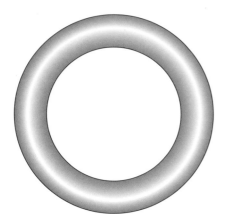

Cock Ring

A ring, usually in metal or leather, that fits around the base of the penis

The cock ring is probably the oldest sex aid dating back to the 13th century (mind you, in those days it went around the top of the penis and was made of goat's eyelashes). The modern cock ring is usually made of metal, rubber or leather and sits snugly under the testicles, which are fed through it one at a time after the penis, which, at this stage, should be limp and malleable. Snap-on cock rings in leather are easier to get on and off but harder to clean.

The point of the cock ring—apart from bringing much needed attention to your genital area—is to help keep the penis hard. As you get erect, the blood floods into the penis. The presence of the cock ring, which is usually fairly tight by the time you get an erection, prevents the blood getting back out again, meaning you stay longer for longer. Strippers employ a technique known as "tying off," where they put a tight band or string around their erect penises keeping them large (and making them turn purple if they're left on too long).

Metal cock rings, which can be tricky to get off (sit in a cold bath and hot foot it to hospital if you can't remove it!), have the added advantage of providing a solid support for cords and leashes during S&M sex play.

Metal cock rings can also be worn as fashion accessories on a string round your neck or through the epaulet of your leather jacket.

Sex

The beginner's guide to getting down, getting dirty and playing it safe

Sex, being the oh-so personal thing that it is, comes in as many shapes and forms as gay men and women. From hardcore S&M to the most vanilla of funny tickles, here are few ways that you can get your rocks off.

SEX STYLES

Bondage
Tied up or tied down, bondage plays on that whole master/servant tip. You lick my boots, I won't lick yours. As well as ropes, chains and impressive homemade pulley systems, bondage festishists even go to the extremes of mummification—where the bottom, or subservient person, is completely restrained, whether just at the head or top-to-toe. Plastic wrap, or clingfilm, is the substance of choice for mummification-lovers, and apparently you need about 75 feet of it to do the full-body enclosure. Other methods of restraint include handcuffs, gags, collars and leads, and cages, and if tied up in the right way it's possible for you to become a veritable human running finger buffet, ready for the pickings of your dominant partner.

CP
CP, or corporal punishment, is physical punishment in a sexual setting—caning, flogging and slapping are all methods of making your play partner's flesh red and sore. Harsh words, as well as a good collection of whips, cat o'nine tails and paddles, and the know-how to inflict short, sharp stinging smacks all help to make CP a very pleasurable/painful experience.

Cyber sex
Who could have known that when the Internet was invented it would attract a smorgasbord of perverts and freaks, all desperate to get their rocks off. As usual, gay folk are way ahead of the heteros when it comes to getting it on online, and whatever your bag there's a website for you—into older folk? No problem. Bondage? Step this way, madam. Jocks minus their jock-straps? Yes sir. As well as websites for specific kinks, you can also get fruity in the chatrooms, chatting with and chatting up fellow homos from all over the world. With the use of a nifty little webcam, you can also see just what it is you're getting, and even bark instructions at your fellow cyber sex chum.

Exhibitionism
Nothing but a sickness! As your mother used to say: "Stop showing off in front of your friends!" We all crave attention, from the mildest forms of exhibitionism—you know those jeans you have that show off your ass oh-so well—to full on, in-your-face soaping yourself ever so slowly in the showers just so that everyone can see you. Homos who like their fun to be seen in public and love the whole idea of being watched while having sex are exhibitionists. Plain and simple. So next time you go wearing those tight-ass jeans, or start emailing pictures of your cock or tits all around the world, remember the real reason, you attention-seeker, you.

S&M
S&M, or S/M, or sadomasochism to give it its proper name, is the umbrella term for all forms of sex play involving a top or a bottom. Sadism is for the folks who like to be on top and in charge, while the masochists amongst us like to be hurt. Bondage, corporal punishment, slaves and masters, domination—if it's kinky, it's S&M.

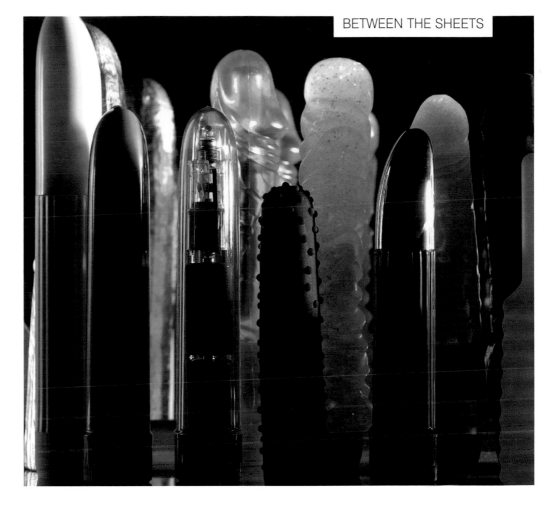

Vanilla

As opposed to the dirty minxes into all things pervy, vanilla homos—and there are a few of them—like it all clean, gentle and without a whiff of anything kinky. Forget a slap, it's all about tickle: it's the missionary position for these girls and boys. While still more than capable of getting down to it, vanilla sex-lovers are often seen as lesser sexual beings than the S&M parade.

SEX TOYS

Beads

Also known as love beads, these strings of marble beads can be inserted into the anus or vagina—if you have one—and are gently pulled out, either by you or someone else, at the point of climax.

Butt plugs

They do exactly what they say on the label—plug your butt. Usually inserted whilst wanking or for the girls, while having vaginal sex as well, the butt plug is a handy, carry-it-anywhere dildo with a wide base to ensure it doesn't get lost up there.

Harness

For the girls, a harness is their dildo's best friend. Made in leather, or easily washable hardy fabrics, the harness sits around the hips and holds the dildo in a holster-like fashion at the front, thus enabling them to go about their business hands-free. Not to be confused with a men's harness, which is worn bikini-top style to give you something to hang onto when you're banging on in there.

Hoist/sling

A favorite for girls and boys into bondage, the hoist—usually found in sex clubs—is a contraption that allows a bottom to be suspended from the ceiling in a leather and chain contraption, putting them at easy access to their top(s). Most professional hoists—because there are such things!—have a "panic snap" that allows the hoistee to quick-release themselves from the contraption in case something goes wrong.

Dildos

The beginners guide to the ultimate toy for girls and boys

Come on, I don't need a dildo.
Listen, if you're not used to getting fucked, a dildo is perfect for working on your technique and finding out which position works best for you. Even if you're getting penetrated on a regular basis, a dildo is indispensable. Every homo should have one.

Why?
Because anyone who wanks will get more out of it with a bit of something inside of themselves. Besides, fucking yourself with a dildo is an entirely different thing to getting fucked.

But I don't want to fork out for an expensive bit of plastic.
Obviously, you don't have to buy a dildo, you can use stuff around the house for times when you're on your own. Bananas are perfect: you can choose the shape and the angle of the curve and, as long as you put a condom on it and hang on tight to the end so it doesn't disappear up there, you have a very inexpensive dildo. Choose an unripe one or it'll break. Don't peel it!

OK, so where do I start?
You start small, that's where you start. I would always advise putting a condom on a dildo, that way not only do you not get it dirty, but you don't damage it with lubrication and you can use it on other people without having to bleach it. I don't have to say that you should never share a dildo without changing condoms or scrubbing it, do I?

OK, so I've got my dildo, it's got its condom on, is "now what?" a silly question?
For a first timer, I actually think a mirror is quite a good idea. Not only does it give you that extra bit of control—though, obviously, you're doing this mostly by touch—but it's actually quite horny to see yourself get fucked. That's another advantage of getting fucked by a dildo instead of a human being, you can do what you like and not have to worry about them.

So how far can I actually take this dildo thing?
Way too far if you ask me. Just look at the show-off dildos, as well as the quick-release harnesses and different colors for every mood.

The Spit Roast
The beginner's guide to having one at both ends

What's that when it's at home?
Think about it. You *are* that suckling pig…

Oh, and they're the spit.
Precisely. One in one end, one in the other. It's also a good trick for the ladies—lunch anyone?

So, we're talking about threesomes? What's so difficult about threesomes?
Are you kidding? Threesomes are a minefield for the inexperienced.

How?
There's only one place to be in a threesome, and that's in the middle, so assert yourself.

Why do you want to be in the middle?
Because otherwise it's just like regular sex. To get the full experience of a threesome you need to have the whole double-barrel experience.

So start me off.
Rule number one is give them both the same amount of attention. You will probably fancy one more than the other, but unless you give it to them both, you are risking pissing one of them off. Snog one, then the other. When you go down, make sure you give attention to both sets of bits.

Sounds OK.
But realize that you're playing with fire. While you're down there noshing, they're probably snogging and bonding and just ignoring you. Which is bad.

How do I make sure they don't end up ignoring me?
Pinch them if need be! Or you can get them to double-nosh you, i.e. suck you off/go down on you at the same time.

I need to get back in the middle of this, don't I?
Too right. Suck one off/go down on one while the other sucks you off/goes down on you, or get rimmed by number one, while snogging number two.

So how do I maneuver a spit-roast situation?
There are variations. If you bend over to suck one of them off/go down on one of them and have your big old butt in the air, number three will hopefully get the message. If they fall into rhythm and they probably will, you'll get that feeling of being invaded on all fronts: in together, out together.

Double penetration
The beginner's guide to two into one does go

Are you crazy?
Listen, everyone has those greedy moods, and if lady porn stars can do it, then why not you?

Yeah, but lady porn stars, correct me if I'm wrong, have two holes.
OK, it's true that your classic DP (double penetration) shot is one up the back and the other up the front, but ladies can and do get two up the poopy-doop at the same time. Haven't you seen *Multiple Anal Slut Bitches Part Three*?

No, I think I'd remember. Alright, you're selling me. Step one…
Step one is get a single cock up there. I'm assuming you know how to do that. A little light action will loosen things up and get you in the mood.

What position are we going to do this in?
First, you need to have one under—sit astride him with his face to you. Choose the guy who can keep his erection hardest for the underneath role—because the guy at the bottom doesn't get much leverage.

Should you have the bigger one at the bottom or the smaller one?
Opt for Mr. Big Stuff. Or, if you really want to ease yourself into this one, have a go with the more modest of your playmates, then switch to the bigger, then go for double glory.

OK, so I'm astride Mr. Big. What now?
Well, you have Mr. Modest approach from behind. He may want to start you off by just slipping a finger or two in before he starts feeding you phallus.

When am I going for the double?
You're going to need per-lenty of lubrication, ultra strong condoms and extra vigilance. This one is going to have more thrust-room than the one at the bottom, so although he's going to have entry issues, he'll get the most out of it (apart from you of course).

Isn't the one underneath going to get bored?
Think about it. Not only is he up your hot little arse, but he also has the sensation of another guy's knob pressed right up to his. Just make sure you don't all put your weight on him.

Anything else I should know?
This isn't one to be doing every weekend. Your poor old back door will need some time to snap back to size.

SEX ACTS

Anal sex, ass fuck, ass games, bum fuck, ram job, sodomizing
The insertion of a part of the body, or at-hand implement, into the anus.

Belly fuck
Non-penetrative sex that involves a boy rubbing his cock on his partner's stomach until he ejaculates. Nice.

Coitus inter femora, dry humping, intercruller sex
For the boys, you put your cock between your partner's thighs, and simulate the act of having sex. For girls, you make thrust movements as if using a strap-on against your partner's groin area.

Cunnilingus, eat out, muff dive, go down, oral sex
From the Latin 'cunnus' meaning vagina, and 'lingus' meaning tongue—put the two together and you've got yourself a lesbian speciality.

Circle jerk, jack-off circle
Popular back in the post-AIDS crisis days, when having sex with anything that moved was no longer an option for some gentlemen. Jack-off parties, usually accompanied by a good quality porn movie, involve the partygoers partaking in simultaneous masturbation, i.e. they all jerked off at the same time.

Doggie style, doggie fashion, from behind
Probably the most popular position for gay boys, the person getting seen to lies on all fours while receiving from behind.

Ejaculate, cum, shoot your load, orgasm
The point of climax for boys and girls.

Felching
Not one for the squeamish amongst you, felching is an English term used to describe the action of the sucking of one's recently deposited semen from the rectum of the receiver.

Fellatio, blow-job, cock sucking, give head, go down, penilingus, gobble, nosh
Oral sex isn't just a thing for the ladies, and fellatio, or more commonly cock sucking, is putting mouth to penis.

Finger

A form of sexual stimulation practiced by teenage boys and lesbians everywhere, it is the insertion of one's finger(s) into the vagina/asshole to stimulate yourself or your partner.

Fisting

The next step up from fingering, fisting requires the entire hand to be put inside the vagina or asshole. Plenty of lube and a slowly-slowly technique are recommended, as is the forming of the fist once inside the intended receptacle. The practice is dangerous as the delicate lining of the ass is of the consistency of wet tissue paper and can easily be torn. Chunky jewelry not recommended.

Gang bang

The performance of a sexual act by a group of men or women on just one person.

Orgy

A sexual free for all involving a whole bunch of folk.

Golden shower, watersports, piss games

For whatever reason that urine is your thang—degradation, the aroma of the toilets where you first got it on, whatever—watersports definitely isn't everyone's cup of tea, so to speak. General rules are: don't get the yellow stuff in your or your partner's eyes (not only will it sting like buggery—or even more than buggery—it's just not good for you.) As far as HIV is concerned, watersports are safe, just don't piss up his/her arse. And as for the obsessives amongst you, some people like (you) to piss in their footwear so they can slosh about in it all day long, or leave a little in an empty water bottle for them to enjoy later. And then there was the guy who cooked his frozen peas in the stuff...

Masturbate, jack off, wank

Self-pleasuring of the most popular order, with toys or without.

69

Two persons engaging in oral sex at the same time, this requires the two partakers to lie or position themselves top-to-tail for easy access.

Rimming

The insertion of one's tongue into your partner's anus. Enough said.

SAFE SEX

Barebacking

Used to describe sex between two gay men who purposely avoid using a condom. While wild arguments exist for the benefits of unsafe sex, aka barebacking—sex feels better without a condom, it leads to a greater intimacy between partners, it's cheaper, it promotes monogamy—quite frankly, is sex really worth the prospect of a nasty infection or hey, even illness resulting in death? Answer: no.

Clap clinic, sexual health clinic

A clinic where you can receive regular check-ups for sexually transmitted infections. Many of them give out free condoms and lube to their clients.

Condoms, rubbers

A sheath for the penis (or a sex toy) made from rubber or latex that is rolled on to the phallus before sex to protect you from sexually transmitted infections, especially HIV.

Dental dam

Not so common now, latex dental dams were used a lot in the midst of the AIDS crisis by gay boys and even gay girls. A square of stinky latex, it could be placed across the vagina or anus before oral sex as a barrier between the mouth and genital area.

Latex gloves

Again, another item used in the middle of the AIDS panic era for fisting and other hand to arse/vagina activites to protect from possible infection. While still used in hardcore sex clubs, they're more of a cleanliness-promoting accessory nowadays.

Abstinence

Gloves, condoms, fiddly dental dams, lubricants... Being safe these days has become something of a full-time pursuit. The safe sex answer for homos in the noughties? Just don't do it, or do it on your own.

Glory Holes

The beginner's guide to cock worship for the boys

Surely no one does that anymore!
Are you kidding! The impact of a fully erect member sticking through a hole in the wall has lost none of its power over the years. Why would it?

But you don't know who it is on the other side of that wall…
And therein lies the deliciousness.

But it might be some crummy old bloke.
Yeah. And it might be someone so gorgeous they would never let you suck their cock if they could see what you looked like.

Point taken. But what if I do want to know at least a bit of what he looks like?
Well, you can hang around outside to see who's going in where or, if you don't want to give up your cubicle, you can always look through the hole.

Aren't there hygiene issues if you're getting your mouth up against some wall blokes have been spunking down?
Yep, but at the end of the day, a lot of old spunk isn't going to do you any harm. But the whole looking-through kind of defeats the object of glory holes anyway.

Go on…
Well, it's the height of phallocentricity, isn't it? Here's this big old cock, no face, no body, no personality. Worship that cock.

How do I let him know I want him to suck my cock? Do I whisper through?
No, it's much easier than that, you just put your cock through the hole and he'll probably get the message.

And if he's not interested?
Then he'll ignore it. Or maybe give it a little tap so you know you can withdraw.

How do I let him know I want to suck his cock?
If you want to hurry him along you can just put your finger—or even your tongue—on the bottom edge of the glory hole. That's a recognized way of asking him to put his cock there.

Is that all you can do through a glory hole?
The whole glory hole thing works really well as a no-strings foreplay. If you get on well sucking each other's cocks and can bear the disappointment when you see him, you can get him to shimmy over to your cubicle and fuck him.

Isn't all this highly illegal?
Now there you do have a point.

Putting a condom on a reluctant partner

The beginner's guide to putting a rubber on someone who doesn't go there

Well, there's not a lot you can do really, is there?
You'd be surprised. The first thing you can do is tell him where to go: no condom, no anus. A shag is a shag, but I've certainly never had one so good I would be prepared to be ill for years and then die for it. But hey, maybe I've just not met the right guy.

So, what can you do?
What apart from knocking him senseless? Well, for a start you have to ask yourself why this guy doesn't want a condom on.

Well, a lot of them say that they lose their erection.
Which is something we can work on. If you can help him keep it up while skinning him up, then there goes his argument.

So, how do I do that?
Well, how do you usually keep a guy's erection? Deft use of tongue and throat, saliva coated palms… if you don't know how to do that, I'm going to send you to the remedial class.

Yeah, but how do I make sure he doesn't lose it before I've got him rubbered up?
Just have the condom to hand. And make sure you know which way it's going to go on.

And if I put some lube on his cock first…
You have much to learn my child. First, who wants to be noshing down on a knob that has Slidey Slick all over it? Not me! And if you put lube on a dick before you rubber it, that rubber is likely to slide right off and up your arse.

OK, so I've got the condom at the ready…
If you can bear the taste of rubber, you can even give him a bit of a nosh when it's on just to firm it all up a bit.

And what if he reckons he doesn't like condoms because his cock is too big?
Condoms are rubber so they're—duh!—stretchy. Anyone who has a dick too big for a condom has a dick too big to fit into any human orifice. Yes, even yours.

Some people are genuinely allergic to latex though, aren't they?
Yep, and everyone's genuinely allergic to sexually transmitted infections so he's just going to have to find one of those plastic condoms.

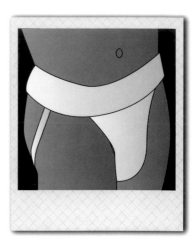

Jockstrap

An item of underwear worn by sportsmen that has become a major gay fetish

Whether the term jockstrap originated from an old English word for cock or from the fact that the first people to wear jockstraps were the "bicycle jockeys" of old Boston town, it first appeared in print around 1886, a good eight years after the Bike Athletic Co. (you see the connection) first started making the things. There are, of course, much older references to athletic supports: in ancient Greece nude athletes would tie their foreskins with a ribbon then attach the ribbon under their testicles to prevent floppiness.

The most obvious appeal to gay men of a simple bit of supportive underwear (usually in off-white cotton) is that it allows the butt to be completely on display. Designed to give maximum physical freedom to sportsmen and prevent sweat building up, the modern jockstrap features a wide elasticated band around the waist and two thinner elasticated straps that connect the waist to the bottom of the pouch across the butt cheeks, allowing total access to one of the main centers of interest to gay men.

Add to this the connection with sports activities—a sure-fire turn-on—and the essential harking back to schooldays spent sneaking peeks at jocks in all their glory, and you have a major clothes fetish which often turns up in personal ads as a prerequisite for sex.

In gay sexual display, the jockstrap often serves as an invite for anal attention (though not always) and is popular with a broad range of gay "types" from skinheads through gym bunnies to hard-core S&Mers.

Crystal Meth

The white powder and tablets which turn gay men and women into crazed sex machines

Active ingredient: Methamphetamine

Appearance: In tablet or powder form. The prescription drug is known as Desoxyn®, though you can get it on the street as a white, bitter-tasting powder that is injected, snorted or swallowed. It's also found in larger crystals, which can be smoked. Although the legal version is odorless, illegal forms of the drug often have a strong ammonia smell, due to incomplete clearing of solvents during manufacture.

What it does: Crystal meth is a supercharged form of speed. Much like other uppers (prescription diet pills, over-the-counter stay-awake tablets, caffeinated colas etc.), it revs up the central nervous system: it's the most potent form of speed. In its prescribed tablet form, it is used to tackle Attention Deficit Disorder or obesity since it boosts alertness and blocks hunger and fatigue at low doses.

Other uses: At higher doses, crystal meth causes exhilaration and euphoria. It's like adrenaline: the physical effects are almost assuredly due to interactions between the amphetamine structure and human physiology. It really took off on the gay scene in the early 90s because it is more powerful than cocaine, but much cheaper. More importantly, it heightens sexual experiences with an intensification of feeling and increased sex drive. Many gay and bi men report that they become less inhibited when they use crystal meth, saying it allows them to do things they ordinarily wouldn't do and for longer! Even days.

Dosage: If you swallow it, it takes about half an hour to work. When smoked or snorted, effects are almost instantaneous. However, a toxic reaction (or overdose) can occur at relatively low levels, 50 milligrams of pure drug for a non-tolerant user. Cost: Half a gram costs around $40 and a $25 hit would probably keep you going a few days.

Warning: Where do you start? When not prescribed in tablet form by your physician, it can cause disturbed sleep patterns, chronic fatigue, disinterest in friends or sex, anorexia, itching, welts on skin, nausea, vomiting, diarrhea, excessive excitation, hyperactivity, shortness of breath, moodiness, nervousness, aggressiveness, involuntary body movements, panic, paranoia, malnutrition, delusions, violence, severe depression and suicidal tendencies.

Meanwhile, long-term effects can include fatal kidney and lung disorders, possible brain damage, permanent psychological problems, lowered resistance to illnesses, liver damage and strokes. Furthermore, there are also risks associated with being high when you have sex; users are more likely to throw caution to the wind. Crystal meth has therefore been a factor in a significant number of AIDS cases among American gay men.

Viagra

Active ingredient: Sildenafil citrate

Appearance: Diamond shaped, pale blue tablet marked with the label Pfizer, the company that makes the mega-selling pill.

What it does: Erectile dysfunction can be a problem for all men, gay or straight, and Viagra hits the spot like no other drug can to help maintain that all important stiffy. The active ingredient (sildenafil citrate) works on enzymes in the body called phosphodiesterases and improves the male's response to sexual stimulation. As these enzymes mainly work in the area around the penis, Viagra's work is done mainly below the waist. By controlling the enzyme, and therefore the blood flow out of the penis, the drug not only helps the patient maintain his hard-on, but also, in cases where the erectile dysfunction is severe, actually helps the boys to get it up.

Other uses: As with many drugs that are meant for clinical purposes, Viagra has found its way onto the recreational drugs market. While it should only be taken as directed by your physician, the drug does improve sexual performance and sexual responsiveness, therefore making it incredibly popular in sex clubs, and with clubbers out on the regular gay scene. Recent studies have shown that women taking the drug in controlled tests (not down London's lesbian Candy Bar on a busy Friday night, then) had improved ability to reach orgasm and became aroused more easily after taking it.

Dosage: Usually 50mg, to be taken one hour before a sexual encounter. No more than one dose should be taken per day. Viagra takes between 30 minutes and an hour to kick in, and the effects (i.e. erection and ultra-sensitivity) can last for a good four to six hours.

Maximum dose: 100mg tablets are also available and are, according to one satisfied customer, "absolutely remarkable."

Cost: Between $12 and $15 a pop.

Warning: Like all drugs, Viagra can react with other regular, and irregular, drugs. For example, poppers, or amyl nitrate as it's medically known, should never be mixed with Viagra, and neither should certain antibiotics.

Body beautiful, 1970s style

Pornography

People doing the dirty for your viewing pleasure

Images of guys frolicking together are as old as the oldest Grecian vase. And even though most of those images are sporty—where have we heard that excuse before?—there are some that are undeniably more, erm, intimate.

As the concept of "gay men" wasn't invented until fairly recently (acts were homosexual, people weren't), pornographic images and literature featuring gay sex appeared alongside those of other forms of sex, as a deviation from the regular man/woman coupling in the way that oral sex and flagellation were deviations. In the 18th century, for instance, the Marquis de Sade wrote extensively about "gay sex" in his *120 Days of Sodom*, where the sex victims are divided into young girls, young boys, older women and older men with huge cocks called "fuckers."

With the invention of photography in the 19th century came the first homoerotic pictures. Baron Wilhelm Von Gloeden turned out endless classical studies of Sicilian youths he had somehow convinced to get their kits off, while much more explicit photographs of men in comedy moustaches tucking into oral, anal and anything else you can think of were appearing on the black market.

In the early 20th century the only images of near-naked men available in the mainstream were available courtesy of a straight bigot called Bernard MacFadden, who published a magazine called *Physical Culture*, which contained

photographs of buff young guys posing in g-strings. When he discovered the pictures were being used for "immoral purposes" by gay men, he freaked. Unwittingly he'd launched the whole concept of homoerotica masquerading as health and fitness that still remains today (*Exercise For Men Only*, hello!), even though the magazines and images were monitored closely by the police and even seized. Ironically, it was after a legal case in 1965 against one of these magazines, which went as far as the Supreme Court, that modern gay pornography was born. The judges found that the magazine in question lacked 'patent offensiveness'. Magazines containing full frontals weren't far behind, while "stag movies" featuring young men masturbating (usually on fur rugs in front of open fires) were already in circulation.

In the 70s—after the sexual revolution of the 60s—pornography went overground with cinemas opening especially to show porno, the gay movie houses providing opportunities for meetings as well as viewings. But it was with the advent of video that pornography really took off, with what would become multi-million dollar gay media companies like Catalina and Falcon becoming established, mainly in California where there was a glut of beautiful guys who didn't quite make it into "legitimate" movies.

Global porn stars like Jeff Stryker and the Brit Aiden Shaw were born, directors like Chi Chi LaRue, Matt Sterling and, in Europe, Cadinot became household names (well, in some households they did), while the porn industry even came up with its own version of the Oscars. And why not? It was, by this time, competing with the "legitimate" film industry in terms of turnover, with current estimates hitting the $10 million mark (although figures are vague and as someone noted, in pornography everything tends to get exaggerated).

The only real crisis to put a spoke in the gay porn industry's ever-spinning wheel was AIDS. With the advent of AIDS, sales were if anything up (in an atmosphere of fear of sex, there was nothing safer than renting some hardcore and enjoying it on your own), but many of the stars who had been having multiple partner sex without the benefit of a condom (it would have looked weird pre-AIDS, and not something paying punters wanted to be confronted with) contracted the virus. Condoms were introduced into gay porn, as was mandatory HIV screening.

Pornography has always been hot on the heels of any technological development, and as the Internet was unrolled so pornography became democratised, especially among gay men who make up an estimated 15% of AOL's clients. Although the major distributors of porn were in on the act with sites eventually offering photographs, streaming movies, and even models involved in live sex sessions that you could "direct" via your keyboard, the most interesting effect of the Internet was in amateur porn. Now any Tom or Dick could become a porn star, posting explicit pictures or movies of himself online, linking up with other guys via webcams across the globe or being paid by having sex on pay-per-view sites.

The beauty of gay porn is that it is largely a guilt-free phenomenon. With the absence of real sexual contact while they were growing up, many gay men built a lasting relationship with porn that stays with them, making them large and unashamed consumers. Add to that the lack of "issues" involved in gay pornography—even the most strident anti-porn feminist finds it hard to come up with any real objections to two men obviously very keen on doing it with each other in front of the camera—and you've got an atmosphere where pornography is not only generally socially acceptable but in certain cases —like with the work of photographer Robert Mapplethorpe—elevated to the status of high art.

Kyle Brandon: Gay Porn Legend

Kyle Brandon is one of the clever porn stars. Having made his name in super hardcore fetish films like the classic *Fallen Angel*, he used his porn fame to brand his name, set up a company and become the, ahem, face of top US phone/internet sex site, *The Number*.

How did you get into porn?
I was in Washington DC, opened up a newspaper and saw an ad for S&M videos by director Bob Jones. I sent him some pictures and he liked them. I was into the S&M scene already and the next thing you know I was doing my first video.

Was it what you expected?
It was really weird because you always hear about the casting couch but there was nothing like that. I was nervous and excited. Just the whole fact of doing the video was great and the idea of being paid on top of it was a bonus.

So you enjoyed doing the sex, it wasn't just work?
Yeah, always. I even had my dick pierced in a video.

Do you end up getting jaded?
I've become more attuned to what the business is. I know the ins and outs, the politics involved and the catfighting and the backstabbing. I'm very careful about what I sign. I'm very professional and some people read that as jaded.

Do people get exploited by the business?
Financially, all the time. Situations where you're supposed to get paid for being on the cover of the video and they don't pay, stuff like that.

What about drugs and manipulation?
I've never heard it, never seen it. I've been involved with all the major companies, and all the smaller companies, and I've never seen anything like that go on. Some people get high to have sex, but it's their choice and to be honest it's frowned upon.

What's the worst porno experience?
Catfighting between the director, the photographer and the porn stars.

How much do you get paid?
Anywhere between a thousand to two thousand dollars per movie. I won't just do any video now. I call myself semi-retired. I have a lot of control over stuff now. I'm very careful with my name, my brand.

Does working in porn click in with prostitution and stripping?
You can earn a lot of money from personal appearances when everyone knows your name and a lot of guys, when they've done some films, make a lot from escorting, so yeah, it does if you want it to.

Lesbian porn
The gay girls just don't get it

While gay boys have turned the porn film into both an art form and a multi-million dollar industry, dykes have got a lot of catching up to do. With just a fistful of titles available that could hardly be described as explicit, lesbian porn is in a sorry old state. Sure, if the need takes you, you can get your hands on the odd homemade girlie beauty knocking around your local lesbian bar, if you know where to ask, and *Bound* does get a bit racy in places, but the snippets of Gershon getting frisky hardly give the girls enough time to get their dungarees undone, let alone the chance to get it on with themselves in the comfort of their own living room.

And while sex shops the world over offer prospective buyers all manner of flicks showing girl-on-girl action, the hot stuff usually involves ladies with big hair, long nails and lip gloss. Sure, some of the "lesbian" sex gets pretty steamy in these made-for-straights porn films, but gay girls and boys alike have to admit that the lack of full-on, bona fide lesbian movies is pretty damn pathetic. Anyone would think that gay girlies don't have sex.

With the Internet starting to offer the odd genuine—and quite raunchy—lesbian porn site, and with dyke erotic novels selling by the bucketload, it seems odd that the girls have not yet ventured into video. While most lesbians with fingers and a computer keyboard seem to be knocking out dreadful homespun tales of nights of lust on silken sheets, the dykes just can't get the filmmaking thing sorted. Perhaps it was the radical feminism of political lesbians of the 70s, who saw pornography as a big no-no due to its patriarchal connotations, that left dykes behind in the dirty movie game, or maybe it's the lack of cock action that makes girlie sex shows just a little bit dull. Whatever it is, it means that the most fun lesbians can have with a VCR is when it's on high-speed rewind.

Rent Boys

Selling it

It's the oldest profession in the world and the oldest trick in the book, and you'd be surprised how many people you know have been there at some time or other.

Prostitution may, in the popular consciousness, be linked with drug addiction, violence and homelessness but somehow gay prostitution has managed to avoid many of the worst features of straight prostitution, with its pimps, its beatings and its rip-offs. Even respected British actor and intimate friend of Madonna Rupert Everett has admitted to "turning tricks" in his younger days, while prostitutes who double up as porn stars are bona fide celebrities with almost no stigma attached. But then, selling it for cash dollars is a time-honored way of, excuse the pun, making ends meet.

There are references to gay prostitution in classical literature, while in the Bible, Corinthians makes clear references to the boys who were employed as live-in hookers for married men or who worked the temples (male temple prostitutes are also referred to in Deuteronomy).

Throughout the centuries, rent boys operated either privately or from brothels. When Oscar Wilde [see page 176] was brought to trial at the end of the 19th century, a whole world of male brothels, where working class lads would congregate for the pleasure of rich patrons, emerged from the shadows.

Nowadays, most rent boys operate via advertisements in the gay press or on the Internet. The customer would once upon a time have to read between the lines of ads for masseurs or escorts, in the days when an escort was someone who would attend an important event with you; now the ads are more explicit and are often accompanied by full frontal pictures of what's on offer. As far as wording goes, the "escorts" (the word has stuck) are

often a bit more coy. "Full service" means you can have anal or oral sex, while "versatile" means you can choose between an "active" or a "passive" service. "Out calls only" means that the escort will only come to your home or hotel room and you can't go to him, while "VGL" means that your escort considers himself very good looking. And beware, it's amazing how many of these guys reckon they are "VWE"—very well endowed—but you can only really rely on such claims if there's a picture attached.

Although street trade, especially among younger, often homeless and occasionally drug-addicted rent boys exists, most male prostitution in urban areas is civilized, safe and even sophisticated. Cute looking guys, most of them fairly intelligent, who wish to fritter away their youth on sex and clubbing have found that a little light "escorting" not only fits perfectly into their way of life, but also provides them with the money to live it up a little before they go back to more conventional careers.

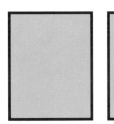  

#01
APRICOT

WORN ON THE
LEFT: "Lose weight now? Don't ask me how." A bona-fide chubby.
WORN ON THE RIGHT: Fan of fat, aka chubby chaser.

#02
BEIGE

WORN ON THE
LEFT: A real hole fan, this guy loves to rim.
WORN ON THE RIGHT: Likes to put out for a good rimming.

#03
BLACK

WORN ON THE
LEFT: Seriously hardcore S&M top.
WORN ON THE RIGHT: Masochist bottom.

#04
BROWN

WORN ON THE
LEFT: There's a clue in the color, this fella is packing a load.
WORN ON THE RIGHT: And this to be at the receiving end of it.

#05
CHECKERED

WORN ON THE
LEFT: This fella plays safe and is carrying a condom.
WORN ON THE RIGHT: Also a safe sex slut, this time the guy's a bottom.

#06
LIGHT BLUE

WORN ON THE
LEFT: This guy wants to get good head.
WORN ON THE RIGHT: Blow jobber.

#07
NAVY BLUE

WORN ON THE
LEFT: Real simple, this one's a top.
WORN ON THE RIGHT: And this guy's a bottom.

Lesbian Hanky Code

The foolproof color coding system for the lesbian hanky-wearing community

The hanky code is an easy way to determine whether your next potential sexual partner is suited to your preferences in the bedroom. Imagine, for example, the faux-pas that would occur if you pulled a prospective partner, only to find that he/she too preferred to give out lashes, rather than receive them. What to do?

Despite the general impression that it's only the boys who employ a hanky code to help rule out embarrassing sexual mismatches, as well as to dress up an outfit, the lady lesbians also like to give potential partners a clue to what's what and who's bottom in the bedroom.

#01
BLACK

WORN ON THE
LEFT: This girl likes S&M and she likes it heavy. She's also into the whipping game and watch out, because she's the one who's on top.
WORN ON THE RIGHT: The same S&M deal, but her ass is ready for that whipping.

#02
GREY

WORN ON THE
LEFT: These girls like to fondle your tits, so wear them proud and you're in there.
WORN ON THE RIGHT: She's got her tits out and ready for action.

Gay Men's Hanky Code

What that handy hanky color code really means

While the hanky code might now simply be a throwback to ye olde worlde gay times, there are actually 138 different shades to signal just exactly what your sexual preference is before you have to engage in any of that stupid chatting-up malarkey.

The code actually originated back in 70s New York to communicate gay men's desires, and world-renowned newspaper, the *Village Voice* is actually credited as its source. In the early 70s they published an article suggesting that it would be easier for gay men in the Village to pick each other up if they didn't only have to rely on wearing their keys in their back pockets, left to denote active, right passive. The feature suggested that they should all get down to the surplus store at the intersection of Christopher and Washington Streets where they could buy color-coded Levi's bandanas.

Yes, it was a joke, but one that gay men took to heart, not only in New York, but eventually on the gay scene across the world. Even if the code is dying out now, you can still pick out a fister from a fistee, for example, if you head to the right kind of clubs.

#08
PALE YELLOW

WORN ON THE **LEFT:** This guy will spit on you—but in a good way.

WORN ON THE **RIGHT:** Also loves to indulge in spit play, he's the bottom.

#09
RED

WORN ON THE **LEFT:** He likes fisting—he's got a hand and knows how to use it.

WORN ON THE **RIGHT:** This guy has a very accommodating bottom.

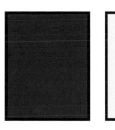

#10
YELLOW

WORN ON THE **LEFT:** Again, a clue in the color. This fella likes to relieve himself on you.

WORN ON THE **RIGHT:** A piss freak, this boy likes to receive the relief.

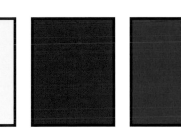

#11
LAVENDER

WORN ON THE **LEFT:** Men who love men who love to dress like a lady.

WORN ON THE **RIGHT:** This is a bona fide drag queen. Like, you couldn't tell, right?

#12
FUSCHIA

WORN ON THE **LEFT:** This fella loves to dish it out with his hands, he's a spanker.

WORN ON THE **RIGHT:** "Oh, Daddy I've been real bad."

#03
DARK RED

WORN ON THE **LEFT:** She's strapping on that dildo and she knows how to use it.

WORN ON THE **RIGHT:** This girl's ready for a good strap-on fucking.

#04
LIME GREEN

WORN ON THE **LEFT:** Not many people can get away with wearing lime green and aptly enough it's girls into humiliation who sport this difficult-to-wear color.

WORN ON THE **RIGHT:** Lime green on the right? She likes to be humiliated.

#05
NAVY BLUE

WORN ON THE **LEFT:** A sensible color that can be worn with most outfits, navy blue denotes a lady partial to some ass fucking.

WORN ON THE **RIGHT:** Again ass fucking, but she likes to lie back and take it.

#06
SARAN WRAP

WORN ON THE **LEFT:** She likes to watch…

WORN ON THE **RIGHT:** …whereas this girl likes to show off.

#07
WHITE

WORN ON THE **LEFT:** White denotes virginal, and this momma likes to break in the novice.

WORN ON THE **RIGHT:** A trainee lesbian strutting her stuff.

#08
LAVENDER

WORN ON THE **LEFT:** You may think lavender is something of an innocent color, but when worn in a back pocket you're talking group sex where this girl's on top.

WORN ON THE **RIGHT:** Another group sex fanatic, this girl's on the bottom of the pile.

#09
ORANGE

WORN ON THE **LEFT:** It's an anything goes scenario for these girls, as long as they're on top.

WORN ON THE **RIGHT:** Anything goes here too, as long as they're on the receiving end of all the naughty goings-on.

Right on Sister

From card-carrying hard-core dykes—on or off bikes—to dollied up drag supermodels, gay liberationistas have come in all shapes, sizes, colors and costumes. Just don't mess with them.

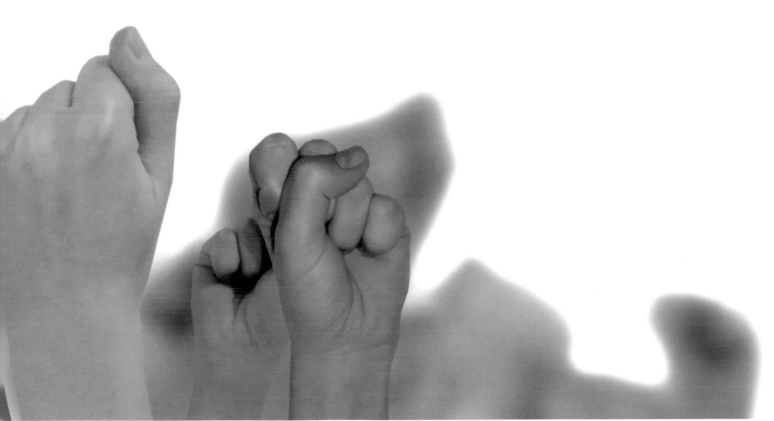

The Stonewall Riots

On June 27th, 1969, police raid a ratty gay bar, the unlikely birthplace of the gay liberation movement

New York, 1969, and it's no fun being gay. Society doesn't acknowledge gay life or experiences. The media only shows stereotypes (communists, sexual deviants, child molesters, that kinda thing) and coming out could mean being fired from your job, no reasons necessary. Verbal and/or physical abuse was par for the course and going to gay bars—all complete with blacked-out windows—meant regular police harassment, which in the summer of 1969 had revved up with a series of raids on illegal clubs.

Prior to the riots, the Stonewall Bar at 53 Christopher Street had been burnt out and remained empty for a year. Its new owners had simply painted the walls black and opened for business. With just two rooms—one a bar, the other a dancefloor—it was a major firetrap, a dope drop, and had even been suspected as the source of a hepatitis outbreak in the city. Still, such was the state of gay nightlife in New York in the late 60s that it was always packed.

The Stonewall Bar was, however, one of very few in operation, with joints like the Sewer and the Snake Pit having been closed down by the authorities. Throw in the death of gay icon Judy Garland [see page 46] on June 22nd—make of that what you will—and this was the backdrop for the police raid on the Stonewall Bar, 53 Christopher Street on June 27th. Gay people weren't taking it anymore…

The only gay riots, like, ever, they lasted for almost a week and by most people's standards, they were pretty small scale. Yet they sparked a global gay liberation movement that would call for pride and action, radically changing gay people's lives in the 30 years since.

THE RIOTS: NIGHT BY NIGHT

Saturday 06.28.69

3am: Nine plainclothes police enter the bar. The lights come on and the doors are sealed. Punters have to show their ID and are led out of the bar, and employees are arrested for selling liquor without a licence. As the police wagon arrives and the bartender, doorman, three drag queens and a lesbian are bundled in, the crowd grows angrier, pelting the police with coins and then bottles.

3.30am: As the 400-strong crowd led by drag queens and gay street people from the Village turns nasty, the police retreat into the bar itself, barricading themselves in. The mob storm the bar, smashing open the door with an uprooted parking meter. A hail of coins, cans and bottles follows.

3.45am: Just as the police are arming themselves, reinforcements arrive en masse in the shape of the Tactical Police Force. There are 13 arrests on charges ranging from harassment and resisting arrest to disorderly conduct.

10pm: Gay people are on the streets in the Village, kissing, hugging and shouting "Gay Power!" and "Liberate Christopher Street!" While these chants may appear comical now, way back then this was pretty radical stuff. Lesbians from the House Of Detention on Greenwich Avenue shout their support. Local police are pelted with bottles from the roofs and small fires are started in trashcans.

Sunday 06.29.69

2.15am: The Tactical Police Force arrives armed and helmeted, and joining arms, they make a sweep of Christopher Street between the Avenue of the Americas and 7th Avenue. The angry crowd continues to antagonize them, dispersing into small side-streets and reforming behind them. The police break rank twice and charge into the crowd. At least two men are clubbed to the ground.

3am: The crowd disperses.

4am: The Tactical Police Force withdraws. Three people are arrested on charges of harassment and disorderly conduct.

Monday 06.30.69
Tuesday 07.01.69

Crowds start to gather again, leading to more stand-offs with the police, some reportedly hilarious and camp.

Wednesday 07.02.69

The last night of riots, but one that takes a more serious turn, with the police attacking the crowds, resulting in serious casualties. Wednesday also sees an article in the *Voice* which brings people to the area intent on taking advantage of the situation and leads to looting.

In The Closet and Coming Out

Being secretive about your homosexuality and then declaring it to the world

The term "in the closet" comes from the concept of having a skeleton in your closet, a dirty secret waiting to come out. And the origin of that expression comes either from the story of Bluebeard, who kept the bodies of his dead wives in his closet, or from the days when dissection was illegal in Great Britain, and students and doctors would hide away human remains among their laundry. If you are "in the closet," you can either stay in there or you can "come out" and add your sexuality to your identity.

Gay activists have always argued that the closet is one of the main barriers to gay men and lesbians working towards equality in the way that other minorities have. While influential gay men and lesbians choose not to be identified, they argue, the movement has much less clout than, say, the black movement. And the very fact that someone would choose not to identify themselves as gay, they say, perpetuates the feeling that there's something shameful about homosexuality, that it's something you should hide.

Outing

Dragging other people out of the closet against their will

Is it right to make someone else's coming out decision for them? Is it politically defensible in a world where we need as many positive gay role models as we can get our hands on? Can someone be a role model for gay men and lesbians if they have been dragged kicking and screaming from the closet? Or is outing simply aping the time-honored blackmailing of homosexuals until they give you what you want? And if you do find it objectionable to reveal the truth about another person's sexuality, where does your respect for their privacy end? Does a gay politician who is happy to sign anti-gay legislation deserve to have his 'privacy' protected? From the early 90s, these were some of the fiercest debates raging in the gay press and in gay and straight bars worldwide as blabbermouths blabbed, sometimes just for the sheer hell of it, and gay celebrities ran for cover or bit the bullet and pipped the outers to the post.

Gay writer Armistead Maupin committed the first ever act to be referred to as "outing" when he revealed that Rock Hudson [see page 184], an ex-lover of his, was in fact gay to the *San Francisco Chronicle*. For this he was taken to task by the gay press who admitted that most people knew all about Rock, who was at the time very ill with AIDS, but insisted it wasn't anyone's place to say so. Maupin had what he described as the worst weeks of his life as he was attacked on all fronts.

That certainly didn't stop him. Apart from going on to an illustrious career dragging reluctant homosexuals out of the closet, he started something of a craze. *USA Today* decided to out publishing mogul Malcolm Forbes, who had once dated Elizabeth Taylor, soon after his death, describing him as "leading a gay lifestyle for at least the last five years." From then on the gloves were off, with gay activists ready to out everyone from athletes to rock stars. No one felt cosy in their closet anymore.

Among those in favor of outing was ACT UP founder [see page 90] and writer Larry Kramer. "I'm HIV-positive and I haven't got time to wait for 25 million people to get their act together to help make the government pay attention to my illness and help save my life," he once said, making it clear, however, that he hated the term 'outing'. "I'm not going to do it to a school-teacher or someone like that, but I get very angry with people who are in a position to do good, like heads of studios, stars, politicians certainly, authors, sports stars—people who could be role models for a community that desperately needs them. We're fighting for our lives now."

UK activist Peter Tatchell waded into the fray when he threatened to out fourteen gay Bishops. "These Bishops are gay in private, but publicly condemn homosexuality and support anti-gay discrimination," he argued in a piece called 'Outing is a Catalyst for Social Change'. The debate raged, with some branding him a blackmailer, while others cheered his stand against hypocrisy.

The National Gay and Lesbian Task Force, however, stood firmly against outing. "The central issue of the national lesbian and gay movement is freedom," said

Top Ten Reasons For Being In The Closet

1. You live under an oppressive regime and risk imprisonment or death if you come out.

2. You live under a semi-oppressive regime and risk losing your job if you come out.

3. You fear violence from homophobes.

4. You fear losing the loving support of your horribly homophobic family.

5. You are a member of a political party/church organisation that makes a point of condemning homosexuality as the devil's own work.

6. You are still trying to come to terms with the enormity of the situation yourself.

7. You are in the army.

8. You are a boy band member and coming out will do nothing to enhance your record sales (plus, your manager will kill you stone dead. See 1.)

9. You have nothing to wear

10. You are a pussy.

Information Director Robert Bray, "and we believe that coming out of the closet is an entirely personal and private decision that only an individual can make."

And in all the fever to out—or not to out—magazines couldn't quite decide whether they'd outed or not. *New York* magazine was accused of outing talk show hostess Rosie O'Donnell in a piece on the conspiracy between gay stars and the press to keep that closet door tightly closed. "The fact that Rosie is gay has been written about extensively in the tabloid press and, to our knowledge, she has never complained about that," said Caroline Miller of *New York* magazine.

The whole subject of outing hit the mainstream when Tom Hanks referred to a gay teacher that had inspired him during an Oscar speech in front of a global audience. Writer Paul Rudnick thought that it was the most spectacular incidence of outing in the history of homosexuality and promptly wrote a movie about it.

Wigstock

The wildest, wiggiest street festival in the world

It could've been anyone—Brian Butterick, Michael "Kitty" Ullman, Wendy Wild, The "Lady" Bunny or one of the members of the Fleshtones—that came up with the idea of Wigstock, the dragstravaganza to end all dragstravaganzas. But the concept was somehow born in the spring of 1984 after a (somewhat messy) night out at the Pyramid Club in Tompkins Square Park, the place Wigstock was first held a year later.

The "Lady" Bunny organized the whole damn thing—think Woodstock but without the matted hair—and she even kicked off what was to become NYC's most happenin' and definitely its most big-haired event on Labor Day, 1985 with a version of Carole King's 'I Feel The Earth Move.' She wore a black double-knit rhinestone-studded pants suit and wedgies. She looked, as usual, stunning.

Nobody gave much of a damn to start with though near-on a thousand folk had mustered some kind of interest by the end of the day. Cut to the following year and the buzz had grown; another year later, and there were as many freaks in the audience as there were on stage lipsynching. Even degenerate folk with body piercings and tattoos were let in.

Soon it was a place of pilgrimage for dragophiliacs the world over, and attended by names from the world of entertainment like Deborah Harry, Deee-Lite, Crystal Waters, Alexis Arquette and RuPaul as well as its stalwart bunch of drag stars like The "Lady" Bunny, Lypsinka, John Kelly, The Duelling Bankheads, Joey Arias, Candis Cayne, Ethel Eichelberger, Wendy Wild, Flotilla DeBarge—Empress Of Large, Leigh Bowery and Jayne County, to name just a few. Its standout moments are many though the bitch fight between the Duelling Bankheads and Deborah Harry is pretty hard to beat.

While Wigstock has also spawned similar festivals in San Francisco, Atlanta, Berlin, Melbourne and Chicago, the original is still the best—whatever anyone else says! But seventeen years, a couple of changes of location (most notably to the piers, an old gay cruising ground at the end of Christopher Street), a sabbatical, an alternative Wignot event and countless Barbras, Dianas, Donnas and Lizas later, the organisers behind the event finally decided to throw in the wig and hang up their stilettos after one last Wigout in 2001.

➪ **Take it further:** Wigstock: The Movie, *directed by Barry Shils. (1995)*

ACT UP

Seminal protest group, the AIDS Coalition To Unleash Power

ACT UP literally does what it says on the box: it acts up. The decentralized political organisation with chapters worldwide has been united in anger and committed to direct action to end the AIDS crisis since March 1987.

It all started in New York as a direct reaction to the US government's mismanagement of the AIDS crisis. The first demonstration took place at 7am on March 24th at Trinity Church, Wall Street to protest about the profiteering of pharmaceutical companies and to demand the immediate release of drugs that might save the lives of people suffering from AIDS. Also on the agenda were calls to increase public education about the disease and policies to prohibit discrimination. While hundreds of demonstrators stayed behind police lines, some sat in the street to block traffic and seventeen protestors were arrested, thereby achieving the goal of drawing both media and public attention to the cause.

Ten years later, at the group's anniversary protest in New York the core purpose still remained: to ensure everyone with HIV and AIDS had access to fundamental rights of healthcare and access to life sustaining medicines. However, the scale of the protest and its significance had grown substantially. This time more than 500 activists from chapters in eight American cities (New York, Los Angeles, San Francisco, Atlanta, Washington DC, Las Vegas, Oberlin, and Philadelphia) attended and there were 73 arrests, two thirds of them women, for acts of civil disobedience.

ACT UP battled under the slogan "Silence=Death" and became one of the most important institutions in the fight against the disease. It regularly made headlines with over-the-top and occasionally violent protests against the government and religious leaders.

However, it also became prone to vicious infighting and power struggles between various factions. The 90s also took their toll with many of ACT UP's leaders dying while AIDS slipped down the headlines with the arrival of cheaper and more effective treatments for the disease.

But in 1998, ACT UP found its feet again when it extended its protests to the major drugs companies' refusal, backed by many Western governments, to allow poorer nations to use generic versions of branded AIDS drugs. Unfortunately, their battle against AIDS both in the richer Northern countries and in poorer countries is still far from over.

Larry Kramer
ACT UP founder and writer

Intellectual and academic Susan Sontag said of him, "Larry Kramer is one of America's most valuable troublemakers. I hope he never lowers his voice." But apart from being the driving force behind ACT UP, he's also responsible for some of the most talked-about films, plays and books dealing with homosexuality and AIDS.

Born on June 25th, 1935 in Bridgeport, Connecticut, he graduated from Yale University in 1957 and spent the 60s in the UK, where he established himself as a screenwriter and producer with the number one movie, *Here We Go Round The Mulberry Bush* and the Academy Award-nominated *Women In Love*, adapted from the D. H. Lawrence classic.

Back in the States, his 1978 novel *Faggots*, one of the biggest gay bestsellers of all time, parodied the sexual carousel that a lot of gay men lived their lives on. It became all too prescient when the AIDS crisis erupted a couple of years later.

The crisis changed Larry Kramer's main role from writer to activist. In 1981, as a direct result of the disease, he co-founded Gay Men's Health Crisis, which is still the world's largest provider of services to those with AIDS. Six years later, he founded ACT UP.

Meanwhile, his activism also found a voice in his work. *The Normal Heart* saw Kramer venting his anger about governmental apathy in the face of the disease: it has gone on to have over 600 productions worldwide and is even used as a text in schools and colleges. Meanwhile, *Just Say No, A Play about a Farce* is an attack on the Reagan administration, which explores how sexual hypocrisy in high places allowed the disease to become an epidemic.

His most recent play, *The Destiny Of Me in 1993*, was a companion piece to *The Normal Heart*, and sees his main character trying to understand his life as a gay man and as a leader of the AIDS activist movement.

As well as writing, Kramer continues to be a pioneer in the field of AIDS. In 1998, he founded the Treatment Data Project to collect information on medical approaches to the disease via the Internet from several hundred thousand people around the world.

"I'm sad that there isn't any real activism anymore, like ACT UP," he says. "I miss that constructive energy that changed things. I think one of the most disheartening things is everyone seems to have forgotten the plague, and not just young people, but older people who lived through it. It's almost like it didn't happen and everybody thinks it's gone away. That's hard to take."
Larry Kramer is currently working on *The American People*, an epic novel about AIDS.

Gore Vidal

Writer, politician, sage, troublemaker and cheeky monkey

When asked whether his first sexual experience had been gay or straight, Gore Vidal replied that he was too polite to ask. No surprise then that this much-venerated intellectual giant is far from your run-of-the-mill gay idol. He even disdains the idea of gay as an identity: "There is no such thing as a homosexual person," he has said. "There are only homosexual acts."

Born into a wealthy family in New York state in 1925, Vidal has always had the whiff of high office about him, even if the nearest he came to a big desk in an important building was in 1960, when he campaigned, unsuccessfully as it turned out, for a place in the House of Representatives, although he was given a seat on the President's Advisory Committee on the Arts during his step-brother John F. Kennedy's administration. And Kennedy was not his only great link to politics: Vidal's grandfather was a U.S. Senator, his distant cousin Al Gore was vice-President and despite the fact that he once told *Time* magazine that "the only thing I've ever really wanted in my life was to be President," he is also on record as saying, "Any American who is prepared to run for President should automatically, by definition, be disqualified from ever doing so."

Having enlisted in the army in 1943 and seeing no real action, Vidal started his first novel *Williwaw*, which became a huge post-war success, but it was with *The City and the Pillar* in 1948 that he started to show his true colors. The story of two regular American Joes who happen to fall in love with each other, *The City and the Pillar* was recognized as the first explicitly gay novel in the American canon. Although it was an instant bestseller, it ultimately marginalized Vidal in a way that has probably since shaped his life and career, excluding him from politics and relegating him to the more useful role of serious critic of the American establishment, both in essays and in his historical novels which include *Washington D.C.* and *Hollywood*.

He returned to controversial territory with his 1968 novel *Myra Breckinridge*, an outrageous yarn about a male to female transsexual who goes about the anal deflowering of an all-American hero. It was dubbed "a virtuoso exercise in kinkiness," and was made into a major flop of a movie starring Raquel Welch and Mae West. In fact, Gore's experience with movies has been patchy: he scripted huge movies like 1959's *Spartacus* (although the gay flavor between Charlton Heston's Ben Hur and Tony Curtis's Messala was suppressed), and the critically acclaimed *Suddenly Last Summer*, after the Tennessee Williams play. But then you have *Caligula*, where Penthouse boss Bob Guccione inserted hardcore scenes so offensive to Gore that he took his name off the film, even though the hardcore scenes work quite well.

Through the 70s and 80s he became a well-known television pundit and chat show host, nurturing very public vendettas with literary luminaries like Truman Capote and Norman Mailer. Having also slept with other authors of note like Jack Kerouac, he became a public champion of sexual liberty, ultimately defending Clinton during the Lewinsky affair by saying, simply and concisely, that what any man does with his dick is his own, and nobody else's affair: "I'm in favor of any form of sexual relationship that gives pleasure to those involved," goes one of his excellent maxims on the subject. "And I have never heard a convincing argument to the contrary."

He now lives in Ravello on the coast of Italy with Howard Austen, a man he met in a bathhouse over 50 years ago, and continues to stir it up—mainly in the magazine *Vanity Fair*—for very carefully chosen targets like the FBI and CIA and hard-core Christians in general, for which he remains very near the top of the Gay Roll of Honor, whether he calls himself gay or not.

⇨ **Take it further:** *Palimpsest, a memoir by Gore Vidal. Sexually Speaking, a collection of essays on sex and sexuality.*

Matthew Shepard

The hate crime murder that shook the world

Twenty-one-year-old Matthew Shepard's life was brought to an untimely end in the fall of 1998. As well as shattering the peace of the small community of Laramie, Wyoming, news of the event reverberated around the world, proving undoubtedly that homophobic violence was still a grim reality in America.

On October 6th, 1998, gay student of the University of Wyoming, Matthew Shepard met Aaron McKinney, 22, and Arthur Henderson, 21, in a bar. Pretending to be gay, they lured him into Aaron's truck where they pistol-whipped and brutally beat him. They then tied him to a fence where he was found 18 hours later in near-freezing temperatures just outside Laramie. Matthew never came out of the coma, but passed away five days later from his injuries.

His horrific death instantly grabbed headlines, and meant that the subsequent funeral received worldwide media coverage.

The funeral took place in his hometown of Casper, Wyoming on October 16th, 1998, and was attended by his friends and family, but it also attracted mourners who identified with him. His cousin, Reverend Anne Kitch, said: "He was not always a winner according to the world's standards. He struggled to fit into a world not always kind to gentle spirits. What was important to Matt was to care, to help nurture, to bring joy to others in his quiet, gentle way."

Meanwhile, the City Council having anticipated demonstrations had voted to prohibit protests on public property within 50 feet of the service. The police presence was heavy and sniffer dogs even had to be used to check for bombs.

This didn't stop the event being hijacked by right-wing Christians and anti-gay protestors however, who stood across the street from the church with hostile placards ("God Hates Fags" and the like), trying to engage passers-by in debate. The Family Research Council even press released the following statement on the day: "Homosexuals are included in a list of sinners, who, if unrepentant, will not inherit the kingdom of God."

A candlelight vigil was held later in the month, attended by members of gay and lesbian groups, names from the world of entertainment and members of congress. Ellen Degeneres said in her speech, "I am so pissed off. I can't stop crying. This is what I was trying to stop—this is why I did what I did."

Justice was served however. Aaron McKinney was convicted of first-degree felony and second-degree murder but was acquitted of aggravated robbery and kidnapping. Arthur Henderson pleaded guilty to felony murder as well as the robbery and kidnapping. Both were sentenced to life terms—though Matthew's parents' intervention in the case of Aaron McKinney helped him escape the death penalty.

After Matthew's murder, President Clinton said: "Crimes of hate and crimes of violence cannot be tolerated in our country. In our shock and grief one thing must remain clear, hate and prejudice are not American values… there is something we can do about this, Congress needs to pass our tough Hate Crimes Legislation."

Unfortunately, Clinton's call to Congress to pass hate crime legislation covering offences based on sexual orientation hasn't been heard as yet.

Brandon Teena

The transsexual who was brutally murdered in Nebraska after his true identity was discovered by local men

On New Year's Eve 1993, Brandon Teena was spending the evening with friends. Lisa Lambert lived in the rural house with her nine-month old son, and was entertaining Brandon and their friend Philip Devine. They sat around, watched TV and drank soft drinks. Not a remarkable New Year's Eve in anyone's book.

Hilary Swank as Brendan Teena in Boys Don't Cry

In the middle of the freezing cold night while they were sleeping, two intruders broke into the small farmhouse and shot and stabbed Brandon, Lisa and Philip. Within minutes of the break-in the three were dead. The two intruders left the crying baby in his crib.

The killers were known to the people they had slain. Just weeks before, Brandon had been a friend of the killers, Tom Nissen and John Lotter. In fact the pair quite liked the affable young Brandon Teena, who had recently moved to town and had already managed to break quite a few girls' hearts in that short time. It was when the two murderers, and the rest of the town, discovered that Brandon Teena was in fact biologically a woman that they became enraged. Brandon had been pulled up for a minor crime by the local police who then released information about Brandon's gender to the local newspaper.

On Christmas Eve, the two men abducted Brandon and raped him. Outraged at his true identity and disgusted at the lies they believed he had told to them, they punished him in a way that they knew would hurt the most. After the brutal attack they threatened to kill him if he told the police about what they'd done. Brandon, nonetheless, reported the crime but despite naming his attackers, Nissen and Lotter were never arrested for Brandon's rape. A week later they'd killed him.

After the killings, it emerged that officers were told not to do anything about the rape by the town's sheriff. Meanwhile, the local authorities, of course, denied that their outing of Brandon Teena in any way contributed to the killers' motives. As the story of this gruesome murder hit the wires, gay and transgendered rights activists up and down the country took up the story of Brandon, who had successfully passed as a man for so long, but who was killed for living his life as he believed he should. Both men were found guilty of first-degree murder. Nissen is now serving consecutive life sentences after plea bargaining his way out of the chair, and Lotter is on death row.

▷ **Take it further:** Boys Don't Cry *starring Hilary Swank*. The Brandon Teena Story *by Susan Muska and Greta Olafsdottir.*

Harvey Milk

The San Francisco Supervisor, the first openly gay official in California, who was assassinated in 1978

Born in 1930 in Long Island, New York, Glimpy Milch aka Harvey Milk (his real, not-so-catchy name coming from his Lithuanian ancestry) moved to San Francisco in the 1970s, along with more than a few coach- and boat-loads of other queer folk, in search of a gay utopia in the hippy West Coast city.

Milk had travelled the US and finally ended up in the Gay Mecca that is The Castro [see page 106]. He opened Castro Camera at 575 Castro (which still has its original frontage and is now a soap shop) and became an important member of the community, acting as an advocate for local businesses. His passion for organizing saw Milk setting up the Castro Village Association (CVA) through which the gay community in San Francisco got its first taster of serious political organization and garnered allies in influential places.

Milk was a natural at this game, and a popular guy to boot, so it was only to be expected that his career in city politics progressed quickly. That's not to say that with his passion for politics he became a bore. His opening line when giving a speech was: "My name's Harvey Milk and I'm here to recruit you"—a cheeky play on the tired old hetero cliché that queers are always out to recruit young, susceptible straight innocents.

His struggle to secure equality for gay men and women was taken on by the city as more than just a token gesture of tolerance. He urged gay men and women to take on positions of power, and on his fourth attempt landed himself a seat on the Board of Supervisors in 1977. It was a brilliant coup for Milk who stood on an unashamed gay rights platform while the state of politics in the rest of the US was undoubtedly dodgy. "Save Our Children" was a regular war cry from anti-gay activists like the infamous Anita Bryant who at that time was stamping her feet about the queers who were, according to her, corrupting her kiddies. During a time in America when homosexuality was seen as a "crime against nature," Milk fought for equality, not just for gay men and lesbians, but for all minorities. He was no longer "the gay politician," he was a politician who just happened to be gay.

Harvey Milk had been in office for eleven months when the unthinkable happened. On November 27th 1978, along with the Mayor of San Francisco, George Moscone, he was murdered in City Hall by a disgruntled former City Supervisor. Dan White had managed to make his way into the government building by clambering in through a basement window, avoiding the metal detectors. White—who had given up his seat on the Board due to his annoyance that he could not support his family on the salary of a Supervisor—now wanted his job back. The Mayor refused, so he shot him. On his way out of the building he sought out Milk and shot him too.

Despite the city being in shock at this act of murder, White was sentenced to just seven years and eight months having had murder charges reduced to voluntary manslaughter. But why such a lenient sentence? White had used what is now known as the "Twinkie Defence"—the preposterous claim that he had eaten far too much junk food on the day of the murders, and therefore could not be held fully accountable for his actions. The gay community reacted to this outrageous sentence by attacking City Hall and rioting in the Civic Center area.

White was released after six years, and was asked by the new Mayor not to return to the city. He did return, but only to commit suicide.

Through his tireless work for gay and lesbian equality, Milk is still a hero, and not just in San Francisco but for gay rights groups the world over. Dubbed the "Mayor of Castro Street," his achievements are marked every year with the Harvey Milk Memorial March on November 27th, the day of his murder, while a branch of the San Francisco Public Library and a square in The Castro have also been named in his honor. There is even a bar, Harvey's, that occupies the space that was once the Elephant Walk bar, which was trashed by off-duty policemen following the rioting in the Civic Center. The Harvey Milk Institute, meanwhile—also based in the city of San Francisco—aims to "foster the development and examination of lesbian, gay, bisexual, transgender and queer culture and community in the Bay Area and beyond."

▷ **Take it further:** The book, The Mayor Of Castro Street *by Randy Shilts and the Oscar-winning documentary,* The Times of Harvey Milk Uncle Donald's Castro Street: www.backdoor.com/castroindex.htm

The Lesbian Avengers

The dyke-rect action group with members all over the world

Formed in 1992 by six angry and political lesbians—not a pretty combination—in New York City, The Lesbian Avengers is a direct action group that at its peak in the mid-90s boasted factions all over the world. Angry with gay groups whose focus was solely on gay male issues, and tired of lesbian politics and visibility being brushed under the carpet, The Lesbian Avengers set out to put a few things straight. So to speak.

Using non-violent tactics and a lot of balls, these women actively promoted lesbian visibility and recruited new members all over America and in Europe. In their heyday they were holding weekly meetings and organizing regular targets for their anger, not only to promote "dykiness" to the gay press and people who'd listen, but also in the mainstream media—the end of the 90s saw the straight media's obsession with lesbian chic [see page 161] grow and grow, so the Avengers were regularly seen both on TV and in major newspapers strutting their stuff. Tabloid papers tried desperately to unearth the leaders in these leader-less groups, and some Avengers were even outed to their parents by journalists. Locally, despite the constant attention, they promoted dyke-only marches before traditional Pride events in many cities and supported under-funded women's groups.

Even though their aims seemed rather dry and goodie-goodie on the surface— attacking institutions and people they saw as patriarchal and anti-lesbian, supporting traditionally gay male groups like ACT UP [see page 90], and promoting the pro-choice cause—what made the Avengers' actions stand out from tired queer groups was their humorous approach to politics. Gone were the serious days of the 1970s lesbian feminists who didn't see fun as something that could be political, or

February 7th 2000: The London Lesbian Avengers attack a Stagecoach red bus whose boss Brian Souter funded an anti-gay campaign in Scotland

personal for that matter. The Avengers dressed up for actions but also took their tops off and got their tits out, had kiss-ins in the most prominent public places, made posters proclaiming "We Recruit," rode around on London in double-decker buses promoting lesbianism to shocked Saturday shoppers and invaded right-wing Christian church services. Some even infiltrated conversion therapy courses held by evangelical Christian groups [see page 122], while others held illegal picnics in the gardens of homophobic politicians. They meant business, and nothing stood in the way of their cause.

The women worked on a real grassroots level—sharing resources, stealing photocopy and fax access from their workplaces, distributing high-end homemade videos to other Avenger groups, giving out eye-catching leaflets, and creating "phone trees" so that they managed to spread secret details of

their next action cheaply and quickly amongst the group.

The dungarees as a political clothing accessory were over—these girls went clubbing, looked hot and actively recruited new members to enlarge their potential pulling circle. Even though serious issues were at their core, partying was just as important. Fundraisers involved go-go girls and lots of alcohol, while the meetings discussed issues as diverse as governmental law, education and the rights of lesbians in the armed forces.

While the heyday of The Avengers has passed, plenty of the groups still exist and are active within their local communities, while the lasting impression that these girls have made on queer politics means that queer actions no longer involve dull old banner waving and polite requests to their politicians.

Ellen Degeneres

The stand-up comic turned unwilling lesbian icon after a global coming out in her popular sitcom series

Ellen Degeneres (pronounced duh-jen-air-ruz) was born in 1958 in Louisiana and first came to prominence on our screens with her eponymous sitcom Ellen. We always knew she was a big old dyke, but it took years for her, and her character Ellen Morgan, to come out of the huge closet that is the American entertainment industry.

She first entered the world of showbiz as a stand-up comic, and a damn good one at that. Her insightful yet goofy shaggy dog stories won her a huge fanbase, and by the time she landed herself a sitcom pilot, called These Friends of Mine, she was a well-respected comedian. This first real foray into television was where the character Ellen Morgan made her screen debut. The station loved her and so did the audiences, and Ms. Degeneres was asked to make a whole series. The ratings grew, the name was changed, and Ellen was born.

No-one was sure just what it was about Ellen Morgan, and in turn Degeneres, that made us all think she was gay. Perhaps it was the chinos-and-tank-top combination wardrobe, or maybe her self-deprecating humor, which we as queers reckon we're all so good at, that made her seem like "one of us". Whatever it was, the rumours spread and after years of gossip, pointed questions and sarcastic answers on talkshows— "No, I'm Lebanese"—and major hints in the series itself, Ellen Degeneres finally came out on the cover of Time magazine's April 1997 edition with the byline "Yep, I'm gay", while Ellen Morgan did the same shortly after in the infamous 'Puppy Episode' on April 30th.

Even though gay characters had been on American television for over 20 years

(Peter was a gay set designer in ABC sit-com The Bar in 1972, while the first proper lesbian was Alice in Soap seven years later), there was something very different and quite spectacular about Ellen's revelations. Not only was the show's coming out episode eagerly anticipated by the world's media, but a whole host of mainstream stars had signed up, and by doing so offered total support to Ellen. 'Coming Out' parties were organised all over the world and as the excitement grew, so did the calibre of the celebrities involved in the 'Puppy Episode.' By the time it was made, the episode boasted the talents of Oprah Winfrey, Laura Dern, kd lang, Melissa Etheridge and dyke model Jenny Shimizu. Even the then-Vice President of the United States, Al Gore, made a statement about the show: "When the character Ellen came out, millions of Americans were forced to look at sexual orientation in a more open light." And that's clout!

Despite scoring the highest ratings that week on American television, winning a Grammy and being voted number one in gay website Planet Out's "GLBT Of The Century," nothing could bolster the ratings for the post-coming out series of Ellen. After the furore that had surrounded the 'Puppy Episode,' viewing figures dropped off and so did the advertising. Some might say the appeal of the show had been lost: without the sneaky in-jokes and the outrageous queer innuendos, there was very little left for Ellen Morgan to do but be loveable. Protests by right-wing Christians in the States hadn't helped. Instead of being a show possibly about a lesbian on mainstream TV, Ellen was now a show about a dyke broadcast to the nation at peak time. Disney, who owns the ABC network, had its products boycotted by

God-fearing Americans and didn't need an excuse to drop the sitcom when the ratings slumped. Despite the extraordinary levels of publicity produced by Ellen out and about with her new girlfriend, the middle-of-the-road actress Anne Heche (pronounced "haytch"— whatever), Ellen bombed and the plug was pulled.

Her untimely departure from TV did nothing to shake her popularity in the queer world and in the gossip columns, however. Ellen and Heche were the golden couple and every lesbian coming out wanted to be just like them. Even without a TV show, her stand-up shows were selling out and she was a regular fixture on talkshows and at award ceremonies, and even started breaking into movies like Ed TV.

The break up with Heche caused outrage and shock, not only because Heche was found wandering in the desert near the couple's former home, naked and bewildered, but also because she later denounced her relationship with Ellen as a big old three-year long mistake. While the couple had been unwilling at first to become spokeswomen for queer rights—"I never wanted to be the lesbian actress. I never wanted to be the spokesperson for the gay community. Ever," grabbing a sneaky kiss at the White House right under Clinton's nose, their appearance on the Capitol steps for Matthew Shepard's memorial and their interviews giving good PR to the legalisation of gay marriage meant that that is exactly what they had become.

Despite the setback of her sitcom being pulled and losing her girlfriend in such a dramatic way, Ellen has bounced back. Not only has her mother become something of a celebrity because of her support for her daughter, but Ellen continues to do television work, act, direct, write, star in films and do stand-up comedy. And she is still the biggest lesbian in Tinseltown. Well, out lesbian.

Sandra Bernhard

Edgy, sexually ambiguous, multi-media entertainer

Lesbians never could pin Sandra Bernhard down. And that was just how Sandy liked it. The comedienne, who also dabbles in music and acting and writing, has always been a slippery customer: she'll admit to being gay if she really has to but she has very little time for the gay community as a community. "I think the most important thing for the gay girl is to be confident, be individual and not dependent on a network of support," she said in one interview. "If you're looking for the gay community to accept you, it's a mistake." For this she has been vilified, not that she cares. On her album *Excuses For Bad Behaviour: Part One* she even lampoons the whiney dyke playing Tracy Chapman records and wondering why Sandra can't be there for the lesbian community. But, hey, that's Sandy. Get used to it.

Born in Michigan in 1955 to a sculptress and a proctologist (how's that for material?), Sandra started her ambiguous, highly ironic schtick at the age of 19 while she was working as a manicurist in L.A, and soon wangled herself a slot on the *Richard Pryor Show*. An ardent fan of Bette Midler when she was still an edgy performer, Bernhard's act has developed along similar lines, taking in music, comedy, observation, all delivered in a borderline aggressive, deadpan tone. A celebrated slaughterer of holy cows, she was the only comedian brave enough to mock the circus that surrounded the death of Princess Diana ("When I heard Tom Cruise speak about how many times he had driven through that same tunnel, it gave me the chills. I said, 'Tom it's the edgy shit that needs to go into your work, baby'"), the only one to lay into the supermodel reaction to Versace's death ("I run into the girls on the streets and their eyes are hollow, listless, they are non-communicative. Naomi is a shadow of a human being"), and by far the finest satiriser of her old sister-in-arms, Madonna. She featured a cheap Madonna lookalike stripper called Shashana in one of her movies and has described Madonna's daughter Lourdes

as, "Cute, very smart and not impressed with her mother. Keeps a real healthy distance."

And yet it could be argued that it was Madonna who brought Bernhard to a mainstream American audience. With a very well-received performance as a crazed fan in Martin Scorcese's *King of Comedy* opposite Robert DeNiro under her belt, she started to date Madonna (well, that's how they seemed to want it to look) with the pair of them winding up talking about being 'gal pals' on *Late Night* with David Letterman and setting up their own all-girl Brat Pack called the Snatch Batch, which cruised the lesbian clubs of New York and LA. Sandy even turned up in the Madonna rockumentary *Truth or Dare* as a slightly bemused voice of reason amidst the madness of a major pop tour. Then they had a big falling out, reportedly over Bernhard's girlfriend of the time Ingrid Casares, and have been mortal enemies ever since.

Bernhard went on to become a major modeliser; she made a movie of her stand-up routine called *Without You I'm Nothing*, became a regular on the *David Letterman Show* and in 1992 landed herself a regular part on *Roseanne* as the lesbian next door, with Morgan Fairchild as her sometime girlfriend. She extended her television career with a regular cameo in *Ally McBeal* and her own talk show *The Sandra Bernhard Experience* and even had a club hit with a cover of Sylvester's gay anthem 'You Make Me Feel (Mighty Real),' developed from a sketch about a straight man who goes to a gay club and discovers poppers and anal sex.

But more than all her TV and film and music, it is Sandra's being Sandra—and refusing to be a lesbian for anyone—that has had the most impact. She gave birth to a daughter—Cicely—in 1998 and made no bones about the fact that she wasn't the result of a donor job but a real life sexual encounter. Now that's queer for you.

The AIDS Quilt

Nobel Peace Prize-nominated memorial to lives lost in the epidemic

Aim: To commemorate loved ones who died with AIDS and to educate the public about the disease. By October 2000, the NAMES Project Foundation had raised over $3 million for AIDS service organisations throughout North America.

Size: As of October 2000, it was 792,000 square feet with 44,000 individual panels, each one memorializing the life of a person lost to the disease. When it was displayed on the National Mall in Washington DC during the National March for Lesbian and Gay Rights in 1987, it covered a space larger than a football field. Now, it's grown too large to be displayed in its entirety, with new panels still continuing to arrive weekly.

History: The idea for the quilt came from gay rights activist, Cleve Jones. In 1985, he discovered that over a thousand San Franciscans had died with AIDS and while helping to organise the annual candlelight march for Harvey Milk [see page 94] and George Moscone, he asked marchers to write the names of their friends and family who'd died from the disease on placards. These were then taped onto the San Francisco Federal Building, which looked like a quilt and provided the inspiration for the memorial, the NAMES Project Foundation. It's now the largest ongoing community arts project in the world, with 50 chapters in the US and 36 affiliates around the world.

Famous AIDS deaths commemorated: Arthur Ashe, tennis player; Tina Chow, clothing designer; Brad Davis, actor; Eazy E, rap artist; Perry Ellis, fashion designer; Wayland Flowers, comedian; Michel Foucault, philosopher; Halston, fashion designer; Keith Haring, artist; Rock Hudson, actor; Liberace, performer; Robert Mapplethorpe, photographer; Freddie Mercury, lead singer of Queen; Rudolf Nureyev, ballet dancer; Anthony Perkins, actor; Vito Russo, writer; Willi Smith, fashion designer; Sylvester, singer; Ryan White, AIDS activist; Ricky Wilson, guitarist with the B-52s.

Materials featured: You name it and it's on there—everything from bubble wrap, through Lego, to wedding rings.

Camille Paglia

Controversial lesbian professor, commentator and writer

Easily the most glamorous thing to happen to the intellectual community since Arthur Miller married Marilyn Monroe, Camille Paglia is a professor, controversialist, media player and one of the most loved and loathed figures operating in gay circles today. Her 'take no prisoners' approach and her willingness to wade deep into the most politically incorrect territory have made her something of a cult, especially with gay men and transsexuals, whom she champions way above lesbians.

In fact it's the insults she has thrown at lesbians, feminism (which is "stuck in an adolescent whining mode, full of puritanism and suffocating ideology") and feminist icons like Andrea Dworkin, Germaine Greer, and Naomi Wolf that have kept her in the news, along with intentionally controversial opinions on issues such as date rape (basically, women have to take some responsibility for the lust they stir up in men), and the death of Matthew Shepard (she says he went after "rough trade" and reaped the consequences). But her bottom line has always been about accepting realities: The realities of our natures (we are animals and our lives are all about the struggle to dominate our own aggressive natures) and the realities of how society functions. In the era of Blame Culture she advocated the taking of responsibility. No wonder she earned herself so many enemies.

Born in 1947 in upstate New York, Paglia left Yale with a PhD in 1974 and immediately began teaching. In 1990 she published her hefty tome (which still managed to become something of a best seller) *Sexual Personae: Art and Decadence from Nefertiti to Emily Dickinson*. She became an overnight celebrity, a role she relished to the extent that she often turned up at lectures flanked by two huge bodyguards, like she was Michael Jackson. Books like *Sex, Art and American Culture* and *Vamps and Tramps*, with their paeans to the likes of Madonna and Princess Di followed, as did articles and TV appearances where she continued to whip cosy lefties into a frenzy by denouncing the liberal gay agenda, warning that the gay disrespect of religion would provoke a backlash and championing the homophobic lyrics of Eminem. She knew that every time she pressed those buttons, all the right people would jump. She was rarely disappointed.

She describes herself as an 'anti-feminist feminist... a 60s free-speech militant' and 'an academic rottweiler' who opposes dogma in all areas. Others just call her a self-publicizing, self-serving nasty bitch. But at least she's fun, and you can't say that about many academics.

▷ **Take it further:** *Sexual Personae: Art and Decadence from Nefertiti to Emily Dickinson*; *Sex, Art and American Culture, and* Vamps and Tramps.

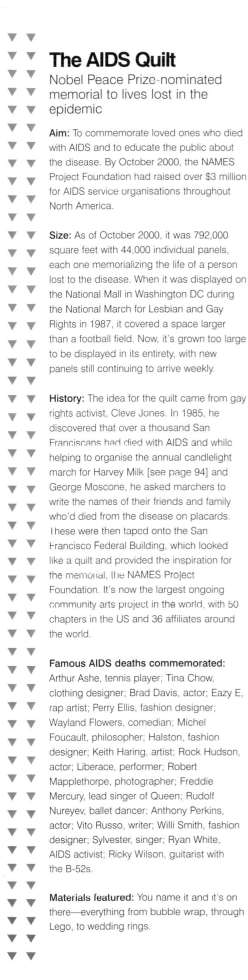

Martina Navratilova

The hard-hitting Czech who became one of the greatest tennis players of all time

As much an idol as a lesbian icon, Martina's strength on the court (she won 168 professional singles titles by the time she retired in 1994) and the way that she revolutionized the women's game, replacing lacy-pantied daintiness with sheer muscular force, meant she became not only a sporting legend, but also one of the first out lesbians. Ever.

Born in what is now the Czech Republic in 1956, Martina became an American citizen in 1981, and while her athleticism raised the game to a new level, her sexuality was causing even more of a stir. It's always been thought that the world of women's tennis has been something of a hotbed of lesbian action, but it was only in 1981, after an affair with the acclaimed author Rita Mae Brown [see page 190],

that Martina eventually came out. As bisexual.

But even this semi-coming out cost her millions. With her dykey cards on the table, even though she was winning more and more competitions, the endorsements that make professional tennis players their fortunes dried up almost completely, with none of the sportswear manufacturers wanting to pin their brand to a girl who was into girls.

The years of rivalry between the dangerously powerful Martina and all-American girl next door Chris Evert saw the two women reach a vast audience, clashing both on and off the court, even though they were, in fact, best buddies. Martina's game hit a real high in 1982

when she became the world number one with the help of her personal trainer Nancy Lieberman and Renee Richards, her coach. Around this time, Martina was adding a certain spice to tournaments by frequently leaping through the crowd to plant a kiss on her then lover Judy Nelson's lips. It was the sort of behavior that had young lesbians rushing to their rooms to hide their embarrassment and glee.

If there was any doubt about Martina's status as a lesbian icon, it was quashed in 1993 when she turned up in person to address the Millennium March in Washington, her first-ever gay and lesbian event. Ironically, despite being the darling of the dykes, Martina had led a sheltered queer life ruled by her tennis career, and admitted to having visited very few lesbian bars in her life.

Even her retirement from international tennis has not shut Martina up. In a speech before her inauguration into the Tennis Hall of Fame Martina proclaimed: "Until we have equal access under the law I'll keep speaking out. I don't want it to be an issue, but it is because we don't have equal rights." And in addition to lending her voice to gay and lesbian political campaigns, Martina, like many a celebrity queer, has taken on fundraising with a passion, raising over a $1 million for lesbian and gay charities with her Red Ribbon Visa card while also finding time to champion animal and children's rights.

And since the golden days of Navratilova, who have lesbians had to swoon over on court? Well, no-one really. The French player Amelie Mauresmo is the only female player to come out since Martina, and for that she was allegedly denounced as "half a man" by fellow player Martina Hingis. Nice.

Billie Jean King

One of the world's greatest tennis players, and one of the first sports stars to come out way back in 1981

Born in 1943 in California, Billie Jean King's career at the top of women's tennis really began back in 1960. Unlike fellow tennis legend and lesbian Martina Navratilova [see page 100] who came out as bisexual in the same year, Billie Jean King's outing was not a celebratory moment. She'd been denying her dykiness for years and was still married to Larry King when her ex-lover, Marilyn Barnett, made history and attempted to sue her for "galimony". In other words, Barnett wanted half of her fortune after the failure of their relationship and she was prepared to go down fighting. Fortunately for King her attempt failed, but it meant that King now had to face the media and her husband, Larry King, whom she was trying to divorce at the time.

Unlike Martina, Billie's career in tennis did not reap millions—she was thirteen years older than the athletic powerhouse and endorsements and prize money for women were a fraction of what Martina would eventually get her hands on, even if King was the first woman to earn over $100,000 in one season.

While you'd have thought that the two world-class players would have sought solace in each other during a time when the media was after them and their dykey stories, Martina and Billie Jean were by no means the best of buddies. Martina's girlfriend of the time, the author Rita Mae Brown, had other ideas as Billie Jean explains: "I wish [Martina Navratilova had] been around more at the time when I was outed but Rita Mae Brown really did not want her to hang out with me at all. Rita Mae didn't like me. When I was outed, Martina called me and said, 'Oh, Rita Mae had me call just to find out the dirt.' That's not being supportive." Even the famous, it seems, cannot escape the jealous girlfriend cliché of lesbian life.

Her outing may have overshadowed the last years of her career, but it was her bout against Bobby Riggs in 1973 that most people will remember. The match, dubbed the "Battle of the Sexes" saw Billie Jean whipping Mr. Riggs's ass in a match that attracted a court-side audience of over 30,000 people—a record that still stands today. Her amazing achievements include 71 singles titles and 20 Wimbledon titles, as well as being only one of eight players to win a singles title in each of the Grand Slam events. Despite a shaky coming out, she now campaigns tirelessly for gay and lesbian rights.

Dungarees
A cover-all item of clothing, usually made of denim

With their name coming from the Hindi word "dungri," a sturdy Indian fabric, these pants, with the add-on extra of a bib-like covering to the chest, are attached to the body with straps over the shoulders. Usually made of denim, or a similarly hardy, unflattering material, they were a la mode with the lesbian population during the 70s and 80s.

While the dungarees' cousin, the jean, falls into fashion whatever the season, the ugly duckling of the denim world, is rarely taken seriously by the fashionista set due to its amazing ability to make the wearer appear to be the size of the back of a large truck. They did, however, cause something of a fashion stir during the 1980s when the dance community, known as ravers, were often seen at dance events sporting dungarees without a shirt underneath. They have been noticeably ignored in recent 1980s fashion revivals.

Lesbians' fond attachment to dungarees comes from the politicized 70s, when dykes were involved in the feminist movement. Dungarees became the preferred trouser as they were both practical and covered most of the body, therefore removing any emphasis from the female form. During the 70s the lesbian uniform often comprised of over-sized dungarees adorned with badges, often including the labrys [see page 50], with Doctor Martens-style boots, a checked shirt and a closely cropped haircut completing the dyke feminists' identity. Not only did the ensemble mirror their political beliefs regarding the female form, but it also enabled political lesbians to spot each other in the street. Their dress sense was often criticized in the reactionary tabloid press for being not only unfeminine, but also ugly.

While dungarees are no longer the preferred pant of modern dykes, old-school lesbians of the banner-waving variety can still be seen wearing them.

Derek Jarman

British film maker, poet, author, gay rights activist, video director, gardener, social commentator and AIDS activist

A man of many talents and passions, Derek Jarman was born in Middlesex, England in 1942. Having studied painting at the illustrious Slade School in London, Jarman got into film almost by accident when artsy filmmaker Ken Russell asked him to design a set for his flick *The Devils*.

Jarman's first feature film in 1976 was the controversial *Sebastiane*—a celebration of all things homo set in Roman times that attracted an underground following and critical respect. When it was first shown on British television many years later in a suitably late night slot, it received a massive number of complaints from shocked viewers who really ought to have been tucked up in bed at that godforsaken hour. With its dialogue completely in Latin, it was the film's beautifully shot gay sex scenes that caught the public's imagination and indignation.

Seen as a true radical in this field, and whichever fields he cared to roam in, Jarman's next film propelled him even further into the spotlight. *Jubilee* was released in 1977, the year of Queen Elizabeth II's Silver Jubilee, and gave the finger to the seemingly dead-in-the-water institution of the British monarchy. A bleak tale that transported the 16th century monarch Elizabeth I to the dangerous streets of London in the late 20th century, it oozed punk ideals and anti-establishment messages and, with star freaks like Adam Ant and Toyah Wilcox, it really did cause something of a stir. Think a celluloid version of 'God Save The Queen' by the Sex Pistols and you're getting close.

In 1987, Jarman tested positive for HIV and in a radical step, at a time when people shied away from pronouncing their status and governments the world over were struggling to come to terms both with HIV and AIDS, Jarman was open, honest and critical of the current climate and people's attitudes to the disease. In the years after his diagnosis, he became an outspoken supporter of HIV/AIDS awareness-raising, and of those activists demanding that people with HIV/AIDS be treated equally. In the 1980s and 1990s he was active within British political gay groups like Outrage! (a group similar to the American ACT UP —see page 90) that fought loudly and cleverly against what Jarman saw as the tabloidization of the disease by right-wing commentators and politicians.

And the filmmaking went on. As well as creating films like 1985's art house classic Caravaggio (for which he secured himself a Turner Prize nomination for "Outstanding Visual Quality in the field of film"), the ultra-pretentious Blue from 1993—which is nothing more than a blue screen that symbolizes the invisibility of the HIV virus, with voiceovers and music—and Edward II, he was working on pop videos for the likes of 1980s supergroups The Smiths and the Pet Shop Boys [see page 174], as well as a whole host of short films, well-received books, set designs for ballets and even a photography tome about his famous seaside garden at Prospect Cottage, Dungeness, Kent, England.

As his illness worsened, Jarman not only fought harder against it and the establishment who wished he'd shut up and, quite frankly, die, but also included themes of the disease within his work. An eloquent, open and amusing man, his work, life and politics became more and more entwined. The prospect of his death and the blindness brought on by HIV inspired Jarman, who was more scared of obscurity and "social ostracism" than his impending demise. In 1987, Jarman, who was fond of frolicking on the infamous cruising grounds of Hampstead Heath in London, met Kevin Collins at the Tyneside Film Festival. Twenty-one year old Collins was a software writer for the Government. Jarman relentlessly pursued the young man with letters and in just a few months Collins had moved down to London and in with Jarman. Collins nursed Jarman until his death in 1994.

With his unashamed use of both gay themes and gay sex, his tireless campaigning for the rights of people with AIDS and the fact that he just would not shut up, Jarman is a true all-round gay icon.

▷ **Take it further:** Derek Jarman's Garden, Photographs by Howard Sooley (Thames and Hudson, 1995), Smiling In Slow Motion, Derek Jarman's personal diary (Vintage, 2001).

The Sisters of Perpetual Indulgence
Queer activists who dress up as nuns

Famous for their canonization of Derek Jarman in 1991 and their black (and no doubt dirty) habits and white faces, the Sisters of Perpetual Indulgence, Inc., if you please, were founded in 1979 in— guess where?—San Francisco.

The queer grapevine has it that some unsuspecting nuns in Iowa lent their old habits to a group of men for a performance of The Sound Of Music in 1976. Three years later, the habits turned up in the Castro on the backs of three homos heading to the city's nude beach, one of whom was smoking a cigar and carrying a machine gun. In the fall of that year they were out on the streets of San Fran recruiting potential followers and habit-wearers, and by 1981 the Sisters had launched a new Order in Sydney, Australia.

Working on a grass roots level and subverting Christian imagery, the Sisters fought against the spread of HIV/AIDS in San Fran, and eventually the world over. Working with local health workers, by 1982 they were in the thick of the crisis in San Francisco. With STIs spreading like proverbial wild fire, and the talk of a 'gay cancer', the Sisters were the first group to produce sex-positive safe sex leaflets with a sense of humor.

Organizing the first AIDS Candlelight Vigil ever in 1983, the Sisters have gone on to promote safe sex, organize fundraisers for queer youth and AIDS charities and spread the word of their Order around the world. Working with all forms of media, including mainstream titles like Newsweek, they pressed for the issues of HIV/AIDS within the gay community to be handled fairly and responsibly.

The Sisters continue their work today and it's been their outspoken attitude to the bigotry and fear of AIDS as well as their amusing and out-there actions that have not only caught the attention of the world's media, but also the respect of queer communities and political groups globally.

"Our common vows are to promulgate universal joy and expiate stigmatic guilt. Our shared ministry is one of public manifestation and habitual preparation. We pledge to support our fellow Sisters toward our personal and collective enlightenment."

Location, Location, Location

Some places are just gayer than others; whether it's New York, London, Sydney or Paris, you can be sure as hell it ain't Boise, Idaho.

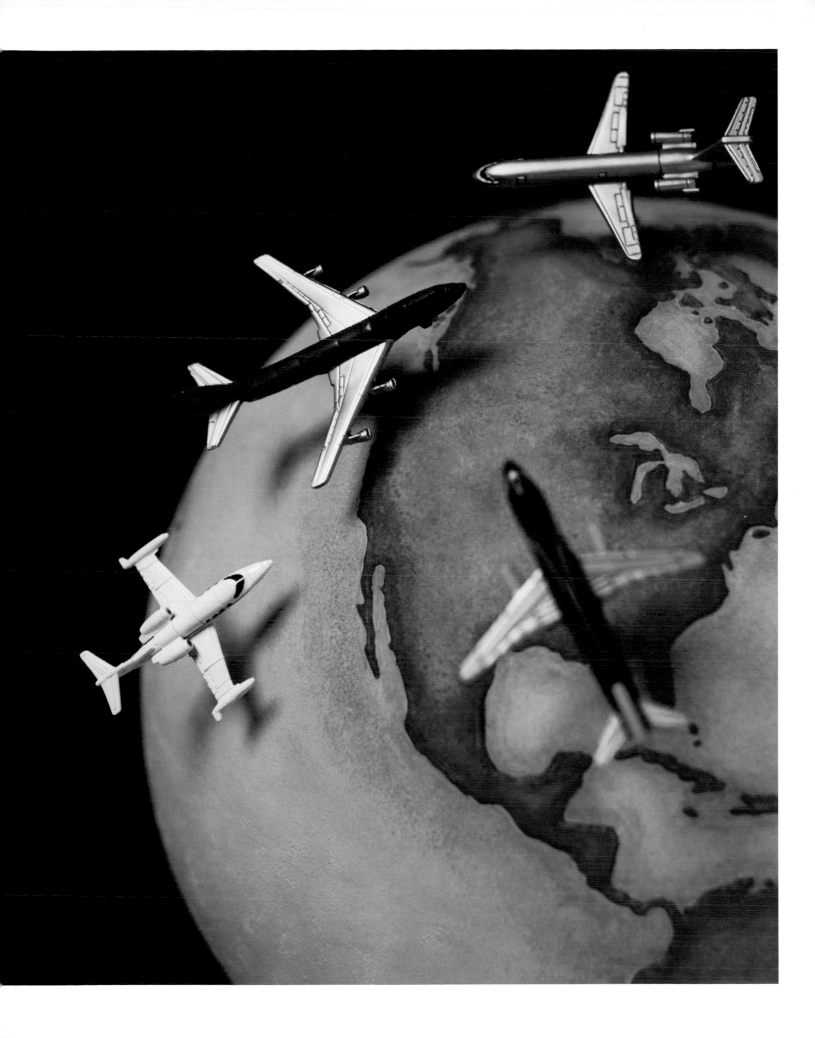

San Francisco

Arguably the best city in the world to be gay in

With a population of 800,000 people, it's reckoned that about of quarter of San Francisco's inhabitants are gay or lesbian. With such an impressive proportion of queers, it's certainly earned its nickname of "Sodom By The Sea." Gay men and women in San Francisco are at the core of its infrastructure—they drive the buses, they sell burgers on the street, they work in the most glamorous stores and are prominent within local government. It's the kind of place that you'd imagine would grind to a standstill if the queer folk of the city were to ever go on strike.

San Francisco has a great history of tolerance, queer activism and radical politics. Sitting pretty right out there on the West Coast of America, it's been the place that for years people have come to in order to reinvent themselves or change their lives for the better. The fact that it's a melting pot of colors, races, religions and creeds means that gay people have embraced San Francisco as their own. And do you know what? It gives them a big old hug right back.

So how did the city get to be such a gay Mecca? At the beginning of the 20th century the city's waterfront was already a popular cruising ground for gay men. While dyke icons like Gertrude Stein and Alice B. Toklas left their hometown, other queers picked up their belongings and headed west. By the 1920s, the first gay bars had opened up in the city, while in the 1930s drag queens and their muses, like Tallulah Bankhead, [see page 205] headed for the North Beach district.

As with many cities that have become popular with gay men and lesbians, San Francisco was a favorite hangout for bohemian arty types. The Beat Generation of the 1950s made the city its home, and in the same decade the all-lesbian Daughters of Bilitis group was founded. The Beat Generation opened the doors for the counter-culture hippie movement in the 1960s, and with the prospect of free love and lots of drugs, the gay population just grew and grew.

Five years before the Stonewall Riots in New York [see page 87] officially kicked off the global gay rights movement in 1969, gay men and women in San Francisco were already organized and fighting back against continual police harassment. At a gay fundraising event in 1964, plainclothes police raided, photographing people inside and eventually arresting four people. The next day the American Civil Liberties Union took up the case of the four who had been detained, and won. This victory not only increased the gay population's confidence, but it also opened the way for gay men and women to win positions of power in local politics and to fight for equality. When Harvey Milk, an out gay man on the city's Board of Supervisors, [see page 94] was assassinated in 1978, the city's gay community became a force to be reckoned with.

The arrival of the AIDS era at the end of the 1970s took a horrific toll on the city and its gay community. Nevertheless, both its queer and straight habitants fought back and it was here that militant AIDS activism groups were born, developing a strong and supportive network for people with HIV/AIDS and setting the standards that we see today.

Nowadays, the city celebrates its gay community unashamedly, and attracts a massive number of gay tourists to boot. With its fabulous Pride events [see page 119], Gay Film Festival, Harvey Milk Memorial March and Castro and Folsom Street fairs, it seems that all-year round there's something thoroughly queer to do. Even the city's tallest flag pole proudly waves a massive rainbow flag.

While the Mission and the world-renowned Castro have an air of the gay ghetto about them—the Mission is dykeville, while the boys rule the Castro—the reason they live, work and party there is because they damn well like it. Each of these areas, instead of being false and plastic like gay districts in other big cities, boast a fabulous diversity. From Hispanic gay bars and transgender meetings, to lesbian mums, book clubs and leather bars, there's a little bit of something for everyone, it seems. And the best thing? Whether you live here, or are merely a wide-eyed visitor, you can get on with your life without your sexuality ever being

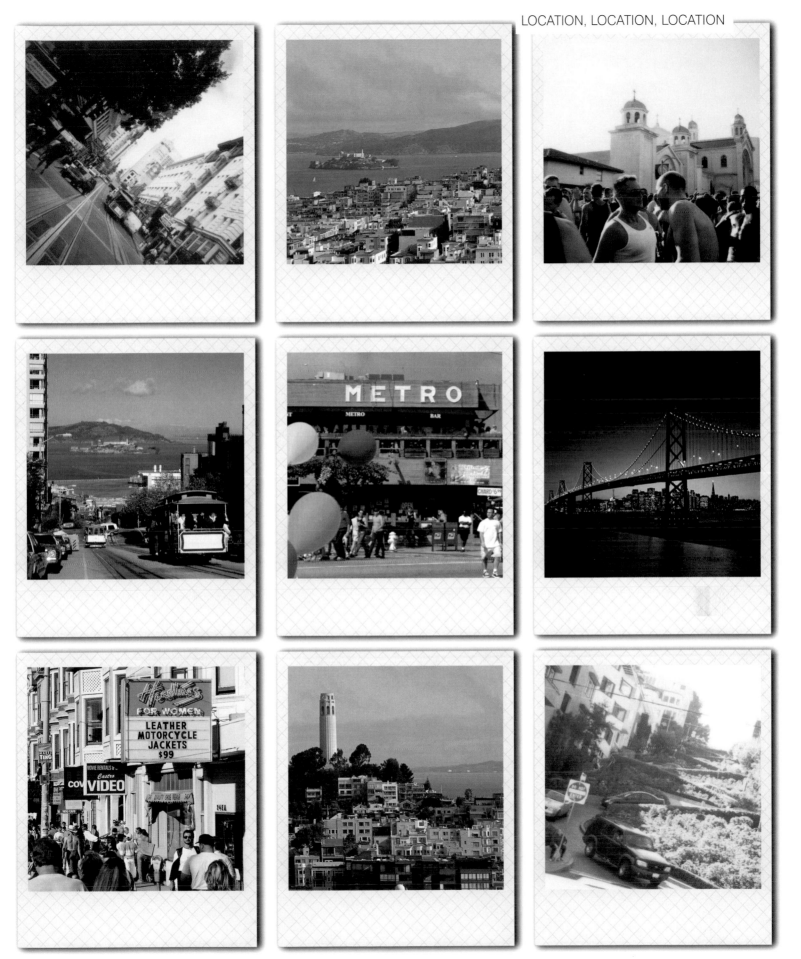

Map #1

The gayest places out there

06 London

Because of strict obscenity laws, London once trailed waaay behind the rest of the world when it came to gay clubs, cinemas, saunas and the like, but now due to a loosening of legalities it's superseding almost any other city. While you won't see many gay guys holding hands in the street—Brits are far too uptight for much of that!—Londoners are generally cool with the whole gay thang; hey, this is one of the most cosmopolitan cities in the world.

Arguably the best nightlife the world has got to offer—if you're a muscle Mary, an indie kid or a chubby chaser with a particular penchant for dolly disco, chances are you'll find it, or someone, here. The melting pot however is the legendary Heaven [see page 115]—after over 20 years in the business of gay business, it's still pulling in the punters, though it does put out for the straight/mixed crowds a couple of times a week. What makes London different is that unlike other destinations, it's not so much about your body as it is your face, your clothes and how well connected you are. [See page 114]

07 Paris

Not only is Paris blessed with being the most "romantic city in the world," after London it is home to the biggest gay scene in Europe with over 200 joints to choose from including the legendary Le Queen club and Le Central bar. While most gay men here sport crew cuts and are gym-toned, the gay scene is hardly in your face, and the majority of Parisians just don't want it rubbed in theirs, even if they don't give a damn what you get up to.

The gay area is now the Marais district. It dates back to the 16th and 17th centuries when it was a Jewish area, though its arrival as a gay ghetto started in the late 80s when it took over from the quartier Sainte-Anne, home to Paris' first gay club which opened there in 1956. Across town, Saint-Germain has been home to many lesbian literary lesbian legends like Nathalie Barney, Janet Flanner, Sylvia Beach and Adrienne Monnier.

Meanwhile, the famous Pere Lachaise Cemetery, located in the 20th arrondissement, is the final resting place for several gay celebrities including Gertrude Stein, Alice B. Toklas and Oscar Wilde.

08 Amsterdam

Whether or not it really is the "Gay Capital Of Europe" as billed, Amsterdam is nevertheless one of the best places to be gay in the world. Like other gay cities, Amsterdam has long been welcoming anyone through its port. Add to that the fact that the Netherlands is the world's most tolerant country and you have a city that can promise all kinds of action for gay men—despite its mere 750,000 population. The Reguliersdwarsstraat caters to the muscle Mary, the Warmoesstraat to the leather queen and the Amstel to everyone else, though the scene doesn't necessarily translate to women who love women. [See page 118]

03 Provincetown

At the very tip of Cape Cod, jutting far out into the Atlantic, Provincetown, or P'town as it is fondly known, is uniquely stunning as it's surrounded by the Atlantic on one side and Cape Cod Bay on the other—with Boston just across the water. Once an artists' colony, now you'll be hard pushed to find so many gay men and lesbians in such a small place anywhere else in the world. Hardly a party town, it is instead on the homey side with bars and clubs closing early, not a whiff of drugs and gay guesthouses hardly likely to offer you the opportunity to get laid by the hot tub.

04 New York & Fire Island

The birthplace of gay liberation, New York is without a doubt a gay Mecca. Home to Truman Capote, Andy Warhol, Robert Mapplethorpe, and pretty much every other key gay mover and shaker from the last century, it's legendary though, if truth be told, the vision has begun to fade somewhat in recent years thanks to the "clean-up" policies of former mayor, Rudy Giuliani. Historically, Greenwich Village has been the center of New York's gay life though in recent years, Chelsea has become the area to cruise, have lunch, work out and buy some gay schmutter. [See page 111]

Fire Island, meanwhile, is a gay holiday village, which starts to see some action from Memorial Day. To be honest, there's not much here—not even a bank—but over the past couple of decades, it's become the gay equivalent of the Hamptons, with the most action happening around Gay Pride, Memorial and Labor Days, the motorcycle run in the second weekend in September and the Miss Fire Island drag queen competition. Infamous too are the tea dances at the Yacht Club, and the cruising area known as the Judy Garland Memorial Park.

05 San Jose, Costa Rica

Costa Rica is fast becoming a gay holiday destination par excellence. A pocket of democracy in the middle of Central America, it has an international reputation for tolerance, so not only does it offer everything geographically from volcanoes and rainforests to miles of beaches, but—shock, horror—it even has a gay scene. San Jose, its capital city, is the home to several discos and more than a dozen gay bars. A well kept secret about to come out.

01 San Francisco

Arguably the gayest city in the world, San Fran has a history of politicism, radicalism and tolerance. Even before Stonewall, the gay community got its first taste of power here when four people were acquitted after the Council on Religion and the Homosexual's New Year's Eve dance was raided by the police in 1964. Since then gay San Franciscans have run with it, first with Harvey Milk [see page 94] and then AIDS activism. It's a city that celebrates its gay community and without it, it wouldn't function properly. Gay men and women are out and proud throughout the city—and not just in the Castro, the city's world famous gay ghetto. [See page 106]

02 Key West, Florida

While Miami's South Beach offers Euro-glamor, Key West, a three-hour drive away, is a more traditional, homey resort with good restaurants, a laidback vibe and one of the world's largest and most varied collections of hotels and b & b's targeted at the gay traveller. It was once *the* gay holiday resort, but is now rivalled by the likes of Provincetown and others further afield. It isn't big on beaches, but all the action takes place along the Old Town's main drag, Duval Street and around the pools and hot tubs of its guesthouses. No attitude and—get this!—no body fascism either.

12 Mykonos

The gayest of the Greek islands, Mykonos is a picture-postcard island once popular with upper class Greek folk before the gays got hold of it. Admittedly, it's not 100 percent gay, but the combination of a laissez-faire attitude, a party-by-the-sea atmosphere and guaranteed sun sees us returning again and again. There are a lot of gay clubs and bars, like the infamous O'Pierros, and heavy cruising on the beaches and through the labyrinth of streets around Panagia Paraportiani church at night.

13 Lesbos

The third largest and one of the most lush of the Greek islands is where dykes come to pay homage to legendary lesbian and poet Sappho, whose reputation has given the word "lesbian" an international currency. The 15th August sees a proliferation of ladies' events at Eressos, home of Sappho, but women visiting at other times have been bemused at the lack of lesbian activity and are not always welcomed with open arms by the local community. Before you ask, people from Lesbos are called Lesbians.

14 Ibiza

This Balearic Island first established itself as an alternative holiday destination in the 70s when it was home to a rag-tag bunch of bohemians and artists. It's since become Europe's party central with superclubs like Space and Pacha, which are generally straight or mixed, and imported gay club nights like Trade. Gay folk do the old town and port area, leaving the rest of the island to low-rent and E-ed up British tourists. Calle de la Virgen is home to a slew of gay bars, Anfora is the island's only gay club and Playa Es Cavallet its most famous gay beach where anything goes. If you like E and men with big tits, you'll be sorted.

15 Cape Town

Since 1996, discrimination on the basis of sexual orientation has been banned here and the gay community in the "Mother City"—always the country's most liberal area—has become more and more visible. As a gay holiday destination, it's right up there with Sydney and San Francisco, since it offers the winning combination of beach, culture and geographic beauty. Most of the action takes place by the sea courtesy of the Sea Point and Green Point neighborhoods and the Camps Bay beaches. On the downside however, crime is high and so is the rate of HIV infection, with 1,600 new cases a day—yes, a day—in the region.

16 Tokyo

With a Buddhist background, there are no prohibitions about homosexuality in Japan, though with minorities largely unrecognised in the country, many Japanese people don't actually believe gay people exist! The scene therefore is mainly covert, but in the increasingly Americanized Tokyo, it's live and kicking in downtown Shinjuku's Ni-Chome district which boasts more than 200 gay bars, including the long-established Kinsmen and Arty Farty, though some of them are indeed very small. Ni-Chome is, however, highly frequented by "gaigen" (foreigners) and Japanese gay men who dig them.

17 Bangkok

Thailand's gay scene has mainly been manufactured by Westerners. While Thais do not make any moral judgment about being gay, it's generally accepted that you will settle down and have a family, however, like elsewhere in the world there is an increasing group of people who identify as gay. Much more accepted is cross-dressing, hence the proliferation of lady boys or 'katoeys' as they're known, whose shows aren't restricted to gay audiences.

The majority of gay places are around the trendy Silom/Suriwong/Patpong area though Silom Soi 2 works for the dance crowd. Venues divide between non-commercial (bars and clubs) and commercial (go-go bars, lounges, karaoke bars and massage/sauna establishments) where sex workers are available. However, due to the 2001 crackdown on living it up, most of the go-go bars are now closing by 2am and no longer have sex shows!

18 Sydney

Not only are gays, transgendered folk and those with HIV/AIDS protected against discrimination and vilification in New South Wales, but Sydney is home to the largest population of gay people in Australasia. Mardi Gras is the city's Unique Selling Point, which sees its gay strip, Oxford Street, cordoned off for the annual parade. While there are gay suburbs like Darlinghurst (through which Oxford Street runs) and the rattier Newtown, all with their own fair share of bars, clubs and vibes, it's the dance parties like Mardi Gras, Sleaze Ball and Pride which will have Sydney gays out in force. [See page 117]

09 Sitges

Half-an-hour away from Barcelona, Sitges is one of Europe's most famous gay resorts, particularly during the summer months—though don't be too surprised if you're working a thong right next to a Spanish family of four. Home to over 20 gay bars and the renowned Trailer nightclub—check out its foam parties—it also has a couple of gay beaches, one in town in front of the Calipolis Hotel, and the other, a nude one, a couple of miles south of the town where folk cruise in the woods behind.

10 Gran Canaria

Top destination on Gran Canaria is undoubtedly Playa del Ingles, home to the gay and nudie beaches, cruisey Maspalomas dunes and the infamous concrete Yumbo centre, which is full of gay bars, restaurants, sex shops and the like. Hardly the most beautiful of gay resorts (Spain had a thing for concrete in the 70s), it appeals to a real mix of gay men (and a few lesbians), probably due to the fact it's dirt cheap.

11 Tangiers

Until 1956, Tangiers was an international zone with loose tax laws, a free port, and an atmosphere of moral permissiveness. No wonder it was attractive to ex-pats like Tennessee Williams, Truman Capote, and Joe Orton, whose adventures are partly responsible for its gay rep. Although there's an old Moroccan proverb: "Women for marriage, boys for love" and a silent tolerance of homosexual acts, the city is Islamic and even men who've had same-sex experiences wouldn't class themselves as "gay," let alone "out."

NYC

If you can't make it there, you can't make it anywhere

Before former Mayor Rudy Giuliani was canonized in the light of the September 11th tragedy, he was largely credited with closing down gay New York. The dance clubs that had led the world were swooped on for drugs and noise offences, while he is alleged to have paid informers to infiltrate gay sex clubs to report on them so that the city could force them to close. Dens of iniquity like The Eagle and The Spike that had been world famous since the early 70s vanished, either because of pressure or due to the introduction of stringent rules about what you could and couldn't get up to, meaning the clientele had no real reason to go anymore. What had been the best city on earth for gay men started to slide down the table of gay cities.

As the birthplace of gay liberation [see page 87], you just know that New York was rocking before most other cities. With establishments like The Aston Bathhouse that date back to the turn of the century (and the Anston was a proper bathhouse, "for the purposes of sodomy," according to one contemporary report), established cruising grounds in Bryant Park by the 1920s and recognized places for sailors to come and get themselves seen to, like The Times Square Building, New York's underground gay scene was swinging even before most of its landmarks were built.

The huge city offered anonymity and, in a country which is still very religious, a relief from the constraints of small town life. Add to that the vibrant theater and arts scene and you've got a honeypot tempting gay men and women from all

over the world. By the end of the Second World War, during which many gay men and women had tasted the freedom of being away from home in New York City, a lot of demobbed service-people decided to stay in the city and start a new life of sexual adventure. The area around Greenwich Village, already popular with bohemians who were unlikely to object to a little light same-sex action, became "the gay area," although gay bars and amenities were still very much an undercover thing.

By the late 60s, with the whole hippy movement well under way, and New York's first gay bookshop and fledgling gay rights movement starting to make inroads, it was high time for the gay community, which had never actually thought of itself like that, to go overground. After Stonewall, the town became the spiritual and political home for gay men and women throughout the world. Gay artists like Warhol were already operating there, gay writers like Truman Capote were based there and—thanks to the art and theater scene—there was never any shortage of new blood.

By the 70s, New York was a gay Babylon. Sex clubs like The Spike started to proliferate, while the gay ghetto burst its Greenwich Village confines and started to spread to Chelsea. And then in the early 80s came AIDS. Much of the progress gay men and women had made seemed to evaporate overnight. While in the 70s clubs like Studio 54 actively sought to have a huge gay

contingent because that's who the famous and the fabulous wanted to hang with, in the 80s the tide started to turn and paranoia reigned. Many of the guys who had made up the brilliant sex scene, among them artists like Robert Mapplethorpe whose photographs reflected the hardcore leather clubs he went to, were getting sick and though they were organizing [see page 90], the life had been kicked out of gay New York. But it hadn't rolled over yet. Sleaze houses like the now legendary Adonis Theater on 8th Avenue where you could see some strippers, buy a big old tub of Crisco and then do the strippers or members of the audience, were still operating and busy, while gay nights like Bump and The Roxy flourished and über-clubs like Twilo and The Tunnel were still to come.

And then came Rudy. With his mandate to clean up New York, Giuliani set about creating the circumstances that would spell the end of the road for some of the best-loved gay establishments in the world. Now New York's gay scene is a shadow of its former self with London and Sydney hosting the huge dance clubs that used to be New York's stock-in-trade. Obviously, on many levels, New York is still as gay as it ever was—those people didn't just go away—and there are vibrant gay neighborhoods. There are even glossy new gay bars like G and Splash and XL, and the edgier establishments—Cock, Fat Cock—of the East Village. But the glory days of gay New York are over. For the time being.

▷ **Take it further:** Like People In History by *Felice Picano;* The Golden Age of

Map #2

Where you can and can't do the gay thing, and the penalties you could face

10 Netherlands
Age of consent for gay men: 16
Age of consent for lesbians: 16
An equal age of consent is just the start of Holland's exemplary record of gay and lesbian rights and it wins hands down as the most tolerant and accepting country in the world. With a law banning discrimination in all areas, allowing gay men and women to serve in the military (and letting them engage in sexual acts off duty and away from military premises) and granting non-Dutch partners residency, it seems that the Netherlands can do no wrong. As well as their partnerships being completely equal to straight marriages, gay couples are also allowed to adopt children. In fact, there are no remaining anti-gay or lesbian laws on the Dutch statute books. Period.

11 Algeria
Age of consent for gay men: illegal
Age of consent for lesbians: illegal
Homosexual activity being illegal is punishable with up to three years imprisonment, as well as a fine of up to 10,000 Algerian dinars, which is roughly US$130.

12 Egypt
Age of consent for gay men: 18
Age of consent for lesbians: 18
There is some dubious wording on the statute books, including "offences against public morals and sensitivities," which could be used against gay men and women, but the age of consent is set at 18 for all. While Egypt has an unimpressive record of deporting HIV-positive visitors, it does allow sex change operations for its citizens.

The highest profile case of anti-gay discrimination took place with the "Cairo 52" trial in May 2001. Police raided the Queen Boat disco, and arrested 52 men for "obscene behavior," with two of the men being accused of acting as ringleaders of a homosexual "cult."

The arrests, and subsequent trial have been viewed as a crackdown on the country's increasingly visible gay community by a government who are keen to be seen to uphold Islamic law. Allegations from the men's lawyers include beatings, electroshock therapy and abuse.

13 Kenya
Age of consent for gay men: illegal
Age of consent for lesbians: not mentioned
Homosexual activity is punishable with between five and 14 years in jail.

14 Zimbabwe
Age of consent for gay men: illegal
Age of consent for lesbians: illegal
Homophobia and bigotry in Zimbabwe has been supported and led by President Mugabe, whose rants against all things queer have included stating that homosexuality is not an African phenomenon, but Western decadence. Among those that have been prosecuted and imprisoned for their gayness is the country's first President, the improbably named Mr Banana. Despite the anti-gay hatred being peddled by Mugabe and his followers, gay groups are incredibly active within the country and have even won several lawsuits against the government.

05 Argentina
Age of consent for gay men: 16
Age of consent for lesbians: 16
The cities of Buenos Aires and Rosario have gay rights laws that ban discrimination against gay men and women. However, nationally the police still have the discretion to apply their own edicts, one of which, the Edict Against Public Dancing, has been used to prosecute proprietors who allow men to dance together in their establishments.

06 Denmark
Age of consent for gay men: 15
Age of consent for lesbians: 15
One of Europe's star turns when it comes to homo equality. Not only does Denmark boast an equal age of consent, it also allows its queer couples to register their partnership and enjoy the same rights as married heteros, as well as offering residency to foreign partners of Danish gay men and women. It also allows gay men and women to serve in the military and has anti-discrimination laws covering employment.

07 Germany
Age of consent for gay men: 14
Age of consent for lesbians: 14
Huge reforms have been made in Germany since 1998, when the Social Democrat and Green Party coalition came to power. As well as an equal age of consent, gay couples can also register their partnership. In addition, German nationality is on offer to non-resident partners and there are even a few parental rights. Gay men and women can also serve in the military, but not at officer or instructor level.

08 Belgium
Age of consent for gay men: 16
Age of consent for lesbians: 16
Belgium, like its neighbor Holland, allows gay men and women to serve in the armed forces. It also boasts a "Statutory Cohabitation Contract" which is available to two adults who are not married or legally contracted, regardless of their gender.

09 Hungary
Age of consent for gay men: 18
Age of consent for lesbians: 18
While the state recommends that gay men should not become teachers or soldiers, the Hungarian Constitutional Court legalized "common law" gay marriage in 1995, making it the first Eastern European country to extend partnership rights to gay men and women.

01 Canada
Age of consent for gay men: 18 for anal sex, 14 for all the other stuff
Age of consent for lesbians: 14
While British Columbia offers queer couples the same rights as straight couples living together, the rest of the country has yet to follow suit.

02 USA
Despite the U S of A boasting some of the world's gayest cities, according to the human rights group Amnesty International, the following states or provinces ban gay sex: Alabama, Florida (ironically home to 'gayville' Key West [see page 108]), Miami, Idaho, Kansas, Louisiana, Massachusetts (where you'll find gay favorite Provincetown [see page 108]), Michigan, Minnesota, Mississippi, Missouri, North Carolina, Oklahoma, Puerto Rico, South Carolina, Texas, Utah, and Virginia.

03 Jamaica
Age of consent for gay men: Illegal
Age of consent for lesbians: not mentioned
With its deeply Christian beliefs, it looks unlikely that Jamaica's laws against homosexuality will change soon. However, gay groups have been set up in this country that punishes sodomy with up to 10 years' imprisonment, including hard labor.

04 Costa Rica
Age of consent for gay men: 15
Age of consent for lesbians: 15
Its popularity as a queer vacation hotspot has managed to upset a few of Costa Rica's Catholic priests, but the country still manages to extend a warm welcome to gay and lesbian holidaymakers.

19 Ethiopa
Age of consent for gay men: illegal
Age of consent for lesbians: illegal
Homosexual activity is punishable with a penalty of between 10 days to three years 'simple imprisonment'.

20 Bahrain
Age of consent for gay men: illegal
Age of consent for lesbians: illegal
Bahrain's laws against "unnatural sexual offences" means that gay men and women are punishable with imprisonment, not exceeding 10 years. This may include corporal punishment.

23 Pakistan
Age of consent for gay men: illegal
Age of consent for lesbians: illegal
Homosexual action is punishable with between two years and life in jail, while Islamic laws can also be called upon to dish out a sentence of death by stoning, or 100 lashes. However, in the Northwest Frontier, Pathan culture allows men to have other men as lovers.

24 Bhutan
Age of consent for gay men: illegal
Age of consent for lesbians: illegal
Sex between two men is punishable with a maximum sentence of life in jail.

21 Iran
Age of consent for gay men: illegal
Age of consent for lesbians: illegal
Iran has adopted the ultra-strict Shari'a Law, which sees homosexuality as one of the worst possible sins that one could commit. Those found guilty of committing sodomy have one of four death penalties chosen for them by the judge—being hanged, stoned, halved by sword or dropped from the highest perch. What's more, if two men, not related by blood, are found naked under one cover without good reason, they will be punished at the judge's discretion. And it's not just the gay boys in trouble with the lawmakers. The punishment for lesbianism is 100 lashes, but if the act is repeated and tried in court three times, the death sentence is passed. As with gay boys, if women are found naked under one cover, they will be punished with up to 100 lashes.

15 Somalia
Age of consent for gay men: illegal
Age of consent for lesbians: not known
With its penal code based loosely on Shari'a Law, gay boys face between two months and two years in jail. Rules regarding lesbianism are unclear. However, a case came to light in 2001 of a lesbian couple being sentenced to death on the grounds of "exercising unnatural behavior."

16 Uganda
Age of consent for gay men: illegal
Age of consent for lesbians: not mentioned
With gay boys going down for a maximum of life, it's hardly surprising that Uganda's President called for the arrest of homos for their "abominable acts."

17 Botswana
Age of consent for gay men: illegal
Age of consent for lesbians: Illegal
Homosexual conduct is punishable with up to seven years in jail.

18 South Africa
Age of consent for gay men: 19
Age of consent for lesbians: 19
Despite its unequal age of consent, with hetero sex at 16 and gay sex at 19, South Africa stands apart from other African countries with its stance on equal rights for gay men and women. With legislation banning discrimination in the areas of employment and adoption rights, as well as the inclusion of queer youth in all youth programs, it looks like the rest of Africa could learn a lot from its southernmost state.

22 Afghanistan
Age of consent for gay men: illegal
Age of consent for lesbians: illegal
Since the Taliban government seized power in 1996—a fact that was frowned upon but largely ignored by the West until the events of September 11th 2001—human rights of any description have been removed from Afghanistan's statute books due to the Taliban's unique interpretation of Islamic Shari'a laws, the rules of conduct set out by the Koran. If women aren't even allowed to ride a bicycle—and this really is no joking matter—then you can imagine that acts of homosexuality aren't up there on Mullah Mohammed Omar's list of favorite pastimes. In March 1998 two young men accused of sodomy were buried alive in the city of Herat, while just a month earlier three men found guilty of the same "crime" were punished by having a stone wall collapsed onto them. Miraculously, they survived the initial 30-minute burial, so according to the Taliban law, they were free to go. However, two of the men later died in hospital. These are just two of the regime's infringements on human rights.

25 Bangladesh
Age of consent for gay men: illegal
Age of consent for lesbians: illegal
A sodomy law includes punishment of fines, along with 10 years to life imprisonment.

26 India
Age of consent for gay men: illegal
Age of consent for lesbians: unknown
Section 377 of the Indian Penal Code treats sodomy, buggery and bestiality as equal crimes with sentences ranging between a 10-year sentence and life in jail. Because of section 377, Indian jails refuse to distribute condoms to inmates, and with the numbers of Indians with HIV/AIDS growing rapidly, and still no sex education in schools, the epidemic is already hitting the country hard.

27 Singapore
Age of consent for gay men: illegal
Age of consent for lesbians: legal in private!
As well as outlawing the chewing of gum in public, the ultimate nanny state punishes homosexual acts with life in jail.

28 Brunei
Age of consent for gay men: illegal
Age of consent for lesbians: illegal
Brunei's sodomy law has a penalty of up to 10 years in jail, or a fine of up to 30,000 Brunei dollars.

*All figures correct at the time of going to press.

London

A gay social history

1533: During Henry VIII's reign, a law was passed to make buggery an offence under English criminal law. It survived in various forms until 1967, though it was amended in 1861, changing death penalties and forfeiture of property to life imprisonment.

Late 1600s: The first real details of homosexual behavior were recorded thanks to the Societies for the Reformation of Manners, a network of "moral guardians" who gathered the names and addresses of offenders against morality.

Theaters were widely recorded as being "frequented by sodomites" and diarist Samuel Pepys wrote: "Sir J Jemmes and Mr Batten both say that buggery is now almost grown as common among our gallants as in Italy."

Early 1700s: Raids were organized by the Societies for Reformation of Manners on "molly" houses—pubs and clubs where gay men met, especially on Sunday nights. On "Festival Nights," they'd even drag up, dance and sing.

Cruising grounds were called "Markets" and could be found in Smithfields, Covent Garden and Lincoln's Inn Fields where the toilets—or bog houses—saw a lot of action. Gay men were already using the terms "pick up" and "trade" while lesbians were known as "tommies."

1709: A prosecution proved that gay men were regarded as part of a subculture and as a different "kind of people."

1726: Margaret Clap was indicted for keeping a molly house in the City of London. The raid on her house also led to three men being hanged at Tyburn, though Mother Clap was sentenced to stand in the pillory in Smithfield market, to pay a fine of 20 marks, and to two years' imprisonment.

1732: London's first recorded drag queen was gentlemen's servant and hustler John Cooper, aka Princess Seraphina, who came to light when he accused another queer of stealing his clothes.

Late 1700s: Lesbian marriages and "female husbands" were known to exist. Sculptor and amateur actress Anne Damer (1749-1848), probably the most famous lesbian of the time, wore men's clothes and her closest lover was Mary Berry, later Horace Walpole's literary executor, with whom she travelled abroad and lived in the Gothic folly Strawberry Hill.

Early 1800s: Evidence exists that in some molly houses there were "marrying rooms" where men could be "married," though this sometimes just meant having sex. There are records of at least half a dozen gay couples, who lived together for long periods.

The Reverend John Church became the first duly ordained minister to celebrate gay rites of Holy Matrimony and presided over ceremonies at the White Swan in Vere Street. In 1816, he was found guilty of attempted sodomy on a 19-year-old servant. There was some public outcry with a huge mob burning his effigy outside his home; however, after 730 days in jail, he returned to preach at his church in Dover Street.

1889: The public learned of a male prostitution ring whose clients included English aristocrats and a member of the Royal Family. The "scandal on Cleveland Street" created a public outcry and saw a real rise in anti-gay sentiment, which culminated in the prosecution of Oscar Wilde six years later.

1920s: Theatrical pubs and members' clubs started appearing, hiding behind a veneer of respectability by featuring drag artists.

1930s: The Gateways, aka The Gates, opened in Chelsea, becoming the longest-running gay women's club in British history. You can see it on film in the 1968 movie, *The Killing Of Sister George*.

1950s: Members' bars and clubs multiplied in Soho and Fitzrovia, becoming much less covert. One of the most famous was Soho's Colony Room frequented by Francis Bacon [see page 216] and other artists. However, after the infamous 1953-54 Montagu case, in which Lord Montagu of Beaulieu and a number of other men were charged with unnatural offences, the police stepped up a campaign to "rip the covers off all London's filth spots," encouraging arrests for homosexual offences.

1960s: Gay men benefit from the change in climate brought about by the civil rights movements and the idea of a "counterculture," which meant sex was now being discussed more openly.

1967: Amendments to the Sexual Offences Act meant gay sex between two men over 21 in private was decriminalized and led to a surge of new gay bars.

1970: After a meeting in the London School of Economics, the London Gay Liberation Front was founded on October 13th with the first gay demonstration held in Highbury Fields, Islington.

1971: The Gay Liberation Front held the first open gay dance at Kensington Town Hall followed by the first gay march through London against the unequal age of consent for gay men.

1972: The first national gay newspaper in the UK, *Gay News*, was launched while July that year saw the first Pride.

1974: London Lesbian and Gay Switchboard starts the first 24-hour line.

Late 1970s: The gay scene intensifies around Old Compton Street with cafés, bars, clubs and fetish boutiques.

1980: Heaven, London's first all-week gay club, opened underneath the arches at Charing Cross.

1982: Gay emporium Clone Zone was opened.

1987: Gay and lesbian newspaper the *Pink Paper* was founded.

1991: *Boyz* magazine is launched, soon to become the biggest gay magazine in Europe, pioneering a new era in gay identity: less political, more self-assured and hedonistic. All the while, Soho was further establishing itself as the city's central gay district, first with the Village, a European-style venue, then a slew of copycat gay bars and cafés.

1992: G.A.Y started on Spectrum Radio, which later translated into the extremely popular nightclub, the hot ticket for Saturday night.

1993: The Age of Consent was reduced to the age of 18, from 21.

1996: The first 'Summer Rites,' an alternative to Pride, took place in Kennington Park, attracting 25,000 people.

1997: The world's first Lesbian Beauty contest took place in London.

1998: Pride 98 was cancelled after poor ticket sales, but an informal event went ahead nevertheless in the streets of Soho.

1999: The Admiral Duncan pub in Soho was targeted in April by nail bomber and self-confessed fascist, David Copeland.

Early 2000s: London has established itself as the gay capital of Europe, if not the world. Together with Soho in the center, there's a gay scene in the south between Vauxhall and Clapham and a lesbian scene in the east around Islington and Stoke Newington. You'd be hard pushed to find the variety of nights, bars and clubs anywhere else; London boasts indie nights, bhangra clubs, muscle Mary fare… well, you name it, it's there.

Sydney

It's big down under!

It's gaudy and trashy, yet it's also classy and beautiful. Like most cities, Sydney is a contradiction in itself, but as a gay destination, it's pretty hard to beat since it combines those guaranteed crowd-pleasers, sun, sea, and sex.

Melbourne might give it a run for its money, but Sydney has the largest gay population in Australia and anywhere in South East Asia. A melting pot of cultures and vibes, it's a draw not only as a holiday destination but as somewhere to emigrate since it boasts strong anti-discrimination laws and rights for gay partners. Same-sex sex is completely legal (the age of consent is currently 16 for women but 18 for men, though it's under review) while those with AIDS and HIV are also protected by law All in all, the gay community is highly visible, audible and—get this!—treasured, even if you only need to travel an hour or so out of the city to find that prejudice is alive and kicking.

Gay people live all across the city, though there are specifically gay suburbs like Darlinghurst and Newtown as well as Leichhardt (also known as "Dykeheart") and Glebe, the latter two favored by lesbians.

Darlinghurst, aka, Darlo, a stone's throw from downtown, is where Oxford Street, the city's main gay drag, runs. Pre-1970s, gay men used to hang in nearby Kings Cross but ironically the straight sleaze pushed them out, as did the heroin.

Oxford Street is where Muriel worked in the video store in *Muriel's Wedding*, and throughout the day its many cafés are ideal for checking out the local talent while at night it sees gay men and women out in force at its many gay bars and clubs. The two-floored Oxfords (with its upstairs cocktail lounge, Gilligans) is legendary as is the Albury Hotel, home to nightly dragstravaganzas though new pretenders like The Stonewall Hotel and dance club Arq are certainly becoming the institutions of the moment.

Across town, the rattier Newtown has a different vibe entirely—and is even more laid back. Its main drag is King Street, is home to students, twentysomethings, feral folk and the big ol' Newtown Hotel, a friendly gay pub. The area also boasts the Imperial Hotel, as seen in the send-off scene in *The Adventures of Priscilla, Queen Of The Desert* [see page 144] and yes, it still celebrates the fact with tribute shows.

Sydney probably begs comparison with San Francisco—after all they're both on the water, have landmark bridges, views to die for and… the list goes on—however the vibe is very, very different. While San Francisco is radical and political, Sydney is laid back and dare we say it, shallow. The emphasis is on pecs and sex, drugs and drag, and it really lets loose with annual dance parties like Mardi Gras, the down 'n' dirtier Sleaze Ball, and the new year Pride, but like, since when was that a bad thing?

Sydney Mardi Gras

Sydney prides itself as a party city and while it does the business throughout the year, its big night out is Mardi Gras, the first Saturday in March.

The largest street event in Australia, it started in June 1978 to commemorate the Stonewall riots and although it's hardly a political event any more, it does hammer home its core message of reclaiming the streets.

The parade sees Oxford Street, the city's main gay drag, cordoned off for a three-hour parade, which starts at its foot and culminates at Fox Studios. Cue dykes on bikes, dragmobiles, jaw-dropping floats and acres of near naked flesh of a highly toned nature—. As many as half a million spectators turn up to check out what is the city's number one tourist draw and at its close, 22,000 of them head off to party hard in five halls until 8am—punctuated only by the biggest and most OTT shows (think Baz Luhrman on LSD) and a performance from the diva of the day, though everyone always assumes it's gonna be Kylie. Drugs, toned bodies, and skimpy costumes are near-on obligatory.

Yet Mardi Gras is far from being a one-night only event. The parties along Oxford Street can run for a couple of days after and the event is preceded by a month-long cultural festival, which showcases the best in local and overseas gay and lesbian arts, as well as sure-fire punter-pulling affairs like handbag tossing on Bondi Beach. No wonder that the whole gay population is a little hazy and more than a bit depressed when it all comes to an end.

Amsterdam

Drugs, dijks and gay rights in Holland's second city

The Netherlands, or Holland as it is also known, is one of the most tolerant countries in the world. With an impressive gay rights record, as well as the legalisation of cannabis and workers rights for prostitutes on its statute books, it's set a precedent for other countries with not so liberal laws.

Amsterdam, with a population of just 750,000, has had a long and colorful history—since the 15th century it's been welcoming immigrants from all over the world and it's this tolerance and acceptance of 'others' that has helped it to become a mini version of San Francisco. Except the weather ain't so good.

Europe's own gay Mecca that never feels like a ghetto attracts queer travelers from all over the world who flock to its melting hotpot of sex, drugs, beer and culture against a backdrop of cutesy canals. They may have put sodomizers to death back in the 18th century, but the gay men and women living in this tiny city are now fully integrated into its daily goings on. Sure, there's a great gay scene, especially if you're partial to a bit of leather, but Amsterdam's promotion of tolerance, equality and acceptance means that being gay really is no big deal. Gay men and women serve in the government, in the armed forces and are allowed to officially register their same-sex marriages, and in doing so receive the same benefits as straight couples. And if you're partial to a bit of homo discrimination, you'd better watch your back—anyone seen to be discriminating against gay men and women here faces harsh penalties enforced by law.

With its stance on homos verging on positive discrimination, the city's queer scene has matured over the years and the pleasures available, mainly to the boys, are pretty much endless. Whether you're into pecs, a bit of leather and

rubber or tranny boys, your needs are catered for. With its hardcore sex and leather scene—which quite easily rivals the daddy of all leather scenes in San Fran—jostling for space on the Warmoesstraat with the Red Light District's prostitutes' windows, Amsterdam's queer and sex hot spots, along with its infamous "coffeeshops" that offer the finest marijuana ready-rolled for $10 a joint, have become something of an alternative tourist draw for the city. Some of the highlights include The Cuckoo's Nest, which boasts Europe's largest "playroom" in its basement (and no, we're not talking climbing frames and trampolines), the Argos's cellar complete with sling and cabins, and the Cockring, whose moniker serves it well. There are even nightly jack-off parties held at The Stablemaster Hotel, so if the cannabis at queer coffeeshop The Otherside, the slings, and Dutch beer-and-boys aren't enough for you, then you can get down to some do-it-yourself action in the company of strangers.

For lesbians, as per, the choice isn't so hot. The COC (pronounced "say-oh-say"), the Dutch Association for the Integration of Homosexuality with a branch located in nearly every town in Holland, is the best bet for girl-on-girl action, as well as for information on all things queer such as club nights for the boys. The association's aims include supplying information on lesbian and gay issues and working with politicians to further the gains reached by queers in Holland. It boasts the most extensive queer social network in the country. Along with its lesbian-only club nights, the COC offers all manner of services to the city's queer residents—from afternoon socials for the city's older gay gentlemen and ladies to Alcoholics Anonymous meetings, S&M parties and free legal advice, it seems that the COC has got the whole Dutch queer thing stitched up.

The Homomonument

As if to prove its gay-friendly ways even further, Amsterdam also boasts the world's only official commemoration of lesbians and gay men who were oppressed and killed in the Second World War at the hands of the Nazis. The Homomonument, on the Keizergracht Canal at Westermarkt, was designed by Karin Daan, and as well as remembering those who died, also it is seen as a celebration of tolerance and hope. Made up of three huge pink granite triangles that represent the past, present and future of gay liberation, one of its tips points out into the canal towards the Liberation Monument that remembers all those who died, while another other tip nods in the direction of the nearby Anne Frank House—the former hiding place and home of the young Dutch Jewish girl who, along with her family, hid from the Nazis during their invasion of Holland, and whose diaries have sold millions of copies globally.

The Homomonument was unveiled in 1987 after nine years in the making, and in addition to being home to the odd bunch of flowers and sodden rainbow flag, also it attracts queer tourists to the city without fail, especially during the city's Pride festivities.

If you're in the city between June and August, check out the Pink Point of Presence (or the PPP, said "pay-pay-pay") nearby—a cutesy booth that offers queer information about all the fun to be had in the city, copies of Holland's queer publications, and free advice.

YOUR HANDY CUT-OUT-AND-KEEP GLOBAL GAY PRIDE CALENDAR

From banner waving and whistle blowing to partying al fresco in the streets, gay pride events have become de rigeur globally

Since those naughty drag queens, butch dykes et al fought off the police in New York City in 1969 [see page 87], Gay Pride has become an annual event in cities and towns all over the world. The first-ever Gay Pride march took place in New York in June 1970, a year after the riots, with 2,000 people stomping their way from Greenwich Village to Central Park. The city's March and Pride events now attract over 750,000 every year to its streets. London's first placard-waving event was in November 1970, organized by the Gay Liberation Front (GLF) on a Friday night and attended by 80 members of the group. London experienced its first official Gay Pride March on 1st July 1972 with 2,000 lesbians and gay men marching through the heart of the city to Hyde Park. London's Pride March and now attracts upward of 100,000 revellers.

While between 8-10 million people attend gay, lesbian, bisexual and transgender Pride events in the States and Canada each year, with three million in Europe and two million in Australia and New Zealand, it's the birth and presence of Pride marches in countries not known for their tolerance of homosexuality that continues to evoke the true spirit of "gay pride" and "gay strength." San Francisco's massive party might attract over one million revellers and inject over $150 million into the local economy, but there was a more political vibe for Pride-goers in Tel Aviv, Israel, in 2001 when both Israelis and Palestinians, dressed in black, linked arms and showed their opposition to the Israeli occupation of the West Bank and Gaza.

Pride is everything for all queers, from drag queens in high heels and glittery performances from top pop stars, to serious political statements and good old fashioned police harassment. So, whether it's an alcohol-fuelled fun day out with your mates or placard-waving, whistle-blowing and consciousness-raising that's on your agenda, there's pretty much something queer and proud going on every month of the year around the world.

JANUARY
Melbourne, Australia

FEBRUARY
Sydney Mardi Gras, Australia
–one of Australia's major tourist attractions and sources of income.
Auckland, New Zealand

MARCH
Sydney Mardi Gras, Australia continues

APRIL
Phoenix, Arizona, USA

MAY
Birmingham, England
–the UK's second city's Pride event attracts thousands of homos.
Las Vegas, Nevada, USA
Brussels, Belgium

JUNE
Berlin, Germany
Caracas, Venezuela
–Caracas's first-ever Pride event took place in July 2001
Dallas, Texas, USA
Los Angeles Black Pride, California, USA
Milan, Italy
San Francisco, California, USA

JULY
London Mardi Gras, England
Los Angeles Black Pride, California, USA continues
St Petersburg, Russia
Ottawa, Ontario, Canada

AUGUST
Copenhagen, Denmark
Reykjavik, Iceland
Stockholm, Sweden
Tokyo, Japan

SEPTEMBER
Johannesburg, South Africa
–since the fall of apartheid, the event attracts over 10,000 people.

OCTOBER
Santa Barbara, California, USA

NOVEMBER
Bangkok, Thailand
Buenos Aires, Argentina

DECEMBER
Cape Town, South Africa
Pattaya, Thailand

The Way We Were

While the 20th century remains the gayest of them all, ye olden days have produced some of the world's most influential and important gay men, lesbians, and folk we like to call our own.

Know Your Enemy

The Christian 'New Right'

Since the 1970s, the Christian 'New Right' in the United States has not only grown in influence, numbers and financial might, but also in its hatred for the gay, lesbian and transgender communities. While Christian ministries' literature barely uttered the word "gay" in the 1960s, homosexuality—and all the evil "sexual doings" supposedly entrenched in its very being—has in recent years become an unhealthy obsession for groups such as Concerned Women for America, the American Family Association, and the Christian Coalition of America.

In the 1970s, the New Right networked furiously, turning itself into a multi-million dollar industry to be reckoned with. Coalitions of groups headed by charismatic figures like Pat Robertson and Jerry Falwell, were by the early 1980s using the latest technology to organize national groups in grassroots-style anti-homo initiatives. Sympathies were won on a lucrative national level by local communities that lashed out at the gays in their midst. By hiding the overtly religious tone of these campaigns with their 'main concern' for the promotion of the family, and by publishing literature that supposedly fairly examined the organizations, activities and the ideology of gay rights groups, they won the support of people whose beliefs were by no means fundamentalist.

The publications that they distributed were often re-worked and reproduced quickly to include topical issues such as the AIDS crisis, which the New Right suspected gay men and women were using for their own political gains. While spouting that gay

Gay rights groups in Britain such as Outrage! (right) have targeted the Church and its leaders, demanding not only that the Church accept homosexuals but also that it change its traditional bigoted laws

men and women "are loved by God as much as anyone else," the New Right was completely committed to fighting against homosexuals receiving any preferential treatment in the eyes of the law—"that would be tantamount to rewarding evil." The AIDS crisis of the mid-80s was used as serious rocket fuel by the hate-mongering groups—never had the

Christian Right been so vocal in its condemnation of homosexuality. During this period, the Right used arguments to attack what they saw as a liberal, overly sympathetic response to HIV/AIDS by the US Government. The old scare stories of gay men preying upon children and the so-called promotion of the gay lifestyle to school kids were spiced up, and fascistic suggestions made for persons with the virus—such as the tattooing of their status and enforced quarantine. For the religious Right, homosexuality was a sin, and AIDS was seen as a fit punishment for this "filthy" lifestyle.

While anti-abortion issues still managed to top the charts for the New Right, homosexuality in the 1990s seemed oh-so easy for the fundamentalists to attack—preying on people's fear and ignorance post-AIDS crisis, they produced videos featuring explicit gay sex to illustrate the 'decline of morality' in the US, and also garnered support for a new movement that was growing in popularity. The 'ex-gay' movement with its 'Conversion Therapy' "cure" for gay men and women pushed the New Right's anti-gay agenda onto even dodgier ground. It is only since the 1990s that the New Right has fully embraced Conversion Therapy, and the thinly-veiled rhetoric about protecting the family has become a relatively minor point now that the New Right can "treat" homosexuality with its version of Scripture. For years, the 'ex-gay' movement—an international network of ministries that claims it can "convert" homos into heteros through "submission to Jesus Christ"— had huge difficulties in convincing the New Right of its worth, since the leaders of the ex-gay ministries were, by definition, 'former homosexuals.'

As the Right's message of outright condemnation and damnation of homosexuals failed to produce further support for their cause, Conversion Therapy seemed the next logical step—caring words and support that cleverly shielded an agenda that included removing any kind of rights for lesbians and gay men. And with the official support for the ex-gay movement from a coalition of New Right groups came millions of dollars. In 1998, one of many new ex-gay advertisements appeared. A full-page ad appeared in the *New York Times* featuring

Anne Paulk—a mother, wife, and, get this, a former lesbian. Sporting a sparkling diamond engagement ring and fat wedding band, Anne claimed in the ad that just by accepting Jesus Christ into your life, you too could repent your sins—i.e., your gay lifestyle. These ads caused a huge controversy and sparked a media debate, propelling the ex-gay movement further than it could ever have dreamed of.

With impressive gains through anti-gay referenda in states like Oregon and Colorado, and the backing of the winning team in the 2000 American elections—effectively putting a halt to any future wins for lesbian and gay rights groups—the New Right has become a force to be reckoned with. No longer can the gay and lesbian community afford to sit back and laugh at the hateful quotes based on lies. The hokey local groups have turned around State votes. Even after the terrorist attacks in New York City on September 11th, 2001, when local politics and religion were seen as no-go areas and unity was supposedly the key, the New Right viciously launched into the gay and lesbian community—along with feminist and pro-choice groups—blaming their immorality for making the US a target for terrorists hell-bent on punishing America's sins.

Bigots To Watch Out For

Jess Helms
"If they had a father who was worth a damn, he would not have gotten AIDS."
On people with AIDS

God Hates Fags website
"Matthew Shepard has been in hell for 1123 days. Deal with it! All else is trivial and unimportant. All the fag caterwauling, candlelight vigils, court orders, etc., can't buy Matt one drop of water to cool his tongue."
On the killing of Matthew Shepard

Pat Robertson
"It's one thing to say, 'We have rights to jobs... we have rights to be left alone in our little corner of the world to do our thing.' It's an entirely different thing to say, well, 'We're not only going to go into the schools and we're going to take your children and your grandchildren and turn them into homosexuals.' Now that's wrong."
700 Club, September 17th, 1992

Jerry Falwell
"[Vice President Gore] recently praised the lesbian actress who plays 'Ellen' on ABC Television... I believe he may even put children, young people, and adults in danger by his public endorsement of deviant homosexual behavior... Our elected leaders are attempting to glorify and legitimize perversion."
People for the American Way, "Hostile Climate," 1998

Leviticus and the gay bits in the Bible
How the Bible has been used to condemn gay men and lesbians

"God Hates Fags," or so claimed the placards of the seething mass of protesters outside the funeral of gay-hate murder victim Matthew Shepard (see page 92). But what evidence is there for this? It's all in the Bible, those people will tell you. And it is, sort of. But just in the crazy bits and the bits that have been badly translated.

Jesus, surely the star at least of the New Testament, never mentions the subject of homosexuality at all while being very hot on the "thou shalt not judge" and the "love one another" approaches to one's neighbors that religious anti-gay protesters choose to ignore.

Even hardcore anti-gay Christians can only ever cite a maximum of four Bible passages which they claim condemn homosexuality. In fact, due to mistranslation, even those passages condemn then-contemporary social phenomena such as temple prostitution rather than your basic same-sex sexiness. In other parts of the Bible—Genesis 19:4-11 for instance—the Sin of Sodom is actually a sin of abuse rather than of homosexuality, sins that are even now often confused.

The Bible quote that nine out of ten anti-gay Christians prefer comes from a particularly barmy bit of the good book called Leviticus, a text created to lay down laws of hygiene for a people that was traveling around the desert with not so much as a Wet Wipe between them.

"You shall not lie with a male as one lies with a female; it is an abomination," says Saint Paul, the guy credited with turning Christianity from a religion based on love to one based on judgment. And while abomination sounds pretty heavy, don't forget the rule on laying down with males was tucked in alongside other laws regarding not eating shellfish, not letting ladies with periods near the temples, and not picking up sticks on a Sunday. The passage is, anyway, a code of holiness for Israelites who want to set themselves apart for special attention from the Lord. And that's not you, is it?

Other passages dragged out to condemn homosexuals come from Corinthians, where the simple mistranslation of the word "malakee" as "effeminate" instead of the intended "morally weak" (you can see the homophobia of the translators, who had their own agendas) has been corralled into divine condemnation, and from Timothy where "arsenokeeteh" refers not to homosexuality but to temple prostitution, of the lady or gentleman variety. All pretty skimpy pickings considering the vehemence with which homosexuals are condemned by many Christians.

And finally, bear in mind that in Leviticus there's even a rule banning cloth made of more than one kind of fiber. Which means the next time someone tells you you're an abomination, you can judge them right back on their use of a polyester mix. If you're a gay man, you probably already have.

Famous Gays and Lesbians in History

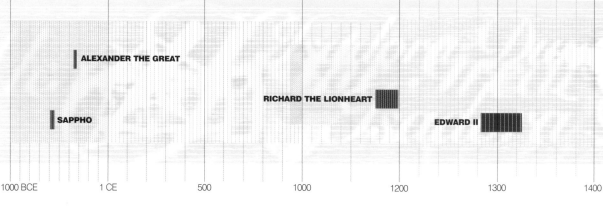

ALEXANDER THE GREAT

RICHARD THE LIONHEART

SAPPHO

EDWARD II

| 1000 BCE | 1 CE | 500 | 1000 | 1200 | 1300 | 1400 |

When you consider that coming out is still an issue for people in places as far flung as Afghanistan, Hollywood and Zambia in the 21st century, just imagine what it was like in ye olde worlde times. Finding evidence of gay and lesbians' existence is one hell of a task since family, friends and historians have rewritten and heterosexualized their stories. What follows, however, is a who's who, who's probably, and who's at least had a serious crack at sleeping with the same sex.

01 Sappho (c. 600 BCE) Greek poetess

Plato called her the tenth muse, but facts are still scanty about this lovely lady. We do know that she was born on Lesbos, wore her hair short, wrote love poetry for her friends and disciples, and is famed for being the first real live lesbian—though it's thought she also had male lovers, including the poet Alcaeus.

02 Alexander The Great (356-323 BCE) Macedonian king and military leader

Though not quite 20 when he came to the throne, Alexander The Great's big achievement was overthrowing the Persian Empire, which meant he ruled from Greece in the north to Egypt in the west to India in the east. While people are still arguing about his sexuality, he was a real looker by all accounts, and his big love was his boyhood friend Hephaeston, who was even hotter. When the two did marry, they married sisters so that their children could be cousins. When Hephaeston died, Alexander ransacked whole districts to assuage his grief, like you do.

03 Richard the Lionheart (1157-1199 CE) English king and Crusader

As well as leading the Crusades against the Muslims, Richard the Lionheart was a poet, an intellectual and thought to be gay to boot. Yes, he married (Berengaria of Navarre, fact fans) but quickly and conveniently dashed off to the Crusades on his wedding night. It's thought he married to appease his mother who was desperate for an heir—he never produced one. However, he is known to have made two confessions about his sexuality in church—one just in his underpants.

04 Edward II (1284-1327) English king

Edward liked gardening and shoeing horses when most other men of the time were into jousting. Ironically, his father, Edward I, unintentionally introduced him to his first boyfriend, Gaveston, who he thought could steer him in a different direction. Yeah, right. After his father's death, Gaveston was having a gay old time, even getting to wear Edward II's wife's wedding jewelry in public. Even when Gaveston was dispatched with (his head was cut off), things went from bad to worse when Edward II continued to heap presents on the usual bunch of sycophants you generally find at court, including his

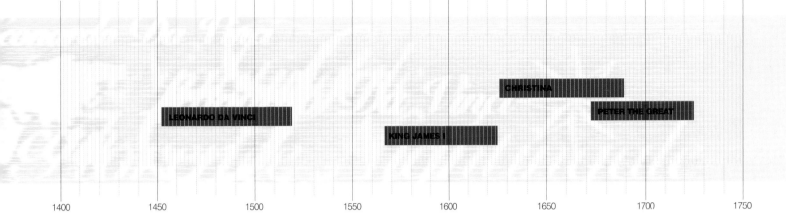

1400   1450   1500   1550   1600   1650   1700   1750

cute new boyfriend Hugh la Desposer. Surprise, surprise, people (and we include his queen Isabella here) soon got really fed up with him and eventually he was ousted from the throne in favor of his son and was bumped off "with a red-hot spit thrust into the anus," probably with the nod from Isabella. Nice.

05 Leonardo da Vinci (1452-1519)
Italian artist, teacher, scientist and inventor
A real all-rounder, Leonardo da Vinci could turn his hand to anything, though he is famous for being one of the greatest painters of the Renaissance. He only left a handful of completed paintings, but they did include the Mona Lisa. Most historians now agree he was gay, since he never married and had no relationships with women. One of the tell-tale signs came when he was arrested, though later released, for sodomy at the age of 24. He is known to have had a couple of long-term companions— Giacomo Caprotti, aka "Little Devil," the subject of some of his work, and aristocrat Francesco Melzi.

06 King James I (1566-1625)
British king
"Long live Queen James!" was a regular cry heard throughout London after he united England and Scotland following Elizabeth I's death in 1603. Though not unsuccessful as a king, there were the usual religious wranglings and even a plot to blow up Parliament during his reign, but he was misunderstood and the fact he was putting it around with the gents at court probably didn't help much. He started as a teen, falling in love with the elegant French courtier, Esmé Stuart, aka Seigneur d'Aubigny, in the Scottish court, but after the couple were forced apart by nobles, he

turned his attention to page boys, bodyguards and the like, who suddenly started to do really well in their careers. The big love of his life however was George Villers, regarded as the most beautiful man in Europe. The son of a penniless Leicestershire squire whom James met in 1614, it took him just three years to become an earl. Earl Buckingham jokingly called himself James's dog, but was soon wielding power, and bringing about a great deal of reform and efficiency to the government. James is buried in Westminster Abbey between George and another boyfriend, Ludovic Stuart, Duke of Richmond and Lennox.

07 Christina (1626-1689)
Swedish queen
The subject of the famous Marlene Dietrich movie, Christina was a tortured soul who didn't dig the role of monarch—even if she did drag Sweden into the 18th century. She did however enjoy her lady-in-waiting, Ebba, until she abdicated the throne and headed to Rome after finding Catholicism.

08 Peter the Great (1672-1725)
Russian czar
A reformer set on making Russia a hot European destination, he was married twice, had 11 children and was also a confirmed party animal thought to lie down with gents. One of his bits of trade reportedly came from the Moscow slums, and was made over into Prince Alexander, the most powerful man in Russia at the time. Ironically, the first laws against homosexual acts appeared in the 18th century, during his reign.

09 Lord Byron (1788-1824)
British poet
Born into an aristocratic family, Lord Byron lived life on his own terms and was by all accounts a slut, having affairs with inappropriate partners like his half-sister, Augusta Leigh. While there are gay love letters written by him, and stories of his unquenchable passion for Greek youths, most of the evidence lies in the subtext of his poetry where he writes of heroes who are "contemptuous of society but haunted by unnameable crimes," i.e., gay.

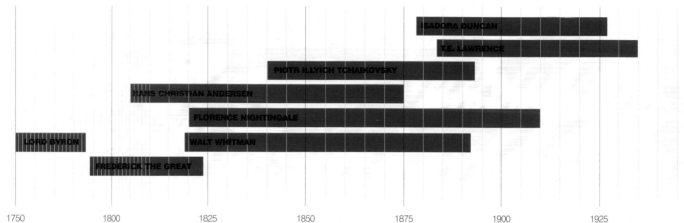

1750	1800	1825	1850	1875	1900	1925	1950

ISADORA DUNCAN

T.E. LAWRENCE

PIOTR ILLYICH TCHAIKOVSKY

HANS CHRISTIAN ANDERSEN

FLORENCE NIGHTINGALE

LORD BYRON

WALT WHITMAN

FREDERICK THE GREAT

10 Frederick the Great (1712-1786) **Prussian king and military leader**

Frederick doubled his land during his reign and tried to make Prussia a much better place—even if he didn't repeal the death penalty for sodomy. There's no question he was a man who loved men, however: the first inkling came at the age of 18 when he conspired with his lover, Katte, and another soldier to get the hell out of there and head for England. He didn't make it and his father had his lover executed in front of him just to teach him a lesson. His affairs with men were an open secret, and his wife didn't see much, if any, action at his retreat, Potsdam Palace.

11 Hans Christian Andersen (1805-1875) **Danish poet and writer**

He didn't write fairy stories for no reason. From the word go, he had "gay" written all over him: his first love was making dolls' clothes. At the age of 14, he was off to Copenhagen where he was "befriended" by two gay musicians. He then became lover to Jonas Collin, director of the Royal Theater who encouraged him to write. The rest is history.

12 Walt Whitman (1819-1892) **Euro-American poet**

Famous for his epic 'Leaves of Grass' and the way his poetry reflected the feelings of a nation, Walt started out as a printer and journalist. His sentiments have since been heterosexualized, but throughout his life Walt was a real rough trade fan. And his notebooks were full of descriptions and addresses of bus drivers, ferry boatmen, and the like whom he used to pick up.

13 Florence Nightingale (1820-1910) **Nurse**

Florence was one serious career gal, famous for her work during the Crimean war and for shaping the nursing profession as we now know it. The gay jury is still out on Flo, but she did write of her close relationship with her aunt as being "like two lovers," and refused all offers of marriage throughout her life. She said, "I have lived and slept in the same bed with English countesses and Prussian farm women.... no woman has excited passions among women more than I have." Go figure.

14 Piotr Illyich Tchaikovsky (1840-1893) **Russian composer**

He might not have made it to the St. Petersburg Conservatory until he was 23, but Piotr was a musical genius whose work was loved by the masses—his biggest hits included *The Nutcracker Suite* and the *1812 Overture*. His sexuality wasn't such a big hit with him however, and he struggled with it all his life, even marrying a female groupie at one point. The marriage only lasted three months, however, after a mental breakdown and attempted suicide. From then on he stuck to men and his final symphony was dedicated to a man he failed to seduce.

15 Isadora Duncan (1878-1927) **Dancer**

For Victorian times, Isadora Duncan was well racy. She showed a bit of ankle and breast, had children out of wedlock, and dabbled with many men and women, and with great frequency. She still managed to find time to shape dance as we know it today, however.

16 T.E. Lawrence, aka **Lawrence of Arabia** (1888-1935) **British soldier**

Lawrence was best known for his activities in the Middle East during the First World War and for being the subject of an epic movie by David Lean. He headed off to the Middle East to do archaeology and got caught up with the cause of Arab independence partly thanks to a guy called Salim Ahmed, aka Dahoum, whom he met at a dig in southern Turkey. They later moved in together and Lawrence made a nude carving of him to put on top of the house. Aww! They lost contact when war broke out and never met again. Any other evidence of Lawrence's sexuality, however, is sketchy at best.

Michelangelo

Renaissance star and the painter behind the Vatican's Sistine Chapel

Michelangelo Buonarotti (1475-1564) is regarded as one of the most important and influential artists of all time, and was thought very highly of even during his own lifetime, which is not always the case with artists. Everyone digs the masculinity, the muscularity (even his female forms look like men with long hair) and gigantic grandeur of his work, from David to the Medici tombs, to the Sistine Chapel, which he was actually coerced into creating—after all, his first love was sculpture.

Looking at his work today, it makes sense that the man who created the downright homoerotic statue of David was a fag, yet art historians have sought to cover up his sexuality since as far back as 1623, when his grand-nephew Michelangelo il Giovane changed all the masculine pronouns in his poetry to feminine.

But cover it up or not, there is no doubt that in his 89 years, he sure got through his fair share of fellas. The handsome and muscular model Gherardo Perini came to work for him around 1520, and they embarked on an affair which at the time was the subject of much gossip. Other lovers may have included: "that little blackmailer," Febo di Poggio, another model who constantly demanded presents from him; his constant companion Francesco Urbino, and Andrea Quaratesi, with whose family he lived for some time. In 1532, he tried to seduce Roman nobleman Tommaso Cavalieri and though Tommaso was having none of it, their relationship was significant since it encouraged Michelangelo to knock out some fine Platonic poetry, and the two men became lifelong friends.

Though he became affected by the Puritanism of the Counter-reformation before his death, and transferred his interest (though not his sexual desires) to Vittorio Colonna, Marchioness of Pescara, testament to his sexuality can be seen in the verse he wrote for the tomb of his lover Francesco de Zanobi Bracci in 1544.

The earthly flesh, and here my bones deprived
Of their charming face and beautiful eyes,
Do yet attest for him how gracious I was in bed
When he embraced, and in what the soul doth live.

Lesbian Pirates

Sapphic love on the high seas

While tales of piracy and thieving on the high seas tend to involve one-legged men or rough types with black beards, there are however some stories of ladies kicking ass on stolen boats and commandeering all-male crews. Anne Bonny and Mary "Mark" Read's story first appeared in 1724, shortly after their trial for piracy, in the book, *A General History of the Robberies and Murders of the Most Notorious Pirates*, written by Charles Johnson—a probable pseudonym of Daniel Defoe.

Anne Bonny, born Anne Cormac, was brought up in South Carolina in the 1700s. A tomboy with short red hair, a dirty face and "rowdy habits," her father was a wealthy lawyer and plantation owner. As historians noted, she had a "fierce and courageous" temper and apparently killed her English maid with a knife while still a youngster.

Anne's boisterous younger years are well-documented by local historians who also report how she used to frequent the bars in the port of Charleston, and how she also put a male admirer into hospital by beating him with a chair. When she eloped with a man called James Bonny her father disinherited her, so she burned down his plantation and fled to Nassau in the Bahamas—a renowned haven for pirates at that time.

No sooner had she arrived, Anne shot off the ear of a sailor who had foolishly tried to stop her from disembarking from her boat. After a short time she'd dumped her husband and had gone off to live with Captain Jennings and his mistress. Thanks to her behavior it was recommended that Anne get herself some male protection, so she bagged herself the richest man on the island, Chidley Bayard.

She soon got bored and decided to land herself a pirate instead. John "Calico Jack" Rackham—whose nickname was thanks to the dubious stripey pants he wore—was the chosen man, and despite having a child together—who mysteriously disappeared—she soon threw Jack out of his captain's quarters and took both the command of the ship and the cabin for herself. After a narrow scrape with officials cracking down on piracy, Anne, Calico Jack and a gay male friend, Pierre Bouspeut—who was a hairdresser and dressmaker—set sail. After a pillage-free journey, Anne and her crew returned to Nassau where she met Mary "Mark" Read.

Mary Read's mother had dressed her as a boy ever since she was young and even called her Mark—the name of her dead brother—in order to ensure she inherited her grandmother's money. Not so odd when you realize that back then only boys were entitled to inheritance. However, it seemed that Mary had a penchant for all this cross-dressing, and when she refused to return to girls' clothes her mother disinherited her. Mark then ran off to join the army.

Later, Mary Read—reverting to girliness—married a soldier, but after just three years her husband died, so she again donned men's clothes and signed up on a Dutch ship as "Mark Read." The ship was captured by pirates, who persuaded Mark to join them and "he" eventually turned up in the Bahamas where "he" met Anne Bonny.

Anne and Mary were already good friends when James Bonny turned up on the scene to reclaim his wife as his property. James Bonny kidnapped Anne and took her to the governor of the island, bound and naked. He charged Anne for the desertion of her husband and recommended "divorce by sale." Anne, naturally, did not take the charge lying down and refused to be "bought and sold like a hog." She was left unsold at the end of the day as no-one dared buy the "hellcat," so she reformed her crew, along with Mark, and the pair became inseparable. Their relationship annoyed Jack Calico, and he threatened to slit Mark's throat in a fit of jealousy, still not realizing that Mark was a girl. One day Jack went into the couple's cabin and discovered Mark lying half-dressed with Anne, and looking a lot like a woman. Many historians attempt to explain that Anne too had only just discovered Mary's real gender at this moment, despite the fact that the two women spent all their time together, donned men's or women's clothing whenever the fancy took them, and took command of and raided other ships and boats.

After a warrant was put out for their arrest, they were captured by Captain Barnet, but not without a fight that ended up with Mary shooting two of her own crew for cowardice, and wounding Calico—it took an hour for Barnet's entire crew to arrest the two women. The girls and their crew were put on trial on November 28th, 1720, and were sentenced to hanging. In a fitting act of cunning, Anne and Mary claimed to be pregnant— despite it being highly unlikely—and escaped the death penalty by "pleading their bellies."

While these feisty girl pirates were obviously bisexual, their relationship is often glossed over by historians, despite Anne and Mary being a strong couple who lived and worked together— admittedly by stealing and killing.

Mary later died of fever in prison and Anne disappeared, with one unlikely story suggesting that she remarried, and another that she became a nun. Whatever her fate, she was one-half of a kick-ass girl duo who ruled the high seas, and was known as the "infamous woman."

Joan of Arc

Dyke icon, army captain, patron saint and pioneer of the pudding bowl haircut

Almost six hundred years after Jeanne d'Arc, aka the Maid Of Orleans, took arms to kick British butt, she is still revered as a dyke icon. However—let's get this straight from the start—there is absolutely no evidence to point to the fact that she was a lesbian. Nevertheless, Jeanne or Joan as we've come to call her, did the unthinkable—she excelled herself in a men-only environment and unfortunately paid for it with her life.

The third of five children, Joan was born in Douremy in 1412, the daughter of a farmer, Jacques d'Arc. She spent an unremarkable childhood tending herds and learning religion until, at the age of twelve, she started hearing the voices of St. Michael, St. Catherine, and St. Margaret. They told her it was her divine mission to help the French Dauphin—the rightful heir to the throne—claim the crown and free France from the tyranny of the English who were then engaged in the 100 Years War. By 1429, Paris and all of France north of the Loire had been occupied.

Those religious voices held some sway back in the day and after being quizzed by theologians on behalf of the Dauphin, seventeen-year-old Joan became a captain and was given a bunch of troops to command. But she was pretty darn good at warfare and at the battle of Orleans in May 1429, she led her troops to victory over the English. This triumph was closely followed by another win at Patay. On July 17th, 1429, she achieved part one of her mission when the Dauphin, Charles VII, was crowned King of France, and Joan was present in a place of honor.

The following year, the Burgundians captured her while she was defending Compiegne near Paris. They sold her to the English who in turn handed her over to the ecclesiastical court at Rouen. Led by the pro-English Bishop of Beauvais, they tried her for witchcraft and heresy. The interrogation lasted fourteen months, after which she was found guilty and was burned at the stake on May 30th, 1431. Charles VII didn't do anything to help her. In 1909, she was beatified and canonized in 1920.

You can blame 20th century English writer Vita Sackville-West [see page 190] for initially suggesting that Joan of Arc was a lesbian. She based her opinion on Simon Beaucroix's testimony during the trial: "Joan slept always with young girls, she did not like to sleep with old women." However, trial records show that she was accused of having sexual relationships with men, not women, and in fact she was actually a virgin—she was examined by the Duchess of Bedford and her matrons while being held in the English prison at Rouen.

Search through the records some more and you discover that there is further evidence—albeit scanty—that she was straight. Apparently in 1428, a young man from her village had proposed marriage to her, meanwhile her squire and bodyguard said she "particularly loved an honorable man whom she knew to be of chaste habits."

There is evidence, however, that Joan cross-dressed—something that was used to convict her. Her cross-dressing has been made much of over the years, however it seems to have been more a matter of necessity—she was commanding troops after all—rather than something she just relished. The only accounts of her wearing armour come from eyewitnesses during her military campaigns, however this was also common procedure to protect women who were going through dangerous territory in war-torn France. It's true that during her trial she refused to remove her male attire. This has been accounted for in several ways: Joan saw her clothes as a symbol of her loyalty to God, and would have changed them if her "voices" had told her to; alternatively, she had to wear soldier's clothing in prison (her pants and tunic could be tied together) because her guards had tried to rape her, or because that's all they'd given her to wear before she was examined by the authorities.

Of course, nearly 600 years later, it's hard to do anything but surmise what the real deal was with Joan. However, we can be sure that as the head of a formidable army she changed the course of history; a feat unmatched by any other female at the time.

authoritatively as President Truman had ended racial segregation back in 1948, Don't Ask, Don't Tell backfired when the numbers of gay men and lesbians discharged by the US military began to rise (597 in 1994, 722 in 1995, 850 in 1996, and 997 in 1997) after its implementation. The policy was an attempt to protect gay men and women, with new recruits no longer being questioned about their sexual orientation during preliminary interviews and, as long as they did not admit to being queer, being allowed to serve. Seen as a positive step by some, it also meant that queers hoping to go on to college with the monetary help of the military now just had to keep their mouths shut. The reality, however, was rather different.

As an institution that is known for turning boys into men, and men into killing machines, for many straight soldiers allowing gay men into the army—and before that, allowing blacks and women to serve—seemed to deny them their rites of passage. And it's these soldiers' views of gay men and women that upheld the Defense Department's original ban for so long. Many believed that "good order, discipline and morale" would disappear, as no straight soldier would

Gays in The Military

Fighting for the right to fight for your country

While a career in the military is not to everyone's taste—hell, who'd want to run around in the cold dressed in khaki killing people for a living?—the right to be able to fight and die for your country has become the subject of one of the most contentious gay rights battles in recent years. While most people would agree that everyone should be able to do whatever job they wish, without prejudice, the time and effort spent fighting for equality within the military

smacks of a waste of time for a large number of queers who see working for a misogynistic old boys' club-cum-killing machine as all wrong.

In 1993, the U.S. government launched its controversial "Don't Ask, Don't Tell" policy—Bill Clinton's compromising attempt to end the US's total ban on gays serving in the military. While many hoped that the policy would stop the armed force's prejudice as

want to serve with, take orders from or share close quarters with a homo.

Instead of removing such stigma from queers in the military, Don't Ask, Don't Tell has managed to create an atmosphere in which discrimination and harassment—and that includes blackmail, violence and sometimes even murder—is not only tolerated and covered up, but also occasionally encouraged by some superiors. For some homophobic servicemen and women, Don't Ask, Don't Tell is the perfect tool to enable them to oust queer colleagues whom they disapprove of—all they have to do is find evidence of their sexuality: For one seventeen-year naval

veteran, the mere fact that his AOL account described his marital status as "gay" saw him being discharged, despite an impeccable service record.

However, put into that mix a wartime situation, and the views of both the government and the soldiers towards gay service people changes. From the Second World War to the Vietnamese War, it seemed that fighting men and women were able to turn a blind eye to their queer comrades when combat was taking place. And while The Pentagon refuses to reassess the Don't Ask, Don't Tell policy, claiming that homo presence is a fundamental danger to the military's effectiveness, at the beginning of the "war against terrorism" in Afghanistan in 2001, it put discharge on the grounds of homosexuality on hold. This outrageous contradiction, making the presence of gay soldiers indispensable at times of conflict, became even more shocking when it was disclosed that those admitting to being gay at that time (in the hope, most probably, of not having to be shipped over Afghanistan to fight) may still face discharge, but only after the war is over.

Don't Ask, Don't Tell clearly discriminates against gay men and women by denying them their right to free speech, and by not protecting them under law. The US government, and The Pentagon in particular, continues to deny queer soldiers, sailors and the like not only their fundamental rights but also the same rights as their straight comrades. And while a large number of gay men and women would argue that such a career is disgusting, what has to be understood is that the military is not only the US's biggest employer, but that the US as a whole is still in the midst of a battle to secure equal rights for gay men and women in all of its states. But until this happens, and until the US government removes the ambiguous Don't Ask, Don't Tell policy, gay servicemen and women will not only have to continue to work in isolation and in fear of discovery; they will also have to face the homophobia of their co-workers in silence.

Despite precedents being set by countries like Israel, the UK, Germany, Australia, Japan, France and The Netherlands which allow gay men and women to serve, America remains a long way behind.

Gay Spies

The centuries-old relationship between gay men and espionage

The last couple of years have seen major changes for gay people in the British secret services. Just like the Cold War and the Berlin Wall, it seems homophobia is a thing of the past with MI5 becoming an equal opportunities employer and actually advertising for staff, while MI6 reportedly sent a gay couple abroad recently.

Anyway, having been forced to lead a "double life" for centuries, gay men make excellent spies, going back to the original spymaster Sir Francis Walsingham who uncovered plots against Elizabeth I in 16th century England, built up a case against Mary, Queen Of Scots and had an affair with spy and playwright Christopher Marlowe.

Writer Somerset Maugham worked for British Intelligence in Russia during the Russian Revolution in 1917, and wrote the first modern spy story, *Ashenden or The British Agent*, while bisexual writer Graham Greene engaged in undercover business during the Second World War.

The most famous spies of all, coincidentally, came out of Trinity College, Cambridge in the 1930s to sell secrets to the KGB. Donald McLean may have been married four times but he was still into man-on-man action while Kim Philby was a practicing transvestite, and Anthony Blunt and Guy Burgess were gay. In 1951, Burgess and McLean defected to the Soviet Union where they continued to work in espionage. Philby fled Britain in 1963, but Blunt remained in the country and was eventually unmasked in 1979. Together they were blamed with having prolonged the Cold War and possibly leading to the deaths of a dozen western agents.

▷ **Take it further:** Another Country, *the play by Julian Mitchell, later turned into a film starring Rupert Everett, deals with English public schoolboys like Burgess and McLean, who turned to spying, while the Alan Bennett television play An Englishman Abroad deals with the real story of Burgess' time living in Moscow.*

1980

AIDS, though yet unnamed, starts to spread through Eastern Africa. The Kinshasa Highway is later nicknamed 'AIDS Highway'.

31 cases of PCP occur in the US. PCP, full name pneumocystsis crinij pneumonia, is a disease where patients' blood lacks T-helper cells, which are part of the immune system. This is later found to be HIV-related.

A doctor in New York notices the rare Kaposi's sarcoma occurring in two young gay men. He contacts two physicians in San Francisco, who have seen a similar case. This new disease is first called "gay cancer", but is soon renamed GRID—gay-related immune deficiency.

Dr. Michael Gottlieb publishes a piece in the catchily-titled *Morbidity and Mortality Weekly* that reviews other seemingly healthy young gay men who are experiencing severe fungal infections and PCP.

May: New York Times announces a "rare cancer seen in 41 gay men." The media backlash and scaremongering begins in earnest.

June: The US federal Centers for Disease Control (CDC) reports the first cases of the disease that will eventually be known as AIDS.

October: CDC declares the new disease an epidemic.

1983

May 19th: The *New England Journal of Medicine* confirms that researchers have found that HIV can be transmitted from males to females.

The first AIDS discrimination trial is held in the US.

The first AIDS Candlelight Vigil is held in San Francisco, lead by the Sisters of Perpetual Indulgence's banner "Fight For Our Lives."

The first Australian death from AIDS is recorded in Melbourne.

Late 1983: The Buddy Program launches as the "Home Health Assistance/Hospice Services", it continues its work for people with HIV/AIDS to this day.

In Europe there are two epidemics—one linked to Africa, and one to gay men who have visited the US. Three people die in the UK in 1983.

1986

The World Health Organization (WHO) launches its global AIDS strategy, recommending that sterile needles and syringes are provided to drug users.

Russia reports its first case of AIDS.

The Ugandan minister for health declares that his country "has AIDS", with other African countries following suit, demanding WHO assistance.

1987

1st June: ACT UP and other groups demonstrate in Washington DC. Police at the demo sport rubber gloves when arresting protestors to 'protect' themselves from HIV.

The US shuts its doors to HIV-infected immigrants.

The AIDS Memorial Quilt [see page 99] is started in San Francisco by Cleve Jones, who sews a panel in memory of his friend Marvin Feldman.

President Ronald Reagan makes his first public address on AIDS, while his Vice President, George Bush Senior, calls for mandatory HIV testing.

The history of AIDS, from 1959 to the year 2000

AIDS

1959

The earliest case of what is now known as HIV is confirmed in the Congo.

1969

The first case of what is now known as HIV is confirmed in the US. A teenage prostitute with Kaposi's sarcoma (once a rare cancer, until its prolific appearance in AIDS patients) and HIV dies.

1979

Gay men in the US and Sweden, and straight men in Tanzania and Haiti start showing signs of Kaposi's sarcoma.

1982

September: The disease is officially named Acquired Immunodeficiency Syndrome, or AIDS.

Many of the original GRID cases are linked to Gaetan Dugas, a Canadian airline steward, who's been dubbed 'Patient Zero'. Patient Zero, or the Index Patient, isn't necessarily the first person to be diagnosed with a disease or illness, and often Patient Zero has died before health authorities get to them. However, he/she is seen to be the person that all subsequent infections come from, whether directly or indirectly.

It is thought that Dugas caught the disease in Africa and then brought it home to Canada, where it spread rapidly to the United States. Mr. Dugas' status as the Index Patient only applies to North America, as he is not seen to be responsible for the spread of the disease in Africa and other countries globally.

By the end of the year, approximately, 1,300 cases of AIDS are reported in the US, with 460 dead.

1983

The HIV virus, then known as HTLV-III, which causes AIDS is isolated by the Pasteur Institute in France.

May: A report wrongly suggests that there is a possibility of casual household transmission of HIV. In San Francisco some bus drivers wear face masks to protect themselves from supposed possible infection.

In the early 1980s, Kaposi's sarcoma was seen in nearly 50% of AIDS patients. Slightly raised red or pink papules or plaques spread across the patient's skin, as well as in the gastrointestinal and respiratory tracts, sometimes causing excessive bleeding. Before its prevalence in AIDS victims, it was a rare cancer linked to a virus of the herpes group.

1987

February 4th: Liberace [see page 186] dies of an AIDS-related illness. Before his illness, despite having his HIV status outed by tabloid newspapers in the US, Liberace's management claim his extreme weight loss is due to a "watermelon diet".

March: ACT UP [see page 90] is formed in New York City. Using non-violent direct action and acts of civil disobedience, ACT UP successfully focuses media and public attention on the crucial issues of the AIDS crisis.

Delta Airlines in the US attempts to bar people with AIDS on their flights. A threatened boycott sees the airline making a u-turn.

March 19th: Zidovudine (AZT, Retrovir®) is launched and approved to fight HIV itself and is marketed at people with AIDS. The cost of a year's supply, however, weighs in at a hefty $10,000, making it the most expensive drug in history. The recommended dose is 100mg every four hours, 24 hours a day.

24th March: The first ACT UP demonstration takes place on Wall Street in New York, against the profiteering of pharmaceutical companies, especially Burroughs Wellcome, makers of AZT. 17 demonstrators are arrested.

The British government launches a major advertising campaign entitled "Don't Die Of Ignorance". A leaflet, since slated for its scare mongering tactics, is delivered to every household in the country.

Princess Diana opens the first specialist AIDS hospital ward in England. She controversially does not wear gloves when shaking patients' hands.

1988

15th January: The women's caucus of ACT UP New York protest against an article in Cosmopolitan magazine that states that straight women who have unprotected vaginal sex with HIV-positive men are at no risk. A documentary about the women's action is shown around the country and is placed on permanent exhibition at New York's Museum of Modern Art.

The US launches a HIV/AIDS education campaign.

The human trials of an anti-HIV vaccine begin.

The World Health Organization announces World AIDS Day—a new annual event on 1st December each year.

The cases of AIDS being transmitted by needles in New York now exceed the number of sexually transmitted new cases.

AIDS

1989

Under huge pressure from the AIDS community, Burroughs Wellcome lowers the price of AZT by 20%.

August: A federal study in the US indicates that AZT slows the progression of HIV infection in those who are asymptomatic or who have few symptoms.

The Sisters of Perpetual Indulgence throw a 10th anniversary party in San Francisco, which helps to raise much-needed cash for the AIDS Emergency Fund.

1990

The AIDS movie *Longtime Companion* opens.

President Bush Senior signs the 'Americans With Disabilities Act',

1992

February 4th: The International Olympic Committee rules that athletes with HIV are eligible to compete.

June: The Food and Drug Administration in the US approves Zalcitabine (ddC, Hivid®) for use in combination with AZT.

49 cases of AIDS without HIV infection are reported to the eighth International AIDS Conference.

Tennis star Arthur Ashe announces that he had been infected with HIV during a blood transfusion in 1983.

1993

January 6th: Rudolph Nureyev [see page 201], the Russian ballet star dies of AIDS, aged 54.

Reports show that AIDS patients have begun to show signs of resistance to AZT.

Arthur Ashe dies less than a year after revealing he is HIV-positive.

A US federal government study shows that giving clean needles to drug users helps prevent the spread of HIV and AIDS.

1995

HIV becomes the leading cause of death of Americans between 25 and 44 years of age.

Gangsta rapper Eazy E dies of AIDS.

Results of the Delta trial conclude that combining AZT with ddI or ddC provides a major improvement in treatment, compared with AZT alone.

The Food and Drug Administration in the US approves the use of Saquinavir, the first of a group of Protease Inhibitor anti-retroviral drugs.

1996

The use of drug 'cocktails', called combination therapy, helps to delay the onset of full-blown AIDS.

Magic Johnson briefly returns to professional basketball.

The United Nations' Joint Program on HIV/AIDS, UNAIDS, reports that the number of new HIV infections has declined in many countries due to safer sex practices. However, the collective worldwide rate of infection continues to grow rapidly.

1999

In the UK, the number of HIV-positive prisoners reaches an all-time high.

HIV infections increase in West Africa.

2000

Morgues in Zimbabwe open all night to cope with deaths from AIDS.

The XIII International AIDS Conference is held in Durban, South Africa—its location is considered to be Ground Zero of the epidemic in the year 2000. 5,000 doctors and scientists sign the 'Durban Declaration', affirming the overwhelming evidence that HIV causes AIDS.

The UN and WHO estimate that 36.1 million people have HIV/AIDS globally, with 25.3 million of these living in Africa. Meanwhile, the infection rate rises in Eastern Europe. Russia, South and Southeast Asia.

It is estimated that nearly 20 million people have died of AIDS since the start of the epidemic; 15 million of them are Africans

According to the World Health Organization's report, AIDS has become the world's fourth largest killer, just 20 years after the epidemic began.

UNAIDS estimates that 33 million people are living with HIV/AIDS globally.

A large-scale study of HIV infection among gay men in New York shows that large numbers have become infected with HIV in the last two years, despite health education campaigns within the gay community.

1998

February 4th: The analysis of a blood sample preserved since 1959, from the oldest documented case of HIV infection, shows that the first infections probably occurred in the late 1940s and early 1950s.

UNAIDS estimates that 70% of all new HIV infections and 80% of deaths from AIDS are occurring in sub-Saharan Africa.

Due to the success of combination therapy, many previously sick HIV-positive people are able to return to work.

1997

The film *Philadelphia*, starring Tom Hanks, opens. It's the first mainstream Hollywood film to broach the subject of AIDS.

AIDS becomes the leading cause of death for young adults in 64 cities in America.

February 17th: Randy Shilts, author of *And The Band Played On*, dies from AIDS, age 42.

Deaths from AIDS drop by 19% in the US.

Approximately 30 million cases of HIV occur worldwide, according to UNAIDS, including 6.5 million deaths.

Reports are made public of the first case of a probable HIV transmission through kissing.

1995

Despite South African Deputy President Thabo Mbeki calling for people to "break the silence about AIDS", an AIDS activist is beaten to death outside her house after revealing her HIV status on Zulu television.

January 3rd: 500 ACT UP activists visit Rudolph Giuliani: the new mayor of New York, demanding he puts the AIDS crisis at the top of his job list.

The four-time Olympic gold medal-winning diver Greg Louganis comes out as gay and HIV-positive on ABC's *20/20* program, in an interview with Barbara Walters.

1994

February 19th: Derek Jarman [see page 102] dies of AIDS.

April 15th: John Curry, the Olympic figure skater, dies of AIDS.

The polyurethane condom goes on sale.

Tom Hanks' performance in the film *Philadelphia*, where he plays a lawyer with AIDS, wins him an Oscar. The actors in attendance at the 1994 Oscars make the red ribbon the fashion and political statement of the moment.

1991

Jeremy Irons is the first celebrity to sport a Red Ribbon at the Tony Awards. The Red Ribbon Campaign, founded in memory of the singer/songwriter Paul Jabara—who conceived the red ribbon idea—begins.

Fox Television becomes the first TV network to broadcast a paid condom commercial.

The basketball player Magic Johnson reveals he is HIV-positive.

November 22nd: Freddie Mercury, lead singer of Queen, announces he has AIDS.

November 24th: Freddie Mercury dies of bronchio-pneumonia, brought on by AIDS, just 24 hours after the announcement of his illness.

Approximately 10 million people have HIV globally.

which protects people with disabilities from discrimination, including those with HIV.

Former US President Ronald Reagan apologizes for his neglect of the AIDS epidemic while he was in office. Deaths from AIDS in the US pass the 100,000 mark, meaning that nearly twice as many Americans have died from AIDS as the number who died in the Vietnam War.

Halston, one of the world's first celebrity fashion designers, who dressed the likes of Jackie O, Lauren Bacall and Liz Taylor, dies of AIDS.

Gay to Straight

Plunder the gays! How gay men and lesbians have added to the greater good, bringing color, movement, fun and dollars to the general commonwealth.

Fag hags

Women who love gay men

Hear the words "fag hag" and you immediately conjure up an image of a feather-boa wearing porker and an emotional car crash to boot: no wonder she can't get a date on a Saturday night and has to resort to a desperately sad and needy friendship with a fag to make up for the sex she should be rightfully getting elsewhere. Cue the gag: "Why did God create gay men? To take fat girls to discotheques!"

Straight male society has cunningly brought together two of the most demeaning words it can pull out of the bag to diss women who just might not be interested in what they've got to offer.

The term fag hag might not be one most women would choose for themselves, but it is now being reclaimed in the same way as "queer." As well as high-profile fag hags like your Madonnas, Kate Mosses and Princess Dianas, you'll find that women who love gay men come from all walks of life, are all shapes and sizes and all colors and creeds—and technically, they no longer work only in the theater. Over the past couple of decades they've been increasingly coming out of the closet and wearing their hearts on their sleeves.

Our friendships have fast become the subject of films like *The Object Of My Affection* and *The Next Best Thing* [see page 150], have appeared on television shows like *Will and Grace* [see page 145] and *Sex And The City* [see page 34] and have been increasingly covered in newspaper editorials.

Our relationships might be dismissed as a new "trend," but they're as old as the hills. Margaret Clap—Molly Clap to you—was Britain's first known example back in 1726: she ran a gay brothel not to make money (like, doh!), but because she just liked it [see page 114]. Likewise, if anyone was a friend to a hostess in the 19th century, it was a gay boy acting as a 'spare man.' Who else would balance the number of men at her dinner party or take her to the theater when her husband wasn't around? Yes, this still goes on today, but it's not like it's a one-way street of a relationship.

It should be remembered that fag hags are not 'beards.' This term refers to the complicit relationships between some women and gay men so that they can enjoy the benefits that heterosexual couples take for granted. Fag hags are too intent on having a great time to ever settle for undercover work. But if sex is out of the question—and it isn't always!— what is it that we dig about each other? Unlike straight men's friendships, which seem to mask out-and-out male competition, we appreciate each others' loyalty, compassion, emotional literacy, the ability to coordinate clothes in a half-decent manner, raise an arched eyebrow and bitch down whoever might have it in for us. Gay men and fag hags are girlfriends and if that means ever so occasionally fighting over men, then so be it.

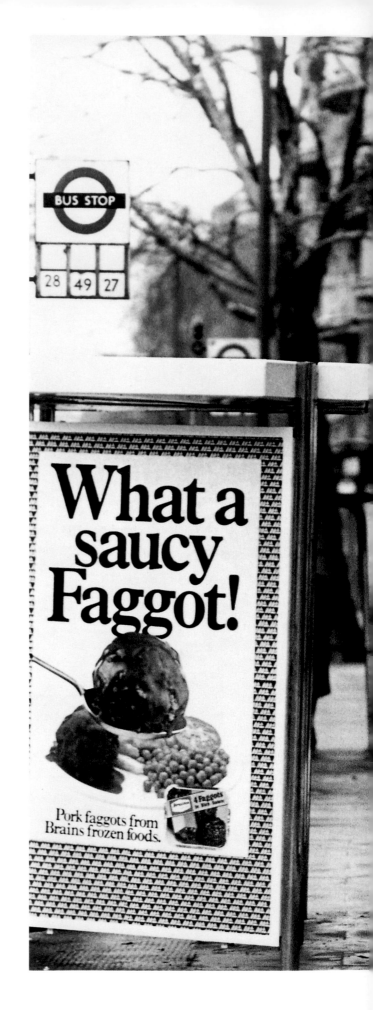

Gay Advertising
Selling to gay men and lesbians

"Apart from notoriety and controversy, there are few benefits to targeting a commercial gay audience," reckons advertising industry bible *Campaign*. The industry obviously agrees, if the very low number of adverts featuring gays going about their daily business is anything to go by. There was the famous IKEA ad featuring two gay men shopping for a dining table, which formed part of the furniture group's non-traditional families campaign, but even that was only shown in New York and Washington DC, and was swiftly withdrawn after outcry.

Despite the myth of gay affluence that makes marketing eyes twinkle, the fear of offending the non-gay audience is overwhelming and is cited by *Campaign* as the main reason advertisers are loath to put their toe into gay waters. A recent campaign for Guinness, which showed two gay men living together, with one giving the other a kiss before he set of to work, was pulled before it was aired after news stories caused a storm of protest among British publicans nervous that a gay ad would scupper sales. Another commercial featuring gay men made by Levi's to advertise their engineered jeans was also pulled before being aired. It featured a bunch of people, including gay men, jumping rope on a beach and included one guy grabbing another guy's ass. Although Levi's pride themselves on being gay friendly, they felt it wasn't getting the right message across.

Where gay men and lesbians excel in advertising is in the field of being exploited to sell to the wider population. "Some companies use gay characters in a bid to appear hip to straight viewers," says Michael Wilke, the journalist behind the *commercialcloset.org* website, which tracks ads featuring gay elements. "Others do it to shock people," he adds. The Diesel print ad by photographer David LaChapelle featuring a port-side scene with two gay sailors French-kissing helped establish Diesel as a cutting edge jeans brand, while designers like Gaultier have no scruples when it comes to playing with images of homosexuality to maintain their out-there-ness.

Clothing company Abercrombie & Fitch have often flirted with gay themes (well, that's what happens when you hire Bruce Weber and Sam Shahid, the guys who invented male physique advertising), most of which boil down to blatant homoeroticism [see page 18] but which occasionally venture into revolutionary territory—such as the shots of Whitney and Beth's wedding, which has two fit babes, both in wedding dresses, kissing the bride (i.e. each other.) A&F's use of homosexuality, like Diesel's, has resulted not only in it becoming a cult brand among gay men and women, but in it becoming so controversial and impactful that their quarterly advertising magazine now has to be sold in a sealed wrapper.

But these are examples of the good side of exploitation. Advertisers have also used gay characters in ads to pander to the sexual appetites of straight viewers (cute lesbian anyone?), or have used denigrating stereotypes to play to their prejudices.

In an award-winning ad for Sprite, three basketball players making the ad are revealed to be just actors. One is very upper-crust British, one is Californian and the third an effeminate homo who proceeds to throw a temper tantrum and storm back to his trailer.

Paydirt for advertisers is a campaign where those monied gay folk can read the ad as gay while the straight potential bigots that view it are left none the wiser. An ad for Beefeater gin featuring two beautiful blondes, for instance, will be seen as lesbian by lesbians but plain horny by men. A&F produced the mother of all these ads, but with a very plucky spin, when they used a young man frolicking with an older guy, an image that was bound to be read as daring and gay by the gay readers of *Vanity Fair*, where it appeared. The couple were in fact John Wayne's son and grandson. It was almost like they were itching for complaints to be made so they could lay that one on them.

The Village People

How a biker, a policeman, a construction worker, a cowboy, a soldier, and a Red Indian became the first crossover "gay" stars

With the benefit of hindsight, it's hard to believe that back in 1978 when literally the whole of the western world was gyrating to 'YMCA,' most of those people were probably unaware of the innuendo in the lyrics: "They have everything for you men to enjoy / You can hang out with all the boys / You can do whatever you feel / It's fun to stay at the Y-M-C-A." Or of the homosexual subtext of the biker, the policeman, the construction worker, the cowboy, the soldier and the Red Indian. So what the hell was going on?

The Village People were dreamt up by French producer Jacques Morali and his partner Henri Belolo. Together, the pair had already had a bit of success with the Ritchie Family, but they were inspired by the gay dance scene, which was new at that time, and the group of party people who made their living by going from club to club creating "an atmosphere." Felipe Rose, the Red Indian, was in one such group and he was the starting point for the Village People. After some initial musical success on FM radio (even though everyone listened to AM radio stations at the time), Jacques pulled together a group from ads in the trade papers.

Taking their name from Greenwich Village, New York's gay ghetto, the original line-up—though it's changed over the years—included Victor Willis, Randy Jones, David "Scar" Hodo, Glenn Hughes, Alexander Briley and Felipe Rose. The assorted mix of sexy, blue-collar characters was conceived to personify the mixing of American social groups—though it didn't

hurt that some were also gay stereotypes. But there's little doubt that initially at least, the band were designed to attract gay audiences; their first singles, 'Fire Island' and 'San Francisco (You've Got Me)', were clearly not aimed at the straight crowd.

'San Francisco' was a hit nevertheless, and an impressive series of others followed including 'YMCA' (Jacques got the inspiration from passing the establishment in New York), 'Macho Man' (1978), and 'In the Navy' (1979), all of which were number ones. 'Go West' (1979) and 'Sleazy' (1979) followed, and during their heyday, the Village People sold 65 million albums.

Like any other pop act, they weren't immune to criticism, being seen as nothing more than a male burlesque act, but as 'construction worker' David Hodo says now, "The music was bright, the Democrats were in office, the country wanted to party and we were the perfect group for that. They thought we were the most outrageous thing they'd seen.

"You just had to have a natural slut factor to work in the group," he continues. "We all had a willingness to behave as cheaply as we possibly could in front of an audience—we were pretty outrageous: bumping and grinding on stage."

At a time when the gay community was seriously under-represented in the media, it's little wonder that few people questioned anyone's sexuality in the group and any reporters who did were

"hung up" on. And even today David Hodo is coy when confronting the question, saying, "The group consists of gay and straight men, black and white men and everything in between. And we've been singing and working together in harmony for 23 years—that's more than I can say for most of the world."

While the band continues to perform today, notching up almost 100 concerts a year at private events, county fairs and theme parks, their career took a downturn in 1980 when they starred in the movie *Can't Stop The Music*, which was savaged by the critics and ignored by the public at large, though gay folk revered it as a camp classic.

The tide had turned and despite a flirtation with New Romanticism, they couldn't rekindle their disco success and songs like 'Do You Wanna Spend The Night' (1981), and '5 O'Clock In The Morning"' were just minor hits. After a couple of years' break, they tried once again but their sexy antics and songs like 'Sex Over The Phone,' although an ode to safe sex, fell flat in the AIDS era.

Yet the Village People will never be forgotten. For some people they'll always be synonymous with the camp classic 'YMCA,' which even gets performed in kindergartens today; for others they're a precursor to the Spice Girls or even the Chippendales; but for gay men, they'll always be monuments to gay pride, celebrating both its positivity, its freedom and its down 'n' dirty sleaziness.

Top 10 Trannie movies

Men playing women, usually for laughs

It's the oldest trick in the book and somehow one of the fastest tracks to hilarity known to movie makers: men done up as women. There's nothing new about it, it goes back to Shakespeare's time (mind you, he had no choice as it was illegal for women to act back then), but done right, putting a guy in a dress can throw a whole new light on issues of homosexuality, gender, bigotry, romance, you name it. Oh, and it can't fail to be hilarious (*To Wong Foo, Thanks for Everything, Love Julie Newmar!* being the obvious exception to that rule). Here are the best movie crossdressers.

1. Daphne and Josephine in *Some Like It Hot* (1959)

The best cross-dressing movie by, well, by much farther than they could walk in those heels, *Some Like It Hot* sees Tony Curtis and Jack Lemmon as Jo and Jerry, done up as Josephine and Daphne so they can join an all-female band and escape the Mob. Josephine, out of skirts but back in drag as Cary Grant, falls in love with Marilyn Monroe's Sugar Kane, while Daphne starts a voyage of discovery with a dirty old man. Classic scenes follows with very pro-gay messages such as when Daphne is showing off her engagement ring and Curtis's Jo asks why a guy would marry another guy—"Security" says Lemmon's Jerry. But then he has been out all night running wild with maracas.

2. Dolly in *Personal Services* (1987)

Maybe the dowdiest cross-dresser in movie history, Dolly (played by Danny Schiller) is the sidekick of Julie Waters' blue collar madam, Christine Painter, and is only revealed not to be a sour-faced old cow but a sour faced old man when Christine surprises her in the toilet during a wedding. It's only a supporting role and Julie Walters pretty much steals any scenes she's in, but Dolly is still an endearing character.

3. Edna Turnblad in *Hairspray* (1988)

Divine had sickened us in *Pink Flamingos*, where he really did eat dog shit, and shocked us in *Female Trouble* as the disfigured freak hungry for fame but it was as Edna Turnblad, the easily shocked mother of Tracy—a teen model for Hefty Hideaway, a boutique for big girls—played by Ricki Lake, that he really came into his own. The story focuses on a lame whites-only TV dance show to which right-on Tracy wants to introduce racial integration. Edna is a bastion of propriety—a big break from Divine's repertoire—who stands by her daughter. Divine's acting was, as always, erm, unique and endearing. [See page 206]

4. Dorothy in *Tootsie* (1982)

When out-of-work actor Michael Dorsey fails to help his friend nab a leading female role in a soap, he hits on the idea that with a little cosmetic help he could bag the part himself. Initially not impressing anyone very much, it's Dorothy's feistiness that wins him not only the part but the love and admiration of the nation. Complications obviously arise as Dorothy falls in love with his co-star Julie (Jessica Lange), whose father falls in love with Dorothy. Brilliantly funny—especially the quick montage of Dorothy becoming a star and posing in a variety of looks for magazine covers—*Tootsie* makes more of a point about women than it does about drag queens. And that's not bad.

5. Victor in *Victor/Victoria* (1982)

The concept seemed a tricky one—a girl who dresses as a boy who dresses as a girl in shows but tries to pass as a boy in real life—but the nicest lady in Hollywood, Julie Andrews, pulled it off with such style that everyone got it. Julie looks better as a man than she does as a girl, and better as a drag queen than she does as a man (if that makes any sense). But even she is upstaged by the brilliant Lesley Anne Warren, who plays the dumb, crass blond whose nose is put out of joint when her mobster boyfriend, played by James Garner, starts a "gay" relationship with Victor. Brilliant musical numbers and a great gay best friend in the shape of Toddy, played by Robert Preston.

6. Mrs Doubtfire in *Mrs Doubtfire* (1993)

Robin Williams resorts to his gay brother's very complete make-up box to solve his domestic problems when his wife files for divorce and he looks like being deprived of contact with his kids. To dodge this, he gets done up as a loveable Irish nanny cum housekeeper and applies for the job of looking after his own children. A very safe use of cross-dressing—the "woman" is so old it is assumed that there are no sexuality issues at play here—Mrs Doubtfire is enjoyable for a limited period only and is upstaged by the gay brother played by the mighty Harvey Fierstien.

7. Rusty in *Flawless* (1999)

The healing powers of a pre-op transsexual are truly remarkable in this Joel Schumacker movie about Walt, a crusty old bigot of a stroke victim, played by Robert DeNiro, who gets landed with Philip Seymour Hoffman's Rusty as his care worker. Rusty, a sensitive and caring soul who just happens to have gender re-alignment on

the cards, goes about the long and gruelling process of teaching Walt not only how to cope with his new disability and speak again, but how to break through his issues. And it's a great performance by Seymour Hoffman, who plays it—and this is a weird one for a movie trannie—way down. Go figure!

8. ZaZa in *La Cage Aux Folles* (1978)

The vastly superior original version of the crass *Birdcage*, ZaZa, played by Michel Serrault, is the drag incarnation of nightclub owner Albin. He and his partner Renato's very happy existence in the south of France comes to a nasty end when Renato's son decides he wants to marry the daughter of an ultra-moral politician. ZaZa decides she will meet the girl's family as a woman with, as you can imagine, hilarious results. ZaZa is not only glamorous and fabulous but such a sweetheart that you never want her to go away. A real classic with a great (if flamboyant) example of a solid gay male partnership.

9. Felicia in *The Adventures of Priscilla, Queen of the Desert* (1994)

An absolute sensation when it opened, this film put Australia on the map as the spiritual home of all things trashy. Guy Pearce, now a major Hollywood star (*LA Confidential*, *Memento*), played Felicia as a bitchy, fierce ruling diva of a drag queen traveling the outback of Oz with fellow performers Bernadette, played by Terence Stamp and Mitzi (Hugo Weaving). As you would expect, they come across any amount of homophobia but Felicia is not one to take anything lying down. Throw in a whole bunch of trash songs and costumes Liberace would have toned down, and you have a great little feelgood film.

10. Big Momma in *Big Momma's House* (2000)

Malcolm Turner, played by Martin Lawrence, goes undercover as a big old lady in order to stake out the house of an escaped convict and tears cinemas apart. OK, it was never going to win any prizes for sophistication and owes one hell of a lot to Eddie Murphy's various female Klumps in *The Nutty Professor*, but Big Momma is a whole pantyhose-full of laughs, especially when she's trying to be sassy.

wallpaper* magazine

wallpaper* is possibly the gayest magazine in the world, like ever

I've never heard of it, what is it?
Call yourself a stylish homo? This opulent mag, launched by über-chic and mega-rich bender Tyler Brulé in 1996, is the ultimate glossy monthly for many a gay boy and girl with aspirations way above their stations.

What, so it's a wank mag for gay boys and gay girls?
No, no, no. You've got it all wrong. It's all about high fashion, first class travel, cutting edge architecture and high end art and design, interspersed with lots of very pretty girls and boys in stunning locations—usually wearing very little—with bodies and suntans to die for.

Sounds like a wank mag to me. So there's nothing about 1970s wallcoverings then?
According to the cover's strapline, it's dedicated to "the stuff that surrounds you." And yeah, if wallcoverings are in that season, they'll treat you to a fashion shoot featuring the most expensive ones available, complete with the right-looking folk draped up against them.

I'm liking the sound of that…
As well as that, this advertising-heavy mag—so thick it could be confused with a coffee table tome—speaks in such homo "more stylish than thou" dialogue that some months it's gayer than *The Advocate*…

And a lot more sexy by the sounds of it.
Just don't read it—presuming you didn't just buy it for the pictures anyway—when you're depressed, broke and hate your life. Ideas in *wallpaper** magazine to counter life's ennui would include buying your own tropical island, hiring a private jet, or swanning off to Damascus on a spending spree. Handy, huh?

Oh, if only I could find a boyfriend/girlfriend to support such a delicious, ridiculous lifestyle…
Well, the last we heard, Mr Brulé was still single… you see—there is a God.

Will & Grace

The odd couple!

Since its first screening in September 1998, *Will & Grace* has fast become the funniest show on television. What's surprising is that it's taken so long for a gay-themed network TV series to cross over to the mainstream, when after all everyone says their best friend is gay, right?

The sitcom's premise is simple: Will (played by Eric McCormack) and Grace (Debra Messing) are best friends, period. Don't expect them to do the *When Harry Met Sally* thang, because he's a gay lawyer and she's a straight interior decorator. In true comic style, both characters have fall guys in the shape of Will's queeny sidekick, Jack (Sean Hayes) and Grace's stuck-up bitch of a PA, Karen (Megan Mullally).

Ellen might have been groundbreaking, but there's no doubt that *Will & Grace* has surpassed it. The show has not only guest-starred Hollywood stalwarts like Debbie Reynolds, Gregory Hines, and Joan Collins, but it's been a massive hit with the critics and the public alike: at the 2001 Emmy Awards, it took home gongs for Outstanding Comedy Series, Outstanding Supporting Actor, and Outstanding Supporting Actress in a Comedy Series.

The show is not without its detractors. Will is a card-playing (yes, really), white, middle class man—hardly a threat to straight masculinity, and hardly a true representative of the varied gay life in New York where the show is set. Even the fact that the sitcom is set in the Big Apple helps "distance" it from the

conservative Midwest, who might take issue if it were set on their own doorstep. Furthermore, there's no getting away from the fact that most of the show's humor is derived from out-there, flamboyant Jack, whose character tends to rely on all the gay clichés of yore. Hmm...

Nevertheless, *Will & Grace* is proof of the changing attitudes, both of the public and of television networks, to gay men onscreen. It also looks like it will pave the way for many more gay-themed primetime shows. At the time of writing, a small-screen version of the 1997 independent movie *Kiss Me, Guido*, about a macho straight guy and his gay actor flatmate, was in the offing as was a sitcom based on Gary Goldstein's *Parental Discretion*, about a father and his gay son. Whether they hit the small screen is another question altogether, but without the crossover appeal of *Will & Grace* the prospect of shows like this would have been just a joke.

The Pink Pound, the Pink Dollar and the Pink Euro

How gay and lesbian big spenders became big business for pink pound- and dollar-hungry companies

Imagine it: a childless couple with two impressive salaries, no kids to support and a rather hefty disposable joint income to spend on a great home, vacations in the sun, and the highest fashions. Sure, not all gay men and women are as upwardly mobile as the advertising man's dream scenario, but more and more often, big businesses—who in the past would shy away from associating themselves with anything queer—are now shamelessly touting their wares for gay boys and girls. While some marketers dismiss the whole Pink Currency as a myth, in the other camp hardened political queers shun such shallow attention from profit-hungry capitalists who are suddenly wearing the rainbow flag with pride. Meanwhile the rest of the homos are embracing their new-found friends in industry and are spending like it's going out of fashion.

The Pink Pound, the Pink Dollar—or the Dorothy Dollar as it is sometimes known—is the potential spending power of the gay community. Depending on contrasting figures, this is anything between one and ten per cent of the population as a whole—and this collective income is a massive spending force to be reckoned with. The unique aspect of the gay community's spending power is that as a group they are fiercely loyal when it comes to splashing out with their hard-earned cash. Whereas the average (straight) consumer is influenced by the latest fashions, gay men and women's spending has a unique factor as it is also directed by whether a company has a "gay friendly" identity—whether that be an employer who offers domestic partner benefits for its workers, or one who uses positive gay imagery within their advertising campaigns. According to ID Research—a gay and lesbian agency that conducted the first ever gay and lesbian census in the UK in 2000—73.2% of queer consumers think that it is important that a company is 'gay friendly', while 77% think it's important that businesses show their support of the gay market by sponsoring lesbian and gay events and festivals.

Even though legal equality has been slow to arrive globally (and we're still waiting), businesses in Europe, the States and Australia were quick to recognize the monetary potential of attracting lesbian and gay consumers—with the gay market in the western world worth an estimated $400 billion (Sydney Mardi Gras alone pumped $99 million into the Australian economy in 1999) and rising, you can see why. While the demographics of other consumer groups are easy to chart, since the number of gay folk is still not really officially known it's a tricky one to put a figure on. But numbers aside, as more and more gay studies are conducted, it's becoming apparent that the queer market not only parties harder and more often than other groups—it's reckoned that homos spend twice as much on alcohol as their straight counterparts—but that gay people take vacations regularly and more frequently, and generally have a higher disposable income. These findings mean that a business that ignores gay people as a potential market is losing out on huge profit potentials. As the breweries in Britain began to take note—Bass Breweries' gay arm has become the most profitable gay company in Europe—so did American airline companies, with United Airlines spotting the potential early, and becoming one of the main sponsors of London's Pride event back in 1998. Many others, including Virgin Atlantic, and British travel agents Thomas Cook, have followed suit, sponsoring major gay festivals, and even publishing guidebooks aimed specifically at the gay male traveler.

But while press and marketing folk are quick to embrace gay men and women with cash, the Christian Right in the US and their fellow God-fearing friends in the rest of the world are threatening homo-friendly companies like Disney—who realize their gay market is far too large to risk losing—with mass boycotts. Despite the continuing controversy surrounding equal rights for gay people, the multinationals continue to court gay people. Whether this will lead to a watering down of the gay culture and its many communities, or a step toward equality in the marketplace at least, the Pink Pound and Pink Dollar will remain a favorite niche of marketers for a long time to come. The hope is that they choose to get to know their consumer before waving a rainbow flag in one hand, while they take homo cash with the other.

Queer As Folk

Groundbreaking and raunchy TV drama series about three gay guys, their friends and families

One thing's for sure: whether you were watching the original *Queer As Folk* series in the UK or how it translated onto American screens, it was a representation of gay life you'd never seen on television before.

In a nutshell, *Queer As Folk* is about three gay guys. The names might have changed but the characters are essentially the same. Stuart (UK version, pictured left)/Brian (US counterpart) is oversexed, totally hot, approaching thirty and not too happy about it. His lifelong best friend, Vince/Michael is a mild-mannered sweet guy totally into Stuart/Brian and always having to pick up the pieces for him—one of which is Nathan/Justin, his teen one-night stand who just won't go away. Throw in Stuart/Brian's fag hag mother, a lesbian couple (one of whom was impregnated by Stuart/Brian) and a menagerie of buddies and you have the makings of what has become a cult television show both sides of the Pond.

Apart from the names, there are other differences in the two series. While the UK's *Queer As Folk* consisted of ten episodes—one eight-episode series, followed by two final episodes the following year, the US had committed to a season and so had to build up the minor characters to accommodate.

The UK version was set in Manchester, a city with a burgeoning gay culture while the US's was located in Pittsburgh, Pennsylvania—an equivalent in theory, it hardly registers on most gay folk's consciousness, however. In the UK, Nathan was fifteen, in the US Justin was seventeen—the American version might have been prepared to push the envelope in some directions but not all of them. And finally, so American ladies didn't feel left out, there was also a full-on lesbian sex scene in the US version.

In fact, there's a lot of sex in *Queer As Folk*—and full-on legs-over-shoulders sex at that. Surprisingly, some of the US series even duplicated the scenes from its UK predecessor.

But despite the differences, there's one thing both series had in common: controversy. As well as the usual "gay men are sickos" moral outrage, criticism also came from some members of the gay community itself who objected to the fact that the characters were only interested in sex, drugs and clubs. But that only misses the point.

While it's nice to see Ellen, Will and some nice non-threatening queers on television, don't we deserve on-screen characters who represent all of who we are with our good points and our bad ones too?

Boy bands

As long as there are little girls and gay men, there will always be boy bands

During the last couple of decades, the music industry has seriously cottoned on not only to the spending power of the teenager, but also to the potential of the pink dollar/pound too, resulting in an almost endless stream of fresh-faced lovelies willing to pout, perform and take their tops off all for our pleasure.

Whatever the musical genre, wherever the territory (to coin music industry-speak), you can be sure there are and have been an endless supply of cute fellas perfecting their moves and their lipsynching. Any of these familiar? The Village People [see page 140], Menudo, New Edition, Boyz II Men, 5ive, O Town… we'll let you fill in the gaps.

While some might argue that the Beatles were the original and the best, don't believe them: John, Paul, George and Ringo might have made the world scream, but they weren't just a male vocal group performing other people's songs. They at least showed some semblance of talent.

The true pioneers of this genre were no doubt the Jacksons and the Osmonds back in the early 70s: cute, plastic and with serious pin-up material in the shape of Michael and Donny. And oh yes, they even had some good tunes.

But this musical genre (if you can call it that) really got a boost in the 80s with the arrival of New Kids On The Block on the erm, block. Highly marketable, they brought the edgy sounds of the street to the charts worldwide but were packaged in a way that teens could identify with. They were killed off, however, by grunge, though the genre mutated in the UK, spawning Take That, who helped shape the whole thing into what it is today—taking those urban grooves and throwing into the mix some heartstring-pulling power ballads worthy of George Michael.

You'd have to be a total cynic to suggest all boy bands are the same, but—hell—they can't help but have some things in common.

For instance: They are always chosen by an "evil" svengali-type manager at an audition, which has been advertised in the local stage press under the headline: ARE YOU GOOD LOOKING? Then in small print: Can you sing?

There are always at least three members, but no more than six—we don't want the kids to get confused.

They are always cute, but not too cute—and to show that there is some artistry at work here for chrissakes, there's always a fat, ugly but "talented" one.

They have zero input in the music… no hang on a minute, they might add the rhyme "glove" to "love" if only to get their name on the credits and ensure a share of the songwriters' cash.

And one of the group has always slept with men… well, at least in gay mythology.

New Kids On The Block

The story: After his success with New Edition, producer Maurice Starr translated the formula to white kids in oversized T-shirts and baggy pants. The oldest was barely sixteen, but Donnie Wahlberg, Jonathan Knight, Jordan Knight, Danny Wood and Joey McIntyre were a winning combo and by their second album in 1988, NKOTB mania had gripped the States. Jordan and Joey now continue with solo projects with varying success.
The hits: 'You Got It (The Right Stuff),' 'Hangin' Tough,' 'I'll Be Loving You (Forever).'

Take That [pictured above]

The story: From the word go, Take That were directly marketed at the gay audience with appearances at gay clubs (in their underwear!), and in gay magazines. Even after they struck the mainstream with their cover of Tavares' 'It Only Takes A Minute,' all the videos were seriously homoerotic. For five years Gary Barlow, Robbie Williams, Mark Owen, Howard Donald and Jason Orange ruled the British charts thanks to their combo of good looks, kitsch appeal, hi-NRG covers and Gary-penned ballads even your mum would like. In July 1995, Robbie, the wild one, left after "artistic differences" and the rest disbanded soon afterwards.
The hits: 'Back For Good,' 'Relight My Fire,' 'Never Forget' and 'Pray.'

Boyzone

The story: Undoubtedly, the poor man's Take That, Irish Boyzone were the brainchild(ren) of theatrical manager Louis Walsh. Ronan Keating, Stephen Gately, Shane Lynch, Keith Duffy, and Mikey Graham nevertheless managed the kind of longevity elusive to most boy bands, notching up a whopping 12 top five singles in the UK from 1994. After a sabbatical to work on solo careers, it's since become kinda bitter with stories that Ronan is unwilling to give a return tour a shot. Boyzone are of note however since they buck boy band trends by having a real live homosexual among their ranks: Stephen Gately was "nudged" into coming out by a British tabloid.
The hits: 'Love Me For A Reason,' 'When The Going Gets Tough,' 'No Matter What,' 'Baby Can I Hold You.'

*N Sync [pictured below]

The story: Like the BSBs, 'N Sync emerged out of Florida to follow an almost identikit route to boy band stardom. Ex-Mickey Mouse Club stars Justin Timberlake and JC Chasez hooked up with Chris Kirkpatrick, Lance Bass and Joe Fatone, got taken on by manager Lou Pearlman, notched up

hits in Europe before translating that success in the States with a tour of roller skating rinks and falling out with management over money.
The hits: 'Tearin' Up My Heart,' 'Pop,' 'Gone.'

Backstreet Boys

The story: Get this: the Backstreet Boys actually put themselves together! It wasn't however until Howie Dorough, AJ McLean, Nick Carter, and cousins Kevin Richardson and Brian Littrell hooked up with heavyweight manager Louis J. Pearlman that it started translating into a viable career. While their 1996 debut album established them in Europe and Canada, the States didn't cotton on until 'Quit Playin' Games (With My Heart),' and 'As Long As You Love Me,' and they've since notched up super-platinum sales.
The hits: 'Everybody (Backstreet's Back),' 'I Want It That Way,' 'Shape of My Heart.'

Westlife [pictured below]

The story: Blame Boyzone. Westlife are a carbon copy boy band—albeit better looking—brought to you by manager Louis Walsh and Boyzone's Ronan Keating (though his involvement was a publicity stunt), who since 1999 have worked a heady mix of power ballads, Irish charm and comfy designer knits. Shane Filan, Nicky Byrne, Bryan McFadden, Mark Feehily, and Kian Egan had notched up an unstoppable record-breaking slew of Number One hits and platinum sales, firmly establishing themselves as the boy band of preference in the UK. Success in the States has so far been minimal despite a collaboration with Mariah Carey, prompting the gag: What do you call a dog with five dicks?
The hits: 'Flying Without Wings,' 'Swear It Again,' 'If I Let You Go.'

Hollywood and Queers

Queers misrepresented, maligned and hidden on and off the silver screen

With the arts and homosexuality so intrinsically linked—"those gays, they're so artistic"—it's odd that mainstream cinema has so shamelessly marginalized, ignored or hounded gay men and women on-screen and off. When one of the earliest films ever made —*The Gay Brothers*, by cinema pioneer Thomas Edison—showed two men dancing with each other, it seemed that cinema and us queers were going to get along great. How wrong could we be.

At the beginning of *The Celluloid Closet*, Lily Tomlin says: "In a hundred years of movies, homosexuality has rarely been depicted on the screen. When it did appear it was something to laugh at or something to pity. Or even something to fear." It's true. Since the beginning of the 20th century we have been forced to read between the lines to find ourselves and our lives represented—even if those lines were written by queer writers like Gore Vidal, who scripted the classic homoerotic flick *Ben Hur*. We clapped and cried when Louise kissed Thelma, hoping that there was something more to it, and we raised a collective eyebrow when we spotted the tenderness between Stan Laurel and Oliver Hardy in those old black and white classics.

Compared to the enormous output of Hollywood's well-oiled movie machine, it was only in the past couple of decades that gay men and lesbians found the power and the finance to make great independent queer movies. Not surprisingly, these made-for-us gay classics began to rake in big bucks at the box offices and Hollywood decided to jump on the queer bandwagon and start making homo movies to line their own pockets.

With the prospect of AIDS difficult to ignore in the 1990s, and with growing support for AIDS charities from A-list celebrities, Hollywood turned its attention to the epidemic. While *Philadelphia* was a groundbreaking mainstream movie because it portrayed the struggle of someone with HIV, it was nevertheless a wealthy, middle class gay lawyer in a long-term relationship played by the likeable and the very straight Tom Hanks. There's not even a gay kiss. Meanwhile, the downright awful remake of the classic flick *La Cage Aux Folles—The Birdcage*, starring Robin Williams—again proved that Hollywood in the 1990s was only comfortable with stereotypical aspects of gay life.

Perhaps we're being too harsh? After all, Hollywood's aim has never been to reflect true life—fantastical images and storylines hardly accurately recount day-to-day happenings in the real world, let alone the queer one. But it's when you add to that mix the fact that for years gay and lesbian actors have been forced to hide their true sexuality with fabricated "womanizing" stories for the boys or faux-marriage ceremonies for the girls—even nowadays, young queer actors are recommended by their agents to stay well back in the closet—that Hollywood begins to smack of homophobia. And you thought the days of closet-cases like Rock Hudson, Montgomery Clift, and Marlene Dietrich were over. Even now, the studios insist that closeted actors appear in public with a member of the opposite sex on their arm so as not to arouse suspicion. So, while queer men and women continue to work in the studios, producing, writing, filming—and hell—starring in some of Hollywood's biggest blockbusters, it seems that, despite the political gains made by gay rights groups, the movie industry is one of the last places to endorse and protect the rights of its queer employees.

⇨ **Take it further:** The Celluloid Closet *by Vito Russo.*

Top 5
Gay best friend
movies

**A romantic lead, a plot
device or a beacon of
sanity in a crazy world,
gay men and lesbians do
have their uses in movies**

Never mind the Chanel chain handbag,
the gay best friend is fast becoming THE
must-have accessory for the smart
movie character about town. Not usually
the star of that movie, the gay best
friend is usually there—as in real life—
putting in a damn fine supporting
performance while the leading
characters get stuck into the main plot
developments. Here we have picked out
five, not necessarily the best, but
probably the highest profile. And yes, of
course Madonna's in there.

1. My Best Friend's Wedding (1997) [right]

This genuinely charming comedy uses
Rupert Everett's character, George, as
the gay best friend who happens to be
the only person in the entire movie to
have his head screwed on. Julianne
(Julia Roberts) has been friends with
Michael, a guy from college, played by
the dreamy Dermot Mulroney, for years.
They have always had a pact that if
neither of them is married by the age of
twenty-eight, they would marry each
other. As the deadline approaches,
Michael meets the girl of his dreams,
played by Cameron Diaz, and it looks like
the deal is off. Unless Julianne can
scupper their wedding plans. Recruiting
George to pose as her boyfriend in an
attempt to make Michael jealous,
Julianne draws her gay best friend into a
web of suburban deceit. The fact that
Everett makes George such a charming,
funny, natural and most of all sane
character among the madness around
him did much to revive his career while
the film's use of a gay character as a
simple plot device, without any hand-
wringing about his gayness, is a real sign
of maturity. Oh, and it's funny.

2. As Good As It Gets (1997)

In this Oscar-laden romantic-comedy-
drama-type thing, the gay best friend
starts out as a gay worst enemy. Jack
Nicholson plays Melvin Udall, a
cantankerous old bastard who makes his

gay neighbor Simon's life a misery. When
Simon, played by Greg Kinnear, is horribly
mugged (spot the gay-as-victim
stereotype), Melvin reluctantly agrees to
look after his dog, Verdell. And that dog
must have been to the Motown Charm
School or something as he weaves his
magic spell over Melvin in such a way that
not only does it look like he might actually
be able to start a love affair with Carol, a
waitress played by Helen Hunt, but may
also stop being a nasty little shit of a
homophobe. Everything comes to a head
when the three of them drive to Baltimore—
in itself, enough to make most people sit up
and take stock—and Melvin confesses to
Carol that she makes him want to be a
better man. Kinnear plays Simon by the
Hollywood fag book and comes over as a
fairly unappealing gay victim, in the early
part of the film at least. Didn't stop him
getting an Oscar nomination, but then why
would it?

3. The Object of My Affection (1998)

Nina Borowski (Jennifer Aniston) meets
George Hanson (Paul Rudd, the step-
brother from Clueless), a gay
schoolteacher, at a dinner party and
inadvertently lets the cat out of the bag
that he's being dumped by his boyfriend.
Mind you, her love life is not much better
with a stinker of a boyfriend who
manages to get her pregnant. The pair of
them move in together, become bosom
buddies and even try to get it on with
each other (very unsuccessfully) before

settling for the kind of straight girl-gay boy relationship we all know and love. The film got fairly poor reviews but is in fact a decent feel-good effort from the man who brought us *The Crucible* and *The Madness of King George*. The fact that it has such a restrained, sensible and non-Hollywood type ending sends you out with a lump in your throat and a thrill in your heart. Well, you feel OK about it.

4. Silkwood (1983) [top left]

Cher, complete with old nose and a very dodgy no-style hair-style, plays the dungaree-wearing lesbian best friend and housemate of Karen Silkwood (Meryl Streep), a nuclear plant worker intent on uncovering the evil company's disregard for the workers' health and safety. The lesbian friendship storyline is peripheral to the high drama of the industrial thriller but with a heart-breaking unrequited love scene on a swing on the porch, the theme is handled sweetly and, when Cher gets a girlfriend who works as a beauty attendant at a mortician's, hilariously. Meryl Streep was nominated for an Oscar for her role in this based-on-a-true-story drama, as was Cher, who managed to walk off with the Golden Globe for what was only her second acting part. It must have been a strange irony for Chastity Bono, Cher's daughter, watching her mum play a dyke, one struggling to come to terms (what else do you expect?) and yet be so reportedly unsupportive when Chastity eventually came out

5. The Next Best Thing (2000) [left]

For Madonna, whose film career is littered with stinkers, this total *The Object of My Affection* rip-off is a new nadir. She is Abbie, a yoga teacher (it was supposed to be swimming teacher but she didn't want to get her hair wet for a whole film) who one drunken evening falls in the sack with Robert, her gay best friend, played by Rupert Everett, who is cornering the market in gay best friend roles. The result is a child. So far, so predictable. Then Madonna falls for Ben (Julia Roberts' ex, Benjamin Bratt) and this non-traditional family goes the way of all families when tall dark dreamboats come on the scene: directly to court, where the whole movie becomes a shoddy re-run of *Kramer vs. Kramer*. Badly done, terribly acted and poorly rated by critics, *Next Best Thing* adds up to a pernicious kind of gaysploitation, even if it was conceived by the very gay Everett and directed by gay Brit John Schlesinger.

Freddie Mercury

The ultimate showman!

Throughout the 70s and 80s, Queen shaped the face of popular rock music. The band's frontman, Freddie Mercury, combined an amazing voice, an innovative talent for songwriting and lyrics— 'Bohemian Rhapsody' anyone?—and an outrageously flamboyant stage persona. He was one of rock's greatest showmen. Yet while he was adored by rock's generic fan base—straight teens to thirty-something males—the gay world was largely unimpressed, even if he was gay.

Freddie was born Farrokh Bulsara on September 5th, 1946, in Zanzibar to Persian parents. He optioned the name Freddie whilst attending an English boarding school where he threw himself into art and music. At the age of eighteen, he moved with his family to London and enrolled in the Ealing College of Art, where he met aspiring musician Tim Staffel, then a member of a band called Smile alongside guitarist Brian May and drummer Roger Taylor. In 1970 when Tim quit, Freddie took his place.

And so Queen were born—though a permanent bassist, John Deacon, wasn't found until just before the recording of their debut album. Inspired by the sounds of Led Zeppelin and Jimi Hendrix and by the era's over-the-top glam rock movement, the band's name and Freddie's new moniker, Mercury, epitomised what they were trying to achieve.

While their 1973 self-titled debut wasn't an instant hit, they built a hardcore male fanbase thanks to constant touring. By 1974, they were starting a run of top ten hits in their native UK that would be the most impressive for any group in history, apart from The Beatles. With 'Bohemian Rhapsody' from their breakthrough album *A Night At The Opera*, their success was assured and hits like 'Somebody to Love,' 'We Are the Champions,' 'Don't Stop Me Now,' and

'Crazy Little Thing Called Love' followed. By the end of the 70s, Freddie had honed his act as the ultimate showman. He wore his hair long, flaunted make-up and nail polish and teamed them with cutting edge designer outfits from Zandra Rhodes. Remember his open-chested, figure-hugging catsuit with wings? It might have prompted the quote: "My hose is my own. No Coke bottle, nothing stuffed down there." What he brought to the stage with his bombastic performances (and his trademark "broken" mic stand) was a blurring of sexuality, which proved endlessly fascinating.

By the 1980s, the image had changed. Gone were the outrageous stage outfits, now replaced with a new gay uniform: jeans and leather teamed with shorn hair and a handlebar moustache. The music changed too as Queen experimented with dance music, evident on the whopper 'Another One Bites The Dust,' but their album output was more hit 'n' miss: while *The Game* was their biggest album to date, the follow-up *Hot Space* proved much less successful as did Freddie's solo outing, *Mr Bad Guy*. The mid-80s saw the band back on track in the UK, if not the in States however, with albums like *The Works* and *A Kind Of Magic* and a show-stealing performance at Live Aid.

Anyone reading between the lines could tell Freddie was gay. Not only were there telltale signs like the flamboyance, the leather and the handlebar moustache, but Freddie often made allusions to his sexuality in his work. In fact, his sexuality was something he was highly preoccupied with: "My sex drive is enormous. I live life to the full." Meanwhile the lyrics and video for 'I Want To Break Free,' which saw him in drag, hardly tried to disguise it!

Nevertheless, Freddie was coy when it came to speaking frankly about his

sexuality throughout his career, even if it was regularly questioned despite a six-year relationship with Mary Austin, who remained a close companion/beard throughout his life.

He did however admit to being "extremely promiscuous" and his aftershow parties were infamous: he'd employ strippers, dwarves and topless waitresses to entertain the guests, and was even known to fly his friends to Munich in Germany (where he lived for a period) to enormous drag balls.

In 1985, he began a relationship with Irish hairdresser Jim Hutton, put his partying hard days behind him "and started growing tulips" instead. Meanwhile, Queen continued to rule the charts in Europe if not the States. Freddie fulfilled a lifelong dream by working with an opera singer, Montserrat Caballe on the album, *Barcelona*, and continued to chart in the UK with Queen on 1989's *The Miracle* and 1991's *Innuendo* albums. But by this time concern had started to grow about Freddie's health: his weight had plummeted from 170 pounds to just over 120 and the band started to scale down their activities.

On November 22nd, 1991, Mercury issued a statement confirming that he had AIDS, two days later he was dead from AIDS-induced bronchial pneumonia.

The following year, the remaining Queen members held a memorial concert at Wembley Stadium, featuring performers like David Bowie, Elton John, Annie Lennox, and Guns N' Roses. It raised millions for the Mercury Phoenix Trust, established for AIDS awareness, and was watched by more than one billion people worldwide.

Freddie Mercury's showmanship and talent remain undisputed today, and he's still much missed by fans, friends and lovers alike. Says his boyfriend, Jim: "Freddie and I never talked about how long we'd be together. Now and then he'd ask me what I wanted from life. 'Contentment and love,' I'd say. I found both in Freddie."

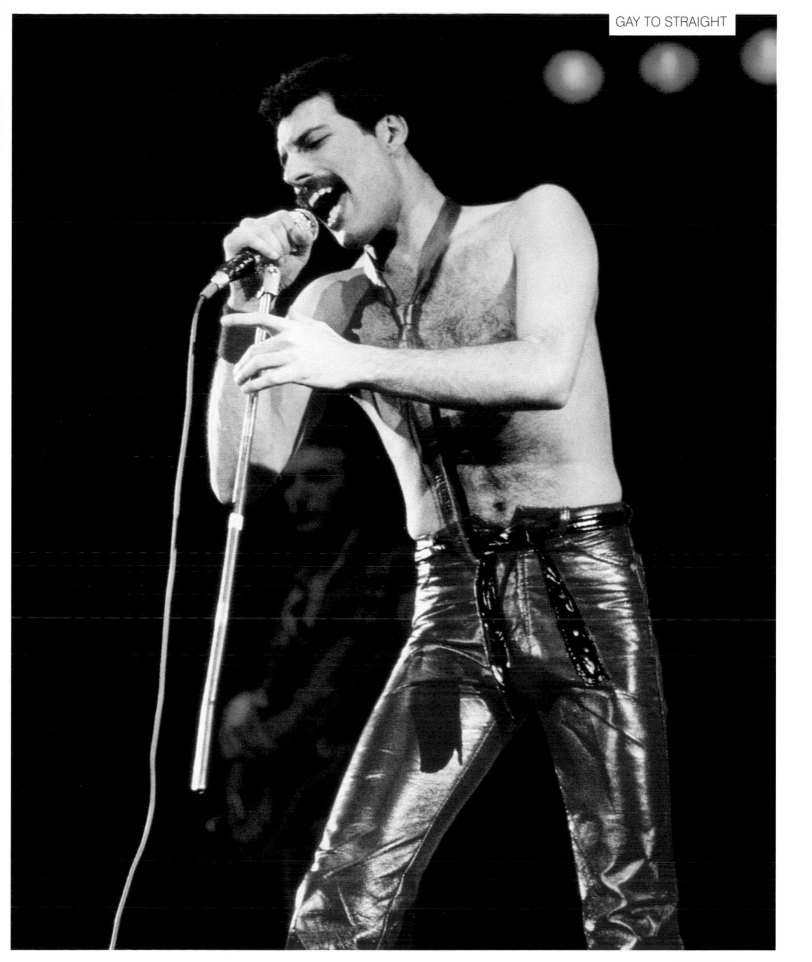

The Look

Famed for their hot-to-trot styles, gay men and lesbians have designed the world and created looks emulated everywhere. So, how do we look?

Alexander McQueen

The bad boy British fashion designer who took over one of Paris's most venerated couture houses

Probably the most unexpected character ever to head up a Paris fashion house, Lee (Alexander was for welfare purposes) is the son of a taxi driver from a deeply unfashionable part of East London. He started his career collecting glasses in a less-than-salubrious pub before enrolling as an apprentice at a Savile Row tailors, where he cut suits for the Prince of Wales (inscribing the legend "I am a cunt" in the lining, according to fashion legend). After more apprentice duties including a stint in Milan with Romeo Gigli he came back to London to study for a Masters Degree at the venerated St Martin's School of Fashion. His MA show was nothing short of a sensation, with every item being snapped up by über-stylist and fashionista Isabella Blow for instant sale in London's West End. He became a star overnight.

Having built a reputation as a fashion visionary, with shows that included a dress filled with moths, amputees running down the catwalk, fire, floods and anything guaranteed to grab a headline, he was signed up to take over from fellow Londoner John Galliano at Givenchy. Reviews were OK, but McQueen hated Paris, hated being told what to do, and soon threw it in, signing a deal with Gucci for his own label.

Despite his blue-collar background, Lee has always been openly—defiantly—gay, and even married a boyfriend aboard the Prince of Gambia's yacht off the Mediterranean party island of Ibiza in 1999. Supermodel Kate Moss was bridesmaid, Jude Law was in attendance. Happy to talk about drug-taking, liposuction, sex and suicide, and how he had clobbered a man in a bar over the head with an ashtray for coming on too strong with his boyfriend, McQueen is not your usual fashion fairy. "I'm not the stereotypical gay man," he says.

He always found it hard to deal with the fame and fortune aspect of the job, turning down a meeting with the Queen, publicly turning his nose up at the Prime Minister and his wife, and banning certain celebrities from his shows: "At the end of the day it's about my clothes and the hard work that everyone backstage puts into it, not about the fucking tosser sitting in the front row lapping it up," he says.

"Mentally, it does fuck you up because you start watching your back, especially when you start looking for a relationship as a gay man. All of a sudden you've got all these queens coming on to you that you've known since the 80s, that didn't take a second look at you and all of a sudden they want to know you. And you're having to deal with all that kind of shit. It's fucking hard to come across a good nut amongst all them bolts but it's been like that since it started going off really."

Gym Culture

How the beefed up body became the biggest gay cliché of them all

Whether it's a reaction to AIDS, a homoerotic reclaiming of our schooldays, a rejection of the camp image or a realistic attempt to get as much sex as we can in a demanding market, there's no doubt that the gay man's body is very different to the way it was just a few decades ago.

In the 50s and 60s, the cliché of a gay man was slim, well dressed and effete. The whole Athletic Model Guild thing just wasn't what we were like. It was what we liked. Then Tom of Finland started drawing pictures of muscleboys having very explicit gay sex with each other and a bell went off: we could be like that.

Throughout the 70s, gay gym culture grew and gay men started to take their eyes off the straight boys to become their own hyper-masculine objects of desire. They developed the biceps; they took the whole horny atmosphere of naked jocks they used to enjoy covertly in high school and made it their own.

But it was only with the advent of AIDS that the gay obsession with looking fit took a darker turn. With affected gay men getting skinny and wasting away, looking buff started to seem like the only way a gay man would ever get any. The bigger they got the less they looked like they'd got, you know, it.

This phenomenon coincided with a new era in popular culture, an era of the man as object. Advertising had begun to make men delicacies, with the whole focus of campaigns shifting onto their physical image and whether he was buff or a loser. And as gay men with money to spend on new clothes and fancy underwear, we were prime targets of this kind of advertising.

By the 90s, gym culture—and remember that by this time there were gay gyms where the boys could flick towels at each other's asses—had become entrenched. Whereas the muscled gay man used to be a special treat, it was now a "type," with the non-muscled gay man beginning to be excluded with phrases like "no pecs, no sex." The slim gay man—even if he had a nice face!—had become a marginalized sex type. Gay men were now kicking sand in their own faces.

Dolce & Gabbana

The most famous gay couple operating in fashion

Domenico argues that sexuality is completely individual, saying that he doesn't like it when people are divided up into hetero and gay, men and women. He also strongly disapproves of the way the media covers events like Gay Pride, choosing to focus on the drag queens and the "freaks" instead of the "normal couples" of gay men who live normal lives and don't feel any need to make an exhibition of themselves.

Dolce and Gabbana's refusal to go on Milan's comparatively pitiful Gay Pride marches has resulted in demonstrations against them but their stance is at the end of the day typically Italian. They say they refuse to live in a gay ghetto and that they believe the only way forward is to educate children to believe that gay men and lesbians are the same as everyone else and that the flaunting of difference runs contrary to that.

But internationally renowned celebrity designers or not, the issues discussed in the opulently decorated Dolce and Gabbana apartment in Milan (think leopard print walls, chairs covered in fur and big, important art) are the exact same issues long-standing gay partners from all walks of life are discussing. The main one recently has been the question of whether or not they will have children. And as is typical with the couple who say they can never agree on anything, how those children are going to be had is turning into a battle of wills and has thrown up some seemingly insuperable difficulties.

Domenico, who says that he loves children and whenever he sees gay couples with a baby he wants one too, says he wants to be like Josephine Baker and adopt 12 babies. But Stefano can't even believe he would entertain the idea and is set on having just one child, but a child of his own. He has even been doing fertility tests to find out where he stands. The problem is that, as a Catholic, he believes that a child should be the fruit of love, and should have both a mother and a father. As a gay man in a long-term relationship, this is obviously something of a problem.

These conflicts apart, Dolce and Gabbana are obviously a very tight couple, both professionally and personally, and twenty years into their relationship are at the height of their game, in all possible senses.

Piercing

No orifice or flap of skin is safe from the piercer's needle

While the art of piercing, or "body modification" as it is known by its aficionados, is an age-old practice, in recent years it seems no homo worth their salt can escape the painful "pleasure" of puncturing their skin with metal.

Gone are the days when the ears, nose and lips were the sole targets for adornment. Nowadays, no part of the body—not even the sacred genitals—are safe. While the more hardcore prefer the relatively new crazy crazes of scarification and branding, piercing is still a must for youngsters with a point to prove, or those who are old enough to know better. For those of you with a nervous disposition, look away now.

Genital piercings

When you've decided which adornment is for you, make sure that once pierced you don't touch your new piercing with dirty hands (like, hello?), but clean it regularly and do not allow any bodily fluids near the wound (that means saliva, semen et al) until it's fully healed. And if your piercer recommends you abstain from sexual liaisons for a certain period of time, take heed.

Intimate piercings for the ladies

Inner Labia

Less painful than getting the outer labia skewered, the inner labia is popular not just because it looks quite pretty, but because it can sometimes offer rather pleasant stimulation for the jewelry-wearer.
Healing time: 4-6 weeks

Outer Labia

A relatively simple procedure, the barbell is thrust right through the ladies' outer lips. And we ain't talking mouth.
Healing time: 8-12 weeks

Clitoral hood piercing

If you feel the desire to get your downstairs regions pierced, the clit hood is probably the least painful, quickest to heal and most stimulating spot. While it puts direct pressure onto the naughty clit, it doesn't actually penetrate it, so pleasure without too much pain. Perfect.
Healing time: 4-6 weeks

Fourchette

A tricky one for the ladies, this. The fourchette is placed over the perineum—that's the area between the anus and the vagina—from the bottom of the vaginal opening. As not all women have the extra flap of tissue here, it's not always possible to pierce. It's also not the most sturdy flap of flesh, so if jewelry is caught, it could tear. Ouch. It's also not the most comfortable piercing to wear during sex.
Healing time: 8-12 weeks

Triangle

Not all girlies can sport the clever little triangle piercing, due to a particular anatomical layout needed. The jewelry is inserted just below the clitoris, and then goes behind the clit itself. Not only does it look pretty fantastic, but when the front of the clit is being stimulated, the piercing works the back end all by itself. Impressive, huh?
Healing time: 8-12 weeks

Christina

Not a very common one, the Christina—what a lovely name!—can take up to 16 weeks to heal and can often be rejected by the body. It is a vertical piercing that goes straight through the V-shape at the top of the point where the outer labia join.
Healing time: A whopping 12-16 weeks

Clitoris Piercing

Possibly the most ultra-sensitive place to have a rod of cold steel rammed through—we're not putting you off are we?—the clitoris piercing is not for everyone as it can either make it super-sensitive or rob it of its sensitivity altogether! If the girl's clit doesn't stick out enough, the piercer won't pierce.
Healing time: 4-6 weeks

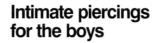

Intimate piercings for the boys

Guiche
The guiche (said "geesh") is a complicated little devil. It's found underneath the scrotal sack, near the anus, but because of a lack of ventilation to said area, plus the chance of heavy perspiration, there's a big chance that the guiche piercing will be rejected. It is also not recommended for men who ride bikes and sit down for most of the day!
Healing time: 4-6 months

Frenum
A great little piercing, and nearly as popular as the Prince Albert, the frenum is quick to heal and relatively painless (considering you're getting your cock stapled, effectively). The needle goes through the loose skin on the underside of the shaft, just behind the head of the penis.
Healing time: 2-4 months

Dydoe
One for the boys who have been circumcised (though not only for them). If the head of your penis is big enough, the dydoe's yours for the taking. The needle is placed against the head, at either the top or sides, and can be a singular or multiple piercing. Loss of sensitivity, due to circumcision, is sometimes restored.
Healing time: 4-6 months

Ampallang
Quite difficult to perform, the ampallang is made horizontally through the head of the penis, and either goes above or below the urethra. It's a tricky one for the piercer who needs to avoid nerves and arteries. Not for the faint-hearted as the needle itself takes longer to push through the penis than others piercings. After-care is crucial.
Healing time: 6-12 months

Apradavya
Easily confused with the term used by magicians, the apradavya is like the ampallang, but goes through the head vertically. Also slow and painful.
Healing time: 6-12 months

Scrotum
Scrotum or 'hafada' piercings are quite painless and can be done pretty much anywhere on the scrotum, but are often difficult to heal and can snag on clothing.
Healing time: 2-4 months

Foreskin
Obviously, not for boys with cut penises, the foreskin can be pierced as often as you like and it helps exaggerate sexual pleasure.
Healing time: 2-4 months

Prince Albert
The most popular and well known of all male genital piercings—a needle receiving tube is inserted down into the urethra and the needle is fed into the tube via the penis itself.
Healing time: 2-4 months

The rest of the body

If the genital piercings seem a little too hardcore for your tastes, there are a bunch of other places suitable for some steel on your bod.

1. Eyebrows
Popular with rock kids, the eyebrow piercing is nowhere near as scary as the lip or nose area. Pretty painless, though definitely not recommended as a do-it-yourself job.

2. Ears
Oh come on. Hardly an original place for a bit of metal, unless you decide to go mad and have every available space on your lobes adorned. Not a good look.

3. Nose
The nose piercing comes with two options the simple-yet-effective nostril piercing, or the septum piercing, which is the bit of cartilage that sits between your two nostrils.

4. Lips
Anywhere on the lips can be pierced, but anything at a jaunty angle usually looks like bits of old food. Metal on the lips often knocks or rubs against the teeth and can cause dental problems.

5. Tongue
An adornment perfect for people who annoyingly like sticking their tongue out in photographs, the tongue piercing means the wearer is off solid food for up to a week. Due to saliva's natural healing properties, however, it's one of the easiest piercings to look after. It's imperative that it's done by a professional, or excessive bleeding can occur.

6. Nipples
Arguably the prettiest and sexiest of all piercings, the nipples look great adorned with a ring or barbell.

7. Belly button
Preferred by the girls, but if not looked after properly, the belly button piercing emits a rather revolting odor.

Lesbian Chic

An obsession of the mainstream press, lesbians became "the new black" in the mid-90s. Or so we were told...

It used to be something of a joke to suggest that lesbians were trendsetters with their fingers apparently on the pulse of fashion (we know where those fingers have been). So when "lesbian chic" became the new buzz phrase of straight journalists, and "lipstick lesbians" became the new cover girls, dykes the world over let out a collective chuckle.

It's now a new millennium and gay girls are wearing hot-to-trot fashions with the best of them, but before the lesbian chic craze hit the pages of the world's press, dykes were more well known for their dungarees [see page 101], Birkenstocks, dodgy haircuts and 'ban the bomb' t-shirts. And any self-respecting lezza wouldn't be caught dead with Chanel lipstick in her cumbersome backpack.

As soon as Ellen Degeneres [see page 97] stepped out of her well-stocked closet with her trophy girlfriend, it seemed that all the media wanted were stories about lipstick lesbians. Soap operas showed off their new lezza characters who didn't necessarily drive trucks for a living (or look like they drove trucks for a living) and fashion mags for straight ladies were encouraging their readership to live out their bisexual fantasies. Instead of the usual cover lines screaming, "Make your man a better lover," suddenly readers of glossy magazines were urged to "Get in touch with your lesbian side" and were being told that it was "hip to be lesbian." Meanwhile, right-wing Christians in the States were getting rather hot under the collar over this promotion of lesbianism and their websites started screaming about "lesbianism gone wild" and vilifying journalists like the famous Liz Smith for daring to proclaim that "hetero is retro."

By 1993, from *Newsweek* to the *New York* magazine, commissioning editors could not get enough of our licking sisters. kd lang, the world's, erm, other famous lesbian appeared on the cover of *Vanity Fair* receiving a rather hot, close shave from supermodel Cindy Crawford, while fame-hungry celebs had to get a piece of the lesbian action: Madge became the most famous "bi-try" of them all. As well as including sexy dykes like nightclub promoter Julie Tolentino in her *SFX* book, she also hinted at an affair with comedienne Sandra Bernhard [see page 98] live on American television. We knew it was all for show, but we loved it anyway.

While lesbians sat by and smugly watched, they already knew really that not only was the whole phenomenon going to fade quite quickly, but that it was also a load of straight fabricated nonsense. It was only ever the pretty, model-skinny supposed lesbians, resplendent in their gorgeous fashions and lipstick that stared out from the pages of glossy publications. These safe, marketing-friendly dykes obscured the real lesbians who were carrying on their daily business unaffected and as ever invisible to the ad men. While *Beverly Hills 90210* boasted a lesbian episode it did nothing for improving gay and lesbian rights, and while dykes may have loved the attention, it did nothing for their collective dress sense.

And those straight journalists who pilfered the lesbian community for stories? They were still scared of real dykes.

Crossing Over, Catch by Leslie Be

Key Lesbian Chic Moments

kd lang on the cover of *Vanity Fair* being shaved by Cindy Crawford.
The Ellen Degeneres' 'coming out' episode.
The first lesbian kiss on primetime British television in the soap opera *Brookside*.
Madonna and Sandra Bernhard flirting outrageously on the *David Letterman* chat show.
Geri Halliwell and Kylie Minogue snogging with tongues and everything on the British chat show *TFI Friday*.
Kylie Minogue's 'What Do I Have To Do?' video.
Flamingo Road star Morgan Fairchild turning up as Sandra Bernhard's girlfriend in *Roseanne*.
Samantha in the über-glamorous *Sex And The City* series doing the dyke thing.

Jean-Paul Gaultier

French fashion designer, noted for inventing Madonna's conical bra

He may be nearing fifty, but it looks as if Jean-Paul (you can get away with JPG) is going to find it hard to shake that *enfant terrible* tag. A lonely child who practiced fancy lingerie designs on his teddy bear Nana, Gaultier's first fashion break was when, having sent sketches to pretty much every designer in Paris, he was taken on by Pierre Cardin at the age of eighteen. At twenty three, with the help of his boyfriend Francis Menuge, he set up on his own and became one of the most recognizable designers of the 80s. Menuge died of an AIDS-related illness in 1990, and Gaultier went into decline. He was back on top in the late 90s when, after having been passed over as head of Dior, he started financing his own couture shows.

A big friend of Madonna, Jean-Paul has proposed marriage to her no fewer than three times:
"She refused all the time. Always in a very polite way."
Were you serious?
"She was the only woman I would ever have married."
What if she had said yes?
"I would have loved it."
Would you have done it with her?
"Yes, I think so. I think a lot of gay men would."

Career highs:

The costumes for Madonna's *Blonde Ambition* tour and for the *Drowned World* tour.
Putting men into skirts and pulling it off.
Cycling shorts and Doctor Martens work boots (especially with their steel toe-caps exposed) enter fashion.
Starring as a presenter on the UK comedy show *Eurotrash*.
The first ever couture show featuring menswear: "It was unique. So unique no-one bought the clothes. I've still got them!"

Tattoos

A tattoo is for life, so make sure your skin art isn't just another queer cliché

People have been permanently inking their bodies for a whole host of reasons since 12,000 BCE. Women in Borneo had their specialist craft tattooed onto their forearms to show off their skills and attract potential husbands, while men in Japan acquired facial tattoos to ward off evil spirits. Even Egyptian mummies uncovered from their tombs have been found sporting fetching skin art. From a ritualistic and tribal marking to a political statement, the tattoo has meant a number of things through the ages—it could signify anything from which gang you belonged to, to having spent time in the slammer—though nowadays skin art has become just another fashion form. Once a rebellious marking, a tattoo now tends to mean you're just another follower of the flock, so make sure you choose your queer tattoo wisely.

Rainbow flag
Instead of that boring old rainbow flag, why not add a cheeky scorpion motif to the billowing symbol of gayness? Perhaps, if this is your choice of personal decoration, you really need some more time to think about your design. Remember: Gay does not necessarily equal rainbow flag.
Cliché rating: 10/10

Pink triangle
The pink triangle can be brightened up with all manner of accessories. While some Americans opt to dress theirs up a little with a patriotic eagle or the stars and stripes, other tattoo freaks add a tiger, rose or even a snake. Scary. The pink triangle is, however, when not messed about with, clearly a political statement. Gay men in the Second World War [see page 50] were made to wear this symbol to show everyone their "deviant" sexuality, so the brandishing of such a symbol now clearly gives the finger to its oppressive history.
Cliché rating: 3/10

Celtic band
Once an unusual emblem, sported by only hardcore tattoo-wearers, the Celtic band has become something of a tired old joke in the land of needle and ink. The band, if drawn properly, should extend around the entire arm, including the incredibly sensitive underarm area. Whether it was the influence of dyke icon Mel C from the Spice Girls [see page 33], or even the well-formed Pamela Anderson in the movie *Barb Wire*, the Celtic band with its intricate knots has become a cheap choice. If it has to be black, why not delve into the history books and check out some funky Maori designs instead?
Cliché rating: 7/10

Anchors
With so many gay boys so desperate to appear macho, the anchor is a popular choice. Sported by sailors without much of an imagination, including Popeye, it's a great way to butch up even the weediest of arms. Some more cheeky queer tattoo-lovers may even throw in a sexy sailor boy to the tableau.
Cliché rating: 2/10

Cats
The ultimate lesbian tattoo? Cat symbols have been used for centuries to represent women and witchcraft, and are no strangers to skin art catalogs. Go for a fierce big cat like a tiger or sleek panther to represent your personality, or a sexy sphinx for that Cleopatra-style inking. When done properly, they can look pretty damn good.
Cliché rating: 4/10

Names of girlfriend/boyfriend
A big no-no. Despite being the first rule of tattooing to never add a girlfriend or boyfriend's name to the skin, even if it is the most solid and perfect relationship in the world, like, ever, there are still some queers who go ahead and do it. Buy

Kathy a bunch of flowers instead. Or perhaps Zack would rather have that lovely Helmut Lang shirt he saw the other day. A tattoo is for life and, invariably, a girlfriend or boyfriend isn't. Looks especially dodgy when one name is crossed out for a new one.
Cliché rating: 10/10

Barcode
So radical for such a very, very short time, the barcode inscribed with your choice of "queer" or "dyke" not only showed the world you were a big old faggot, but also gave a nod to the anti-capitalist movement. Clever, but rather ugly as a skin motif.
Cliché rating: 6/10

Muscle Mary
A Muscle Mary with a picture of a Muscle Mary on his big arms or beefed up chest. Cute, huh? No, not really. A popular one for those boys with more muscles than brains, it's a cheeky nod to straight lads who sport lady mermaids and sexy waitresses on their skin.
Cliché rating: 7/10

Cartoon characters
However much you adored the cross-dressing Bugs Bunny as a kid, or Pluto the dog for his happy-go-lucky personality, a cartoon character on the flesh really isn't cute. Time to grow up.
Cliché rating: 8/10

Nike swoosh or any other logo
Surely wearing a big swoosh or CK on your sweater is enough to show the world that you adore the apparel that these clever designers who take all your money produce? An inked-up sneaker logo, whether ironic or not, is just sad.
Cliché rating: 10/10

Anything from Eastern culture
You could have the word 'peace' tattooed in Japanese, embellished with a pretty yin and yang. Or how about your name? But think about it—what if a tattooist with a weak grasp of the Japanese language spells it wrong, making you look stupid? Or worse still, if they punish you for your unoriginality by writing "asshole" instead?
Cliché rating: 9/10

Drag Kings

The art of drag is taken, shaken and stirred up by the ladies

Drag kings first came to light in the mid-1980s, but it wasn't until the 90s that the art of drag really became a plaything of the dykes. While women have been cross-dressing for centuries and dykes have been doing butch between the sheets *and* on the streets for decades, it was only recently that girls in drag became a popular performance art.

The cities of San Francisco and New York kick-started a colorful and exciting drag king scene, and pretty soon lesbians the world over were sticking on false moustaches, stuffing socks down their panties and walking with a swagger while boys' toilets in clubs were filled with handsome dykes with fantastic sideburns teaching each other how to pee standing up. Butch dykes continued on-stage what they've been doing in public for years, while femme dykes took up drag and started dressing as androgynous boys, and adopted the walk and the talk.

And it wasn't just other dykes who came in their numbers to stare at these outrageous lesbians who were dressing themselves up in all manner of male regalia, from gay boy clones and gigolos, to drunken men in suits with piss-stained trousers. While the drag queens had been dressing everything up in lipstick and glitter for decades, the drag kings were showing a seedier, dirtier, sexier and more dangerous side to drag. They were borrowing from all forms of masculinity and were refusing to give it back. In the mid-90s, when it was becoming cool to be a dyke whether you wore lipstick or not (according to the mainstream press who promoted bisexuality and lesbian chic to their readers), the audiences in these packed-out drag king clubs included straight men and women, gay boys, drag queens and more often than not, journalists from the glossy magazines who had come to watch the chicks with false cocks mess around with gender and stereotypes. They desperately wanted the story on these butch girls with, as they thought, penis envy and a desperate urge to be men with dicks who knew how to use them. Little did they know.

Men's fashion magazine *Arena* photographed lesbian icon Demi Moore decked out in a suit and facial hair, while *Vanity Fair*'s cover showed a suited and booted kd lang getting a close shave from a scantily clad Cindy Crawford. Even the *Pirelli Calendar*, the shiny, soft focus soft porn calendar from the makers of tires which annually features photographs by the likes of Herb Ritts, boasted Linda Evangelista and Naomi Campbell sporting drag king get-up in 1994. Gutter chat shows featured drag kings before and after their makeovers, much to the amusement and shock of the horrified middle-American trailer trash audience.

By the end of the 1990s drag kings ruled. In New York, the masters of drag—Mo B. Dick and Dred King—were performing to audiences filled with screaming girls. In Italy, George Michael lookalikes, complete with red lipstick, performed to audiences of a thousand screaming fans—gay and straight—who were peeling off their panties and throwing them at the performing kings like they were Tom Jones. In London, clubs like Naïve and Knave saw femme dykes and butch lesbians sporting suits, slicked back hair, moustaches and realistic-looking facial hair. Drag King Contests were being held everywhere, with many a dyke crowned the king of their city. Camp, badly behaved, butch and dangerous, somehow the likes of Buster Hymen, Elvis Herselvis, Svar Tomcat, Harry Dodge, Uncle Louie, Lizerace, Jewels and Dred managed to overthrow the media hype surrounding lipstick lesbianism, and became the young and cheeky pretenders to the drag throne. The Queens are dead. Long live the Kings!

⏵ **Take it further:** The Drag King Book *by Del LaGrace Volcano and Judith "Jack" Halberstam, published by Serpent's Tail, 1999. Check out the sexy shots of drag kings from New York, London, and San Francisco*

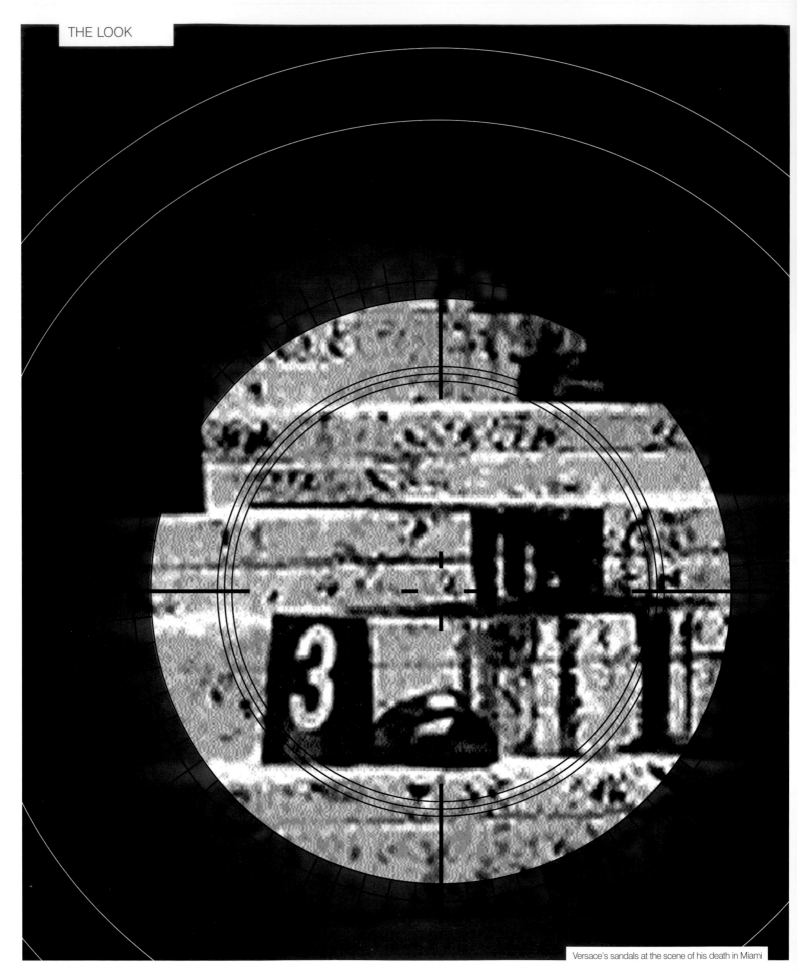

Versace's sandals at the scene of his death in Miami

Versace

The flamboyant head of the world's most opulent fashion house who was murdered in 1997 by a gay serial killer

Gianni Versace was one of the world's most successful and famous fashion designers and the head of his eponymous multi-million dollar fashion house when he was killed in front of his Miami home by Andrew Cunanan in 1997. Born into a relatively poor family in Reggio Calabria, southern Italy in 1946, Versace launched the Gianni Versace label in 1978. The rest is big business and history.

Instead of safe designs for the ladies that lunch, Versace created sexy, flashy, outrageous clothes for women and, unusually for a couture designer, men, that reflected his rock star role in the world of fashion. And he wasn't just a designer, he played the media at their own game and spent millions on self-publicity every year. While the glamor set adored his work, some critics saw his clothes as tasteless and vulgar with his signature low-cut dresses and use of expensive fabrics winning him both admirers and detractors.

Unlike fellow designers who were careful to hide their sexuality, Versace was out, proud and shameless. He lived an idyllic life in the eyes of his many queer fashion followers—a playboy lifestyle without the bunnies. He lived in a vast villa in Miami which more than comfortably housed him and his long-term boyfriend, Antonio D'Amico. His name appeared on the guest list for all the important parties and A-list celebrities called him their friend.

The clothes that helped build the Versace Empire to a business that was making profits of $900 million in 1995 alone appeared on all the right bodies. "That dress" kick-started the career of Elizabeth Hurley back in 1994, while former grunge princess Courtney Love made her supermodel-style debut in a snow white Versace gown. At Versace's funeral, Elton John was consoled by his boyfriend David Furnish, while Princess Diana issued a statement saying she was "devastated" at the news of his murder, ironically just months before her own untimely death.

Despite the murder of Gianni, the Versace fashion house has continued successfully under the rule of his sister and muse Donatella. Donatella had always designed the lower-price diffusion range Versus, but after his death, Gianni's deep-tanned, blond-haired sibling seamlessly took over as head designer of all of the Versace couture ranges. While many obituaries honored his skills as a great designer, the majority ignored the presence of his long-term partner, D'Amico. Many commentators questioned this, raising the point that if a straight designer of this calibre were murdered (for example, Calvin Klein), their partner would never be omitted from a tribute.

Andrew Cunanan

The slaying of Gianni Versace wasn't Andrew Cunanan's first killing [see page 63]. He was already on the FBI's Most Wanted List when he hunted down Versace at his exclusive South Beach home.

The once-handsome Cunanan, who had "let himself go" in recent months, had already murdered four men that year, including two of his former lovers, and was being tracked across the States by the police. No one knew why he'd started his killing spree, but commentators and onlookers of his murderous journey blamed jealousy and his possible HIV-positive status.

Despite being tracked up and down the country, Cunanan managed to move to Miami without difficulty on May 10th, 1997. There he checked into the scruffy Normandy Plaza hotel for a month. Even though he knew the police were watching the gay venues in the city, he regularly visited clubs like The Twist, which he knew Versace frequented when he was in town. Some say that Cunanan was an acquaintance of Versace's, others have alleged that they were lovers, but these rumours have all been strenuously denied by the Versace family.

Gianni had just got back from a hectic tour of Europe and was keen to settle in to his relaxed Miami life, but Cunanan had different ideas. Having watched the millionaire designer's villa during his stay in the city, he knew that Gianni left his palatial home every morning to visit the News Café for coffee. On the morning of July 15th, despite the police being given confirmed sightings of Cunanan in the Miami area, he caught up with Versace when he was undoing the lock on the gates to his home and shot him twice in the back of the head with .40 calibre bullets. Versace was found dead wearing shorts and sandals.

The murder of Versace propelled Cunanan into the limelight—a news story from heaven, it was the twisted tale of a gay serial killer on the run who once courted rich and beautiful men. And killed them. A man who had the cunning to escape the police four times over, and who had killed, apparently without reason, one of the world's highest profile and richest gay men.

The manhunt that ensued, with the eyes of the world's media watching, resulted in the police eventually finding Cunanan on July 23rd, 1997 in a houseboat that he had broken into for refuge. It was later found out that this houseboat belonged to a gay club owner who fled the States due to his alleged involvement with the killer.

The FBI and police pulled out all the stops, and after a three-hour stand off, they stormed the barge. They found Cunanan already dead. He had killed himself with a .40 calibre bullet to the head.

⇨ **Take it further:** Three Month Fever, *by Gary Indiana.*

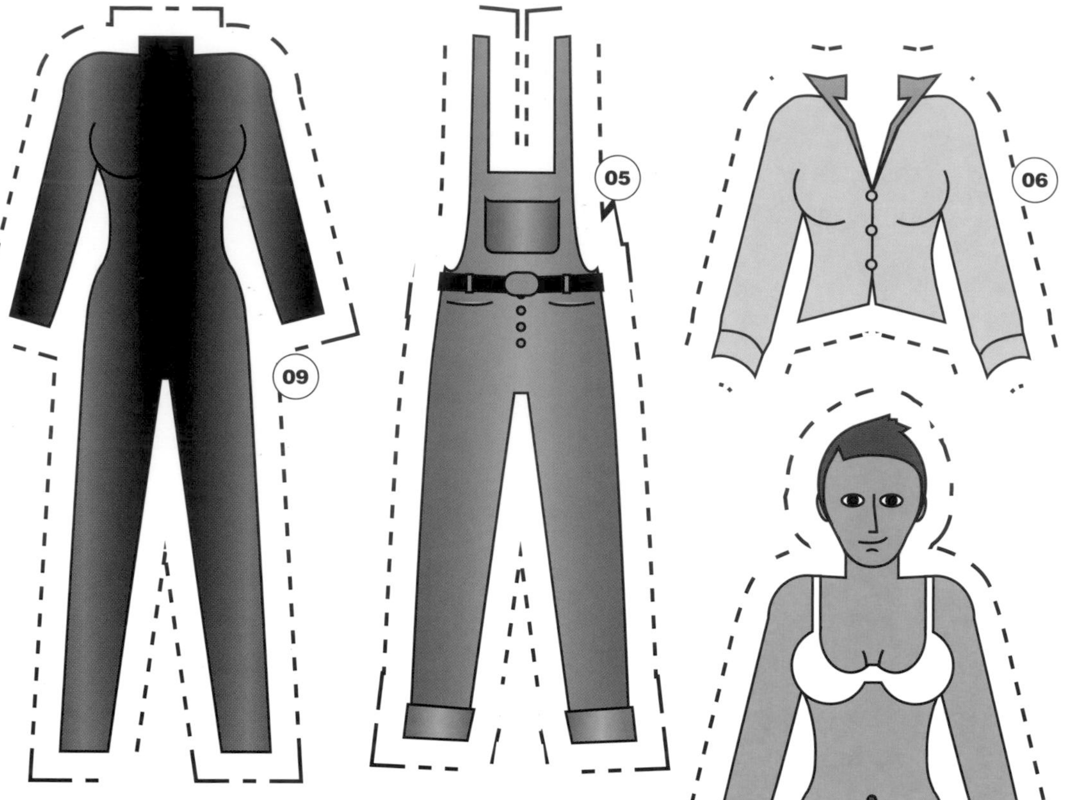

Gay Uniform

We may be a stylish bunch, but even those of us into our Dolce & Gabbana and Versace ensembles can't help reverting to the gay uniform classic pieces every now and then

GIRLS

01 Tracksuit pants
02 Cat
03 Funky trainers
04 Lumberjack shirt
05 Dungarees
06 Shirt with collars turned up
07 Waistcoat
08 Skinny disco t-shirt
09 Rubber catsuit
10 Prada handbag
11 Black tailored suit

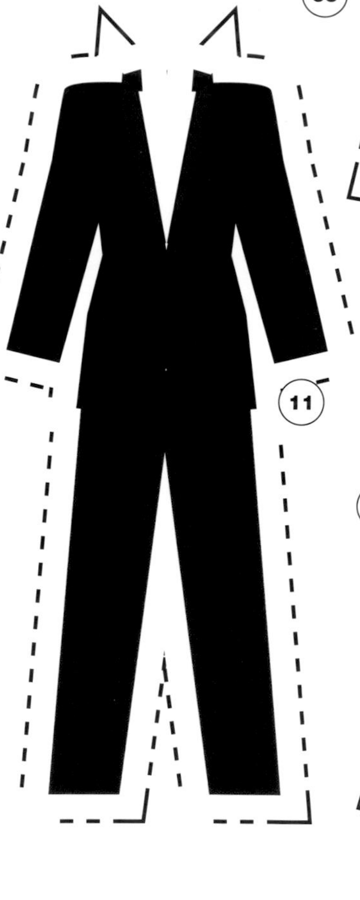

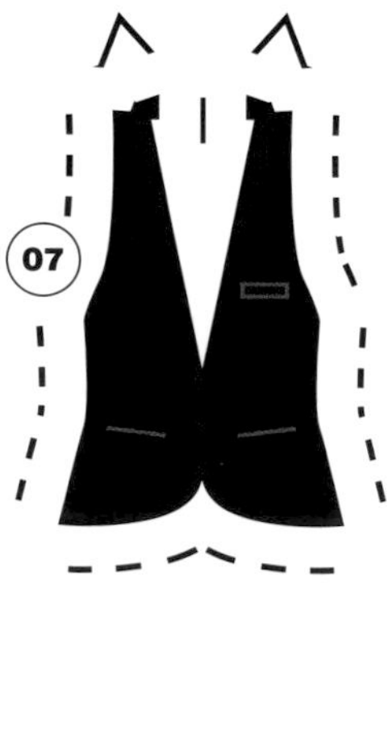

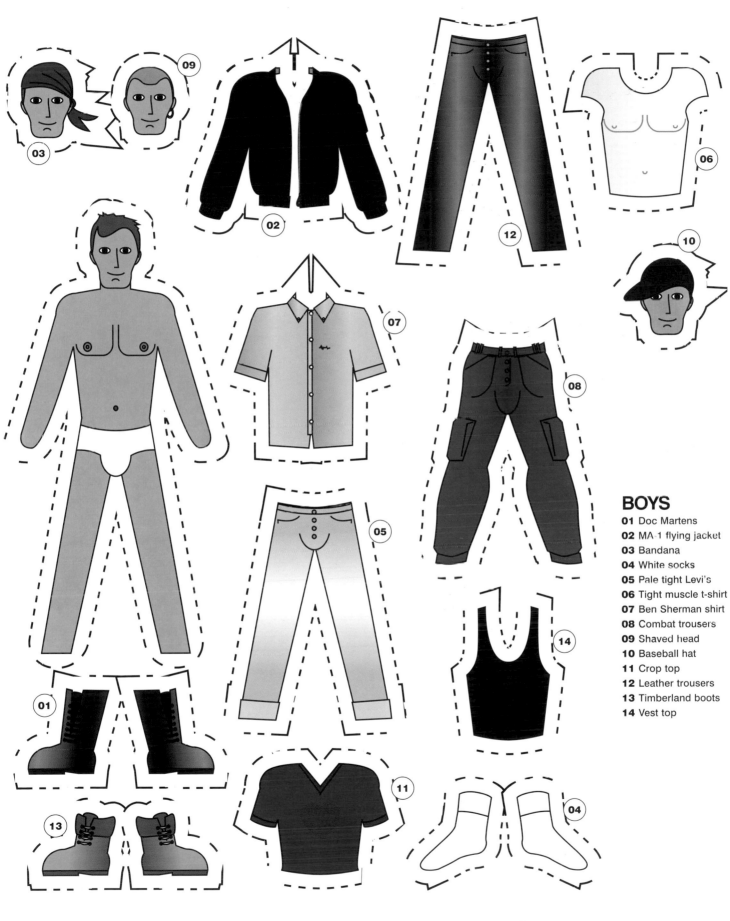

BOYS

01 Doc Martens
02 MA-1 flying jacket
03 Bandana
04 White socks
05 Pale tight Levi's
06 Tight muscle t-shirt
07 Ben Sherman shirt
08 Combat trousers
09 Shaved head
10 Baseball hat
11 Crop top
12 Leather trousers
13 Timberland boots
14 Vest top

Let Me Entertain You

From showgirls to supermodels, lank-haired chanteuses to high-haired drag queens, gay men and lesbians have always given great value for money.

Top 10 Gay movies

The cream of same-sex celluloid

While Hollywood pretty much ignored, maligned, and hell, even banned portrayals of homo folk way back when [see page 149], in recent years queer cinema has become a respected and money-making genre made by homos—and occasionally straight folk—desperate to offer some kind of cinematic representation of gay men. Here are some of the best examples of homo cinema.

1. La Cage Aux Folles (1978)

One of the first queer flicks that unashamedly portrayed a loving gay couple with humor, queeniness and a good helping of farce. The tale of two French gay men, Renato and Zaza, whose son is about to tie the knot, the comedy starts when it's revealed that the son, Laurent, has not told his future in-laws about the 'colorful' life that his two dads lead. So as not to ruin the future wedded bliss of his son, Renato decides to hide the nature of his business—an outrageous drag club—and pose as Laurent's straight, respectable father, while Zaza opts for the role of wifey. Of course things don't go to plan. Check the original before you opt for the dubious 1996 remake, The Birdcage, starring Robin Williams. It also spawned a musical.

2. Ma Vie En Rose (1997)

Boys will be girls in this gorgeous, and beautifully filmed Belgian flick about an adorable seven-year-old, Ludovic, who decides he wants to be a girl when he grows up. Alain Berliner's tender film, which bagged itself a Golden Globe, gets inside the head of a young boy whose dream it is to marry the boy next door. An uncomprising work that is not only a sharp social satire, but also a damn fine film.

3. Parting Glances (1986)

A refreshing addition to the gay flicks of the AIDS-hit 1980s, this is an indie-esque flick about two gorgeous gay men who are about to go their separate ways—gay yuppie Robert is about to quit Manhattan for an assignment in Africa, leaving behind his lover, Michael. As we follow them around the chic NYC lofts and chi-chi dinner parties that the pair attend in their last few hours together, they are completely overshadowed by Steve Buscemi (in his debut movie), who plays Nick, Michael's best friend and former lover who's HIV-positive. The tête-a-têtes that the couple go through prior to Robert's departure provide an insight into late 1980s Manhattan, readying itself for the onset and impact of AIDS.

4. Maurice (1987)

The perfect combination of a period dramarama and top English eye candy, Maurice—the E. M. Forester novel that remained unpublished until after his

death because of its queer theme—is given the Merchant Ivory costume drama treatment and a happy ending. Starring the very dapper Hugh Grant as Clive, an English aristocrat who confesses his love for his posh close friend Maurice, played by the foppish James Wilby, it's set during the First World War in England— a time when homosexuality was illegal. After initial shock, Maurice requites the love but in doing so drives away Clive, who's more interested in an intellectual head fuck than full-on, boy-on-boy passion. After much scandal and shock, Maurice eventually falls for Clive's working class gardener Scudder, played by Rupert Graves.

5. The Wedding Banquet (1993)
Ang Lee's fabulous flick centers around Gao Wai Tung, a Taiwanese gay man happily settled in New York who arranges a marriage of convenience to satisfy his devoutly traditional parents, whose constant haranguing about girlfriends and weddings are wearing him down. Things run smoothly until his parents fly into New York for the ceremony to surprise their son, his faux wife-to-be—an illegal immigrant desperate for a Green Card—and Gao's white boyfriend, Simon. A gay film, primarily, but with the superb direction of Ang—the guy who directed the acclaimed *Crouching Tiger, Hidden Dragon*—and no shortage of comedy moments, it offers up a hilarious plot to straight and queer cinema-goers alike.

6. Beautiful Thing (1996) [right]
Based on Jonathan Harvey's stage production, *Beautiful Thing* is one of the most realistic gay films ever made. Based around the blossoming love story of two working class London teenagers who live on a rough housing estate, it's one of those warm coming-of-age dramas that really hits the spot—no Manhattan lawyers, dinner parties or rich friends, this is true life as it happens. Jamie (Glen Berry) is a quiet sensitive soul who lives with his mother and next door to Ste (Scott Neal), a popular sporty lad in the same year at school who often sees the back of his abusive and drunken father's hand. After being locked out by his father one night, Jamie's mother invites Ste to stay in their flat, and while sleeping in the same bed

together Jamie's feelings for the boy are stirred. A love affair that manages to block out all the shit and grit around them eventually develops into a full-blown romance that fills queer viewers with hope.

7. Torch Song Trilogy (1988) [top right]
This gorgeous three-parter is based on Harvey Fierstein's Pulitzer Prize winning Broadway show all crammed into a 117-minute running time. Covering all the queer bases, it's a coming out, looking-for-love story set over ten years in the life of Arnold Beckoff, a drag queen performer desperate for a long-term relationship. With perfect comic timing, as well as some highly emotive scenes between Arnold and his mother, played by Anne Bancroft, Arnold finds love—in the shape of Mr. Sarah Jessica Parker, Matthew Broderick—but then loses it when the guy is queerbashed to death, and is left to bring up their son. A tear-jerker in places, hilarious in others, its anti-homophobia message still works today.

8. Philadelphia (1993) [bottom right]
Ground-breaking in so many ways, disappointing in so many others, *Philadelphia* was Hollywood's first big bash at a gay movie with bonafide stars and a fairly impressive budget. It was director Jonathan Demme's apology for the homophobia-ridden *Silence Of The Lambs* that riled so many queer viewers. In return we got Tom Hanks as the high-flying lawyer who finds himself HIV-positive and without a job. Denzel Washington plays the lawyer who takes Hanks' old law firm to court for dismissing him because of his status, while Antonio Banderas plays Hanks' boyfriend. Even though it did bring the prejudice and hatred towards people with HIV/AIDS out into the open, it was criticized for the lack of emotion between Hanks and his partner: without even a sniff of a lips-on-lips kiss, there is just one slow dance that sees the pair actually get close for a moment. It won Hanks the Oscar and gave him a global platform to make a very moving pro-gay speech.

9. My Beautiful Launderette (1985)
This tale of mixed race, working class love set against a background of drug-running, squalid London, and Thatcher's

Britain was taken from Hanif Kureshi's book of the same name, and while the fashions appear dated—don't let that put you off—the message is just as pertinent. Omar, played brilliantly by Gordon Warnecke, takes a job in his decidedly dodgy uncle's laundromat and while there, he reunites with an old school friend Johnny (Daniel Day Lewis), whose flirtation with fascist politics doesn't hinder the pair's ensuing relationship. Very timely, and pretty damn sexy.

10. Longtime Companion (1990)
While named after possibly one of the worst metaphors for a bender partner, this was one of the first well-made movies to look into the devastating effects of the AIDS epidemic. Following the lives of seven friends over a nine-year period in, you guessed it, New York City—although director Norman Rene adds: "It was essential that the people we encounter are human and identifiable, so that the film is not about New Yorkers and gays, but about people with whom audiences could identify."—it follows the human impact of the disease, as well as looking at their love and sex lives unapologetically for the first time on celluloid. The great thing about *Longtime Companion* was that it was a gay film made for gay men, without ever trying to be palatable for a potential straight audience. A rare thing way back then.

Pet Shop Boys and Gay Electronica
80s electronica pioneers

Following the free-living and loving 70s and a more lax attitude to the horrors of homosexuality in the 80s, it's no wonder that British record companies were less scared of signing performers and acts who were so obviously gay. After all, gay people had their own clubs and their own type of music and here was a visible trend, which could be exploited for cash dollar—though it's unlikely that the Pet Shop Boys, Erasure, Bronski Beat, Soft Cell or Frankie Goes To Hollywood could really have been broken after the impact of AIDS on social attitudes to gay men in the mid-80s.

The Pet Shop Boys are still the most successful of this slew of Euro-disco-cum-electronica outfits. For the past twenty years or so, Neil Tennant and Chris Lowe have navigated the latest sonic trends (whether it's disco, house or techno) with a knack for wry observation, a cynical smile, dead pan vocals, and oh yeah, some damn fine if melancholic pop songs.

They formed in London in 1981, after Neil, a journalist for teen pop mag, Smash Hits, met Chris, a one-time architecture student, in an electronics shop on London's King Road. Their passion for cheap dance music and musical gadgetry launched a pop career, which although initially stalling, hit the big time with the infectious 'West End Girls' in 1985, their first UK hit single.

Their music has always had mainstream appeal—although their success in the States has been limited—and they've notched up hit after hit, including 'It's A Sin,' 'Left To My Own Devices,' and 'Being Boring.' Although Neil Tennant didn't come out until the early 90s, the duo have always had legions of gay fans reading between the lines, and there have certainly been enough lines to read between: not only were there stories about the name relating to a kooky sex practice, there was the homosexual innuendo of their lyrics, the relentless dressing up, the covers of gay anthems like 'Go West,' and 'Can't Take My Eyes Off You,' and the collaborations with gay icons like Dusty Springfield and Liza Minnelli, gay filmmaker Derek Jarman [see page 102], and gay photographer and filmmaker Bruce Weber [see page 194].

Throughout their career, which is still going—if not particularly strong—the Pet Shop Boys have continually done their own thing, whether it's wearing ridiculous pointy hats, cavorting with muscle boys, or writing the gayest stage musical out there (*Closer To Heaven* was launched in London's West End in 2001). What's more, they've somehow managed to stay one step ahead of the game—and that's some feat in the stupidly fickle world of pop music.

Erasure

Erasure's Andy Bell was one of the first out stars in pop music. He formed the duo with ex-Depeche Mode and Yazoo member Vince Clark, and their mix of a belting voice, synth wizardry, a love of theatricality and the occasional basque struck it lucky throughout the 80s and early 90s. After a failed first album, they hit in 1986 with the single 'Sometimes,' followed by a slew of others including the US hits 'Chains Of Love,' and 'A Little Respect,' as well as five number one UK albums. They continue to record, although their recent outings have failed to match past successes.

Jimmy Somerville/Bronski Beat/The Communards

Glaswegian Jimmy Somerville led both Bronski Beat and the Communards to success in the 80s. His high falsetto and gay autobiographical lyrics met with very little resistance, propelling singles like 'Smalltown Boy' and 'Why?' and the album *The Age of Consent* into the UK top ten. After leaving Bronski Beat, Somerville was immediately back on top again with his new group the Communards, a cover of Thelma Houston's 'Don't Leave Me This Way,' and two successful albums. As a solo artist Somerville couldn't quite crack it except with a handful of covers, though he's always very welcome at Gay Pride festivals.

Marc Almond/Soft Cell

Marc Almond first found fame as one half of duo Soft Cell in 1981 when their cover of Gloria Jones's Northern Soul classic 'Tainted Love' took them to number one in the UK and made an immediate star out of the mincing vocalist. Two albums and an urban myth followed, but Soft Cell disbanded in 1984, and Marc launched a new career

via the Marc and the Mambas project. His solo career has been characterized by a selection of dark but campy cabaret torch songs, although chart success has been marginal. He's since morphed into a sinewy, tattooed cult icon and continues to record, having recently teamed up again with Soft Cell partner Dave Ball. In 2000, he wrote a warts 'n' all autobiography about his descent into drink, drugs, and debauchery.

▷ **Take it further:** *Tainted Life* by Marc Almond

Frankie Goes To Hollywood

Essentially five scallies from Liverpool, FGTH combined the creepy camp of vocalist Holly Johnson, the dancing skills of Paul Rutherford and the instrumental skills of erm, those other three with the big-sound Hi-NRG production of über-producer Trevor Horn. In 1983 on the release of their debut single, 'Relax,' they had the UK by the balls. The sexual nature of the lyrics meant the single was banned, as was the video with its gay orgy. 'Relax' was, of course, a massive hit both in the UK and the States, aided and propelled by the T-shirt slogan campaign of "Frankie Says."

But the success was shortlived with a sophomore album dumping from a great height. Holly Johnson moved onto a short-lived solo career, but was diagnosed with HIV in the early 90s and has subsequently all but retired.

Oscar Wilde

Smart-mouthed Irish writer who became a gay martyr

Oscar Wilde was not the gay hero you think he is. He wasn't a freedom fighter, taking his love of liberty and his right to have sex with whomsoever he wanted through the courts. In fact, the first time he went through the courts it was by his own choice in order to prove he wasn't a fag, but a respectable society gentleman who just happened to enjoy the company of good-looking pieces of rough trade because he liked the way they spoke. Nice try, big guy.

In Victorian England, if you did appreciate the finer qualities of the male form, especially bent over your brass bedstead, you were pretty much forced to live a double life. And master of the double life was Oscar Wilde, who by the end of the 19th century was one of the biggest celebrities in the English speaking world, with smash hit plays, lecture tours of the United States, a novel, children's stories and gimmicks galore: a green carnation always in his buttonhole, a bon mot—usually of a very controversial nature—always on his lips. He was Madonna, only fatter, fiercer and much, much cleverer.

Born in Dublin to an eccentric mother, Wilde was a scholar, poet and esthete (and that means, in today's language, being remarkably camp), who soon dazzled the London scene with his smart talk, his erudition, and his ability to shock and titillate with literature. Married with two sons, Wilde had a string of relationships with young men, the most important—and disastrous—of which was with a spoilt young rich kid known as Bosie.

While Wilde's overblown poetry left most people cold, his novel *The Portrait of Dorian Gray*, about a debauched aristocrat who remained spritely due to a magical picture of himself which aged in his place, was a scandalous success. His plays, comedies like *An Ideal Husband*, *Lady Windermere's Fan* and, above all, *The Importance of Being Earnest*, were absolute hits, drawing high society audiences who came to laugh at satires of their own vanity and shallowness. Oscar Wilde was the funniest and cleverest man in London, but his unshakeable belief in his own cleverness would lead to arrogance and the feeling that he was untouchable. That, in turn, would lead to disaster.

Wilde's downfall came in 1895, when having received a card from the Marquis of Queensbury inscribed "For Oscar Wilde, posing Somdomite" (he meant "sodomite" but wasn't very clever), Wilde decided to sue him for libel. It wasn't a great idea, especially as evidence of Wilde's "somdomy" was pretty thick on the ground and the boys he'd committed it with more than ready to talk for cash inducements.

Queensbury, a notorious bully and the father of Wilde's boyfriend Bosie, or Lord Alfred Douglas to give him his full title, was found not guilty at the trial and the evidence he had gathered for it was turned over to the Director of Public Prosecutions, who would use it to have Wilde for "gross indecency," legalese for dirty homo acts.

The details gathered by Queensbury were juicy and explicit, even if, in Victorian England, most of them were unsuitable for public discussion, even in a court of law. There was the chambermaid's evidence of a "common boy, rough looking, about 14 years of age" in Wilde's dirty bed with sheets "in a most disgusting state… [with] traces of vaseline, soil and semen." Then there was the evidence of Wallis Grainger, an apprentice electrician, that Wilde had, at a cottage where he was writing *An Ideal Husband*, acted inappropriately: "He worked me up with his hand and made me spend in his mouth," said Grainger.

By the time the trial for twenty-five counts of gross indecency and conspiracy to commit gross indecency started on April 26th, 1895, Oscar didn't have a hope in hell. Young men were paraded in and out of the witness box, each of them with their own story of how they'd been hired by Wilde to act out his sexual fantasies. They all, understandably, said how ashamed and remorseful they now felt. Wilde, who had dazzled in the first trial, was in a much less smart mood and tried to deny that any impropriety had taken place. Despite the quantity of evidence, and maybe due to a reluctance to nail one of the country's most enjoyable celebrities, the jury found they could not reach a verdict, meaning that Wilde was released on bail pending a second trial. During this time, many of his friends begged him—for the sake of his wife and children, if not for his own delicate skin—to skip the country and escape to Paris, where a much lighter view was taken of such carryings-on. He didn't, whether through bravery, arrogance or a simple misunderstanding of how bad things had got.

Meanwhile, Queensbury was urging the government to come down hard on Wilde and there is even evidence that the Prime Minister, Rosebury, had been implicated in a relationship with Queensbury's other son, Francis (who had died mysteriously), and was therefore almost blackmailed into insisting that the trial, which many thought should be dropped, go ahead. And with vigor.

The second trial was disastrous. Not only was Wilde found guilty on all but one of the charges, but attitudes to homosexuality, which had been remarkably indulgent, hardened after sordid tales of young lads being bought and sold got into the public domain. Culturally, effeminacy—campness if you like—was linked with homosexuality perhaps for the first time, while the

shadow of Wilde fell over the whole country for at least half a century. British attitudes to homosexuality remained rigid, and Wilde's plays almost unperformable, such was the taint attached to his name.

Wilde, who had at times used beautiful language from the dock—including his defence of "the love that dare not speak its name"—served two years hard labor for his crimes and was released broken, broke, and such a social pariah that he was forced to flee to Paris, where he died in November 1900.

The trial of Oscar Wilde remains one of the most famous in British legal history, a matter of national shame on one hand, an example of absolute arrogance on the other. Gay men have claimed Oscar as their martyr, and there is no doubt that he was sacrificed for behavior that wouldn't have raised an eyebrow had the participants been foxy chambermaids instead of electricians' apprentices. But what many gay men choose to overlook is Wilde's stupidity, arrogance and naïvety and the selfishness of Bosie, author of Oscar's downfall. It's not a beautiful story of love martyred at the altar of society's hypocritical morality, but a shabby tale and the beautiful jail poem *De Profundis* is scant compensation for a very clever and funny man cut down in his prime.

Michael Alig and the Club Kids

Sex, drugs and murder on the New York dancefloor

The late 1980s and early 1990s saw New York's clubs at their hedonistic height. The Limelight—the most famous New York club since Studio 54—the Tunnel and Club USA—with its interior designed by Thierry Mugler and Jean-Paul Gaultier [see page 162]—were bursting at the seams with hip, young queer New Yorkers dancing for three days straight and taking drugs like they were going out of fashion. Think platform shoes, crazy hair colors, dilated pupils, homemade outfits, and a cocktail of chemicals including ketamine, Ecstasy and Rohypnol, and you're getting somewhere.

The rag-tag bunch of crazy party-goers included gay boys and girls, rebellious straight kids and practically anyone with a penchant for drugs. The scene, ready and waiting for rave culture to begin in earnest, was dominated by a clique known as the Club Kids, who threw some of the wildest parties that Manhattan has ever seen. Loathed and feared throughout the city, the Club Kid freakshow was led by their self-appointed leader—an Andy Warhol wannabe—Michael Alig. A gorgeous, sweet, mischievous gay boy with an evil streak, his escapades, including peeing in people's drinks and holding impromptu parties in local fast food joints and on subway platforms, earned him something of a reputation both on the club scene and in the press.

Starting his New York life as a busboy at the cool Danceteria club, Alig persisted and pursued his dream of becoming a club promoter. Blatantly and shamelessly begging club owners for nights at their establishments, he began to throw badly-attended theme parties— including his now infamous Filthy Mouth contest, where the winner was the brat who cussed the most—that were largely ignored by the club-going elite. By no means an overnight success, no-one is sure how, why or when Alig suddenly became the hottest ticket in town. Rather than joining the scene, Alig

created one all of his very own that boasted a bunch of wackily-dressed hangers-on, including Jonathan Junkie, Jennytalia, and Screaming Rachel, who couldn't get enough of the free drugs, sex and bagfuls of drink tickets that Alig handed out to make friends and influence people.

Disco 2000 was where Alig and his gang of drugged-up Club Kids ruled on a weekly basis. With stolen fancy dress outfits, including a chicken, a dog and a bear spawning the biggest star, Clara The Carefree Chicken, the club was packed every week. With the fashions including tiaras, flowerpots as millinery, and body parts painted with polka dots, these kids didn't know the meaning of

the expression "less is more." Which is probably how they got themselves into so much trouble.

Amputees, drag kings and queens, hardcore ravers, and even Michael's mum flocked to the club that was being touted as the place to be seen. Alig had somehow pulled it off, much to the disbelief of Manhattan's social circles. Disco 2000 had turned the etiquette of clubland on its head. Unlike the strict door policy of wonder club Studio 54 way back when, where you had to be sophisticated to get past the velvet rope, Alig's door policy was that you had to be a little bit crazy but mostly just plain weird to get in. As one of Alig's sidekicks, James St James, put it in the Club Kid documentary *Party Monster*: "If you feel like you're a freak and if you've got a hunchback, throw a little glitter on it honey and show the world that it's OK."

Cool no longer ruled in Manhattan, and the wackier and goofier Alig got, the more the Kids loved him. Falling into people while pretending to be drunk, looking ridiculous in wigs and "unitards"—an all-in-one outfit, preferably in some psychedelic pattern, with the ass cut out—and inviting Ernie The Pee Drinker to perform on-stage all added to the subversive atmosphere. The powers that be began to take note.

Club tsar Peter Gatien was persuaded to inject millions of dollars into Club USA, Alig's newest venture, and suddenly the Club Kids were making TV commercials and appearing on the trashy chat show *Geraldo*. It was at this point that the drug-taking and partying got out of hand. Heroin chic was the new look, and despite the previous mockery of the "sad" junkies, Alig became one. During this time the rumors began to spread through clubland that Alig had killed someone— that someone being his former boyfriend and current drug dealer, Angel Melendez. Because of his drug-addled state, Alig missed the seriousness of the situation and the implications of telling too many people about what he had done (and of turning up one night with a bloody hammer as a nightclub accessory).

The story goes that on Sunday March 17th, 1996, Alig had been arguing with Angel about drug money that he owed. The argument had gotten out of hand, and Alig was being strangled by Angel. Handily, at this moment, in strolled Alig's roommate, Freeze, who hit Angel on the head with a hammer that happened to by lying around their apartment. Fuelled by ten bags of heroin, Alig and Freeze injected Angel with Drano—a drain cleaning substance—cut off his legs, and put the body in a TV box, which was later unceremoniously dumped in the Hudson River. After weeks of speculation, the *Village Voice*'s social columnist Michael Musto retold the story, with the names changed to protect the guilty. It was then that the media, the police desperate to clamp down on the drugs, and clubland's socialites really got interested.

As the sheen began to wear off the Club Kid phenomenon, the net closed in on Alig and his clique. The authorities believed the Kids were protecting him, but they were soon seen for what they had become: the years of excess, fun and outrageousness had left the Club Kids as nothing more than drug addicts, and far from protecting him, they were simply too messed up to find a policeman, let alone tell them the story of Michael Alig killing Angel.

The media interest grew and it became more and more apparent that Alig was guilty. The body still hadn't turned up, and Alig had left town. As more articles began to appear in the press, Alig, oddly, returned to Manhattan. Even with Angel's brother in town, looking for his missing sibling, it didn't stop Alig trying to pull off one last gig: his hunger for attention knew no bounds and he used the publicity surrounding the murder to open a new club, the Honey Trap.

In December of 1996, after a police cock-up, it was discovered that Angel's body had actually been found way back in April on Staten Island. They now had a body, and their suspects, and it was only a matter of time before Alig and Freeze were arrested. Freeze and Michael were eventually found guilty of homicide and were sentenced to twenty two years in jail.

Gay hip hop

Music for the homeboys goes homo

The first ever rap number one in the UK might have been by Blondie— 'Rapture,' fact fans—but hip hop is very much a black thing with roots stretching back to African tribal music, which came to the States with slavery. By the middle of the 20th century, this African music had already provided the basis for jazz, gospel and soul, but in the 1970s a new trend had emerged: MCs (Master of Ceremonies, i.e. the men with the microphones) had started talking over reggae tunes in clubs, a practice which, over time, developed into a genre of its own. Rappers would acknowledge people at clubs and praise the DJs' skills. These "shout outs" and "in the house" greetings became more elaborate, incorporating social commentary and stories—anything from talking about their neighborhood to their sexual prowess.

Machismo, misogyny and violence have since become synonymous with the bustin' beats and the fierce rappers that have carved a name for themselves within the music industry and on the streets, helping them to make some serious dollars. With rap and hip hop now equalling big, big business, it's seen as the ultimate way out and up for kids living in deprived inner city areas.

Born out of a frustration at the white-dominated, sometimes racist gay clubs that refused to spin decent hip hop grooves or "black tunes," and the intrinsic homophobia of the hip hop scene, gay rappers got together and began setting up their own club nights—evoking disgust from their straight black brothers and sisters, and contempt from the white gay club-owners and goers.

The emergence of these hip hop clubs, which played the hottest new tunes to a gay crowd, and the coming out of gay rappers and gay people within the hip hop business has been painfully slow. Even with prominent figures such as Biff Warren—one of the original members of the Def Jam team who brought acts like Public Enemy and LL Cool J to the fore—the reaction in straight hip hop joints to the suggestion of queerness is still hostile. As Warren, who publishes two gay hip hop magazines, puts it: "If Lil' Kim said in a song that she wanted to see two brothers getting busy with each other, what would happen? I'll tell you. Brothers would lose their minds!"

With the high profile and admittedly talent-lite rapper Will Smith feeling the homophobic after-effects of playing a gay role in the film *Six Degrees Of Separation*, and rap tracks by the likes of stars such as Ice Cube and Chuck D—to name just two of many guilty of homophobia—liberally sprinkled with anti gay, "faggot"-littered lyrics, it's proof there's a long way to go before gay fans, let alone gay rappers, are accepted and respected in the homeboy-run land of hip hop—even if a lot of "straight" hip-hoppers are certainly not above a little boy-ass every once in a while.

But it's by no means a lost cause. With the help of the groundbreaking website *gayhiphop.com* run by Phukup and Mr. Maker, whose mission is to allow fans and performers alike a space to enjoy and promote their music without prejudice and without their sexuality being scrutinized, it looks like the gay hip hop crew are becoming a force to be reckoned with. And with the gay hip hop community becoming more visible, with rappers like Caushun coming out, the straight rappers are going to have to sit up and take notice soon—the media circus has already jumped onto the gay hip hop bandwagon. While it's going to be a long time before gay homies are welcomed into straight hip hop clubs, and in turn before black queers feel comfortable on such a white-dominated queer scene, we can at least give a big shout out to clubs like Café Con Leche and collectives like Rainbow Flava who are flying, and fly, in the face of deep-seated homophobia on the hip hop scene, and racism on the queer circuits.

Elton John

The musical gay icon who's still standing despite everything

Born into middle-class English stock in 1947, who knew that Reginald Kenneth Dwight would become, quite literally, one of the biggest gay celebrities in the world? After watching and emulating the camp tinklings of pianists Little Richard and Liberace [see page 186], Elton—that's Sir Elton to you—won himself a place at the Royal Academy of Music at the age of eleven, and began climbing the spangly rungs of the showbiz ladder.

Elton's music, written with his long-term writing partner, Bernie Taupin—who was known to bang out the lyrics to a song every hour—has been inspiring and influencing musicians and songwriters for decades. His debut, *Empty Sky*, clocked up miserable sales, but his self-titled album from 1970 was released to critical acclaim, and marked the beginning of his unstoppable progress towards bagging the title of one of the biggest selling solo artists in American recording history.

Between 1972 and 1976, John and Taupin were something of a hit factory, turning out sixteen top 20 hits, including classics like 'Rocket Man,' 'Bennie And The Jets,' and 'Crocodile Rock' in the four-year period. Despite his outrageous outfits at this time including comedy glasses and platform shoes, all done in an attempt to distract from what he thought of as an unattractive appearance, a fair few of his fans were shocked when, in 1976, he announced in an interview with *Rolling Stone* magazine that he was bisexual. From this brave partial coming out, Elton's audience began to shrink. And as well as being jilted by large swathes of his fanbase, Elton also announced his retirement from live performing in 1977, and the cutback to just one album a year—a decision made due to the deterioration of his relationship with Taupin.

From 1976, Elton was known to partake in the excesses of the rock'n'roll lifestyle, as well as revel in the high camp style that his predecessor Liberace had worked so well. Drugs, drink, sex and shopping saw Elton descend into a chaotic lifestyle, with tempers, outbursts and paranoia, including a phone call to his management to get them to turn off the wind which was irritating him.

The 80s MTV era kicked John back into the limelight, with some of his most memorable singles—'I Guess That's Why They Call It The Blues,' 'I'm Still Standing,' and 'Nikita'—propelling his long-players into the gold sales league. But despite the chart success, his personal life was a mess. Never mind the popular belief that Elton was gay, not bisexual as he claimed, he went ahead and married his recording engineer Renate Blauel in 1984. Defying all expectations, the pair stayed married for four years, although Elton has subsequently admitted he knew he
was gay before they tied the knot.

In 1988, after a run playing live at Madison Square Garden in New York for five nights, Elton decided to sell off his entire wardrobe of camp stage outfits, as well as his record collection in an attempt to regain some control over his life. He was battling drug and alcohol addiction, bulimia, and was having desperate surgery to turn back the tide of his hair loss. The sale of everything that made him Elton proved to be a turning point. By 1991 he was clean and back on form. The following year he launched the Elton John AIDS Foundation, which would receive the royalties from all of his singles sales. The Foundation would grow to become one of the world's largest private non-profit AIDS organizations.

In fact, the early 90s proved something of comeback for Elton, now in his 40s, and amongst his key moments was the soundtrack to the musical *The Lion King*, and his return-to-form album *The One*. However, despite his healthy and happy relationship with film producer David Furnish, which had started after a party in 1993, the late 90s were overshadowed by the death of two of Elton's closest friends: designer Gianni Versace [see page 167] and Princess Diana [see page 16].

Ironically, it was Diana who had helped comfort Elton at Versace's funeral. Just months later, he was getting up in front of billions to play a newly written version of his classic 'Candle In The Wind.' He released the single—hastily re-written by Taupin—as a charity record with donations going to the Princess's charities and it promptly became the biggest selling record of all time.

In 2000 Elton became embroiled in a $28 million legal battle with his accountants. It was a case that brought to light an incredible spending of $57 million in just twenty months. His flower bill alone was enough to sustain a small country!

Living a flamboyant, glamorous and out gay lifestyle with his partner David Furnish has made Elton John one of the most famous queers on the planet. As well as rubbing shoulders with A-list celebrities and throwing outrageous parties, he's famous for courting controversy: he did a duet at the Grammies in 2001 with controversial rapper Eminem, of whom Elton announced: "I don't think he's homophobic. I wouldn't have done it if I thought he was, and he wouldn't have asked me to do it."

Despite his standing in the music industry Elton has never shied away from fighting for the causes he believes in: as well as his contributions to AIDS charities, he recorded 'American Triangle' in memory of the savage killing of Matthew Shepard [see page 92]: "I did a concert at the University of Wyoming in Laramie, and I met Matthew's parents," says Elton. "I set up a scholarship in his name. I did a fund-raiser for anti-hate groups. I'm a gay man, and whether it had been a girl [or a boy], I would have done the same thing."

He may be a blousy old tart with a past riddled with drug addiction, dodgy hair, and a suspect marriage, but you've got to hand to it Elton, he really has come out the other side. Currently not only the Stately Homo of England but the first emergency service for any waif or stray pop star in their hour of need, Elton has become an institution.

Gay Clubbing

Whatever you wear, whoever you do, there's a club night out there waiting for your Pink Pound and Dollar. This is your booty call

Whether scantily-clad go-go boys dancing to hi-energy choons atop a podium, or mullet-haired pool-playing lesbians in women-only spaces get your rocks off, the queer scene has got it covered. Here are the ways you can get can get down or get down and dirty.

Underwear parties/boot parties

Leave your clothes in a locker, slip your wallet, mobile phone and keys into your socks, strap on your boots and pray that you've got your whitest white Calvin Klein underwear on—or if you're doing the boot party, that you've got that personal hygiene thang going on. Basically a sex club, where you can sit and sip a beer and watch the panties—or more—walk by or get down to some naughtier fun, at least it means you've got very little to peel off in preparation for some serious backroom action should the occasion arise.

Tip: Stablemaster, in Amsterdam

S&M clubs

Usually with a strict dress code only permitting queers decked out in leather, rubber or uniform, S&M clubs—that's sadomasochism to you play hard house tunes for a horny, up-for-it crowd. They certainly ain't just your regular sex clubs, and chatting with friends over a martini is the last thing on the clientele's collective mind. Eye-popping, mind blowing "cabaret" is often performed for a worked-up crowd dressed in some pretty scary outfits—gas masks, soldiers uniforms, gags and the like—who use every dark corner available for sexual shenanigans of a hardcore nature.

Tip: Fist in London

Drag clubs

Here the drag queens rule. Boasting a mixed-up crowd, usually including a few straight nosey tourists, drag clubs are all about entertainment and attitude. Expect a floorshow by a bitch with legs and perma-sneer, and never be surprised if they don't like the look of your face—famed for cheap jokes aimed at audience members, and bad lipsynching to 'Goldfinger' the world over, drag clubs are never about you and are always all about the hostess with the most-est in charge.

Tip: Tranny Shack in San Francisco

Saunas

Another one for the boys, although of late the lady lesbians in San Francisco and London have been getting a look in with their very own girl-only, lesbian-run steamy sessions. Thinly disguised as a place to relax and hang out in towels, you're more likely to find private cabins where you can enjoy boy-on-boy action with like-minded males with the same dirty thing on their mind (not aromatherapy treatments and cold plunges). And if you do go looking for a massage, expect added-extras to the usual head and shoulder rub. Globally, saunas are renowned for their uncleanliness, but there are a few around that not only pride themselves on their hygienic "facilities" but also their 24-hour opening times.

Tip: Hollywood Spa, Los Angeles

Circuit parties

Circuit parties are one-off gay events organized by big-name party people, and at one time the only way to get invited was to know the right people or get your name down on an elusive and exclusive mailing list. Kicking off in some of the biggest gay towns in the US, they generally attract big-titted, Muscle Mary types who fill their social calendar with parties all over the world. With gay ski weekends, New Year's Eve events, and all of the global Pride events covered, circuit party promotion has become mega-buck business. The biggest and best on the circuit are the color-themed gigs that have become not only legendary, but also copied the world over, with most major cities now boasting their own version of a white, black, blue or the kinkier red gig. Many of the party organizers donate takings to local HIV/AIDS charities, and queer tourists from all over the world are willing to travel miles to shake their booty at some of the more well-renowned dance fests.

Tip: Miami White Party, Vizcaya, Coconut Grove, Florida

Tea dances

Inspired by the same-sex balls of the 19th century, gay Tea Dances, despite their hokey-sounding moniker, have become institutional in the gay clubbing scene the world over. Usually held on a Sunday afternoon, it's a cheeky way of squeezing yet another day out of a homo's social calendar. Some Tea Dance events, especially those in gay resorts and cities like Key West and San Francisco, have become queer tourist hotspots, and locals will often be seen cruising the fresh meat in town for one week only. Oh, and despite the name, tea isn't usually what's drunk.

Tip: Atlantic Shores, Key West, Florida

Linedancing

You'd think that homo boys and girls would have more taste than this, but linedancing is big, big, big in the land of queer. With linedancing spaces even popping up at lesbian and gay pride events the world over, it seems that the appeal of donning a stetson and Madonna-style checked cowboy shirt is still as popular as ever. It may have been something to laugh at, but linedancing homos take their country and western fancy dance moves extremely seriously indeed.

Tip: Any hokey town, like anywhere

Women-only nights

With the growth of feminism in the 1970s came a demand for women-only spaces—where women could be, well, women, and the men were not allowed. While the gay guys and girls have now learned to play nicely, women-only spaces are still in demand due to a general lack of women-dominated, women-run spaces the world over. Now, rather than being driven by political motives, women-only spaces are set-up to guarantee the girls a chance of spotting a few other ladies-that-lunch-on-ladies on the scene. A rare thing, sadly.

Tip: Clit Club, New York

Dolly pop clubs

If you want pop, you may as well make it disco dolly pop. Crop-topped young things with glitter on their faces and in their spiky young hair-dos ram clubs like Pop Rocks in New York, and G.A.Y in London to unashamedly enjoy crap popular tunes by the likes of Britney, Kylie, and whichever boy band is currently riding high in the charts. Expect a just-out-of-diapers crowd of oh-so young queens with their fag hag school friends in tow. Sucking on a lollipop all night is optional.

Tip: G.A.Y, London

Indie and alternative clubs

Despite the popular belief, not all gay men and women long for the weekend to be filled with tops-off clubs and pumping house. Since the days of The Smiths, queer indie/alternative/goth kids have longed for a space of their own. Offering guitar tunes that require jumping up and down dance routines, as opposed to hands in the air movements, the queer indie scene exploded in the 1990s in London with Club Vaseline—no longer with us—and Popstarz, packing in the punters every week with a soundtrack by Blur, REM and Nirvana. There's even the odd awful queer band with loud guitars and screechy vocals performing, or some whacky performance artist who covers themselves with their own shit and calls it art.

Tip: Poptastic, Manchester

Fetish club

Slightly dirtier and more specialized than its filthy younger brother the S&M club, the fetish club attracts those with specific sexual interests—whether you like to get peed on, pierced, electrocuted or like to play puppy, they've got pretty much every perversion covered. Prepare to have your eyes well and truly opened.

Tip: Headquarters, Sydney

Amateur strip clubs

As opposed to the professional strip night, where a cute young thing with his dick tied up with elastic bands wiggles and jiggles in front of a disinterested looking crowd, amateur strip nights—like karaoke—give the paying punters a chance to shake their non-professional booty after a few too many drinks.

Tip: Provincial bars the world over

Hard house/tops off clubs

Tanned, muscled, shaven flesh dancing to the deep, pulsating, hard beats of house and techno are a sure-fire winner in gay club land. Usually after-hours and with boys definitely in the majority, the clientele are here for the chance to dance their ample tits off, as opposed to picking up—although both can and normally does happen. A bottle of water, no T-shirt and cropped hairdo are de rigeur for these club kids, as are top name DJs and strobe effect lighting.

Tip: Trade, London

Rock Hudson

A-list Hollywood stud muffin and the first celebrity to die of AIDS

Classically tall, dark and handsome, everyone wanted to be/do Rock Hudson (originally Roy Scherer), which was why the news that he was a) gay and b) suffering from AIDS in 1985, the dark days of the epidemic, was met with such surprise and horror from the public at large. The discovery, protégé and lover of (gay) talent agent Henry Willson, who gave him his name, he secured a series of small film parts until *Magnificent Obsession* in 1954 launched him into the big time.

Behind the scenes, Rock had been sleeping with fading star Tyrone Power as well as a number of other actors, but Willson was able to protect Rock's all-American image, and when rumors of the star's sexuality threatened to creep out he encouraged him to marry his secretary, Phyllis Gates in 1955 (though they were divorced three years later).

Rock was now on a roll. His standout movies followed, like 1956's *Giant* (with James Dean and Elizabeth Taylor) and *Pillow Talk*, the first of several profitable gigs opposite the squeaky clean Doris Day. In 1974, Rock met writer Armistead Maupin [see page 190] through his lover, and the two started an occasional affair. The character Blank Blank in Armistead's *Tales Of The City* books was suspected to be based on Rock, although the author claims it was actually about a "type."

Rock resisted the lure of TV for some time, but finally relented in 1971 with the detective series, *McMillan and Wife*, alongside Susan St.James. A guest-role in *Dynasty* [see page 21] followed in the early 80s, when he hit headlines after he confirmed that he'd contracted AIDS, and much was made about his screen kiss with Linda Evans.

With his death, AIDS finally came out of the closet, his close friend Elizabeth Taylor became an AIDS activist and the public began to learn about the disease and give to charity. To his friends in the business, he was a hardworking likeable guy; to the public he was the epitome of Hollywood stud, and yet his death from AIDS has overshadowed what a damn fine actor he was.

David Hockney

Brit artist who captured gay California

God bless David Hockney, the artist who was even out about his gay status at school and whose paintings—the best-known of which are beautifully colored portraits—breathe with a freshness and honesty that make them fit in perfectly with many a modern room. His paintings of sexy Californian boys clambering naked out of wiggly line swimming pools or showering are probably among the most popular, and accessible gay paintings there are. They are simple portraits of gay men looking great and having a fantastic time.

Born just before the Second World War in Yorkshire, England, Hockney came from an over-achieving middle-class family. His father was an accountant, his mother a shop assistant, and from an early age David was registering as a conscientious objector, and sending off letters to world leaders telling them how they could sort things out (he's not changed by the way: in 2000, he fired across the bows of a supposedly liberal left-wing British government, calling them "a load of philistines. And that's not surprising. What is surprising is that they are a lot more philistine than the last lot." The last lot being hard right-wing Tories.)

Just before the swinging 60s took off, David took off to London to study at the Royal College of Art, where his eccentricities and drive marked him out from the pack. And in the deeply homophobic society that England was at the time, his production of works with titles like *We 2 Boys Together Clinging* [above] also raised more than an eyebrow or two. The Young Contemporaries Exhibition in 1961 marked the emergence of what was to become the Pop Art phenomenon, with Hockney seated firmly at its head.

Within a couple of years, Hockney's fascination with all things American led him to visit New York for the first time, followed by California where he found his spiritual home. The boy from the grimmest town among the "Satanic mills" of northern England was at last in the sun and surrounded by the swimming pools, tanned boys and an atmosphere of relaxation that he'd never found in England. California was simply "more sexy", he said at the time.

"Within a week of arriving there in this strange big city, not knowing a soul, I'd passed the driving test, bought a car, driven to Las Vegas and won some money, got myself a studio, started painting, all within a week," he recalled. "And I thought, it's just how I imagined it would be."

The influence of the Los Angeles lifestyle also found its way onto Hockney's canvasses. The brightly colored, practically two-dimensional works he painted during this time were unashamedly homoerotic, featuring boys taking showers, boys sleeping displaying their asses to the viewer, and boys lying in bed together. And all this came at a time when the UK was still coming to terms with the idea that homosexuality would have to be decriminalized. Despite Hockney's early political activism, these works didn't take an overtly political stance. They were just images of men loving each other. It was the social context that made them political.

By now Hockney's star was in the ascendant, with one-man shows of his work being held all over Europe. Already a recognizable celebrity with his trademark bleached white hair, big-framed glasses and natty jackets, David met Peter Schlesinger, a Californian art student, who became his lover and model. This period of his life, including those swimming pools, the boys and his break-up with Peter, was captured in a then ground-breaking British television documentary called *A Bigger Splash*, the name of one of his best loved paintings, which was filmed in 1970. It transformed him from merely the most successful British painter since the war into a household name throughout the UK.

Hockney was never just a painter. He had always experimented with photography and, like his contemporary, Andy Warhol, was drawn more and more towards working with Polaroids, pioneering the overlapping build of a wider image, photo collage-style, to give a composite landscape or panorama. It's a look you'll still find being ripped off on many an album cover thirty years later. The 70s also found Hockney adding further strings to his bow, dedicating a series of etchings to Picasso while in Paris, and designing theater and opera sets in London and New York. Almost inevitably, the 80s found Hockney working with the cutting edge technology of the day, including photocopied prints and computer-generated images. So you'd expect him to be busy redesigning the worldwide web as we speak, right? Wrong. Recent years have seen the ever contrary Hockney devoting himself to painting huge canvases of (what else?) the Grand Canyon. "Often it looks like I'm going off on a tangent but it's really exploring in another way. But I always saw that, which was why I was a little bit immune to criticism. I'm confident enough to be a bit immune to it, yes."

Hockney achieved further mainstream recognition in the 90s, and currently divides his time between his LA studio and an apartment in Malibu.

Liberace

Piano player

Somewhere between Jack Nicholson's Joker and Dame Edna Everage sits rancid queen and showbiz legend Liberace, who made a name for himself peddling a heady mix of showy extravagance and unadulterated cheese.

Lee, as he was known to his fans and friends (yes, he did have some) was born on May 16th, 1919, in West Allis, Wisconsin to an Italian French-horn player and bit-part silent movie actor father and ex-concert pianist Polish mother. Showbiz was in his blood and he was a childhood piano prodigy, who even performed for the Polish pianist Ignace Jan Paderweski at the age of seven. By high school he'd renamed himself Walter Busterkeys and was playing in lounges and nightclubs.

In 1939, he ended a classical performance with an encore of 'Three Little Fishes,' which he delivered with a wink and a smile—the audience lapped it up. It was a turnaround moment that was to shape his career and when he moved to New York in 1940, he began to work on the flamboyant image that was to make him a megastar: the rhinestones, the gold lamé, the furs, the gilt candelabra, the perma-grin—they all became trademark fixtures and certainly translated onto television in the 50s, where he played a mix of Gershwin, lounge jazz and classical-lite, earning him the nickname 'Mr Showmanship.'

To an America weaned on war rations, he symbolized the ultimate in extravagance and elegance, even if he didn't know the difference between class and downright tack—who else would have a piano-shaped swimming pool? Nevertheless, he developed a hardcore fanbase of middle-class conservative housewives, and was soon being invited to royal dinners, presidential evenings, and celebrity birthdays. He was, of course, a big old faggot, but one smart enough to know that any revelation about his sexuality would be disastrous to his career. Despite what is now perceived as a wall of silence, biographers have since denied he was self-hating, and was actually not very discreet about his gay liaisons.

Not only was he known to have had an affair with writer John Rechy, and actor Rock Hudson before he became a star [see page 184], but there was the endless succession of young chauffeurs, the cruising of Mexican boys on Sunset Boulevard, and flings with weightlifters and men from various chorus lines. This homosexual promiscuity was of course kept firmly behind the smoke screen of "affairs" with the likes of Joanne Rio, Sonja Henie, and Mae West, the latter two gay icons.

In 1956, columnist William Connor of British tabloid the *Daily Mirror* wrote: "He reeks with emetic language that can only make grown men long for a quiet corner, an aspidistra, a handkerchief and the old heave-ho."

The piece was picked up on by the States' *Confidential* tabloid who wrote a piece: 'Why Liberace's Theme Song Should be "Mad About the Boy."' Liberace successfully sued for libel against both publications, and in Britain won the largest settlement of any libel case in British history. The legal cases did nothing to damage his career however, and throughout the 1960s and 1970s, Liberace was the world's single highest paid performer, selling out concerts around the world, and notching up five million-selling albums even though he was the biggest joke in showbusiness. Liberace always shrugged off his critics, saying he "laughed all the way to the bank." Later he quipped, "You know that bank I used to cry all the way to? Well, now I own it."

In 1982, he was dogged by scandal once again when his ex-boyfriend, Scott Thorson, a live-in secretary and chauffeur for six years, brought a "palimony" suit against Liberace, which was settled out of court four years later.

The next year, on February 4th, 1987, Liberace died in Palm Springs, California, and even though he couldn't continue to deny his homosexuality from beyond the grave, his family took the baton and refused point blank to acknowledge that it was AIDS that had killed him. The local coroner, however, insisted on an autopsy, which brought to light the real facts: Liberace had died of a cardiac arrest brought on by AIDS-related subacute encephalopathy.

RuPaul

The drag queen that ate America

There was always much more to RuPaul than met the eye (and, let's face it, there was plenty to meet the eye). His almost hokey message of love ("If you can't love yourself, how the hell you going to love anyone else") may have been lapped up by the daytime talk show brigade, who were ironically in the vanguard of RuPaul's success, but gay men and lesbians knew there was something very much edgier going on. A drag queen preaching peace and love? That would be a first.

Unlike the character in his biggest hit 'Supermodel,' RuPaul was not born a poor black child in the projects of Detroit, Michigan, but in a hospital in San Diego where his mother named him RuPaul Andre Charles, and immediately proclaimed him a star: "Cause there ain't another motherf****er alive with a name like that." By the time he was five, RuPaul was proving her right, performing as Diana Ross in a long pink dress. He was a pre-school sensation. By the age of sixteen, his parents having messily divorced, he moved with his sister to Atlanta, or Hotlanta, even today his spiritual home, where he enrolled in a school for the performing arts and became a part-time used car salesman. In 1982, he caught *The American Music Show* on Public Access cable, and his showbusiness career took off.

Debuting as RuPaul and the U-Hauls with a couple of his friends, RuPaul's first performances were enthusiastic but hardly polished and, though weird, were not strictly speaking drag. Giddy on the success of his cable appearances, that same year RuPaul moved to midtown Manhattan (with his first boyfriend Todd) and started appearing at the legendary Pyramid club. But for his drag career to truly get under way, RuPaul went back to Atlanta, where he started to make underground movies with his brother-in-law's camera, and recorded his first mini-EP, called *RuPaul: Sex Freak*. It wasn't until Ru returned to Manhattan, ditched his punk drag for a new black hooker look that things really started to take off, with club bookings coming in fast, and RuPaul ending the year voted Queen of Manhattan by club owners.

Coming off booze and pills (quite a few of which had been consumed during his reign as Queen of Manhattan), RuPaul eventually got a record deal with Tommy Boy and on his birthday in 1992, 'Supermodel' was released. With its hilarious video—a parody of the Diana Ross movie *Mahogany*—and a string of appearances on TV shows, RuPaul did what had seemed impossible: he became the first mainstream drag superstar the world had really seen. It was partly due to a truly great song, partly due to how gorgeous a creation RuPaul was and partly due to the bizarro "love" message RuPaul was putting across, a message that neutralized the fear mainstream America would naturally have felt for a cross-dresser.

Celebrities clamored for a bit of Ru. Elton John snapped him up for a duet on the old Elton/Kiki Dee hit 'Don't Go Breaking My Heart' and a co-presenting gig at the Brits (the UK version of the Grammies), Diana Ross worked him into the video for her lame "I love the gays" reworking of 'I Will Survive,' while kd lang became co-face of cosmetics brand MAC. Cameo performances in mainstream movies like *The Brady Bunch*, Spike Lee's *Crooklyn*, and dragstravaganza *To Wong Foo, Thanks For Everything, Love Julie Newmar!* with Wesley Snipes and Patrick Swayze followed. The world was crazy for the six-foot-something drag queen who had better legs than any Hollywood star and a face to stop traffic.

But RuPaul's celebrity was to be of the fifteen-minute variety. The public didn't go for his follow-up album, the disappointing *Foxy Lady*. He got his own show on VH-1 but the way forward for RuPaul, who brought the mentality of the gay club to the mainstream, albeit in a very sanitized incarnation, is still not clear. He better work.

Queer Authors

Classics

In a league of their own, these classic authors have gone down in history

Oscar Wilde

[see page 176]

Virginia Woolf
1882-1941

Born in London, Woolf was one of the founding members of the Bloomsbury Group—essentially a bunch of English toffs who fancied themselves as writers. She married Leonard Woolf in 1912, and following continuing bouts of depression, tried to commit suicide in 1913.
Overshadowing her novel *Mrs Dalloway* from 1925, her most famous work, *Orlando: A Biography*, was published in 1928. Basically a love letter to her then-lover, Vita Sackville-West [see page 190], it follows the life of a young woman over four centuries, from an incarnation as a favorite of Queen Elizabeth I in 1600, through changing sex and then finally becoming Lady Orlando centuries later. It was made into an acclaimed feature-length film in 1993 starring Tilda Swinton and Quentin Crisp [see page 216]. Woolf eventually committed suicide in 1941.

Langston Hughes
1902-1967

A writer of poetry and fiction, Hughes, who was something of a drifter, wrote about the life of young Black Americans, and was in fact one of the first black writers to be taken seriously by the white-run literary world. In the award-winning film, *Looking For Langston*, Isaac Julian explores the writer's sexuality, his alleged gayness having long been played down by scholars and fans of the important writer, who is seen as America's most original black poet.

Christopher Isherwood
1904-1986

Isherwood went to school with W. H. Auden, and knew him all of his life—their friendship also included casual sex whenever they "felt like it." After attending college in Cambridge and London, Isherwood moved to Berlin to teach English between 1930 and 1933, and it was here that he wrote *Mr. Norris Changes Trains* and *Goodbye To Berlin*. The latter was turned into the play, *I Am Camera*, which eventually became the Kander and Ebb stage musical and Oscar-winning Bob Fosse movie *Cabaret* [see page 44], starring Liza Minnelli. In 1953 Isherwood began a relationship with the then 18-year-old Don Bachardy—who went on to become a famous painter in his own right—and the pair stayed together until Isherwood's death in 1986. In his later years, he was actively involved in gay politics, and his writing became more homo. In his autobiography, *Christopher And His Kind*, he wrote candidly about his gay life, as well as listing his many sexual liaisons.

Walt Whitman
1819-1892

Walt Whitman is seen as the great American poet but regardless of his status as a household word (well, practically) and the shining star of American literature, the flag-waving Americans that hold him so dear to their patriotic hearts know little of Walt Whitman the gay man. Despite being cast out by his contemporaries for his apparent homosexuality, and the racier work published later in his life, Whitman remained a devout patriot. While his notebooks may be crammed with over 100 descriptions of men that he met on the streets of Manhattan and "slept" with, his queer side has been well hidden by American scholars and teachers. They mistakenly believe that Whitman couldn't have been involved in any kind of gay subculture of cruising, as such a culture didn't exist way back then. They are wrong. A writer of charged and pretty damn sensual poetry at that time (check out *I Sing The Body Electric*) he wrote about homosexuality 20 years before it was even called that.

Gore Vidal
Born 1925

Vidal's time spent serving in the Army gave him the inspiration to write his first novel in 1946, entitled *Williwaw*, which boasted an openly gay character way back then. The book was championed by Eleanor Roosevelt, and Vidal's work gained notoriety. His breakthrough book was *The City And The Pillar* in 1948, one of the first novels to contain gay characters, it was acclaimed by gay and straight audiences alike. In the 1950s he worked in television, wrote dramas, and became something of a social commentator. Another literary success was *Myra Breckinridge*—the story of a transsexual that was later made into a film starring Mae West and Raquel Welch. Vidal reckons everyone is bisexual, and doesn't believe in the term "gay"—through most of his sexual relations have been with men. More recently he has been in the press for his correspondence with the Oklahoma bomber Timothy McVeigh, who invited Vidal to his execution on May 16th, 2001. Vidal wrote a piece about his exchange with the bomber for *Vanity Fair*, for which he is a regular contributor.

Tennessee Williams 1911-1983

Born Thomas Lanier, Williams became one of the 20th century's most renowned playwrights, novelists and poets. Coming from a messed up home—his father was never there, while his mother, who was considered unstable ordered his sister to have a lobotomy—he dropped out of college where he was studying journalism, but continued to write in his spare time. In the 1940s he wrote his first play, moved to New Orleans, and had his first affair with a man, called Kit, who then married a woman, and died an untimely death in 1944. He was awarded the Pulitzer Prize in 1948 for A Streetcar Named Desire, and won the Pulitzer Prize again in 1955 for Cat On A Hot Tin Roof—which featured alcoholism, homosexuality and child prostitution—but despite this success still suffered from bouts of depression that led to alcohol and drug abuse. He was outed in the 1950s, after which he openly discussed his gayness, and wrote his autobiography Memoirs. He died in 1983—drunk in a hotel room, he choked on the cap from a nasal spray.

Truman Capote 1924-1984

Born Truman Streckfus Persons, Mr Capote was out and proud about his queerness way back in the 1940s when it certainly wasn't fashionable to be a flagrant homo. But with acclaimed works like Other Voices, Other Rooms (1948)—about a gay boy's sexual awakening in the Deep South of America—his travel writings for The New Yorker and his damn good looks, Capote became a favorite on New York's artsy scene. In 1958 he wrote Breakfast At Tiffany's, which was immortalized on screen by the legendary Audrey Hepburn. An absolute smash, it propelled Capote's career even further. His non-fiction investigation of the murder of a family in Kansas, called In Cold Blood, put him on TV screens and in magazines everywhere, where he was a hit with his witty repartee. In the 1970s he languished on the New York gay scene, and was a regular at Studio 54 and The Limelight. Towards the end of his life, Capote became a social pariah after blowing the lid on high society shenanigans in his book Answered Prayers.

Contemporary classics
Smart young things whose books have crowded queer sections in book shops the world over

Patricia Highsmith 1921-1995

An American writer, Highsmith's nomadic life saw her moving to Europe in 1949. Her first novel, Strangers On A Train, was turned into a film by Alfred Hitchcock, and while she was very private about her personal life, the fact that she penned the 1952 lesbian novel The Price Of Salt (one of the first gay-themed books to have a happy ending) under the pseudonym Claire Morgan says it all. In her diaries she also wrote about several lady lovers, including living with the novelist Ann Aldrich in the 1950s and, according to British journalist Andrew Wilson, "In her diaries and notebooks she left clues to the identities of several, mainly female lovers, who were often listed by their initials, thereby necessitating a great deal of detective work." She is most famed for her five novels about the criminal psychotic Tom Ripley, one of which was turned into the movie The Talented Mr Ripley, starring Jude Law and Matt Damon.

Andrew Holleran Born 1943

Andrew Holleran, whose real name is Eric Gerber, had his first novel—and biggest success—Dancer From The Dance published in 1978. A sort of male version of Rubyfruit Jungle [see page 190], it depicted the hedonistic-yet lonely days of the 70s in NYC—boys who went to bathhouses, danced under the glitter ball in the hope of finding true love and holidayed in Key West or Fire Island. It became a gay classic. His follow-ups, including books of short stories, saw Holleran becoming a literary force in queer publishing.

David Leavitt Born 1961

Possibly one of the queerest of the contemporary queer writers, a hip young upstart on the New York literary scene, his first novel The Lost Language Of Cranes about a gay son's coming out to his then closeted gay father won him instant acclaim. Other novels and short story collections include Martin Bauman and The Marble Quilt.

Felice Picano Born 1944

The queer author of 19 books, Picano's most celebrated work is Like People In History. A writer in post-Stonewall New York, his works reflect the hedonistic disco days and bathhouse shenanigans, all written in an unabashed and shameless homo manner. As well as acclaimed queer novels, he is also the coauthor of The New Joy of Gay Sex. With his contemporaries, including Andrew Holleran and Edmund White, he founded the Violet Quill Club in order to promote the visibility of gay authors and their work.

Leslie Feinberg Born 1949

A writer and political activist whose work debates and brings to light the issues of transgender people, Feinberg's breakthrough novel Stone Butch Blues caused a stir in the queer communities and won her a LAMBDA Literary Award in 1994. As well as Stone Butch Blues, which introduced us to the Feinberg protagonist Jessie, Feinberg has also produced works of non-fiction that were some of the first to spotlight the issues of the trans community often ignored by gay men and dykes.

The Talented Mr Ripley   Patricia Highsmith

LIKE PEOPLE IN HISTORY Felice Picano

DAVID LEAVITT   The Lost Language Of Cranes

Page turners
Plain good reads, these have few literary pretensions but are classics in their own right

Literary
Whether old school or modern literary geniuses, these scribes have been using their queerness to create high-brow classics

Armistead Maupin
Born 1949

With four million copies of Maupin's celebrated series *Tales Of The City* in circulation, it's no wonder that he's one of the world's best-known queer writers. The series began as a serial in the *San Francisco Chronicle*, and caused such a stir amongst its readers—both gay and straight—that in 1976 Maupin turned the San Francisco-based stories into a book, which was in turn made into a television series that attracted millions of viewers globally. The series of six books, set at the 28 Barbary Lane apartment block include *Tales Of The City, More Tales Of The City, Further Tales Of The City, Babycakes, Significant Others* and *Sure Of You*. They have become so popular that people have even asked to be buried with them. Post-*Tales*, and because of *Tales*, Maupin has managed to forge himself a reputation as a storyteller of the highest order with books like *The Night Listener* and *Maybe The Moon*. He is also something of a controversial figure, having been at the forefront of the Outing movement [see page 88].

Rita Mae Brown
Born 1944

The mega-smash novel *Rubyfruit Jungle* from 1973 deservedly won Brown critical acclaim. However, even with this, and an impressive political background, having been part of the kick ass Stonewall Riots in 1969, as well as being involved as an out-dyke in women's groups in the 1970s, Brown faced a backlash after the publication of *Rubyfruit*. She received "threats on my life including two bomb threats. Straight people were mad because I was gay. The dykes were mad because I wasn't gay enough." Her outspoken ways, including slamming the Republican and Democratic parties, as well as her failed relationships—first with Martina Navratilova [see page 100] and then with Martina's ex-girlfriend Judy Nelson—have only added to the writer's notoriety. Add to that her split up with Fannie Flagg, author of *Fried Green Tomatoes At The Whistlestop Café* [see page 31] who was "so homophobic" and you realize you've got a cheeky madam with a loose mouth whose work has won her a fervent queer fanbase.

Alison Bechdel
Born 1949

Not a writer as such, Bechdel's *Dykes To Watch Out For* cartoon series made her a queer bestseller. The exploits of her laughably stereo-typical lesbian characters—bitter Mo, the heroine looking for love; Clarice her ex-lover who's still on the scene; Sparrow who works in a women's shelter; Jezanna who owns a "wimmin's" bookstore—have had lesbian fans hooked the world over. Think veganism, feminist politics, and hapless love lives and you've got the perfect drawn soap opera.

Dorothy Allison
Born 1949

Allison's first novel, the semi-autobiographical *Bastard Out Of Carolina* from 1992 paved the way for her works around the theme of po'white trash. Born into a dirt poor family in the Deep South of the States, Allison's childhood was littered with sexual and physical abuse, a drunken stepfather, and abject poverty. These roots led her to put finger to typewriter and with *Bastard* she became an international bestseller. Allison-the-outsider became famous, and her later oeuvre, *Cavedweller*, propelled her career even further.

Vita Sackville-West
1892-1962

Brought up in Knole Castle in Kent—a gift to her ancestors from Queen Elizabeth I—posh Ms. West was educated privately and began writing plays and novels as a child. She married in 1913 and had two sons with her husband, Harold Nicholson, who was also gay. Despite a string of affairs with several ladies, including Virginia Woolf and Violet Keppel—their lovematch was fictionalized in Sackville-West's work *Challenge*, about the pair's respective husbands coming to get the two from Paris, where they'd gone off together—the marriage survived. A poet, as well the writer of over 50 novels, including the acclaimed *The Edwardians*, and the prose poem *The Land*, she is actually more well-known for her dykey persuasion than her literary works.

Marguerite Radclyffe-Hall
1880-1943

Born in 1880, in Bournemouth, on the south coast of England, Ms. Hall was known as Peter as a child, later calling herself John. This gender terrorist had a way with words and published several tomes of poetry, all dedicated to the love that dare not speak its name, aka lesbianism. She wrote the semi-autobiographical *The Well of Loneliness* in 1928, and it became the first in-your-face lesbian novel ever. Despite its miserablist writings on how tragic same-sex desire is, and that the "loneliest place in the world is the no-man's land of sex" it became a hit with gay ladies everywhere. The then-outrageous content of the book saw it being banned in the UK, while its defenders included authors of note like Virginia Woolf [see page 188] and E. M. Forster [see page 173]. Despite—and probably because of—the furore surrounding it, it went on to sell over one million copies during her lifetime, and was published in eleven languages.

Jeanette Winterson
Born 1959

A writer and a preacher by the age of eight—due to the overpowering influence of her evangelical father—Winterson came out as a lesbian at the age of 15 and was promptly dumped by her parents. She supported herself through higher education, and attended Oxford University. Her 1985 breakthrough first novel—and still arguably the best of her output—was *Oranges Are Not The Only Fruit*, a semi-autobiographical work about a young dyke in the North of England growing up with religious fanatics for parents. Her other works, including *Sexing The Cherry* and *The Passion*, were published to critical praise, but her out and out self-publicism, along with the outing of her agent—who was married at the time and having an affair with Winterson—put her in bad favor with other writers and book folk. She has, however, been lauded as something of a literary genius by some, going even so far as to call herself "the only true heir to Virginia Woolf."

Non-English
They do gay books abroad, you know

Gertrude Stein
1874-1946

Stein's only explicitly dykey book, *Q.E.D.* was not published in her lifetime although there can never have been much doubt as to the nature of the writer's sexuality. She traveled Europe extensively with her brother Leo Stein, and hung out with and bought art from painters like Henri Matisse and Pablo Picasso, who also painted her portrait. Her group of friends in Paris also included writers and painters of note, including Ernest Hemingway and Jean Cocteau. Liaisons with friends like May Bookstaver and Etta Cone have been hinted at by literary scholars, and her relationship with Alice B.Toklas—whose biography Stein wrote—lasted 38 years and was punctuated by poetry published after Stein's death.

James Baldwin
1924-1987

Brought up in Harlem as the eldest of nine brothers and sisters, Baldwin's family were religious devotees and by the age of 14 he was preaching his ass around the churches of Manhattan. By the age of 17 he'd begun writing book reviews and essays, one of the first of which looked at homosexuality and homophobia, and in 1948, at the age of 24, he moved to Paris, where he met Lucien Happersberger and fell in love. He stayed in Paris until 1957, mainly due to his fury at the racism in America, and while there wrote *Giovanni's Room*, his greatest novel, which dealt openly with gayness—one of the first novels to do so. It was because of his openness that Baldwin was often rejected by black-focussed, homophobic Civil Rights groups.

Audre Lorde
1934-1992

Raised in Harlem, Lorde's first work was published while she was still at high school. From 1968 to 1992 she produced poetry about her life as a "black lesbian, mother, warrior." A writer and a dedicated campaigner against human rights abuses, Lorde was one of the speakers at the first ever march for gay and lesbian liberation that took place in Washington DC. Her book, *The Cancer Journals*, was a chronicle of her 14-year fight against the disease, which she eventually lost in 1992.

Reinaldo Arenas
1943-1990

The Cuban poet and writer was imprisoned for his homosexuality and his opposition to Fidel Castro's political regime in 1973, eventually escaping to the United States, where he committed suicide in 1980 upon discovering he was HIV-positive. His work was brought to a wider audience in 2000, when the filmmaker Julian Schnabel made a movie based on his autobiographical *Before Night Falls*. His works include the four-part *Pentagonia*, about his childhood, adolescent rebellion and growing up closeted in a macho world.

Jean Cocteau
1889-1963

A master of the arts, Cocteau was an accomplished novelist, film director, poet and fine artist. Hanging out with all the right people, like Picasso—who was his friend for over 50 years—Stravinsky and di Chirico, Cocteau was a true renaissance man, the writer of ballets, the founder of a publishing house, decorator of churches and an acclaimed novelist, with works including the novel *Les Enfants Terribles* and films like *Beauty and the Beast* (not the Disney version!). Famous for his relationship with French actor Jean Marais and his friendship with writer Colette, he was also a notorious opium taker.

Yukio Mishima
1925-1970

One of the most talented writers to come out of Japan in the last century, Mishima produced 23 novels and over 40 plays in his lifetime—add to that some short stories, travel volumes and a few hundred essays, and you can see why he's on the list. His second novel, *Confessions Of A Mask*, the story of a boy who realizes he's gay and has to hide his sexuality behind a mask, was lauded by Japanese audiences who seemed to have missed the gay plot. Although he was married, Mishima was a regular punter in the gay bars in Tokyo, where he was known as the "bearer of two swords," meaning that he swung both ways. In 1970 he broke into the National Defence Headquarters in Tokyo and made a speech to the servicemen in the building, attacking Japan's constitution. After this scathing ten-minute diatribe, in true Samurai tradition, he committed suicide.

Federico Garcia Lorca
1898-1936

One of the most well-known and popular poets and playwrights in Spain like ever, Lorca moved to Madrid when he was 20 and hung out with a bunch of young intellectuals that included the saucy Surrealist, Salvador Dali (apparently Lorca lusted after the moustached artist, and there are rumours that skin hit skin). His 1928 poem *Romancero Gitano* made him a firm favorite in his homeland, and in 1929 he went to the States to study English, with some of his work at this time expressing his loathing for the "squalor and racism" he found there. His *Ode To Walt Whitman* told of his hatred for "maricas" (or fairies)—effeminate men, as opposed to the closeted, straight-acting butch guys he preferred. Already a national hero on the back of dramas such as *The House of Bernarda Alba*, it was during the Spanish Civil War that Lorca was arrested by right-wing soldiers, tortured and shot dead. The nature of the killing has led historians to believe that he was killed more for his homosexuality than for his left-wing beliefs.

Oranges Are Not The Only Fruit JEANETTE WINTERSON

The Well Of Loneliness Marguerite Radclyffe-Hall

Before Night Falls Reinaldo Arenas

Les Enfants Terribles

Confessions Of A Mask Jean Cocteau

ODE TO WALT WHITMAN YUKIO MISHIMA

FEDERICO GARCIA LORCA

Edmund White
Writer

Edmund White will always be known for his groundbreaking novels *A Boy's Own Story* (1982) and *The Beautiful Room Is Empty* (1988), and although, admittedly, his best work is of an autobiographical nature, he's notched up enough critical and commercial successes to warrant his status as a pink writer par excellence.

After graduating from University of Michigan where he studied Chinese, he moved to New York where he worked for Time-Life books, then *The Saturday Review* and *Horizon*. During the mid-70s, as well as working on *The Joy Of Gay Sex* (with Dr. Charles Silverstein) and *Nocturnes For The King Of Naples*, he helped found the Violet Quill alongside Andrew Holleran, Robert Ferro, Felice Picano, George Whitmore, Christopher Cox, and Michael Grumley, who regularly met to critique each others' work.

After the release of the critically acclaimed and highly successful *A Boy's Own Story*, he moved to Paris where he met his lover Hubert Sorin, who at the time was married. Like many American gay men at the time, he seriously suffered the repercussions of AIDS: while he was diagnosed as HIV-positive in 1985, most of his friends died during the decade as did Hubert—Edmund's book *The Married Man* (2000) was based on that relationship. In 1995, by this time back in New York, Edmund started a relationship with writer Michael Carroll, and they moved in together four years later.

Edmund White says, "The true duty of gay writers is to remind readers of the wealth of gay accomplishments."

Tom of Finland
Gay illustrator and designer of the modern gay body

You can feel the influence of Tom of Finland every time you set foot inside a gay club: the heavy-set bodies, the massive pectorals, the tight jeans with huge, prominently displayed dicks, the short hair, the tattoos, the boots, the jeans, the uniforms, the leather, the rubber, the very masculinity that gay men adopted as their own, can all be traced back to a former advertising artist from a Northern European country with an obsession for hard-faced guys, preferably in uniform, with dicks the size of baby pigs and libidos to make the Marquis de Sade hanker after a quiet night in.

Born Touko in 1920, Tom first came in contact with the hyper-masculine specimens that would populate his art while living among farmers and lumberjacks in his native— guess where— Finland. Later, during the Second World War, in which he served as a lieutenant, he became infatuated by men in uniforms and, after a lot of great sex during blackouts, started to see the erotic side of the occupying Nazi army, with their jackboots and propensity towards rape and torture. It was all prime inspiration for the guy who started drawing while masturbating.

In 1957 a friend of Touko's sent one of his images to muscle mag *Physique Pictorial* in the States; they used it on the cover and Tom of Finland—Touko would have been too confusing—was born. Over the following decades Tom's trademark men took over. With their anuses gaping and their huge members dripping, they were everywhere, getting screwed in jail, having motorcycle cops bend them over their bikes, having mammoth cocks shoved up their willing asses, being tied up, hung from trees, tattooed, trodden on. Tom's men showed up in magazines, on T-shirts, in cards, in books and increasingly—especially with the on-set of AIDS when every gay man wanted to look healthy—in real life.

There were obviously the expected criticisms that Tom of Finland was perpetuating a gay myth and that there were no tender images of gay love (even though there were, just not very many). But what critics refused to recognize, apart from the fact that Tom's men always had very friendly faces, was that Tom of Finland was drawing from the cutting edge of male desire, an unpoliceable area where rape fantasies roamed, and where members so huge they would actually kill you were at the top of everyone's wish list.

Tom became an established part of the gay New York scene, with friends like Robert Mapplethorpe [see page 194], who did a portrait of him, but having lost his lover of twenty-eight years to cancer, Tom of Finland finally succumbed to an emphysema-induced stroke on November 7th, 1991.

Image: Tom of Finland Foundation © 2002

Gilbert and George

The art world's shit-obsessed odd couple

Gilbert Proesch and George Passmore met on the Advanced Sculpture course at Central St. Martin's School Of Art in London in 1967. Gilbert, born in Italy and unable to speak English when he first arrived, teamed up with George, who was born in Devon, England, to perform their now infamous double act, the *Singing Sculptures*. Rather than making the art, the comical duo became the art. They would paint their faces, stand on tables and move to music for up to eight hours at a time! After eight years of performing this particular piece, the duo decided they needed a new canvas other than themselves.

Despite their austere appearance—the pair are only ever seen in public wearing formal matching tweed suits—Gilbert and George not only use humor in their work, they also constantly push the boundaries of what the conservative art world sees as acceptable. With works entitled 'Bum Holes,' 'Sperm Eaters,' and 'New Horny Pictures,' their almost childish wording and representation of sexual themes often distract from the fact that the art they produce is visually and intellectually pleasing: their huge, brightly colored photo collages on black grids, usually starring themselves, are gorgeously harmonious pieces representing a couple at work—using advertising speak and fonts, they strive to create art that is accessible to the general public, and not just the gallery-going elite, with "Art For All" being their battle cry against the conservative hierarchy of the art world.

While they may look the perfect middle-aged besuited queer couple, Gilbert and George have been out-doing young pretenders to the "shock art" throne for years. Often posing nude, and looking menacingly like the classic British

comedians Morecambe and Wise, the backdrop to their photographic portraits can be anything from feces and piss, to blood, semen and spit—everyday human excreta all dressed up in pretty colors.

Like all good queer artists, their shows have caused outrage amongst religious folk. As recently as 1999, their art was branded "impure filth" by priests in Belfast who took offence not only to their work, but also to their homosexuality. As one British newspaper reported from the picket lines outside the gallery,

George was actually more insulted by protestors shouting "Sodom and Gomorrah" at him, saying it was the anti-gay protests that were "beyond the pale and not their pictures." And while some may recoil in horror at the images of blow jobs, assholes and fists—entitled 'Coloured Friends' from 1982—it's undeniable that the art-producing queer couple have been influencing, entertaining, and mocking the art world since 1970: "Our whole lives must be about creating an impact and making our mark. Otherwise there would be no point."

Bruce Weber

The photographer responsible for mainstreaming homoerotica

A photographer first and foremost, Bruce Weber—the big, beardy guy with the bandana—is also an acclaimed filmmaker with his Chet Baker documentary, *Let's Get Lost*, earning him an Oscar nomination and state-of-the-art music videos for Chris Isaak and the Pet Shop Boys [see page 174] to his name. A dynamic force in fashion and art photography, with an almost unrivaled commercial reputation, he has, over the past couple of decades, become one of the best-known American photographers ever.

Born in Pennsylvania in 1946, Weber moved to New York when he was twenty to study photography. His first big break came in 1981 when he was inadvertently responsible for shaping the way that fashion houses advertised their products forever: while working with the advertising agency Shahid & Company, and the creative director Sam Shahid in particular, he was hired to photograph a Calvin Klein campaign that unusually adopted a gay male gaze and put the sexualised male form center stage for the first time in commercial history. As well as some shots featuring boys in bed together, Weber's most famous look for Mr. Klein featured rapper and future actor "Marky" Mark Wahlberg, with his Calvins showing way above the waistband of his jeans. It was a style popular among black men that took off in gay ghettos worldwide on the strength of that one shot.

Weber went on to create imagery for Banana Republic and Abercrombie & Fitch [see page 139], where his over-sexed shots of beautiful boys and girls not only used subtle homoerotic themes such as wrestling, but also full-on, in-your-face queer poses, and to such an extent that the company was obliged to put its catalog inside a sealed wrapper.

Famed for his use of real people instead of supermodels, Weber has been known to pluck potential poseurs off the street and off the playing fields to appear in high-end advertising campaigns for the likes of Ralph Lauren, as well as in his films (*Let's Get Lost* was peopled by a host of unfeasibly great looking extras). Peter Johnson, who Weber discovered wrestling, has been propelled into campaigns for Versace and Lagerfield, and appears in Weber's autobiographical movie *Chop Suey*, which also charts Johnson's rise from a cute young thing into an internationally recognized model.

Parallel to his commercial work, but not always entirely distinguishable from it, Weber has created fine art photography by the gallery-full, most of it black and white and featuring young men, often in a summer camp setting, and often with vaguely Hitler Youth-y connotations, over which he has messily painted messages. With over sixteen books to his name, Weber has also photographed Newfoundland dogs, landscapes, and Hollywood celebrities like Madonna, Kate Moss and Leonardo DiCaprio. Without him the world would be a less sexy place.

▷ **Take it further**: *Chop Suey*, a film by Bruce Weber

Robert Mapplethorpe

A taboo-busting master of photography

Famous for his technically superb black and white photographs of cock in a still life setting, Robert Mapplethorpe was born in middle-class suburbia, on Long Island, in 1946, and relished leaving his quiet hometown to move to Brooklyn. The bright lights, big city and veritable feast of queerness drew him in.

As a student of painting at the Pratt Institute in Brooklyn, he shared a room with life-long close friend, muse and occasional lover, Patti Smith. Mapplethorpe became one of the most talked about photographic artists of the 20th century. He lived the life that encapsulated the spirit of the hedonistic days of 1970s and 1980s New York, a time when the art world was at the very core of the social whirl of Manhattan. Warhol, Mapplethorpe and Haring were the boys for whom the velvet rope was pushed aside, and film stars, musicians and models were their closest friends.

After bagging himself a mover and shaker in the art world as his boyfriend—the older and very handsome art curator Samuel Wagstaff—his career as a photographer began its impressive trajectory. Starting off using Polaroid, by 1977 he had moved to a large format camera and made his name exhibiting classically themed still lives (mainly flowers), society portraits and S&M sex scenes simultaneously. He pushed the boundaries of what was proper and acceptable in the art world, and kicked up a storm doing it.

The 1980s saw Mapplethorpe's thorough exploration of the male nude begin in earnest. Black men were one of his favorite subjects—one of the most famous being that of a rather impressively endowed black man, wearing a polyester suit with his semi-erect cock on full view—and these overtly homoerotic and sexual images drew both positive and negative criticism from the African American community, especially when it was alleged that Mapplethorpe was something of a racist himself. Another of his favorite themes was himself—the most memorable being Mapplethorpe dressed up in a cowboy outfit with a bullwhip protruding from his asshole, while others depict his physical demise as HIV/AIDS set in.

During the 1980s, at the fervorous height of reactionary Reaganism, Senator Jesse Helms was getting very hot under the collar about the funding of such "filth" with government money by the National Endowment for the Arts: it seemed that the ultra-conservative USA wasn't quite ready for in-your-face images showing full-on gay sex acts. As the AIDS epidemic began to attract media interest and support from celebrities and artists, Mapplethorpe set up the Robert Mapplethorpe Foundation to support AIDS research. As right-wingers took much-needed funding money away from artists who were daring to confront their prejudices, Maplethorpe was injecting money right back into his community by supporting the arts and photography.

After his death from AIDS at the age of forty-two in 1988, Mapplethorpe's notoriety increased when galleries exhibiting his retrospective were charged with obscenity and the misuse of a minor in photography. Ironically, these charges and the censoring of his shows catapulted the dead artist into the mainstream, making this technically brilliant, cutting-edge homo photographer something of a household name.

▷ **Take it further**: *Robert Mapplethorpe* by Patricia Morisroe

Leigh Bowery

The legendary queer performance artist, designer, musician and all-round weird guy

A nude model for the painter Lucien Freud, a muse for designers John Galliano and Vivienne Westwood, and an infamous nightclub performer, Leigh Bowery was a legend on the London club scene in the 1980s and early 1990s.

Born in Australia in 1959, Bowery moved to London in the early 80s where he became a big star on the underground freaky club scene. An accomplished designer, his outlandish, boundary-pushing outfits saw him being photographed incessantly by the scene's snappers desperate to catch some of the hedonism, gender-bending, drug-fuelled fun for posterity. Railing against the ultra-conservative era of Thatcherism and Reaganism, Bowery's taste for the outlandish stood him good stead for his role as a designer for Boy George, who called him "modern art on legs."

Known for covering himself in blood and shit, and dressing up in drag and Saran Wrap, Bowery's body became his canvas. With the look of the evil clown about him, one of his scene-stealing moments came in the film *Wigstock* [see page 89] when he came on stage to perform a blood-curdling rendition of 'All You Need Is Love.' As he leapt around the stage, Bowery fainted and out from between his spread legs came a bald-headed woman—Bowery was giving birth live on stage! Forget the Debbie Harry impersonators and drag queen bitchiness, Bowery had not only stolen the show, but he'd also shut up the mouthy drag queens. Blood, guts and meat had transformed the lite-trash stage of *Wigstock* in an instant. Other on-stage Bowery stunts included spraying the audience with the contents of an enema. Nice. As well as walking the catwalk for Galliano, Bowery

also ran his own legendary club, Taboo, just off Leicester Square in central London. A scary affair, as you can imagine, it attracted the club kids, freaks, and movers and shakers of the queer club scene at that time. All dressed in weird gear—baby doll nightdresses and platform boots were de rigeur—Bowery out-fashioned them all with his polka dot-painted face and crazy wigs. Following the demise of the club, and the demise of Taboo regular and roommate Trojan, Bowery into live music and performance, where, as well as designing the costumes, he performed as a dancer for queer choreographer and punk ballet dancer Michael Clark's extravaganzas.

Bowery lived a life as whacky and mysterious as his on-stage persona—and very few people were ever to see him without full make-up. As well as secretly getting married to his close friend and art collaborator Nicola, despite being a big old homo—it was her that was seen being born from Bowery's faux-vagina at Wigstock—Bowery hid his HIV status from his friends and wife. Noting that his biggest regret was "having unsafe sex with 1000 men," Bowery died from an AIDS-related illness on New Year's Eve, 1994.

Boy George

The gayest superstar in the world

There are not many pop stars your grandmother would recognize. She wouldn't be able to pick Justin Timberlake out of a police line-up, and would probably get Britney mixed up with that nice girl at the deli counter. But she'd recognize Boy George. And not only would she recognize him, she'd probably love him, never mind that he's a cross-dressing homosexual with a serious drugs history. Everyone loves Boy George. It's what he's there for.

Boy George, or George O'Dowd, was born to an anglo-Irish family in south London in 1961. After a fairly straightforward gay childhood (Bowie fixation, hair dying dramas, girlfriends), he moved away from home and into a series of squats, from where he fell into the London punk scene and then, as it evolved, the New Romantic scene, with its emphasis on big hair and scary make up. George was a natural and soon had the biggest hair and the scariest make-up in town becoming a clubland celebrity and, having got a taste for recognition, he eventually decided to have a bash at real stardom. He'd tried being a bit actor in films but it hadn't quite panned out, so he plumped for music and—who knew?, turned out to have a really great soft soul voice.

In 1982, while working in a clothes store and after a couple of false starts, Culture Club, the band George fronted, crashed into the British charts, going all the way to number one with 'Do You Really Want To Hurt Me,' a lilting, reggae-tinged beauty of a single as popular with the mums and dads and the smart set as it was with the majority of record buying kids. But that was before they'd seen what he looked like. The band was already an unusual one, with the name reflecting the diversity of backgrounds within it: there was a black member (Mikey Craig), a white one (Roy Hay), a Jewish one (Jon Moss), and, well, George. But when George appeared on British music show *Top of the Pops*, you could almost hear the shout go up across the land: "What is it?"

But even though he looked like a china doll, George was no muppet. While his edgy dressing, heavy make-up and feminine posturing won the favour of the young and the rebellious, his smart talking and non-confrontational interviews, including the infamous "I'd rather have a cup of tea than sex," helped convince the rest of the population—especially grandmothers for some reason—that he was a nice boy. The only group that seemed immune to George's charm were hard-core gay activists who criticized his refusal to come out properly (like there could ever be any doubt about his leanings), and talk about his homosexuality.

After 'Do You Really Want To Hurt Me,' came a string of hits which made Boy George and Culture Club huge and on a global scale, with 'Karma Chameleon,' the first single from their second album, *Colour By Numbers* making it to number one almost everywhere. But it wasn't to last. A hectic schedule criss-crossing the world, George's abusive relationship with the band's drummer Jon Moss, fame on a life-wrecking scale and drugs all played a part in the bringing down of Culture Club. But it wasn't only the music that was suffering. George had fallen in with transvestite pop wannabe Marilyn, who, riding in on George's coat-tails, had his own top five hit, 'Calling Your Name' in the UK in 1993. Although never lovers, the two were the best of friends and the deadliest of enemies. They were also the worst possible influence on each other and by 1986, having been taking copious amounts of drugs at home and abroad, with and without Marilyn, and after a lengthy game of cat and mouse in the press, George was arrested and charged with crimes relating to heroin abuse. A high-profile court case ensued starring George, who rather than the dazzling creature we'd grown to love, looked pale and drawn. He looked like a drug addict.

In a Britain (and an America) fixated on the drugs menace, this seemed like the most sure-fire way to throw away his popularity but somehow it didn't work like that for George. When he released 'Everything I Own,' a version of an old Bread song, in 1987 it was an immediate number one smash hit in the UK. But George's solo career was never going to do much and totally failed to get off the ground in the States, except for a solitary American hit with a Pet Shop Boys produced version of 'The Crying Game,' which was used as the theme to the Neil Jordan film of the same name. Even in the UK, where he was, and still is, a national institution, George's solo albums—though good—would never excite any of the interest the Culture Club albums did. What would excite interest, however, would be George's autobiography, *Take It Like A Man*, which was received with the kind of reviews he would have been embarrassed to write for himself. It was generally considered to be one of the best rock 'n' roll autobiographies ever written, laced as it was with juicy stories and George's trademark wit. It even brought a court case from Spear of Destiny singer Kirk Brandon, who denied George's claims that they had had a relationship. This time round Boy George looked fabulous in court. He also won.

As well as the book, George also started a column in national UK newspaper *The Sunday Express*, but writing wasn't his only new talent. Having started his own record label More Protein, with its spermatozoa-design logo, George got heavily into dance music, and has become one of the most sought-after DJs in the world. He has also produced a new musical based on the craziness of the 80s club scene, called *Taboo*. Oh, and he still looks fierce.

Top 10 Lesbian movies

The best dyke flicks made especially for the ladies

While films of a lesbian nature—whether you want full-on naughtiness or not—are hard to come by, there are a few classics that any self-respecting, card-carrying lesbian should own. Kick back, slip that video into your slot and enjoy the lady lesbians frolicking on celluloid.

1. Boys On The Side (1995)

Hardly an out and out girl-on-girl action flick, it's the subtext that gets the old juices flowing for this classic road movie film. Starring Whoopi Goldberg—who's scored as many column inches in the "is she, isn't she?" stakes as our dear Miss Jodie Foster—the ever-so delicious Drew Barrymore, and Brat Pack throwback Mary Louise Parker, it's a feelgood, girlie movie with an unrequited lesbian love theme that really hits the spot, without ever getting too cheesy, or too saucy unfortunately.

Mary Louise Parker plays Robin, an uptight real estate executive who's HIV-positive. She hooks up with Jane, an out-of-work lesbian singer (someone's conducted their lesbian research well) played by Goldberg, who has decided to head West to begin a new life and find fame and fortune. En route, as well as hooking up with Barrymore's pregnant character, Holly, who keeps falling for abusive men, the three become close, with Jane falling for Robin big time. A sweet, slushy-in-a-good-way and pretty damn funny film, with a lesbian sub-plot that could have done with more of an airing.

2. The Children's Hour (1961)

Starring two of Hollywood's old heavyweights, Shirley MacClaine and the iconic Audrey Hepburn,

The Children's Hour is the classic tale of a love that dare not speak its name. It's the story of two teachers accused of an evil perversion that we've all grown to know and love as lesbianism. The pair fight in court against the claims of an "unnatural relationship," and attempt to sue the malicious pupil who made up the lies.

However, as the trial continues, MacClaine finally admits to Hepburn that she is actually in love with her in one of the most powerful coming out scenes, like, ever. Due to the era, and due to the film industry's overbearing censorship code and prejudice at the time, MacClaine's character promptly hangs herself. All in all, it's a pretty sad and sorry tale that completely epitomizes a time of prejudice and fear of representing homosexuality in Hollywood.

3. Bound (1996) [right]

This film set lesbians' panties on fire. The hot-to-trot Gina Gershon stars, with those lips and dykey vest tops, alongside Jennifer Tilly in a damn decent modern film noir that twists and turns to keep you on the edge of your seat for the full 108 minutes. Directed by Andy and Larry Wachowski, this girl-powered and rather clever thriller sees Gershon's ex-con character, Corky, doing up an apartment next door to that of a psychotic Mob gangster. Corky is called next door to help out the wife of the gangster, Violet played by Jennifer Tilly, and the sparks begin to fly. Gershon out-butches the so-called Mobster hard men at every turn, in her cute white vests and with her labrys tattoo—the scene where Tilly boasts to Corky that she knows what it means is a classic moment in lesbian cinema—she wins over Tilly, with sex scenes verging on raunchy (but only at the beginning). Despite it being man-made, the Wachowski boys did get in lesbian "sexpert" Susie Bright to call the bedroom shots, and she certainly knows her stuff. While the lesbian sub-plot is tasty, so is the script and filming,

and it's all topped off nicely with some scenes of graphic violence and no end of bloodletting Bound ends up a decent crime thriller with some seriously hot lesbian action.

4. Go Fish! (1994)

One of the first films to look like dykes actually turn up for classes at film school, *Go Fish!* is a grainy black and white number that follows a rag-tag bunch of lesbian friends as they go looking for love. Gossip, sex, arguments, sleeping with men, trying to bag the perfect girl, cutting nails before a date—it's all covered here. Rose Troche's Chicago-based debut stars the irresistible dyke actress, writer and producer, Guinevere Turner, who plays Max—the girl in search of a girl. Set up on a blind date with V. S. Brodie's character, Ely—a lesbian who goes through the from-long-hair-to-dodgy-lesbian-hair process in the midst of the movie—Max ain't interested at first. The film, with cameos from lesbian-on-the-horn Daria and other friends of the two match-made girls, follows their blossoming relationship with cheeky humor and lesbian in-jokes. A thoroughly modern-looking treat of a lesbian flick.

5. Better Than Chocolate (1999)

Nothing more, nothing less than a good old lesbian love story, with some amusing comic touches and a damn good, compelling story that follows sexy 19-year-old baby dyke Maggie, played by Karen Dwyer, as she quits law school, gets a job in a dykey bookshop, and goes on the search for girls. Handling more than just one coming out story, the film sees Maggie falling for Kim, played by Christina Cox, an arty type who lives in a van. The pair get it on while Maggie's recently divorced mother, along with Maggie's brother, turn up on her doorstep. The sexual awakening of her younger brother (with one of the bisexual girls in the bookstore) and her mother—the scene with the box of vibrators is hilarious—as well as Maggie's coming out to her mum are sweet and really touching, and also really funny in places. And those sex scenes? Let's just say that for a 19 year-old, she knows her stuff!

6. Desert Hearts (1985) [left]

Based on the 1964 lesbian novel, *Desert Of The Heart* by Jane Rule, Donna

Deitch's first feature-length flick has gone down as a true dykey classic in the heart of cinema-going girls everywhere. Set in 1950s American, it's the typical tale of chalk falling for cheese. Vivian, an uptight professor is stationed in Reno waiting for her divorce to come through—cue cowboys and a girl, big shiny automobiles and country and western tunes. In her mid-thirties, with a failed marriage to her name, and despite trying to resist, Vivian falls for the advances of Cay, a younger cute casino worker who woos the straight-laced Vivian right into the bedroom. While the sex scenes are slow-burning and romantic rather than full throttle, it's still seen as a groundbreaking queer movie—one of the first out-and-out dykey films to be produced, cast and filmed with a respectable budget, and the first lesbian movie to be written and directed by a woman.

7. High Art (1998)

Quite simply one of the best returns to form for an overlooked actress in filmdom. Ally Sheedy—looking fine in her must-be-a-lesbian white vest and no bra —as the Nan Goldin-esque former photographer, romps home in this Sapphic, arty beauty that abuses fabulous cinematography, hot new actresses and a great, drug-infused storyline. While the lezza sex is overshadowed by the heavy drug consumption, the tenderness between Ally's character, Lucy Berliner, and the naïve-but-pretty underling Syd, played by up-and-coming Aussie actress Radha Mitchell—who's no virgin to dyke roles—is nothing but delicious. Second only to Sheedy's performance, though, is that of her heroin addict girlfriend, Greta, played by Patricia Clarkson. Arty, fierce, sexy, grungey and downright addictive, it's deserving of its Sundance Film Festival accolades.

8. Butterfly Kiss (1995)

Another lesbian film, another take on the road movie genre—this time it's set in the grim north of England, and as well as a whiff of lesbianism, there's serial killing a-go-go in this feature from respected Brit director Michael Winterbottom. Amanda Plummer plays a slightly crazed lesbian—another piece of good research—who's roaming the grey towns of North England in search of her departed lover. She stumbles upon the gorgeous Saskia Reeves, who plays gas station attendant Miriam, and the two end up traveling the countryside killing men who stand for the degradation they've experienced all their lives. Dark, slightly menacing and thoroughly watchable, the girls' on-the-road killing spree is a weird but delicious look at an odd lesbian couple.

9. When Night Is Falling (1995)

From the maker of lesbian fave, *I've Heard The Mermaids Singing*, this lesbian flick starts off slowly but builds into a little beauty of a film. It, again, goes for the "uptight woman falls for sexy young girl" plot, and makes use of a circus backdrop along the way. The film's lead, Camille, played by Pascale Bussières, has her pet dog run over, and her laundry "mistakenly" swapped by minx-like trapeze girl Petra, whose lesbian predatory skills need much praise heaped upon them. Petra, skillfully played by the actress Rachael Crawford, manages to get the girl, while Camille not only obliges in bed, but gives wild child Petra the stability that she needs.

10. Heavenly Creatures (1994)

Starring Kate Winslet before she did *Titanic*, *Heavenly Creatures* is a New Zealand flick based on the true story about two murderous schoolgirls in the 1950s— Pauline Parker, played by Melanie Lynskey, and Juliet Hulme, played by Winslet—who develop an intense and obsessive friendship, based on their own dream world Borovnia, which is fanned and fuelled by their intellectualism and feelings of being outsiders.

When their parents spot the whole thing turning slightly "unhealthy" (their sexual relationship is only hinted at in the film, as opposed to the girls' true life dykey fling) they're separated "for their own good." This doesn't stop their fantasy life and relationship continuing, however, and their masterplan to stop them being parted by Winslet's enforced departure to South Africa is a grisly one that involved the pair killing Pauline's mother while out on a walk in the country. A cult classic of a film. Following a short period in jail the real-life Juliet Hulme now lives in Scotland, under the name Anne Perry, and writes murder fiction, while Pauline Parker has also moved to the UK. As a condition of their sentencing, the two young women were ordered to never see each other again.

Nureyev

Man in pantyhose

It's not too difficult to work out why gay men have always been attracted to color and movement—particularly in a Communist country like the USSR. Following in the footsteps—geddit?— of Sergei Diaghileff and Vaslav Nijinsky, Rudolf Nureyev was however a genius who brought pure sex appeal to ballet in a way hitherto unseen—why else would he have had groupies at the stage door screaming, "We want Rudi, in the nudie!"

But as well as being a great talent admired by everyone from Jackie Onassis to Madonna [see page 22], Rudolf's life story is so remarkable, you couldn't dream it up.

The son of a committed Communist, he was born on the Trans-Siberian Express train in 1938. He grew up struggling to dance against his father's wishes, but persisted, studying in Ufa and St. Petersburg where he was continually criticized for his lack of technique. Despite this, he became a soloist with the Kirov ballet in 1958, and by the time of his defection to the West three years later, he had interpreted every lead role and become a megastar in his own right.

In 1961, at the height of the Cold War, Rudolf angered the Communist Party and KGB by associating too freely with westerners on tour in Europe. When it came to fly to London from Paris, KGB agents were dispatched to bring him home. However, in a dramatic scene in the airport bar he was able to flee into the protection of the French police.

He went on to score himself a slew of lead roles around the world, and also became a permanent guest artist of the Royal Ballet, all of which firmly established him as the leading classical ballet dancer of his generation. He even revised and staged several ballets himself.

But it was together with legendary ballerina Margot Fonteyn that he'll be forever remembered. Together they epitomized romance and passion, though it seems unlikely they actually had a fling even if Rudolf slept with both men and women (including Jackie Kennedy's sister Lee Radziwil.) The love of his life, however, was Danish

dancer Erik Bruhn, ten years his senior, with whom he had a tumultuous affair.

He said, "With women, you have to work so hard and that is not very satisfying for me," he said. "With men, it's very quick. Big pleasure."

While his defection to the West had gained him endless media attention, it was something Nureyev didn't shy away from during his life. He was the star and subject of a movie, had a Broadway show in the mid-70s, toured the US in a revival of the Broadway musical *The King and I*, and was frequently on television— he was a bona fide celebrity, if not an icon, who moved and shook in all the right circles.

In 1983, he became ballet director of the Paris Opera, where he spent most of his time, but ten years later on January 6th, 1993, he was back in the headlines when his death became the subject of media controversy.

Michel Canesi, his personal friend and physician, broke the news to the media, stating he'd died of a "cardiac complication following a grievous illness." He refused to say anything else, citing he was following Rudolf's wishes. Nevertheless, rumors that he had AIDS had circulated years earlier after he'd taken an HIV test, and some people with the disease dissed him as a coward.

Seven days later however, Michel spoke to French newspaper, *Le Figaro* and confirmed that Rudolf had indeed died because of AIDS, having lived with the virus for 13-14 years. The reason he'd not come out earlier is that some countries refused entry to people with the disease.

The controversy didn't stop there however. Rudolf had left his financial affairs in a mess. His personal things were later auctioned off at Christie's in New York, becoming the biggest celebrity sale the auction house had known.

Rudolf Nureyev was more than just a dancer, he was a larger than life personality and without him ballet would be a very different creature today.

George Michael

From big-haired 80s heartthrob to the queen of public sex

For every Melissa Etheridge and kd lang [see page 215], there's a George Michael, whose career has been killed dead—at least in America—by coming out.

It all kicked off in 1998 when singer George Michael, a huge star on both sides of the Atlantic, was arrested for lewd behavior in a Los Angeles public restroom. The media went wild. But after reportedly declining an interview with *Dateline*, he decided to tell his side of the story three days later when he also acknowledged he was gay. He said: "This is as good a time as any... I want to say that I have no problem with people knowing that I'm in a relationship with a man right now. I have not been in a relationship with a woman for almost 10 years."

As to the toilet incident, he revealed: "I don't feel any shame. I feel stupid and I feel reckless and weak for having allowed my sexuality to be exposed this way."

In the resulting suit, George entered a plea of "no contest" and was fined $810, ordered to perform eighty hours of community service, and seek counselling. He was banned from the park in question.

George has since been able to turn the incident around with a sense of humor. Quizzed on the Internet about whether he now felt like a role model, he said not "unless gay youths are looking for advice on how to get arrested." Meanwhile, invitations to his 35th-birthday party asked guests to use the bathroom before they arrived as "all conveniences will be locked to protect the host." With tongue still firmly in cheek, the video for the single 'Outside' from the double album *Ladies and Gentlemen… The Best Of George Michael*, released around the same time, saw George donning police uniform and leading a choreographed dance routine in a public convenience. Hilarious. The

fact that he refused to feel any remorse for what he'd done won George Michael the hearts of gay men everywhere.

However, winning the hearts of the general public everywhere has been a different matter. In Europe, and particularly Britain, it's been easy: the UK warmed to its homegrown star's self-deprecating humor and honesty, and his *Best Of* collection was the runaway success of 1998, clocking up staggering eight-times platinum sales. In the States though, it seriously underachieved while 'As', his duet with Mary J. Blige, was removed from her album altogether by her record label. That kind of scandal doesn't sell to r'n'b fans in the US.

But all in all, it's surprising that George was able to keep his sexuality under wraps for so long. Anybody reading between the lines should have guessed it—hell, there was even a veiled reference to his dead boyfriend on the *Older* album. Although, he'd been out to his friends and family for a long time, he chose privacy when it came to the media. As to his fans, he says: "I think I tried to tell them everything through my work, as opposed to using the media. But in all honesty I think I blew that particular strategy in a big way."

Yorgos Kyriatou Panayioutou, aka George Michael, first came to fame in 1986 as half of teen pin-up duo Wham! Together with Andrew Ridgeley they scored hit after hit with white boy soul singles like 'Young Guns (Go For It),' 'Freedom,' and 'Wake Me Up Before You Go Go,' which were propelled by big hair, Fila sportswear, and a working class joie-de-vivre embodied by their "Choose Freedom" T-shirts.

But although Andrew was waaay cuter, it was ultimately all about George—what with his songwriting talent and all—so it came as no real surprise when in 1985 they split (amicably) with a sell-out concert in front of 72,000 fans in

London's Wembley Arena. While Andrew went on to have a feeble and unsuccessful stab at a solo career, and move in with girl group Bananarama star, Keren Woodward, George had much bigger fish to fry, and when the album *Faith* was launched two years later, he instantly became a massive star not only in the UK but in the States too, notching up impressive album sales of ten million there.

That's not to say his sexuality wasn't under scrutiny at the time. George was the subject of tabloid speculation, something his image of leather jacket, ripped jeans and stubble did nothing to dispel (though the video for 'I Want Your Sex,' which saw him cavorting with a lady at least tried).

By the follow-up, *Listen Without Prejudice Vol 1*, George had disappeared behind a bevy of beautiful supermodels lipsynching his words in the videos. Despite unleashing two top ten hits, receiving much acclaim and selling one million Stateside, the album was regarded as a commercial failure, and prompted George to enter into a legal battle with his record company for not properly promoting it. He vowed not to release any more records if he lost. He lost, but bought his way out of his contract and released the album *Older* in 1996, by which time he'd oddly transformed his image into that of a smarmy Greek waiter. Yet again, sales were disappointing in the US.

Two years later, George was forced out of the closet in the most spectacular style. Despite massive media attention, his fourth solo album, *Songs From The Last Century*, was released at the end of 1999, once again meeting with fewer sales than previous albums during his heyday. Whether this has to do with a poorer product or the scandal, is anyone's guess, but without a doubt, the scandal is sure to throw a shadow over his work for a long time.

Drag Queens
Cocks in frocks

"You're born naked, the rest is drag," said RuPaul [see page 187], the supermodel credited with dragging drag into the mainstream. But while he had his beautifully manicured finger on a very good point—that everyone is dragged up as something, even if it is just as a man—he understates the explosive nature of drag and the effect it has on an almost visceral level.

"When you meet a human being, the first distinction you make is 'male or female,' and you are accustomed to making the distinction with unhesitating certainty," said Sigmund Freud, the granddaddy of psychiatry, in *Femininity*. The fact that with drag queens you do not know with any certainty at all what you are being confronted with, and by extension how you're supposed to react in such a gender-specific world, is the seat of the drag queen's power. She is like the third sex with all the allure of a woman, but all the power of a man.

The phenomenon of men dressing up in women's clothes is not new or necessarily confined to the "decadent" West. There are records of men swishing around in ladies' apparel in Inca, Aztec and ancient Egyptian history, while Native Americans conferred special status on "berdashes" or transvestites. Masai youths are forced into women's clothing between circumcision and the healing of their wounds, while in Ceylon women's clothing is used to call up the gods. In India the Hijra are intersexed persons, sometimes born that way, sometimes created through castration, a process which endows them with the powers of the Goddess. The tradition goes back a good 2000 years and was only looked down upon when the British colonized the subcontinent.

And in Western culture there's really no shortage of men in women's clothing. In Elizabethan times, it was illegal for women to act, meaning that all the female parts had to be taken by men, something Shakespeare had fun with by getting female characters to cross dress—leading to a whole Victor/Victoria scenario, with men dressed as women dressed as men. Or something like that. A century or so later Bonnie Prince Charlie, pretender to the British throne, went undercover in the Scottish Highlands dressed as a woman; Edward Hynde, New York and New Jersey governor between 1702 and 1708, liked nothing better than to parade the streets in female fancywork; and early silent movie actor and drag queen Julian Eltidge was a massive star of screen and stage back in the early years of the 20th century.

Of course, dressing in women's clothing is not by any means the preserve of gay men. In fact, most transvestites who cross-dress for sexual gratification are straight (British comedian Eddie Izzard for instance), and should not be confused with your drag queen: a fierce, ruling homosexual, wearing women's clothes in an assertive way for the power they afford him as part of his performance either on-stage or off-. (Barry Humphreys, the man behind Dame Edna Everage, may be straight but he uses drag in the same way as a gay drag queen).

While drag queens have always played their part on the gay scene, it was in the 80s and 90s that the phenomenon really went crazy, with drag festival Wigstock [see page 89] kicking off in 1985, and a new generation of high-glamour, high-visibility, high-energy drag queens taking over nightclubs from New York to Sydney to London. Their trademark was bitchiness, sharpness of tongue, a lexicon of African American put downs ("girlfrieeeeend"), and real big and expensive designer fashions. Heck, even New York mayor Rudi Giuliani was turning up in drag to some parties despite the fact that kill-joy feminists were denouncing drag as a parodying of women. (The intellectual drag queen would argue right back that the whole concept of drag was about gender constructs, therefore they were battling on the same side as the feminists, affirming that high hair and heels had nothing necessarily to do with femaleness).

In the early 90s, drag's answer to blaxploitation, RuPaul, was crowned Queen of Manhattan, wangled himself a record deal, and really took the big frocks to the little people, getting drag accepted across the board [see page 187]. And it was around this time that Hollywood cottoned on to the comic/tragic possibilities of the drag queen and, in the wake of *Priscilla, Queen of the Desert* [see page 144], started slipping drag queens into movies, while intellectuals like Camille Paglia were defending drag queens as the most powerful sexual icons of our age.

But by the late 90s—after the drag films, drag records, drag clubs, drag superstars, drag porn movie directors (Chi Chi LaRue)—drag was on the wane, mainly because female fashion had finally caught up and girls were coming out of dowdy combats and T-shirts, and getting back into giddy heels and short skirts. In 2001, though New York drag trio The Ones were enjoying a huge UK smash hit with 'Flawless,' the ladies from Wigstock were slapping up for the very last time, and it was looking like the drag party was well and truly over.

But then again, you can never write off a drag queen. Who knows when they will be back.

The ten most influential drag queens of our time

RuPaul
Global Starbooty [see page 187].

The Lady Bunny
She brought you Wigstock and, erm, 'Wuthering Heights.'

Jayne County
Formerly Wayne, the gal behind the classic 'If You Don't Wanna Fuck Me (Then Baby Fuck Off).'

Joey Arias
Channelling Billie Holiday and scaring the hell out of everybody.

Raven A
Fearsome Joey Arias side-kick and mistress of New York's Bar d'O.

The Duelling Bankheads
Double the trouble Tallulah impersonators.

Lypsinka
A whole act based on lipsynching to songs and movie snatches.

The Very Miss Dusty O
The most glamorous drag DJ and hostess in London history. Tight with Boy George.

Lily Savage
From local pubs to primetime TV, Lily savage is one of the highest paid performers on British television.

Eva Destruction
Alter-ego of Hollywood star Alexis Arquette.

John Waters

Filmmaker and Baron of Bad Taste

"To me, bad taste is what entertainment is all about," claims John Waters, the self-styled Pope of Trash and the auteur behind such classic works as *Pink Flamingos*, *Mondo Trasho* and *Pecker*. "If someone vomits watching one of my films, it's like getting a standing ovation. But one must remember that there is such a thing as good bad taste and bad bad taste." Waters made good bad taste his own and ruffled many a feather, sometimes a gay feather, while doing it.

"My movies are politically correct, although I hate to admit it, in a weird way," he says. "The people that win deserve to win." Those people have been a selection of misfits from his freaky ensemble—people like the outsize Divine [see right], an old school chum of his, Mink Stole, Edith Massey—to the celebrities that have been sucked into the weird world of Waters, characters such as Blondie's Debbie Harry, ex-terror victim Patty Hearst, 50s pin-up Tab Hunter, and major stars like Kathleen Turner (*Serial Mom*), and Melanie Griffith, who sent herself up brilliantly in *Cecil B. Demented*.

It all started back in Baltimore where John Waters became fascinated with gore having seen some in a car wreck. When he was given an 8mm camera for his seventeenth birthday there was little doubt that blood, guts and violence in general would play a part in his oeuvre. Using his ensemble, known as the Dreamland Players, Waters turned out early bad taste amateur movies like *Hag In Black Leather* and *Eat Your Make Up* before going overground (well, relatively) with *Pink Flamingos*, a shocking white trash drama where Divine and Mink Stole go head to head for the title of Filthiest Person in the World. The final denouement has Divine proving that she deserves the title, when she bends down to eat freshly produced dog excrement. And there was no trick photography: the dog was followed around until it relieved itself, and Divine was seen scooping the result into her mouth, chomping it and showing her brown tongue, all in one shot. From that famous scene, there was no going back. In subsequent movies like *Female Trouble* (where Divine played a man to "rape" himself) there were motifs such as facial disfigurement, while *Polyester* in 1981 became the world's first ever scratch 'n' sniff movie, where cinemagoers were provided with numbered cards which they would be asked to use during certain scenes.

Polyester saw Waters put his toe into the mainstream, while his next films, *Hairspray* in 1988, which starred Ricki Lake and *Crybaby* in 1990, with Johnny Depp, saw him creep further and further towards the multiplex, even though the content of his films was still, compared to the real mainstream, bizarre to say the least.

"They always think I'm kidding when I'm not," is how he explains the strange immunity he enjoys, despite coming out with statements describing terrorism as sexy and saying of murderers, "I like them, plain and simple. I like to be around them." This predilection for killers led to Waters' creepiest experience, however, when one man he met on a filmmaking course he was giving in jail was released, came to stay and then went on to murder two more people.

Although openly gay from the outset, Waters has never been much of a friend to the gay liberation movement, something he puts down to his distaste for separatism: "I like confusion when everybody's together and it's all mixed and you don't know who's who," he says.

From the perspective of the 21st century, Waters' high point was undoubtedly 1994's *Serial Mom*, starring Kathleen Turner as a deranged suburban housewife running amok. He continues to make films, and has even become an actor in his own right, appearing in Woody Allen's 1999 comedy, *Sweet and Lowdown*. When he's not making the world a sicker place through the magic of cinema, John can be found writing books such as *Shock Value* and *Crackpot*.

Divine

Protégé and muse of John Waters, Divine—or Harris Glenn Millstead, to use his real name—was an old school friend of Waters, and someone who shared his bad taste aesthetic. Starring in all of John Waters' early films, even while he was still working as a hairdresser, Divine's size, growly voice, and sheer yuckiness made him an instant cult figure among the largely gay audiences of works such as *Pink Flamingos* and *Mondo Trasho*.

As Waters went more mainstream, Divine started to attract the attention of filmmakers like Paul Bartell and Alan Rudolph, both of whom used Divine to great effect, but it wasn't only film folk who could see past the rolls of fat. By the early 80s, Divine was using the ridiculously gravely voice to record dance hits like 'Native Love,' 'You Think You're A Man (But You're Only A Boy),' and 'Walk Like A Man,' all huge hits on the gay scene. Above all, Divine was a master of creating a stir: when he performed on the UK's flagship pop show *Top of the Pops*, there was outcry while his appearance at a London nightclub riding a baby elephant was the sensation of the whole season.

Divine eventually died of an enlarged heart in 1989 at the age of forty-two. He was mourned as a great actor, an OK singer, and a magnificent freak.

Andy Warhol

The pop artist whose fame has lasted longer than fifteen minutes

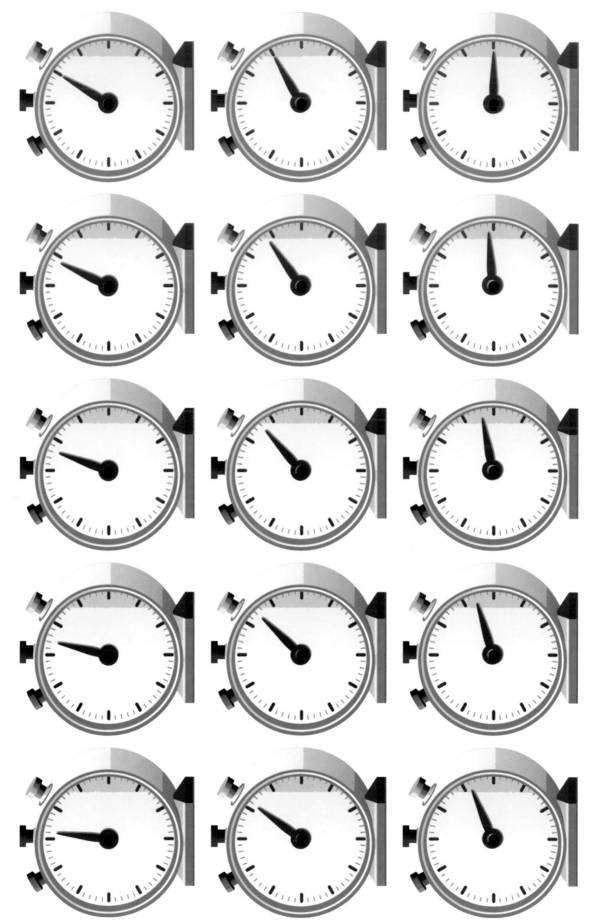

Born Andrew Warhola sometime between 1928 and 1930—no-one is really sure—the man who would become known as Andy Warhol arrived in Manhattan in 1949 with nothing more than a suitcase full of movie magazines. When he checked out of the city—after dying following a gall bladder operation in February 1987—his estate was worth a cool half a billion dollars.

Andy Warhol started his career as a fashion illustrator—and a very good one at that. Before the fine art world came calling, he'd already made a fair bit of cash creating adverts for *Glamour, Vogue* and *Harper's & Queen*. In spite of this success, Warhol always wanted to be recognized as a "real artist."

As something of a celebrity in Manhattan thanks to his penchant for wearing tight-fitting suits, a white-blond wig to hide his baldness, and dark glasses, Warhol always felt like an ugly duckling in this über-beautiful setting, and even had his bulbous red nose sanded down in an attempt to fit in.

However, as Warhol the artist developed, he transformed his image, from an opera-loving cosmopolitan faggot into a gum-chewing artist who dug the lowest forms of popular culture. In the 1960s he traded his images of expensive shoes on Fifth Avenue for those plucked from supermarket shelves in the Bronx. As his illustrative skills developed into those trademark silkscreens, Warhol began depicting items like Campbell's soup tins and Brillo Pad boxes, turning them into iconic images. His repetitive, manufactured "paintings" of popular celebrities like Elvis and Liz Taylor had the Manhattan art world divided, and caused an excited stir in hip NYC.

The 1960s became his most prolific—and drug-fuelled—era. He produced thousands of pieces of work, somehow pre-guessing new fads. Just days after Marilyn Monroe committed suicide with a drug cocktail, Warhol began producing silkscreens taken from a publicity shot of the actress, and helped turn her from a popular but not well respected film star into the cinema icon she is today. Marilyn belonged to Warhol's already controversial "death series," which included air crashes, electric chairs and car wrecks, and was soon to be joined by prints of Jackie Kennedy crying beside the coffin of President John F. Kennedy.

Warhol's life and background became more mysterious the more famous he became. Being ultra-sensitive to touch (due to neurological surgery he'd had when he was a kid), Warhol's sexual profile is a weird and uncatalogued one. With the backdrop of the inhibition-free 1960s, it is known he had boyfriends, many of whom described him as "asexual." Warhol often confessed to finding everything sexual—stillness, being looked at, watching people, you name it—and critics often say that this is because he found his own body so "unsexual." While some critics debate whether he was indeed gay his biographer Wayne Koestenbaum retorts that Warhol was "as gay as you can get."

Warhol began experimenting with film during the early 60s in his studio cum apartment cum legendary art space, the Factory, collaborating with the group of people who had materialized and somehow stayed. Some were artists and filmmakers in their own right, others were just gay boys and dykes who hung out with the creative mix of freaks that was fast becoming an art powerhouse. Warhol used the electric atmosphere in the Factory, and sucked ideas from the people who hung out there, described as "space debris" by the critic Robert Hughes. The productivity of Warhol's "boys and girls" was sky-high, and, though he didn't necessarily work on all the pieces, nothing left the Factory without his seal of approval. As the infamy and the output of the Factory grew, so did the celebrity of the people who dropped by—Jack Kerouac, Jane Fonda, the Rolling Stones, and Judy Garland were just some of the people who popped by while proto-punks The Velvet Underground rehearsed in another part of the building.

His first commercial movie success was *Chelsea Girls* in 1966, but there was a back catalogue of more experimental films. His six-hour cinematic debut *Sleep* (1963) was just that—a 20-minute piece of film of one of his boyfriends sleeping looped over and over, while *Empire* from 1964 was an eight-hour view of the Empire State Building. All of his movies, whether they were boringly long, badly acted or poorly filmed, turned the idea of the Hollywood movie on its head. For some reason, it was this deliberate lack of professionalism that made them feel so fresh.

On June 3rd, 1968, Valerie Solanis—one of the Factory crowd, a lesbian and sole member of S.C.U.M., the Society for Cutting Up Men—attempted to assassinate Warhol in the Factory. Two bullets hit him and penetrated his stomach, lungs, liver and throat. He spent two months in hospital recovering.

Once recovered one of his assistants took over film production, while Andy concentrated on his work with The Velvet Underground, producing a multimedia show that included the appearance of the German singer, actress and model, Nico. In 1970 Warhol began to publish the magazine *Interview*. Having always been fascinated by taping conversations, Warhol would invite someone over for a chat and publish the printed transcript, something which was revolutionary at the time.

Warhol, a permanent guest at all the right parties in Manhattan, met every celebrity of that era: Muhammad Ali, Liza Minnelli, Henry Kissinger, who all competed to get—the ultimate accolade—their portrait done by him. And if he wasn't at the Factory, Warhol was either at Studio 54, or snapping away with his Polaroid (sometimes at the genitals of a cute boy who crossed his path), or hanging out with fashion designer to the stars, Halston.

By the 1980s, he had become a true star—even going so far as to place himself alongside American legends such as Mickey Mouse and Superman. Along with self-portraits, he re-painted the Campbell's soup packaging while tackling subversive images including Mao Tse Tung, the Soviet hammer and sickle and even The Last Supper. Immersed in the easy life of money, celebrity and art—the subjects of much of his work—Warhol died a legend in 1987 after a routine operation.

Gay Magazines

Read all about "It"

Go into the magazine department of any decent-sized bookstore and you will find more gay magazines than you can seriously be expected to read. Some of them will have come the community route, growing up from news-sheets sweated over by radicals in someone's basement; others will have emerged from gay porn companies eager to get a little credibility. And then there are those that have been put out by large straight publishing houses, keen to get in on what they see as a key niche market with readers their advertisers go moist over.

The very concept of magazines specifically for gay men and lesbians is a relatively new one. In the early 1900s, health enthusiast Bernarr Macfadden produced *Physical Culture*, the United States' first bodybuilding magazine, a magazine he later—to his absolute horror!—discovered had become more or less the first gay magazine, in that it was gay men who were buying it to drool over. Other magazines targeting a gay market (though never saying so) followed, including the now legendary *Athletic Model Guild* titles published by Bob Mizer, who would scour the country looking for likely looking lads willing to whack it out in the name of art, health and beauty. His *Physique Pictorial,* which he started to distribute in 1951, was a pocket-sized magazine with men very much in mind, while other publications were launched to emulate its success (words such as "Grecian" in the title indicated that the magazine was for a gay readership).

But parallel to these early sex magazines, political groups such as the Mattachine Society, which had branches all over the United States, were putting out pamphlets with information relevant to gay men and lesbians. *ONE* Magazine was launched in 1953, with the intention of educating the general public about all matters concerning homosexuality and throwing out a lifeline to isolated gay men and lesbians. Circulation was low—around 5,000 at its peak—but it was a groundbreaker, surviving until the late 60s, by which time it had been superseded by more professional gay magazines. Parallel to *ONE* was the *Mattachine Review*, a more scholarly magazine that was in operation between 1955 and 1965. By this time, although most urban queers were still getting their news from publications like the *Village Voice*, it was time for a proper gay magazine to come along. *The Advocate* was launched in 1967 and had ambitions to become a gay *Time* or *Newsweek*, ambitions which it has largely realized.

Meanwhile, in the UK, where anti-gay laws had been even more draconian (homosexuality was in fact illegal until 1967), gay publishing was obviously much slower to take off. In June 1972, Denis Lemon and Andrew Lumsden launched *Gay News* with the help of figures like Peter Tatchell and Jackie Forster. And it was a huge success even if it was hokey and a little on the worthy side. Two years later it was charged with obscenity for a cover featuring two men kissing. It won the case but was not so lucky three years later when crazed British obscenity campaigner Mary Whitehouse took the publication to the High Court for blasphemy, after a frankly ridiculous poem by James Kirkup called 'The Love That Dares To Speak Its Name' about a Roman Centurion having sex with Christ as they take him from the cross. Lemon was found guilty, fined and given a suspended sentence; *Gay News* meanwhile improved circulation from 8,000 to 40,000, and was championed by writers and artists around the world. Nice one Mary!

In 1984—following the example of excellent French title *Gai Pied*—a group of breakaway *Gay News* writers set up *Gay Times*, the first glossy (well, kind of) monthly to be sold on mainstream newsstands. There was no turning back: there was already a popular free gay newspaper in London called *Capital Gay* and within three years *The Pink Paper* became the first free gay national newspaper to be distributed in bars and clubs throughout the UK. But gay men and lesbians had undergone a revolution, largely thanks to publications like these. They were confident enough and comfortable enough with their sexuality to want lifestyle magazines that didn't campaign or protest, but which entertained. In 1991, the publishers behind *The Pink Paper* launched *Boyz* and changed the face of gay publishing in the UK forever. Light, fluffy and with the emphasis on bars, clubs, sex, fashion and celebrity, *Boyz*' success was cited for the burgeoning scene in London and blamed for the closing of *Capital Gay*. With their eye on the sort of advertising revenue the free *Boyz* was pulling in (even though it was printed on newspaper), publishers started to round up teams of gay journalists to create glossy gay magazines. Northern and Shell, a mega-publishing house used to producing pornographic titles such as *Asian Babes*, came up with *Attitude*, a bright, smart, great-looking magazine for gay men and anyone else interested in high glamour, snappy interviews and great journalism. It was a smash hit and gave *Gay Times*, which prided itself on being the biggest gay mag outside North America, a real run for its money.

Meanwhile, back in the States, *The Advocate* was going from strength to strength and had created such a strong identity that there were niches for magazines such as *Out*, which were launched with great success. But by this time American gay men and lesbians were being well and truly spoilt with a whole raft of free local magazines, all serving their communities with the latest information on bars, clubs and sometimes even hookers. What had started out as an inspiring if slightly stifling cottage-industry press had turned into a squillion-dollar industry. And it was all our own work!

Legendary gay clubs
Some of the best queer clubs in the history of the world

New York

Once the gayest Mecca on earth, due to stringent controls on nightclubbing and after-hours shenanigans by former Mayor of New York Rudolph Guiliani, New York's hot spots have fallen out of favor with global gays. With the scene desperately trying to claw back queer tourists, its past glories are still fondly remembered by international club-goers.

Tunnel

Back in the mid-1990s, Tunnel was one of Manhattan's super clubs—with legends like Junior Vasquez and Danny Tenaglia at the decks, Tunnel would pack in the punters week after week. Owned by Peter Gatien whose business dealings have been under scrutiny of late, it will go down as one of New York's finest.

Clit Club

One of the most famous all-girl clubs in the world, lesbian institution Clit Club, owned and run by Julie Tolentino—the sexy dancer who appeared in Madonna's *Sex* book—has moved to a new location recently. With midnight performances, some kick-ass girl DJs and raucous bar-top go-go dancers, you'll get more than a sniff of NYC's varied dyke population at the Clit, with boys welcome as guests to the girlies. Long-running, but never boring.

Beige at B Bar

Once the be-all-and-end-all must-do Tuesday nighter, Beige is still enticing a fashionista crowd. While the queues used to stretch round the block to be the lucky ones to get in and be seen, it's still worth a visit just to check out the once-famous Bowery Bar.

Studio 54

Probably the most famous disco ever, Studio 54 was, in its late 70s heyday, *the* place to see and be seen. With everyone from movie stars to President's wives shaking a tail feather in among the largely gay, sometimes naked and painted gold party set, it got wild, it got druggy, and it got sexy up in the balcony. With the basement a VVIP only area—the rest was just regular VIP—the club was run by Ian Schrager, now owner of hotels like The Paramount and London's St. Martin's, and his gay partner Steve Rubell.

Hellfire

The original, and still the best sex club in Manhattan, the underground meat-packing district Hellfire club dates back to the late 70s, and is still packing in the pervs for hot action of a variety of flavors. It boasts some of the queerest of rules including no drugs or alcohol, no oral sex, no anal or vaginal sex, no tongues and ass play only with fingers and toys; rules are made for breaking even when they're adhered to and you're guaranteed hours of fun at this legendary nightspot. Not gay the whole week round, the Sunday afternoon nude party is especially hot.

Twilo

Arguably one of the best dance clubs in the world from 1995, when it opened in the old Sound Factory building, Twilo was always the host to top name DJs like Carl Cox and Sacha, and was just getting its multimedia act together with albums and magazines when it fell victim to Giuliani's purge of nightclubs in New York.

Sound Factory

Frankie Knuckles among others ruled this legendary 80s club, with its mad sirens and police lights, emphasis on Ecstasy and a cool mix, it was mainly gay but there were loads of Hispanic straight kids coming down for the party. The birthplace of gay house, no gay music club would have made it without the Sound Factory laying the foundations.

San Francisco

Blow Buddies

A notorious and very effective sex club, Blow Buddies is a legend and still offers specialist nooky nights no matter what your predilection. Very safe sex oriented, the condoms are plentiful.

The End Up

Immortalized in Armistead Maupin's *Tales of the City* [see page 190], The End Up's Sunday tea dance is still going strong. It's after-hours Saturday night/Sunday morning dance club is also worth a visit, if only to say you've been to one of San Fran's famous gay hangouts.

The Stud

Generic gay bar/club The Stud has been packing them in (or not, depending on the night) for the last thirty-odd years. Formerly, as the name suggests, something of a hardcore pick-up joint, it's now still picky-uppy but there is a little light dancing too. There are also dyke nights these days.

London

Gateways

One of the longest running dyke bars in Britain, it opened in Chelsea in the 1930s, and was made famous by its appearance in the dykey flick *The Killing Of Sister George* back in 1968. While not exclusively gay, it did tend to attract punters who were rejected by the rest of society, so lesbians were there in abundance. A windowless cellar room with steep, steep stairs, it was a members-only affair.

Heaven

Heaven celebrated its twenty-first birthday back in 2000, and is still one of the biggest gay nightclubs in Europe. When it opened, it was ruled by Hi-NRG DJ Ian Levine, who span frantic tracks for a poppers-fuelled male-only crowd. As times changed, so did Heaven, eventually admitting women and taking its place as one of the UK's most famous gay clubs, not least for live performances by the likes of Madonna and Cher

Candy Bar

Not actually a club, the Candy Bar was the UK's first seven days a week lesbian bar, and also opened the first weekly girls-only strip night. Opening in 1997, it has since moved from its original venue, and now boasts another venue in Brighton.

G.A.Y

Choose a night out at G.A.Y and you're guaranteed performances from some of the biggest names around. Anyone who wants to be someone has performed here, from Donna Summer through Kylie Minogue to the Spice Girls.

Trade

A real mold-breaker, this techno club established by the charismatic Lawrence Malice has become a legend of the London club scene. Expect wall-to-wall muscle, a hard soundtrack and crazy dancing until lunchtime Sunday morning.

Hippodrome

The huge but now defunct gay Monday nighter run by Peter Stringfellow, the Hippodrome is famed for Divine's appearance on a baby elephant!

International

Le Queen, Paris

Le Queen on Paris's swanky Champs Elysees is now the best-established gay club in town, and even if the attitude is a little hard to bear (this is Paris after all), and the drinks on the very expensive side (this is Paris etc.), there is still fun to be had. Probably not quite as much as at sexy-club Le Depot, but hey...

Martin's, Barcelona

Now overtaken by the much more popular Metro, Martin's was, in the 80s and early 90s, *the* place to see, be seen, take, be taken in Barcelona. A huge, three-storey affair with copious backroom facilities, porno screens and a bathroom with a two-way mirror, it's now just a sad shadow of its previous self.

Cockring, Amsterdam

The legendary gay sex club in the heart of Amsterdam's leather district, Cockring is famous for its nude parties, its sex shows and its general dirty atmosphere. Men-only with a hot under-40s crowd, there are queues round the block even into the wee hours of the morning.

IT, Amsterdam

One of the most famous gay clubs in Europe in the 1990s, IT has since, however, lost some of its sheen since a much-publicized drugs bust in 1999. In a converted cinema, despite it being, like, over, it is still rammed at the weekends, especially on a Saturday when it's gay boys only. Famous swimming pool party in July.

Manto, Manchester

Its reputation is bigger than the actual place but Manto's is the center of the whole gay Canal Street scene that really took off in the 90s, made even more famous by the British version of *Queer As Folk*. The only trouble is, post-*Queer As Folk*, you'll be hard pushed to find any queer folk in there.

Tom's Bar, Berlin

A classic, almost by-numbers gay sex bar (expect men in leather with loads of moustaches), Tom's Bar has been pulling them in since before anyone cares to remember. Small and squashy, the action is all towards the back and down the stairs. And when we say action...

The Albury, Sydney

Australia's (and possibly south-east Asia's) most famous drag bar, this huge location has been giving drag addicts their fix for years. With its huge oval central bar where those shows take place, and drip-fed girlie disco, it could probably lay claim to the title 'dolliest bar south of the equator.'

kd lang

From mullet-haired hokey country singer to sexy lesbian megastar

Considering her small-town beginnings, kd lang has come a very long way indeed. It's not every dyke brought up on a farm in rural Alberta, Canada who finds themselves on the front cover of global magazine *Vanity Fair* being shaved—for chrissakes—by supermodel Cindy Crawford. Now the ultimate lesbian icon and one of the celebrities most dykes would give their right arm to sleep with, she's chucked in her ten-gallon hat and gone all cool on our asses.

Starting her musical career as a country singer, lang's androgynous look and velvety vocals caught the eye of music critics, and ruffled a few feathers down in Nashville. Hardly your typical country-singing lady's image, lang shied away from the big hair, big tits look, and opted for a cropped coiff teamed with cut-off cowboy boots, as well as anti-meat-eating politics. Not good in the land where a cow equals dinner and big business. Her refusal to conform with Nashville's straight-laced requirements saw lang being omitted from the Country Music Awards year after year.

In 1988, lang released *Shadowland* and critics outside of the country music community began to take note. Typically, where there's a whiff of a lesbian celebrity—however minor—up crops a fervent dyke fanbase desperate to launch their new-found love into the limelight. It was her openness and humor about her sexuality from the beginning that propelled lang into the elusive land of lesbian icon.

In 1992 she released the acclaimed torch song album *Ingenue* and confirmed in *The Advocate* what all the girls already knew—she was a big old dyke. The confirmation of her sexuality did nothing to affect the publicity and praise her new long-player was receiving. *Ingenue* not only hit the Top 40 all over the world, but lang was nominated and won the MTV Music Award for Best Female Video—which sat nicely alongside her Grammy from 1990. With, as lang confesses, a girl in every port, she became the ultimate lesbian lust-after—sexier than Martina, and with better tunes than Melissa (Ellen was still hanging out in her closet at this point),

lang became the poster girl for a new generation of gay girls, and even a few boys, who were hungry for an out, proud and talented role model. Not only that, but she also gave closeted gay celebs the confidence to come out. The mid-1990s saw every lesbian worth her salt in possession of a kd lang album—whether they were willing to admit to it or not.

lang never took on the role of spokesperson for the lesbian and gay community—despite the pressure being put upon her time and time again—and while she readily admitted her preference for girls in interviews, she didn't want to have to constantly speak out against lesbian and gay discrimination, and the fight for equality: "I don't feel political about my preference. I just don't. I'm sorry! I'm sorry to disappoint you hardcores, but I don't!"

Even though she refused to become a mouthpiece, lang not only appeared at all the right queer events, she also gave her followers a lot to think about, especially when they were alone at night. Always gorgeously suited and booted, photo shoots saw her sat astride a fat, purring Harley Davidson motorbike. Madonna—when it was still cool to flirt with dykes in the heady days of lesbian chic [see page 161]—said: "I have seen Elvis, and she's beautiful;" lang appeared on Ellen's coming out episode, and hung with some of the world's biggest stars. It was the life that lesbians in the sticks, and hell even in the big cities, yearned for, and we were watching her get out there and live it.

While post-*Ingenue* albums didn't fare so well in the charts, lang—partly because of her openness, partly because of her intriguing persona—has managed to keep a Prada-clad foot in the limelight. Still up there on all the queer mags' "Top 100 Gay People Who We Just Love, Love, Love," she's become one of the tick boxes on the "Are You A Lesbian?" quiz—along with owning a cat, wearing your collars upturned and playing golf—it's only a shame that other queer musicians, actors and the like didn't follow her example to be out and happy about their sexuality without ever needing to make a big old fuss.

Francis Bacon

Painter

One of the greatest and most important painters of the 20th century, Francis Bacon's work is unique, infused as it is by his extraordinary life. No appreciation of his work can ignore the fact he had a brutal upbringing and was a serious alcoholic with a thing for rough gay sex. His paintings are both serene and nihilistic, beautiful and grotesque, vivid and distorted, but whatever they're undeniably attention-grabbing and unforgettable.

Francis Bacon was born in Dublin to English parents, on October 28th, 1909, the second of five children, and grew up a sickly child. His father, whom he didn't get on with, hoped to toughen him up by having him horsewhipped; instead Francis got it on with the grooms, which instilled in him a lifelong lust for rough trade.

Following a series of arguments with his father and having been discovered dancing in his mother's panties, he was kicked out in 1925. After initially heading for London, he was soon traveling to Berlin and Paris, where he decided he wanted to be a painter after working on interior decoration commissions. On his return to London in 1929, he held a small exhibition of oil and watercolor paintings and furniture. Francis was entirely self-taught as an artist and wasn't immediately embraced by the art world, though by 1937 he was featured in the Young British Painters Exhibition in London.

During the Second World War, in which he didn't serve due to his asthma, he destroyed all the paintings he felt didn't live up to his standards, something he continually did throughout his life. Then in 1945, he unleashed his infamous *Three Studies for Figures At the Base of a Crucifiction* on a horrified world. "It was a thing I did in about a fortnight, when I was in a bad mood of drinking," he explained. The paintings got him noticed, since they were a shock reminder of the horror and evil of war for a country trying to get back to normal.

His exhibitions, which included his infamous study of six heads featuring the screaming pope, continued to produce "extreme reactions, mostly revulsion," according to critics of the time, but he had begun to make his mark and in 1951 he briefly took a teaching position at the Royal College of Art.

All the while, Francis had started to visit Tangiers in Morocco, a xanadu for gay men who were unable to live openly at home. This is where he met and fell in love with Peter Lacy, a test pilot who had flown combat missions during the Battle of Britain. The relationship however was doomed: Francis felt a masochistic passion for Peter and both drank heavily—it did however provide an inspiration for Francis's work, which started being toured around the world after his first major retrospective in 1955.

In 1964, Francis met petty-criminal George Dyer when he was breaking into his flat. It was an aphrodisiac encounter for the man obsessed with rough and they became lovers. However, seven years later in 1971, on the eve of a major retrospective of his work at the Grand Palais in Paris, George committed suicide in the hotel room they were sharing. Francis blamed himself for the suicide as, by having helped him out of a life of crime, he felt he'd robbed him of his raison d'être. Once again, Francis thrust himself into his work and returned to the scene of George's death for three triptychs. From the 70s on, retrospectives of his work proliferated and Francis continued to paint, though his portraits became less obscure. In the mid-80s, during a major retrospective at the Tate in London, he was proclaimed the "greatest living painter" by the media. In 1992, at the age of eight-two, he visited friends in Madrid where, feeling unwell, he was taken into hospital. He later died from a heart attack.

⇨ **Take it further**: *Love Is The Devil*, a film directed by John Maybury
The Gilded Gutter Life of Francis Bacon, a biography by Daniel Farson

Quentin Crisp

Writer, English eccentric, self-styled stately homo and all-round dolly whatsit

It's fair to say that Quentin Crisp stretched a little a very long way. More famous for just "being," he was nevertheless "out" from the word go (1908), and worked it in a time when being gay was not just frowned upon but got you beaten up and/or thrown in the slammer.

Because of his ambiguous appearance and obvious sexuality, holding down a job was difficult. Only a career in the arts was possible, and he became an illustrator and book cover designer, but even that was difficult. One day he stood in for a friend as an art school life model, which became his career for thirty-five years, until remarks on a radio show led to the commissioning of his autobiography.

The Naked Civil Servant was published in 1968, but didn't become a bestseller until it was turned into a telemovie starring John Hurt four years later. It was critically well received, broadcast worldwide and made Quentin Crisp a global curiosity. On the back of his new celebrity, he started writing about lifestyle and film, and in 1978 made his Off Broadway debut in *An Evening With…* It brought his lifelong love affair with America to a climax and at the age of seventy-two, he left his one-room apartment in London's Chelsea (which he never cleaned, meaning the dust was piled up like snowdrifts), and emigrated to New York City.

There he continued to write, but also turned his hand to other careers like cameo appearances in movies such as *Orlando*, *To Wong Foo, Thanks For Everything, Julie Newmar*, a role as Lady Bracknell in Soho Repertory Theatre's production of *The Importance Of Being Earnest*, and appearances in ads for Levi's and Calvin Klein perfume. His last book was *Resident Alien* in 1997. He died two years later.

⇨ **Take it further**: *The Naked Civil Servant* and *Resident Alien* by Quentin Crisp

picture credits

The Publisher has made every effort to obtain the necessary permissions for all images in this work. If any individual or organization believes images to have been incorrectly credited, please contact the Publisher and the correct credit will be placed in all future editions.

P2 Boy and Girl, Sara Press
P6 Boy George, courtesy of Boy George

GAY UNIVERSE

P12-13 illustration, Chris Tate
P14 Bette Midler, Pictorial Press, still from "The Rose"
P15 Donna Summer, Pictorial Press
P16 Princess Diana, Pictorial Press
P17 Princess Diana's Funeral, London, September 6th, 1997 GAZE/Paul Vallance
P18 Kitsch illustration, Jonathan White
P18 Homoerotic, GAZE/James Stafford
P19 Skinhead, GAZE/Paul Vallance
P20 Camp illustration, Chris Tate
P21 Dynasty, Pictorial Press
P23 Madonna, Pictorial Press
P24 Shirley Bassey, Pictorial Press/Rob Verhost
P26 Mariah Carey, Pictorial Press, 1997, at VH1 Fashion Awards
P26 CD Anthems, Chris Tate
P27 Cagney & Lacey, Pictorial Press
P28 Tracy Chapman, Pictorial Press/Rob Verhost, at Amnesty Concert, 1988
P29 Ani DiFranco, Lisa Richards
P30 Salute You Movies, video shot, Chris Tate
P31 Serial Mom, Pictorial Press
P32 Spice Girls, Pictorial Press/AP
P33 Spice Girls, Pictorial Press/Zuma/Kaszerman, at the MTV Video Awards, New York, 1997
P34 Sex And The City, Pictorial Press, the cast at the 7th Annual SAG Awards, Los Angeles, CA, November 3rd, 2001
P35 Golden Girls, Pictorial Press
P36 Barbra Streisand, Pictorial Press
P40 Jodie Foster, Pictorial Press/Jeffrey Mayer
P41 Xena, Pictorial Press
P42 Absolutely Fabulous, Chris Tate
P43 Absolutely Fabulous, Chris Tate
P44 Kaberet, Pictorial Press
P45 My Fair Lady, Pictorial Press
P45 Calamity Jane, Pictorial Press
P47 Judy Garland, Pictorial Press

NATURE/NURTURE

P48-49 Baby, Digital Vision
P50 Signs and Symbols, Chris Tate

P51 Slogans, Chris Tate
P52 Gay Gene, Jonathan White
P53 Turkey Baster, Chris Tate
P54 F TO Ms, 'Matt and Eric,' San Franscisco, 1996, Del LaGrace Volcano from "Sublime Mutations," Konkursbuchverlag 2000
P55 Gay Animals, Dog with Funky Hat, Foodpix/Paula Friedland
P56 Gaydar, Chris Tate
P57 A Gays, Group of Paparazzi photographers, FPG International, Vcl/Spencer Rowell
P58-59 Sex types, illustrations, Chris Tate
P60-61 Slang, illustrations, Chris Tate
P62-63 Serial Killer, Chris Tate
P64-65 Bisexuality, Digital Vision
P66-67 Gay Marriage, Stone/Thomas J Peterson
P68-69 Stereotypes, illustrations, Chris Tate

BETWEEN THE SHEETS

P70-71 Chris Tate
P72 Cock ring illustration, Chris Tate
P73 Dildos, Stone
P75 Safe Sex, Lisa Richards
P76 Jock strap illustration, Chris Tate
P77 Viagra, Chris Tate
P78 Pornography, Robert Workman/GAZE/Publishers of HIM EXCLUSIVE, March 1976
P79 Lesbian Porn, Couple Kissing, FPG International/Christoph Wilheim
P80 Rent Boy, Chris Tate
P81 Rent Boy, Paul Vallance/GAZE
P82-83 Hanky Code, illustrations, Chris Tate

RIGHT ON SISTER

P84-85 Chris Tate
P86 Stonewall, Pictorial Press/Metro films
P87 Stonewall Bar, PP Hartnett/GAZE
P88 Closet, Chris Tate
P89 Wigstock, Lisa Richards
P90 ACT UP, Paul Vallance/GAZE
P91 Gore Vidal, Gordon Rainsford/GAZE
P92 Candlelight vigil for Matthew Shepard, Steve Liss/TimePix
P93 Brandon Teena, Boys Don't Cry, Pictorial Press
P94 Harvey Milk, courtesy of Uncle Donald
P95 Lesbian Avengers, James & James/GAZE
P96 Ellen & Anne, Pictorial Press/Jeffrey Mayer, at the Oscars, 1999
P98 Sandra Bernard, Pictorial Press/Jeffrey Mayer
P99 Camile Paglia, courtesy of Millivres picture archive
P100 Martina Navratilova, tennis balls illustration, Chris Tate
P101 Billie Jean King, Pictorial Press
P102 Derek Jarman, GAZE
P103 Sisters, Paul Vallance/GAZE

LOCATION, LOCATION, LOCATION

P104-105 Toy planes flying over North America on
 a globe, PhotoDisc/The Studio Dog
P106 Golden Gate Bridge, Chris Tate
P107 San Fransisco neighborhood, EyeWire Collection; San
Fransisco street car, EyeWire Collection; Bay Bridge at twilight,
PhotoDisc/Robert Glusic; Metro Bar, Bob Jones/GAZE; view of
Castro, Sunil Gupta/GAZE; Chris Tate; Lisa Richards
P108-109 Map One, illustration, Chris Tate
P110 NYC Lisa Richards (Guggenheim, Brooklyn Bridge, Drag
kings, Statue of Liberty, NY buildings); NYC Pride flag, Lola
Flash/GAZE; New York by night, Pictorial Press/David Corio; Wall
Street, Pictorial Press; Yellow cab at night, PhotoDisc/Jayme
Thornton; NY sidewalk, Pictorial Press/Nick Wright
P111 Statue of Liberty, Chris Tate
P112-113 Map Two, illustration, Chris Tate
P114 Nelson's column, Chris Tate
P115 Nelson's Column, Annie Bungeroth/GAZE; London at night,
PhotoDisc/Andre Ward/Life File; Doubledecker, PhotoDisc/Doug
Menuez; Guards at Buckingham Palace, PhotoDisc/Albert J.
Copley; Piccadilly Circus, Chris Tate; Tower Bridge,
PhotoDisc/David Buffington
P116 Sydney Bridge, C Moore/GAZE; Sydney night skyline,
C Moore/GAZE; Bondi Beach, C Moore/GAZE; View of Sydney
Opera House from the wharf, Pictorial Press; Sydney skyline,
PhotoDisc/Jeremy Woodhouse; Sydney skyscrapers from the
Royal Botanical Gardens, PhotoDisc/Flora Torrance/Life File; view
of Sydney skyline, Pictorial Press; Sydney Opera House,
PhotoDisc/Izzy Schwartz; kangaroo road sign, Getty Images
P117 Bridge statue, Chris Tate
P118 Homomonument, Lisa Richards
P119 Magere Brug Bridge, Amsterdam, PhotoDisc/Glen Allison;
Canal in Amsterdam, PhotoDisc/Andrew Ward/Life File;
Amsterdam, Lisa Richards

HISTORY

P120 Stack of old books, PhotoDisc/Steve Cole
P122 Right wing Christians, GAZE
P127 Michelangelo's Statue of David, PhotoDisc/David
 Buffington
P128 Lesbian Pirates, illustration, Chris Tate
P129 Joan of Arc, flame illustration, Chris Tate
P130 Gays in Military, Chris Tate
P131 Gay Spies, PhotoDisc/Lawrence Lawry
P132-135 AIDS timeline illustration, Chris Tate

GAY TO STRAIGHT

P140-141 Gay money illustration, Chris Tate
P138-139 Gay adverts, Robert Workman/GAZE
P141 Village People, Pictorial Press
P142 Trannie movies, video image, Chris Tate
P143 Some Like It Hot, Pictorial Press
P144 Mrs Doubtfire, Pictorial Press; Flawless, Pictorial
 Press; Tootsie, Pictorial Press; Priscilla, Pictorial Press;
 Victor Victoria Pictorial Press
P144 Wallpaper* magazine, Chris Tate
P145 Will and Grace, Pictorial Press

P146 Pink pound, illustration, Chris Tate
P147 "Stuart" in Queer As Folk, Joss Barratt
P148 Take That, Pictorial Press; 'N Sync, Pictorial Press;
 Westlife, Pictorial Press
P149 James Dean, Pictorial Press
P150 Gay best friend videos image, Chris Tate
P150 Silkwood, Pictorial Press; The Next Best Thing, Pictorial
 Press;
P151 My Best Friend's Wedding, Pictorial Press
P153 Freddie Mercury, Pictorial Press/van Houten

THE LOOK

P155 Row of wooden hangers, EyeWire Collection
P156 Alexander McQueen, Pictorial Press/Robert Lewis
P157 Dolce & Gabbana, Chris Tate; Gym Culture, Image Source
 Collection
P158-159 Piercing illustrations, Chris Tate
P160 Lesbian Chic, Chris Tate (Vanity Fair cover),
 polaroids courtesy of Lisa Richards
P162 Jean Paul Gaultier, Piers Allardyce/GAZE
P163 Tattoos, Ashley/ GAZE
P164 "Hogs and Hiefers, NYC," Del LaGrace Volcano
P165 "Mo B Dick and Villain, NYC, November 1996,
 Del LaGrace Volcano (GAZE)
P166 Versace steps, Chris Tate
P168-69 Gay Uniform, Chris Tate

LET ME ENTERTAIN YOU

P171 Microphone, PhotoDisk/Thomas Brummett
P172 Gay films, Chris Tate
P173 Beautiful Thing, Pictorial Press
P174 Torch Song Trilogy, Pictorial Press; Philadelphia,
 Pictorial Press
P175 Pet Shop Boys, Pictorial Press
P177 Oscar Wilde, Pictorial Press
P178 Club Kids, Chris Tate
P181 Elton John, Pictorial Press
P182 Gay clubbing, Gordon Rainsford/ GAZE
P184 Rock Hudson, Pictorial Press
P185 David Hockney, Bridgeman Art Library
P186 Liberace, Pictorial Press
P187 Rupaul, Anne Maniglier/GAZE
P192 Tom Of Finland, Tom of Finland Foundation 2002
P193 Gilbert and George, Piers Allardyce/GAZE,
P195 Leigh Bowery, PP Hartnett/GAZE
P197 Boy George, Pictorial Press/Pat Lyttle
P198 Lesbian films, Chris Tate
P199 Bound, Pictorial Press
P200 Desert Hearts, Pictorial Press
P202 George Michael, Pictorial Press/George Chin
P204 Drag Queens, Annie Bungeroth/GAZE
P207 Divine, Pictorial Press
P208 Andy Warholesque, Chris Tate
P213 Gay Clubs, Gordon Rainsford/GAZE
P214 kd lang, Pictorial Press
P217 Quentin Crisp, Piers Allardyce/GAZE

index

Lisa Richards would like to thank Liz Hatton for her constant support. Simon Gage would like to thank Eric Charge. Howard Wilmot would like to thank Alex Sanz.

Warwick Worldwide would like to thank Anna Lawson for research, back-up and the office soundtrack, Chris Tate for the design, and MQP/Unanimous for their direction and knowledge.